T0248202

WHAT REALLY WENT WRONG

WHAT REALLY WENT WRONG

The West and the
Failure of Democracy
in the Middle East

FAWAZ A. GERGES

Yale

UNIVERSITY PRESS

New Haven and London

Yale University Press books may be purchased in quantity for
educational, business, or promotional use. For information,
please e-mail sales.press@yale.edu (U.S. office) or sales@yaleup.co.uk
(U.K. office).

Set in Janson type by IDS Infotech, Ltd.
Printed in the United States of America.

Library of Congress Control Number: 2023951281
ISBN 978-0-300-25957-5 (hardcover: alk. paper)
A catalogue record for this book is available from the British Library.

This paper meets the requirements of ANSI/NISO Z39.48-1992
(Permanence of Paper).

10 9 8 7 6 5 4 3 2 1

To my beloved mother, Sara Bachour

Contents

Preface   ix

Acknowledgments   xiii

INTRODUCTION: Narrating History   1

1.   Mossadegh, Nasser, and What Could Have Been   17

2.   A Portrait of Mossadegh   38

3.   Saving Iran from Democracy   58

4.   From the Cusp of Democracy to the Abyss of
       Absolute Monarchy   83

5.   What Did the Overthrow of Mossadegh Mean for
       Iran and the Middle East?   108

6.   Nasser: The Pan-Arab Icon   126

7.   Nasser in "Little Hollywood": Losing Egypt,
       Losing the Peace   150

8.   The Suez Crisis   171

9.   Frustrating Nasser's Arab Nationalism   190

10.   What Have Egypt and the Arab World Lost by the
       Defeat of Nasser's Secular Nationalism?   214

11.   From Iran to Guatemala: The Fabrication of a
      Communist Threat   228

CONCLUSION   247

Notes   259
Index   301

Preface

As a scholar of the Middle East, I have long been captivated by a singular, hopeful moment in the region's history—the late 1940s and early 1950s, when European imperialism was in the rearview mirror and the region was on the cusp of a new political awakening. Middle Eastern people and their brethren across the decolonized Global South were inspired to modernize their societies and economies and look beyond their differences to unite for a better common future.

This hope proved evanescent, for in later years, the region became synonymous with authoritarianism, superpowers' rivalry, and proxy wars.

I see this as history's greatest loss. As the cradle of civilization, the homeland of talented people, and the site of abundant natural resources, the Middle East could have charted a peaceful future.

What happened to darken such a bright dawn? Did a tipping point set the stage for subsequent turbulent years?

After decades of study and reflection, I have concluded that the legacy of the global Cold War on the nascent postcolonial Middle Eastern state and society was profound and its impact transformational. Although the Cold War, an extension of European colonialism, has received considerable scrutiny, its lasting effects and consequences on the region have never been fully understood.

The United States and the Soviet Union reinforced the legacy of dysfunction left by European imperialism and turned the

Middle East and other regions into proxy battlegrounds. The two superpowers crushed the early hopes of the newly emancipated Middle Eastern states and deprived them of their right to self-determination. The hoped-for peace dividends after decolonization never materialized. Resources that should have gone to development were directed to the security-military sector.

Much of this can be traced to America's fixation with Soviet communism and desire to fold the Middle East into global capital and financial markets. These forces drove the C.I.A. to back a coup that toppled Iran's first democratic government in 1953. Three years later, America undermined and tried to oust Egyptian President Gamal Abdel Nasser, triggering the Suez Crisis, which provoked ire across the Arab world and almost catalyzed a world war. The squandering of this goodwill by the U.S. Cold Warriors had grave consequences that echoed beyond the region's borders. The aftershocks of these events still reverberate in the region today.

Looking closely at the histories of Iran, Egypt, Syria, Lebanon, and Guatemala (the last for comparative reasons), I saw how these and other inciting events radically altered the trajectory of politics and development in the region and wanted to explore what might have been had the Middle East charted its own postcolonial development. Might different decisions at key historical junctures have made the region more peaceful and democratic? Might that have spared lives and spurred global progress?

Revisiting this chapter in Middle Eastern history illuminates what transpired subsequently in relations between the United States and Middle Eastern states. This early chapter in the global Cold War has defined U.S. foreign policy toward the region for decades to come. Obsessed with Soviet communism, addicted to oil, and determined to establish a Pax Americana, U.S. leaders made a devil's pact with potentates, autocrats, and strongmen around the world. Washington protected repressive Middle Eastern regimes in return for compliance with American hegemonic designs and uninterrupted flows of cheap oil and gas.

When genuinely patriotic leaders like Muhammad Mossadegh and Gamal Abdel Nasser emerged, their desires for meaningful independence, territorial, and economic sovereignty, and modernization were branded as thinly veiled communism. Entrenched political interests therefore devised plans to undermine and topple them. The resultant policy of backing authoritarian strongmen in the name of stability took hold, establishing a pattern for Western governments dealing with the Middle East today. That so-called authoritarian stability came at a terrible cost for the region's peoples.

Although America felt the pernicious effects of this complicity on September 11, 2001, conservative scholars eschewed the West's responsibility for the region's current predicament, divesting that from its colonial past and U.S. support for authoritarian regimes. Instead, the region's problems were attributed to the myth of its unchangeable, inherently backward nature.

A prime example of this came shortly after the 9/11 attacks, when the Princeton historian Bernard Lewis published the *New York Times* best seller *What Went Wrong? Western Impact and Middle Eastern Response*, which claimed that Islam had trailed the West owing to its complicated relationship with modernity and freedom and legitimized George W. Bush's global war on terror. This argument provided ballast for neoconservatives who justified America's wars in Iraq and beyond.

This book counters that view with a trenchant examination of the roots of political authoritarianism and underdevelopment in the Middle East. Focusing on watershed moments, it shows that early attempts to create modern political systems, establish national sovereignty, and develop prosperous economies independent from the West were frustrated by Washington's obsession with Soviet communism and its desire to build a new (informal) empire. Rather than encouraging pluralism and genuine independence, this hawkish foreign policy approach quashed it. Understanding the flaws in this approach is fundamental to imagining a new future for the region.

Acknowledgments

As ALWAYS, I SINCERELY appreciate the input of many colleagues who read either the entire manuscript or individual chapters and helped improve the final script. There is not enough space to thank everyone who has done so, and any shortcomings that remain are mine alone.

Special thanks are owed to Professor Nader Hashemi of Georgetown University, who carefully read the manuscript and helped strengthen the arguments. I also appreciate the keen edits of Dr. Nicola Degli Esposti of the University of Padua.

I am grateful to Professor Ali Ansari of St. Andrews University for his critical feedback on the Iran chapters; Professor Pejman Abdolmohammadi of the University of Trento and Dr. Ali Fathollah-Nejad of the American University of Beirut for their astute comments on the Iran chapters; Dr. Walid Abdelnasser for his helpful input on the Egypt drafts; as well as Stephen Kinzer, a journalist and scholar at Brown University, for reading the chapter on Guatemala and providing valuable suggestions. This work benefited greatly from conversations with the historian M. E. McMillan about ideas and books on alternative history.

I am indebted to Jessica Jiji, a scrupulous and a brilliant editor, who improved both the style and substance of the book. Jessica's rich knowledge of the Middle East contributed greatly to the flow of the narrative. Her input and feedback were critical. I am grateful to Jennifer Lyons, my longtime agent, for her commitment and friendship. I also owe thanks to my research assistants, Ferhat Gurini and Euan Ward, who diligently assisted me in researching this book, and I want to recognize Mohid Rehman for organizing the footnotes and Mohamed Elhag for fact-checking chapters 6 through 9. I want to thank my editors at Yale University Press, Jaya Aninda Chatterjee and Ann Twombly, for their diligence and care which improved the manuscript.

I could not have written this book without the support of my family. Over the years my wife, Nora, has selflessly given me the time and space to research and write. I would not have succeeded without her love and affection. My children (Bassam, Annie-Marie, Hannah, and Laith) provided encouragement as well as contrary views. I am proud to be the father of such a beautiful and intelligent crew.

Finally, I dedicate this book to my late and beloved mother, Sara Bachour. My mother was a courageous woman who, as a single parent, gave her all to her children while facing poverty, a decades-long civil war, and the devastating loss of an adult son. In very tough circumstances, my mother fought to ensure that her children would obtain a first-rate education, believing that this was the pathway to better lives. I was heartbroken when my mother passed away while I was researching this book.

WHAT REALLY WENT WRONG

Introduction

Narrating History

THE MIDDLE EAST HAS always enticed Westerners, from opportunists engaged in petro-diplomacy to Hollywood producers animating tales from *One Thousand and One Nights*. The magic and the madness, the romance and the poignancy, the colossal suffering and the breathtaking promise—these depictions of the Middle East cry out for an ambitious, authentic, and original vision based on a rich historical understanding of the region.

There is also a public thirst for a truthful, unbiased account of the region's recent history. Every dramatic turn of events, from the killing of Jamal Khashoggi in the Saudi consulate in Turkey, to Israel's frequent onslaughts on Gaza, to the corruption charges against Benjamin Netanyahu in Israel, to Donald Trump's "deal of the century," increases the public's interest in a credible corrective to the idea that the region lurches from one disaster to the next.

The stakes rise above any intellectual exercise. A realistic portrayal of the Middle East can humanize its people; acknowledge and affirm their dignity, their struggles for justice and freedom, and their aspirations; and inspire reconciliation and peace within and beyond the region. Underlining this potential future is the purpose of this book.

Doing the Middle East Justice

When we drill deep enough, we learn that the heart of the Middle East is neither sectarian nor doomed to fail. Recognizing the humanity of Arabs, Persians, Turks, Kurds, and Jews paves the way for greater investment in the characters that define the Middle East. This means discovering its people and articulating a constructive narrative that does justice to the complexity and color of the region.

For this nuanced understanding to take hold, we must look beyond oil, arms sales, and even the region's outsize religious landmarks and narratives to the Middle East's historical record and current predicament. Forgotten and distorted early historical ruptures and junctures will be consolidated and interrogated for the first time in this book, filling a gap in scholarship. Guided by a strong command of the region's history, culture, language, and present-day realities as well as an interdisciplinary approach, these pages will show that newly independent countries were not allowed to chart their own development immediately after the end of European colonial rule.

The following pages will also show how the West lost the Middle East, and how choosing domination over solidarity brought about a crisis of political legitimacy in the region. It is now increasingly hard to hide from this historical reality and to continue to deflect blame from the West.

In her recent groundbreaking book, the historian Elizabeth Thompson shed light on the pivotal years that followed World War I, when the Arab forces that had contributed to the defeat of the Ottoman Empire tried to establish the first democracy in the region. Led by Emir Faisal, the Syrian National Congress approved a liberal democratic constitution that enshrined the rights of all people, Muslims and non-Muslims, Arabs and non-Arabs.[1] Yet democracy and sovereignty did not fit into the plans of Britain and France, the self-appointed tutors of the post-Ottoman Middle East. Arab democracy was crushed, which left room for the partition of the region between the two colonial powers. These events would shape the relationship between the Arab people and the West for decades.

At the end of the colonial era after World War II, the Middle East was on the cusp of a new awakening. Imperial Britain, France, and Italy were discredited and exhausted. Hope filled the air in newly independent countries around the world. People looked to the United States, the newly ascendant Western superpower, as a progressive oasis in a sea of European reaction. Like people across the decolonized Global South, Middle Easterners had great expectations as well as the material and spiritual energy needed to seize their destiny and modernize their societies. Few could have imagined events unfolding as disastrously as they did. Yet by the late 1950s, the Middle East had descended into geostrategic rivalries, authoritarianism, and civil strife.

What could have clouded this promising horizon? A careful historical analysis unveils both squandered chances and dormant possibilities.

Two interrelated arguments will be woven throughout the book. First, against great odds, the people of the Middle East have consistently and persistently struggled to attain freedom and dignity. Second, the countries of the Middle East have not been able to chart their own course because of factors such as imperialism, the West's coveting of the region's petroleum, the global Cold War, and interrelated geostrategic rivalries and conflicts.

My story examines the post–World War II period. Digging deep into the historical record, the book will critically examine flash points like the C.I.A.'s ouster of Iranian Prime Minister Muhammad Mossadegh in 1953 and the U.S. confrontation with Egyptian President Gamal Abdel Nasser in the mid-1950s. My argument is that such flash points sowed the seeds of subsequent discontent, hubris, and conflict. I zero in on these historical ruptures to reconstruct a radically different story of what went wrong in the region, thus correcting the dominant narrative. My goal is to engender a debate about the past that can make us see the present differently.

Interrogating these events also helps us chart a path forward.

After the in-depth analysis of the Iran and Egypt cases, the book will travel to Central America to show that similar dynamics were at play there. The C.I.A. overthrew Guatemalan President Jacobo Árbenz in 1954 using Cold War and anticommunist tactics and defending global corporate interests at the expense of the peoples. Although the Guatemalan case demonstrates that America's

Cold Warriors targeted postcolonial leaders across the Global South, my book explores the specific historical trajectory of the Middle East.

The puzzle that the book attempts to answer is why the Middle East is gripped by disillusionment, despair, lack of political legitimacy, and distrust of politics. What explains the visceral popular opposition to U.S. foreign policy? What are the impact and legacy of the global Cold War on the Middle East? What if the region had been allowed to chart its own development? If different decisions had been made at key historical junctures, might the Middle East be more stable, prosperous, and pluralistic today?

I argue that the defeat and marginalization of secular-leaning nationalist visions in Iran and Egypt in the 1950s and 1960s allowed for Sunni and Shia puritanical religious narratives and movements to gain momentum throughout the Middle East and beyond. Because of bad decisions that were made in the White House, power passed from popular leaders and sincere patriots to unpopular and subservient rulers, and the sympathy of the people was hijacked by Islamist leaders and movements. The consequences of events in both Iran and Egypt still haunt the Middle East today.

My Own Starting Point: Beirut

Strategically located at the intersection of Africa, Asia, and Europe, the Middle East has always been a dynamic and adaptive region. Since the dawn of civilization, it has developed cultural, economic, and political links with the outside world. All its ancient civilizations were at the peak of human progress. Arguably, few places in the world have experienced as much cross-border fertilization as this region. That history has been defined mostly by multiculturalism and coexistence. Only very recently has the region steered off this course.

Having grown up in Beirut, I can recall the cosmopolitan potential of a country known for its mix of Arab, European, and Asian influences, where intellectuals mingled with merchants and progress was born. As the home of a multiethnic, multireligious, and multicultural society, Lebanon was celebrated as an example of coexistence and tolerance from the 1940s until the 1970s. The lived experience of tolerance is deeply rooted in this ancient land, as well as in neighboring Arab lands.

I vividly remember that my secondary school classmates included Sunnis, Shias, Christians, Druze, and Jews. I knew them not by their religious faiths but simply as my friends. Our disagreements were mostly along ideological rather than political, religious, or ethnic lines. The key divide within the student body was left versus right and rich versus poor. We were more worldly and cosmopolitan than sectarian. We were idealistic, engaging with our aspirations, hopes, and fears for the future of our world.

Our country was outstanding for the vibrancy of its civil society, its openness, and its cosmopolitanism. Until the civil war of 1975, Lebanon was defined by its demographic diversity rather than sectarian strife.

Within this world of diversity and coexistence, however, was the reality of economic cronyism and injustice. Social and economic inequities fueled a growing wave of student activism in the early 1970s, which sought to give voice to the grievances of the underprivileged in the more remote northern and southern areas of Lebanon. The unwillingness of the ruling elites to address these concerns allowed identity-based politics to flourish. This in turn gave rise to a heightened awareness of the social inequities that pervaded our country. Lebanon's elite was dominated by those clinging to and exploiting sectarian identities (which are intimately linked to Lebanon's colonial construction). The country is in a volatile area, surrounded by regional bullies.

The convergence of all these vulnerabilities weighed Lebanon down, triggering a revolution in 1975 that was centered on tangible socioeconomic grievances, not vague notions of identity. Indeed, at least initially, the conflict pitted a coalition of radical leftist groups against state-centric status quo–oriented elites. At the heart of the struggle were two competing visions, one radical-secular and the other conservative-sectarian.

After less than a year, what started as a social revolution in Lebanon evolved into an outright civil war. The intervening years brought successive wars, conflicts, and civil turmoil that demoralized the Lebanese and demonized the country's image. Lebanon became an example of the phenomenon seen throughout this century:

clans and warlords would never have let members of their sects join ranks with others in a call for real change.

And yet, in 2019, in a country of just 5 million people, more than a million individuals from all religious, social, and political persuasions joined forces to call for an end to the hereditary sectarian system that has been in place since the republic was established in the 1920s. It took a tax on WhatsApp in Lebanon to spark the wave of nonsectarian protests that revealed that the Lebanese have more in common with each other than not, just like their sisters and brothers across the Middle East. Protestors shattered the artificial sectarian walls that had been constructed by their tormentors, pitting families against each other. The people of Lebanon have broken their sectarian chains, even though they have not yet succeeded in enacting real change. Rallying under the cry "All of them means all of them," these protestors believe that the sectarian-based elite must go. This revolutionary demand has the potential to spark transformative change in the future. The inscription of love for their homeland is indelible, and it reads: tribalism and sectarianism are not destiny.

By shining a light on the case of Lebanon, we can see an agitation for change that has gripped the country for decades. Similarly, led by their youth, people in Tunisia, Iraq, Sudan, Iran, and Algeria have taken to the streets to demand freedom, justice, and dignity. Just as Christians and Muslims stand side by side in Lebanon, so too do protestors in Iraq. Sunnis, Shias, Arabs, and Kurds join together against a corrupt and failed regime. In the process, they are shattering the myth of perpetual sectarian strife and laying the foundation for a better future. Those in the West so quick to write the obituary of the Arab Spring were premature in their prognosis. The protestors who come from such diverse backgrounds hold the promise of a new political dawn in the Middle East. It is time for the world to catch up with their vision, even though their aspirations have been crushed so far.

The starting point is to radically rethink the Middle East. This requires a new understanding that this book will strive to impart: a discovery story, doing away with conventional patterns of thinking, of what could have been as well as of what the way forward might be. The historian's responsibility is not only to demolish false narratives but also to help build a solid foundation for the future. Managing the transition is in everyone's interest. What will this transition look like? What is the region transitioning to?

The following pages will address the theme of managing the political transition and change in the Middle East. The revolt of the youth contains an implied puzzle: if the Middle East had been allowed to chart its own course of development in the postcolonial era, the people and the region could have fared better and become more prosperous, stable, and democratic. Outside powers repeatedly subverted popular, legitimate leaders and institutions that did not play by their rules and serve their interests. Consequently, the people of the region have been denied freedom and pluralism by both the Great Powers and their local autocratic patrons. Among all foreign powers, the United States played a preponderant role in frustrating and undermining Middle Eastern leaders who fought for independence and economic sovereignty in the postwar era.

A Century-Long Arab Spring

The struggle for freedom, justice, and dignity did not begin with the Arab Spring in 2010; it has been an enduring goal since the establishment of the modern state system in the Middle East after World War I. Thousands of people have paid with their lives, struggling against colonial rule, foreign domination, settler colonialism, political authoritarianism, and militarism. Of all the people in the region, the Palestinians have struggled against great odds to end Israeli military occupation of their lands and to gain freedom and independence. Despite being battered, imprisoned, and killed, the Palestinians have shown *sumud* (steadfast perseverance) and determination in the face of the U.S.–backed Israeli military apparatus. The prisons and dungeons of the Pahlavi monarchy in Iran, Saddam Hussein in Iraq, the Assad family in Syria, Muammar Qaddafi in Libya, the mullahs of the Islamic Republic of Iran, Israel, the monarchies in the Gulf, and other autocrats clearly show that Middle Eastern people aspire to a better life, even at the risk of death. Students of American history should recognize this struggle for freedom. It echoes that famous line from Patrick Henry during the American Revolution: "Give me liberty or give me death."

Donald Trump's xenophobia might be perceived as representing discontinuity, but the forty-fifth president's Islamophobia and anti-Arab sentiment build on a long heritage passed down by other U.S. leaders. Even the erudite and cosmopolitan Barack Obama said that the Middle East's conflicts "date back millennia." He once remarked, "The default position for a lot of folks is to organize tightly in the tribe and to push back or strike out against those who are different."[2]

Blaming the region's problems on tribalism or supposedly ancient conflicts between Sunni and Shia Muslims exonerates the West, which is partly responsible for the turmoil. The mistaken view expressed by Obama and twisted by Trump is widely shared in Western policy circles across the political spectrum. What flows from this binary depiction is the pretext for supporting authoritarian strongmen to preserve "stability." In addition to striking more blows against the Middle East, the West's very act of betraying its own principles extracted and imposed a far higher cost than whatever was gained materially through advantageous commodities pricing, strategic bases, and other geopolitical spoils.

My story provides a corrective to the binary portrayals that overlook difference and diversity in the Middle East and deny centuries of coexistence and tolerance between peoples of different creeds and ethnicities. As Edward Said noted, the othering of Arabs and Muslims has resulted in a dynamic in which the crimes of a minority of strongmen and extremists have eclipsed the good works of millions of humane and compassionate people.[3] Rather than being judged on merit, their very existence comes to stand for violence, backwardness, and otherness.

Doing Away with Cherry-Picking

A coterie of foreign policy experts sees the Middle East as a backward region resistant to change. The rise of political Islam in the Middle East is portrayed as the antithesis of modernity rather than a product of and reaction to it. Even Sayyid Qutb, considered the father of Salafi Jihadism, was socialized within a British education system. Instead of viewing this modern ideology as a byproduct of modernity, Westerners reduce political Islam to an all-pervasive, immutable "essence" that traces its roots back to 600 BC. Even more important, authoritarian political Islam might not have risen to the extent it has today if the legitimacy of the state systems from the 1950s onward had not been hollowed out by foreign interference and subversion of democracy.

Dominant Western narratives cherry-pick from history. The dissonance between lofty rhetoric about American values and the dismal reality of U.S. foreign policy is ascribed to an American leadership stuck in a "mental bog" and a "faulty" reading of history, argues the conservative Catholic scholar and retired army officer Andrew Bacevich.[4] Democracy, prosperity, empowerment, and the rule of law, on the one hand, and total war, slavery, imperialism, and genocide, on the other hand, are all linked to the diffusion of Western modernity, but the latter are rejected as anomalies.

When such "anomalies" occur in the Middle East, however, they are presented as the norm and analyzed not according to the same social scientific standards applied to "the West," but according to outdated discourses and Orientalist stereotypes. This simplistic view denies the region's immense contributions to our collective civilization. It does not consider the colonial and postcolonial effects, the roads not taken, and the agency of millions of people who struggle for a better future. This struggle, dating back to revolts against the Ottoman Empire, has been driven by antipathy to both foreign domination and domestic political repression, as well as a longing for emancipation and self-determination. Yet what they got was polarization, fragmentation, and radicalization, accompanied by a rise in ethnocentric and religion-based rhetoric used as a tool for political mobilization—in the Middle East and, tellingly, in Western societies as well. From the United States to India, Hungary, Italy, Brazil, and beyond, the tide of authoritarian populism, ethnonationalism, and religious fundamentalism is rising, ominously echoing developments that preceded World War II.

All these global developments have broader reverberations that affect the Middle East. If we want to halt the march along this destructive path, we must understand how we got here. The only way to do so is to revisit our history to show that the havoc wreaked on Arab societies is a modern phenomenon, incited and fueled by the Great Powers and their local authoritarian clients.

I also bring to life the story of human agency in the region. Far from being impotent and powerless, local leaders played superpowers off each other to obtain money, arms, and protection. The fascinating figures of Mossadegh, the shah of Iran, Ayatollah Khomeini, Nasser, Anwar Sadat, and others are shown in all their dimensions as they lose sight of the collateral damage and strategic costs to their countries. I take a hard look at the Middle East's manmade crises resulting from unrelenting foreign intervention as well as monstrous miscalculation by indigenous leaders during the postcolonial period. But my story also demonstrates that there was nothing inevitable or culturally determined about the current mess. Radically rethinking the past offers revelations about the present and future.

America's Informal Empire

The history of the Middle East cannot be understood without two major pieces of the puzzle, momentous events in Iran and Egypt in which America played a decisive role. Within living memory, the peoples of the Middle East viewed the United States with awe and optimism. Unlike its European allies, America had never ruled over Muslim lands and appeared to have no imperial ambitions. Instead, Americans had built hospitals and major universities in the region. Washington had the potential to build relations on the basis of mutual interests and respect, not dependency and domination. When the United States signed an agreement with Saudi Arabia to begin oil exploration in 1933, the people of the region saw it as an opportunity to decrease their dependence on the "imperial colossus," Great Britain.[5] If America had lived up to its popular image as a force for good, it might have taken the world by storm, transforming the destiny of the Middle East and the planet as a whole.

From the Middle East to Africa and Asia, newly decolonized countries discovered that formal independence did not translate into full sovereignty. A creeping form of colonialism kept tying these countries to their old European masters and, when the latter were not powerful enough, to the new American power. Kwame Nkrumah, leader of Ghana's liberation from British shackles and a worldwide symbol of the anticolonial struggle, warned his fellow African leaders of this new peril that he named "neo-colonialism." In

Nkrumah's words, "The essence of neo-colonialism is that the State which is subject to it is, in theory, independent. . . . In reality its economic system and thus its political policy is directed from outside."[6]

Like Nkrumah, many leaders of three continents of the Global South discovered that a new, insidious form of empire was taking shape. As the historian Rashid Khalidi noted, the United States was following in the footprints of European colonialism, but in its own way.[7] The American way made the distinction between a formal empire and an informal one. Effectively arguing this point, Atul Kohli, in his book *Imperialism and the Developing World: How Britain and the United States Shaped the Global Periphery*, compares British imperialism during the nineteenth century with America's informal empire in the twentieth.[8] Although not overtly, the United States exploited pliant local regimes, established extensive military bases, penetrated national economies, staged military interventions, and imposed punishing multilateral sanctions. It might not have gone by the formal name *colonialism*, but the effects were the same: Washington—often backed by London—pursued its interests at the cost of the right to self-determination and sovereignty of other peoples and countries.[9]

Kohli offers the example of America's relationship with the shah of Iran to make his point that, unlike colonial empires, informal empires are based on "an alliance in which elites in the imperial country allow elites on the global periphery to share in economic growth in exchange for establishing stable but ultimately subservient governments there." The American relationship with the shah of Iran during the global Cold War is cited as a "classic . . . example" of an informal empire.[10] Egyptian President Anwar Sadat is another example, who sided with Pax Americana in return for economic, military, and political rewards. This is more than an observation about decades-old history. The unspoken hegemony that prevailed then still exists today with respect to America and the Middle East. There is more historical continuity than discontinuity in U.S. foreign policy toward the Middle East. The Truman and Eisenhower administrations laid the foundation of an imperial foreign policy which was hardened by the Richard Nixon and Ronald Reagan presidencies. Even after the end of the Cold War in 1989, U.S. imperial foreign policy persisted with George W. Bush, waging a global war on terror that saw the United States invade and occupy Afghanistan and Iraq.

The arrangement provided a financial reward for the local collabora-
tors. Kohli documents how multinational corporations and financial
flows across national boundaries grew in importance in the second
half of the twentieth century, giving peripheral elites who supported
U.S. interests opportunities to reap enormous rewards from opening
their economies to global finance. The United States and its Western
allies compensated these elites and their rulers across the postcolonial world.

In the case of the Middle East, the United States provided
arms, aid, and security protection to the shah, Saudi rulers, Sadat,
and Israel. The economic growth achieved by these semi-sovereign
countries was not equally distributed across economic, regional,
and ethnoreligious divides, Kohli notes.[11]

On the other side of the equation, the United States as the
dominant capitalistic superpower built the postwar international
financial and trading and security institutions that allowed its competitive corporations to outperform others. This global system of
open, imperial economies disproportionately steered the fruits of
the world economy growth to the citizens of the West, particularly
Americans.[12] Kohli argues that the United States sought to tame
sovereign and effective state power in the newly decolonized
world. Regime change, covert and overt military interventions,
sanctions to create open economies, and acquiescent governments
were all among the weapons of the informal Cold War imperialism, all wielded with the soundtrack of piercing alarm about the
specter of a Soviet communist threat.[13]

The project was not without opposition, however. Nationalist
forces resisted the new imperialism, and U.S. leaders escalated
their military efforts to defeat indigenous opposition. This strategy
ultimately failed to address the root cause of the problem and increased anger at the new, thinly veiled imperialism. Absent enough
justification for using military force, the United States sowed un-
founded fears about its credibility or even an impending threat to
the homeland.[14] As Kohli points out, Washington's shortsighted
views ultimately backfired, undermining security globally and fore-
stalling good governance in the Middle East and beyond.[15]

Added to Iran and Egypt as cases in point are Guatemala, dis-
cussed later in the book, but also Syria, Lebanon, and others. The

sovereignty of these countries was on a collision course with the new imperialism. Countries that attempted to control their own resources for the benefit of their own people risked confrontation with the new informal empires, the United States and Britain.[16]

I present Kohli's framework because it provides helpful context for understanding relations between the United States and the Middle East during the first decades of the global Cold War.[17] I would go further than Kohli, however, who notes that national economic interests were important drivers behind Anglo-American actions, to contend that Western national security interests were equally important. The specter of Soviet communism held Eisenhower's Cold Warriors in such thrall that they myopically focused on that threat. Kohli implies that fighting communism was just "an excuse" for American intervention in developing nations, but to those concerned, it was real. Kohli emphasizes material interests but acknowledges that a multiplicity of events culminating in McCarthyism in the early 1950s led Americans to view the developing world through the prism of the Cold War.[18] In a nutshell, by the early 1950s, the Truman and Eisenhower administrations had launched an all-out war against "godless communism" as well as socialism—in both real and, crucially, imagined manifestations—extending their definitions to Third World nonalignment. This became a cardinal rule of U.S. foreign policy, particularly with the Nixon and Reagan presidencies.

American leaders reacted to feeling on the defensive by going on the offensive, choosing military over diplomatic action and rollback over détente and containment of the Soviet Union.[19] The security strategy of the United States was spelled out in 1950 in a sixty-six-page top-secret National Security Council policy document called NSC-68, which "provided the blueprint for the militarization of the Cold War from 1950 to the collapse of the Soviet Union at the beginning of the 1990s," noted the historian Ernest R. May.[20] The effects would be profound and lasting. Under the new policy, the United States vastly increased military spending, pursued the hydrogen bomb, and promised to undermine "totalitarianism" and to roll back global communist expansion.[21] In a nutshell, by the early 1950s, the Truman and Eisenhower administrations had launched an all-out war against "godless communism" as well as socialism—in both real and, crucially, imagined manifestations—extending their definitions to Third World nonalignment.

The U.S. foreign policy establishment saw the world through imperial lenses that divided everything into binary terms—black and white, good and evil. In their eyes, the existential struggle against Soviet communism justified violence, collective punishment, and all other means to achieve their ideological ends. The C.I.A.'s director at the time, Allen Dulles, who did the empire's dirty work, declared in June 1961 that the destruction of the "system of colonialism" was the first step to defeat the "Free World."[22] Instead of seeing the end of European imperialism as an opportunity for the West to build new relations with the recently independent states that were based on mutual respect and common interests, Dulles sought to curtail political progress. The aim of U.S. leaders following the end of the Second World War was to create an informal empire, or Pax Americana, that would succeed European imperialism.[23] This ambitious aim still animates American foreign policy long after the end of the global Cold War.

Setting up defense pacts in the Middle East in the early 1950s to encircle Russia's southern flank, Eisenhower's Cold Warriors pressured friends and foes to join in America's network of alliances against Soviet communism. Newly decolonized states like Iraq, Egypt, Iran (which was not formally colonized), and Pakistan had to choose between jumping on Uncle Sam's informal empire bandwagon and being trampled under its wheels. Suddenly, the historically nonimperial Western power was mimicking colonial Europe.

Although America's tactics differed, it used neo-imperial divide-and-control devices and covert and overt military methods to force compliance and establish a Pax Americana in the region.[24] Among these was the narrative of backward tribalism, ancient divisions, and congenital violence. In fact, the instability was engendered by policies exploiting the region's resources and peoples in the name of that narrative. The only way a liberal democracy could justify such methods was through such narratives.

America's imperial vision had ramifications back home. Americans would have escaped the decades of militarist and interventionist tendency that afflicted U.S. foreign policy and prolonged costly wars. In addition to the tragic lives lost in conflict, the absence of what would have been a peace dividend takes its toll on the health and welfare of millions of people who have nothing to do with the military-industrial complex itself. Above all, the United States would have been spared its first and worst casualty: democracy at home.

Nowhere is the irony of all that America lost clearer than in the farewell address given by Eisenhower, the premier militaristic and imperial Cold Warrior, who authorized C.I.A.–sponsored coups in many countries. Eisenhower warned of the growing influence of the military-industrial complex and its grave implications for liberty and democracy at home: "We must guard against the acquisition of unwarranted influence, whether sought or unsought, by the military-industrial complex."[25] Heeding this warning might have kept America out of debt and bitter conflicts with other countries and avoided polarization at home. President Eisenhower and his Secretary of State, John Foster Dulles, were trailblazers in pursuing an imperial system on which subsequent Administrations built and augmented.

This book's core concern is with the legacy and impact of U.S. foreign policy during the early years of the Cold War on political and economic development in the Middle East. It shows how Anglo-American interventions in the internal affairs of the Middle East arrested and stunted political development and social change there and led the region down the wrong path to authoritarianism, militarism, and Sunni and Shia pan-Islamism. The Middle East was reimagined as a Cold War chessboard, which left a legacy marked by dependencies, weak political institutions, low levels of civil and human rights protection, lopsided economic growth, and political systems prone to authoritarianism. This is the antithesis of often-stated Western values rooted in democracy, human rights, and the rule of law.

Developing countries emerged into independence from a history that left its mark on their future. With the foundations of imperialism far from completely dismantled, it is no surprise that new structures took their shape if not their names. In some cases, it was more than just persisting structures perpetuated dependence. It was the very leaders and their descendants who were co-opted into a neocolonial reality. Anyone challenging that order was swiftly marked as an enemy of democracy and free markets. Dependencies were reinforced and hierarchies were entrenched.

The Middle East between Two Spaces:
Unique, Not Fixed

It is worth noting here that this book does not argue that democracy was bound to flourish in the Middle East if the United States had not subverted the nascent democratic and anticolonial movements. Rather, America's military intervention, its backing of authoritarian, reactionary regimes and neglect of local concerns, and its imperial ambitions created conditions that undermined the lengthy, turbulent processes that constitutionalism, inclusive economic progress, and democratization require. The political scientist Lisa Anderson notes that "it is usually decades, if not centuries, of slow, subtle, and often violent change" that create the conditions for meaningful state sovereignty.[26]

This book does not suggest that the experiences of the Middle East are wholly unique when compared to those of other regions in the twentieth century. Some characteristics are specific to the Middle East, however, such as its contiguity to Europe and the fact that its vast quantities of petroleum, strategic waterways, markets, and the surplus cash from oil sales have proved irresistible to Western powers. Western powers have thus persistently intervened in the internal affairs of Middle Eastern countries as they have not in other parts of the world. This "oil curse" has triggered a similar geostrategic curse in the Middle East, pitting external and local powers against each other in a struggle for competitive advantage and influence. This convergence of curses has far-reaching and lasting political consequences.

My story eschews historical determinism and offers a robust reconstruction of the international relations of the Middle East as well as social and political developments in the region. It also encourages us to reimagine the present in light of revisiting the past. In so doing, we can begin to see lost opportunities and new possibilities for healing and reconciliation.

CHAPTER ONE

Mossadegh, Nasser, and What Could Have Been

T HIS CHAPTER WILL TELL the story of the two post–
World War II transformative events: the overthrow of
Muhammad Mossadegh in August 1953 and the Eisenhower administration's attempt to cut Nasser to size,
which led to the Suez Crisis in 1956. Each of these flash points will
be rich with detail. Far from being a simple argument that different
decisions would have led to different outcomes, this chapter will lay
out the puzzle of the book, arguing that these inciting ruptures set
off a chain of reactions and counterreactions that dramatically
changed the face of the Middle East. Although I do not draw causal
links between what happened in Iran and Egypt in the 1950s and
the 1960s and subsequent events, the overthrow of Mossadegh and
the confrontation with Nasser provided a trigger, a chain of crises
that radically altered the trajectory of change in the region. These
transformative incidents were great inflection points in that change.

The First Wrong Turns

Iran's first democratic government was toppled by a C.I.A.–backed
coup in 1953. Three years later, America humiliated Egypt's President Gamal Abdel Nasser in order to undermine him and eventually

oust him, triggering the Suez Crisis, which almost precipitated a world war. These two incidents struck Middle Easterners just at a moment of hope for their region, making the blow all the more dramatic and destructive. The events corroded U.S. relations with the Arab and Muslim world, shaking the positive view that many people of these lands held of the United States in a sign of impending future trouble. The coup in Iran was the initial American foray into the dangerous role it would come to play far beyond the Middle East, making our understanding of this origins story critical to unpacking similar events in Latin America, Asia, and Africa.

In contrast to other newly independent states, the Middle East was exceptional in that external powers intensely and repeatedly intervened in its internal affairs, making it, in the words of L. Carl Brown, "the most penetrated region in the world."[1]

When genuinely patriotic leaders, like Mossadegh and Nasser, emerged, their desires for meaningful independence and modernization were branded as disguised communism. While this approach was used in other regions, when it came to the Middle East, U.S. leaders rationalized their neo-imperial mission by asserting that Islam and Arab culture were incompatible with democracy. What emerged from this was a policy of backing authoritarian strongmen in the name of stability, which has become a cardinal rule of how Western governments deal with the Middle East today. Unable to quench its appetite for oil and control over the world economy, the American republic made a conscious choice to become an informal empire—and in the process damaged American democracy and the world. But Western powers became dependent on an undemocratic Middle East.

This cynical and mutually reinforcing relationship, which the sociologist Timothy Mitchell dubbed "carbon democracy," was toxic to both the American republic and the nascent postindependence nation-states in the Middle East.[2] According to Mitchell, the relationship was based on "the pipelines, oil agreements and oligarchies that organised the supply and pricing of oil" but, crucially, "was accompanied by the construction of the Cold War, which provided a framework for the policing of the postwar Middle East that replaced the need for mandates, trusteeships, development programmes and other scaffoldings for imperial power."[3] Mitchell argues that increased American interests in these postindependence Middle Eastern states during the Cold War played a key role in their slow, unstable, and lopsided development.

America embarked on what amounted to an "informal empire" that was modeled on the dominant geopolitical paradigm reigning before it: European imperialism. Studying the history of the Cold War period will lack all context unless it is understood in the larger scheme of British and French imperialism, which drew the map of the Middle East with an eye to the ruling powers' interests. Local rulers gained, maintained, and increased power by doing the bidding of the colonial masters. These pro-Western rulers enabled the integration of the Middle East into the global capitalist economy on terms favorable to the imperialists. It was difficult enough for countries emerging from colonialism to build sound institutions, gain public trust, and extend state authority, and America's actions during the Cold War made this all the more difficult, if not impossible. The Middle East was launched on the trajectory it continues today first by European imperialism and then by American interventions. Local rulers then and now are complicit in perpetuating the region's current predicament.

Since these events were contemporaneous with the global Cold War, naturally communist Russia had a strong hand. That said, there are important reasons to focus on how the United States interfered with and influenced the Middle East. The United States played a preponderant role, inheriting the colonial mantle of its European allies and building an informal empire of its own with a network of friends like the shah of Iran, Israel, and Saudi Arabia.[4]

There were signs on the road of the conflagration that would erupt. The fallout from the Six-Day Arab-Israeli War of June 1967, the continued dispossession of the Palestinians, and America's preponderant support of Israeli settler colonialism are some. Then there was the taking of American hostages in Iran in 1979, the Iran-Contra affair, and the successive wars in Iraq. The culmination came in the September 11, 2001, attacks on the American homeland. The subsequent U.S. global war on terror caused at least 4.5–4.6 million in direct and indirect deaths across conflicts in Afghanistan, Pakistan, Iraq, Syria, Libya, Somalia, and Yemen, according to the Costs of War study by Brown University's Watson Institute for International and Public Affairs. Moreover, 38 million people have been displaced or made refugees, and the United States has spent more than $8 trillion on these wars, the Costs of War research suggests.[5] There were also the resulting seismic waves across Arab societies and not least in the West, where antiterror laws implemented to fend off "the invisible enemy" came at the cost of civil rights.

I do not mean, however, to suggest that there is a direct, straightforward line between events in the 1950s and 1960s and those in the contemporary Middle East. My story interrogates key flash points and inciting incidents and shows how these ruptures set off a chain of reactions and counterreactions that dramatically changed the face of the Middle East. The implications for the entire world were grave and lasting. American democracy was undermined. The venomous effect of colonial European discourse on Middle Eastern minorities has deepened and led to even more societal division and polarization. Without the United States as a beacon of democratic values, lesser powers worldwide were inspired not by Washington's admirable idealism but by its cynical self-interest and imperial overreach. This had serious consequences for people who suffered from the actions of less prominent but no less damaging governments.

More specifically, the West's self-appointed role as the leader of the free world and defender of human rights has been deeply corroded, the ramifications going well beyond reputation. Mistrust in the international liberal order has weakened international institutions and eroded deference to norms such as respect for human rights. What unfolds in Guantánamo Bay or Gaza, Palestine, hurts more than individuals unjustly subject to illegal torture or civilians slaughtered by the thousands; it raises the global public's tolerance for such abhorrent acts by having them unfold in the heart of the democratic West.

This is not an exercise in wishful thinking and feel-good idealism; it is a rediscovery of the historical Middle East and its contentious love-hate relationship with the West. This is a transformation story because it shows how and why the Middle East was (and still is) fundamentally changed by Anglo-America's imperial meddling and intervention. Although formal colonialism ended at the end of World War II, imperialism did not.[6]

It will come as a surprise for those who like to use the Middle East as shorthand for violence—those who might casually write, "It looked like Beirut," or "It was more explosive than Fallujah"—but the region over the past century and a half has been comparatively far less violent than even Europe, which witnessed some of the greatest crimes in world history, particularly the Holocaust and, subsequently, genocide in Bosnia. Death tolls per capita even by conservative estimates show how blood-soaked conflicts beyond the region have left their respective battlefields, whether the two World Wars, the Korean War, the Vietnam War, the Balkans wars, or the U.S. war on terror. Ultimately, though instability persists, the Middle East's level and proportion of violence have not reached such scales.

There is nothing exceptional about the region's supposed ideological differences from the rest of the world, particularly the democratic deficit. The assumption that democracy is the pinnacle of state-society development, its institutions immediately and universally transferable to all contexts, is not empirically valid, especially in developing countries. The political theorist S. N. Eisenstadt argues against viewing the contemporary world through the lens of the cultural program of Western modernity, as most classical sociologists do. Instead, Eisenstadt suggests that the idea of "multiple modernities" best explains the actual development of modernizing societies that have refuted the homogenizing and hegemonic Western program of modernity. In this sense, modernizing countries in the Global South have a multiplicity of ideological and institutional patterns that differ from those of their Western counterparts.[7] This premise of democratic hegemony also ignores the long and treacherous and violent context-specific path all "developed" Western democratic nation-states take to reach the summit, if they can even be said to have reached it yet.[8]

Instead, the differences lie in the way the Middle East has been repeatedly penetrated under various pretexts and how this intense foreign intervention has shaped how politics is done in the region and the way outsiders deal with the region. The formative period of the postcolonial Middle East ran from 1947 to 1958. This was the season when the perennials that still bloom today were planted. Had the United States acted differently during that time, as opposed to resurrecting an informal empire, the destiny of the Middle East as well as America's standing in the Islamic world would have been radically altered and strikingly enhanced.

Enter Iran: The Gateway to
Reimagining the Middle East

Imagine you're on a spaceship orbiting earth. Try to imagine the Middle East as it looked in the late 1940s, and now look at Iran. The first thing that will spring to your eyes is most likely the summit of Mount Damavand, Asia's second-most prominent peak, after Mount Everest, towering above the clouds. Mount Damavand has a special place in Persian folklore. It symbolizes Iranian resistance to foreign domination and despotism. Zahhāk, a foreign ruler who terrorized the Iranians for a thousand years, is said to have been chained up with a lion's pelt fixed to the walls of the mountain's cavern until the end of days. He was overthrown in a popular revolt organized by the nobleman Fereydun, legitimate heir and future king, and led by the blacksmith Kāva. This legend tells us that, stretching back thousands of years, the Iranians, like every other people in the world, have wanted to be free of foreign rule and despotism.

Granted, there probably never existed in Iran an immortal foreign demonic ruler with three mouths, six eyes, and three heads, two of which were snakes that had to be fed human bodies daily—but to suggest that Mossadegh was inspired by this myth in the late 1940s and early 1950s is not completely out of place, the story bearing some resemblance to his brief premiership. Mossadegh, a nobleman, nationalized oil as a means of strengthening Iranian economic sovereignty and wresting itself free of quasi-colonial British control. The people wanted him to nationalize the oil sector, just as the people wanted Fereydun to free them of Zahhāk. Arguably, the biggest difference between the overthrow of Zahhāk and Mossadegh's nationalization of oil was the ending: in Fereydun's case, Zahhāk remained imprisoned within the walls of Mount Damavand forever. The people got their will and Iran was free again. But in Mossadegh's case, the oil soon came under foreign control once again, and the Iranian people went back to even heavier foreign-sponsored despotism. Spillovers of that struggle still haunt them to this day.

The country, which would come to be known as the enduring enemy of the United States, subject to repeated and increasingly stringent sanctions and sirens of wars, was an emerging democracy in the late 1940s and early 1950s. By any objective measure, the prospects for democracy consolidating in Iran at this time looked promising. But rather than allowing the flourishing of this legitimately liberal government, led by Prime Minister Mossadegh, the C.I.A. orchestrated a coup and deposed him. In the process, the U.S. spy agency toppled much more than the Iranian people's choice of leader; it dealt a body blow to America's moral compass and democratic soul.

The reverberations were felt far beyond the Middle East, lending weight to this reconstructed history as a valuable prism through which to view the globe. By the early 1950s, American democracy was stealthily hijacked by the creeping military-industrial complex and imperial seekers. The coup in Tehran also undermined the legitimacy and potency of international institutions, such as the United Nations Security Council.⁹

This was more than a policy miscalculation—it was a neon sign flashing an unmistakable message: the United States would oppose independent and legitimate leaders like Mossadegh—and later the assertive Nasser—who insisted on full political autonomy and who sought to mobilize natural resources and economic assets to lift their peoples out of abject poverty and misery. In his book *Oil and the World Order: American Foreign Oil Policy*, the scholar Svante Karlsson argues that the wave of nationalization that took place in the Middle East after World War II "infringed one of the basic rules of the world economic order, private enterprise and ownership." He points out that in the second half of the twentieth century, "control of the international oil market was one of the most important keys to the control of the world order."¹⁰

Instead, America backed acquiescent or subservient ruling elites, a continuing pattern of U.S. foreign policy today: political and economic interests matter more to the United States than the values it preaches. America's unconscionable removal of Iran's legitimate leader sowed the seeds of the 1979 Iranian revolution and set the course for acrimonious relations that still exist now.

Of course, there is no direct line between 1953 and 1979. But values were corrupted; constitutionalism, liberalism, and pluralism in Iran suffered a critical blow, and, as a result, Iran's political and developmental trajectory was disrupted and altered, which empowered radical and revolutionary ideologies like Marxism and Shia pan-Islamism.

Although Iran experienced some economic growth under the shah, it was uneven, lopsided, fueled by oil wealth, and not based on a diversified and productive economy. Iran under the shah neglected agriculture, which turned this rich-soiled country into a food importer and a commodity-dependent economy.[11] The legacy was an Iran dominated by political authoritarianism under both the repressive rule of the Pahlavi monarchy and the subsequent clerical takeover in the early 1980s.

One aspect of this reconstruction of the history of the Middle East asks how different Iran might have been today if there had been no C.I.A. coup in 1953. Imagining an Iran without oil as a prominent feature in its internal and external affairs offers a vast and vastly different trove of outcomes. A democratic Iran could have been at peace with itself as well as an example for neighboring states. Iranians generally agree that the coup against Mossadegh derailed an emergent democratic sensibility. Others go further by arguing that democracy and political secularism—values that are routinely invoked by the United States—would have established deep roots in their country. Without this transformative event, Ayatollah Khomeini, who would spearhead the Islamic takeover of Iran in 1979, might never have gone into exile in Iraq in the 1960s or gained national and international stardom.

The C.I.A.–sponsored coup against Mossadegh arrested Iran's political and social development. The country veered off course, never regaining its democratic spirit. Or, rather, it was steered off course—aided a great deal by the United States in developing its repressive institutional design in the forms of secret police and maximum-security prisons. These repressive apparatuses were later inherited by the Iranian theocracy from 1979 onward and, ironically, now fuel U.S. narratives on Tehran's cruelty and despotism.

My reconstruction of the Middle East allows readers to enter a world where Iran follows its rightful and proper path to develop into a secular-leaning, modernized, and industrialized nation. Its petroleum reserves and skilled labor force could have allowed a genuinely representative government to support the diversification of a commodity-dependent economy and a better distribution of wealth. This diverse and inclusive economic choice could have ushered in a future as an economic power and an emerging market following the path of the Four Asian Tigers (Taiwan, Singapore, Hong Kong, and South Korea), a wealthy, high-tech, industrialized club of impressive economic development, rather than that of an oil-dependent economy. Greater opportunity could have fostered a culture of respect for human rights and the rule of law as well as women's empowerment. Instead of the present image of a "rogue" and "dangerous" country so successfully manufactured and sold to Western audiences, Iran might have taken its place as a responsible member of the international community, a civilization rich not only in petroleum, but also in history, culture, and diversity.

Egypt's Seeds of Peace

If Iran is the gateway to imagining a new future, Egypt is the garden where we could find peace if only the seeds had been nurtured. Nasser had been positively predisposed toward the United States, but this potential friend was turned into an embittered foe when, in July 1956, President Eisenhower delivered a humiliating public smack when he revoked an offer of nearly $70 million in aid to Egypt for the construction of the Aswan Dam on the Nile River. This was not a miscalculation on the part of the Eisenhower administration; rather, it was a conscious strategy to force a newly decolonized leader to align with the U.S.–led capitalist camp against Soviet communism and eschew state-led development. Absent this ill-fated move, the Egyptian leader would arguably not have entered a tactical relationship with the Soviet Union, and all the fallout that ensued might have been avoided: namely, the Suez Crisis later in 1956 and, even more crucially, the Six-Day War in June 1967. In their stead, the world could have benefited from a more stable region led by a prosperous and peaceful Egypt, and many lives would have been spared.

There is ample evidence of rich soil in this garden. Nasser had no ideological prejudice against the United States and admired American culture. Soon after the overthrow of the pro-British monarchy in Egypt in 1952, he watched Esther Williams movies in the American embassy and wished for his people the same level of prosperity that he saw in those films. Spending time there, Nasser tried to build a close relationship with U.S. diplomats, who then had the foresight to recommend that Washington befriend the new Egyptian leader. The divisions between those in Washington and American officials in Cairo soured U.S.–Egyptian relations. The U.S. media irresponsibly and provocatively poured gasoline on a raging fire by painting the young Egyptian colonel as an expansionist dictator in the mold of Hitler and Mussolini.

This stood in sharp contrast to how Nasser was viewed by the Americans who personally knew him from their long social encounters in the U.S. embassy in Cairo. At this early stage of the Egyptian revolution, Nasser, a young, mild colonel, had not developed a radical sensibility yet, and his worldview was fluid and evolving. Even before the revolution, Nasser and other army officers hoped that America could help in deterring Britain from sabotaging the nascent republican order in Cairo. "Nasser said that America was the only power capable of stopping any British intervention against the revolution," a close army officer friend of Nasser told me.[12]

My argument in this book is that American officials could have capitalized on opportunities to engage with Nasser, a proud, authentic leader who struggled to modernize his country and free it from imperial British control. The seeds of peace sowed by these acts could have flowered into a harvest of goodwill and powerful friends for the United States in the region in the form of leaders who possessed internal political legitimacy and presided over calm, stable, and prosperous polities.

Readers might find my analysis of Egypt's Nasser controversial because he is often portrayed in the West as simply another Arab authoritarian leader with pro-Soviet leanings. My goal is to advance a more nuanced portrait of his rule and political legacy while not exonerating him for cracking down on opposition and all forms of political dissent. Unlike Mossadegh, Nasser was not a democrat. But like Mossadegh, he was a developmentalist genuinely concerned about improving the severe social and economic conditions under which most Egyptians lived—and against the odds and external pressure, he achieved results.

Nasser was also an Egyptian nationalist who believed that the question of political independence is critical to the question of development at home and in neighboring Arab countries. It was this grand and principled vision that earned him legend status from Morocco to

Yemen and beyond. Despite his political authoritarianism, Nasser was a unifying and inspirational leader in Egypt.

Like Iran, a peaceful, prosperous, and strong Egypt could have been the cornerstone of the Arab foundation for democracy. To many people in Egypt and the Arab world, Nasser was an authentic leader, in touch with the grassroots sentiments of the average citizen and fighting for their dignity. Evidence of this is in our lived history. Many countries of the postcolonial world that are democracies today first experienced a period of authoritarian rule after independence before they underwent a transition to democracy. South Korea, Taiwan, Indonesia, Ghana, and Senegal come to mind. Moreover, the Western states' own road to democracy had not been linear or peaceful. It had been long and treacherous, evolving over centuries and taking many forms.[13]

If the postindependence international and regional context had been more propitious, could Egypt's political and economic development trajectory have been different? This book guides the reader in contemplating this critical question.

While it is difficult to precisely determine the unlimited potential of the peace dividend, we can say for sure that the United States would have avoided deadly military entanglements in the region, keeping its troops home instead of sending thousands of boots on the ground to defend the status quo and suffering substantial financial, moral, and physical losses. Middle Eastern peoples would have continued to view the United States as an extension of the philanthropical and progressive American civil society, entrepreneurship, and missionaries that had operated in the region before the 1950s. Then the waste and destruction wrought by the informal empire's military-industrial complex would have been replaced by the gain and value of investments in people engendering greater national prosperity and progress.

As I mentioned in the introduction, in the early 1950s, a sharp turn away from the road taken would have steered the United States away from its embrace and nourishment of authoritarian regimes and strongmen. Instead, sleaze and corruption spread as some of those regimes became wealthy, bought think tanks in Washington, and lobbied Congress and the White House for access and influence. They metastasized the cancer in U.S. politics of allowing private money, special political and corporate interests, and lobbies to shape American foreign policy at the cost of democratic values and respect for human rights and the rule of law. America's full-throated backing of Israeli occupation of Palestinian lands is a case in point.

A Geostrategic Curse

Like its sponsored coup against Mossadegh, America's decision to confront Nasser in the mid-1950s not only changed the trajectory of U.S.–Egyptian relations but also deeply shaped questions of war and peace in the Middle East. By targeting Nasser's Egypt, the United States went against a pivotal state that held great sway among Arab countries and the broader decolonizing world. Nasser retaliated by trying to discredit the Arab monarchs and presidents who joined U.S. imperial networks and defense pacts, which led to a prolonged proxy conflict known as the Arab cold war.[14] This strife between Arab countries had local roots, but the United States blew on the fire; the consequences were compromising inter-Arab cooperation and weakening the newly established Arab League. Not unlike Iran after 1953, the Arab state system never recovered its balance and equilibrium. Geopolitical rivalries tore up plans and hopes for regional economic cooperation and integration.

At the risk of being simplistic, I argue that America's post–World War II imperial ambitions and its offensive conduct in the early decades of the global Cold War triggered something resembling a geostrategic curse in the Middle East. This geostrategic curse has afflicted the region since the 1950s, which coincided with U.S. grand strategy to build an informal empire and roll back Soviet communism.

The internationalization of local and regional politics has played a major role in the maintenance of the status quo, blocking political progress and transformative social change. Immediately after World War II and the onset of the global Cold War, the United States together with Britain aimed to establish a mini–Middle Eastern NATO in order to contain and strangulate the Soviet Union and to control the region's oil and energy supplies and strategic waterways. This neocolonial agenda, or informal empire, clashed with the aspirations of local leaders like Mossadegh and Nasser who prioritized sovereignty, state-led development, independence, and nonalignment in foreign policy. Mossadegh's and Nasser's noncompliance with the Anglo-American demands and even resistance pitted them against the United States, which intervened covertly and overtly in an offensive to undermine their regimes.

The result was to intensify geopolitical rivalries that weighed down the nascent and fragile nation-states in the region. For example, when Nasser and his Free Officer comrades seized power in 1952, their priorities were bread and butter and jobs. They sought to use state power to lift most of the Egyptian people out of punishing poverty and modernize and industrialize the country. Yet by the second half of the 1950s, the Free Officers' agenda shifted radically from an internal focus to a regional focus, entangling the country in costly international rivalries. It would not be an exaggeration to argue that a geostrategic curse afflicted Egyptian foreign policy and led to overextension and miscalculation. The Six-Day War in June 1967 between Israel and Egypt was a case in point. As I will show, in May 1967, preoccupied with challenges by pan-Arab nationalist rivals in Syria and Iraq, Nasser miscalculated and fell into Israel's trap and suffered a catastrophic defeat.

America's imperial overreach and Cold War crusade were the spark that ignited and escalated geostrategic rivalries in the region. Writers view the global Cold War struggle between the United States and the Soviet Union as representing a philosophical and ideological fault line in international relations. In the Middle East, however, there was more convergence than divergence between the two rival superpowers when it came to social and political change. They shared a common goal of preserving the authoritarian status quo and preventing socioeconomic transformation, which allowed them to expand their influence and exercise control. When Nasser and other radical pan-Arab nationalists suppressed Marxists and socialists at home in the 1950s and 1960s, Soviet leaders turned a blind eye. They sacrificed their ideological allies on the altar of realpolitik and national security interests. Similarly, the United States backed brutal authoritarian rulers like the shah of Iran and allied itself with ultraconservative, far-right religious groups and acquiescent regimes like Saudi Arabia and the Afghan mujahideen. American officials sought to combat godless communists and socialists and to tame progressive and radical nationalists.

Far from disappearing, this geostrategic curse is alive and well. From the beginning of the global Cold War to today the Middle East has been a battlefield for intense geopolitical rivalries involving both external and regional powers. Time and again these rivalries have blocked social and political change, consumed financial resources, and sustained the repressive status quo. This is not to say that if the United States had acted differently, the Middle East would not have been gripped by geopolitical rivalries. My contention is that the intensity, potency, and lasting consequences of these rivalries could easily be traced to the U.S. effort to establish a Pax Americana in the early 1950s and to confront nationalist leaders who pursued an independent posture at home and abroad. This U.S. tendency to stir up regional rivalries persists, pitting Iraq against Iran and now "moderate" Sunni Arab states against Shia-dominated Iran.

Looking at today's most salient geostrategic struggle between Shia-dominated Iran and Sunni-majority Saudi Arabia through the lens of social and political change, we see more similarities than differences. Like the United States and the Soviet Union during the Cold War, both Iran and Saudi Arabia share the fundamental strategic goal of maintaining the balance of social forces and crushing dissent. A core concern for Tehran's clerics and Riyad's royals is to prevent radical change in the region, which could threaten the sectarian interests of their ruling coalitions. For instance, Iran and Saudi Arabia have fought hard to crush the Arab Spring revolts that erupted in 2010. Both regional heavyweights are leading counterrevolutionary powers. The Islamic Republic in Iran has invested blood and treasure to keep the secular nationalist Bashar al-Assad in power in Syria. The pro-Iranian Hezbollah in Lebanon, a resistance movement, justifies its defense of the Assad regime on geostrategic grounds. Saudi Arabia and its Gulf allies have spent tens of billions of U.S. dollars in a concerted campaign to thwart the Arab Spring revolutions in Tunisia, Egypt, Bahrain, Yemen, and Libya, and later in Sudan, Iraq, and Syria.

There is no doubt that this geostrategic curse is one of the significant factors that have contributed to crushing the aspirations of millions of Arabs for freedom, justice, and dignity. Likewise, geostrategic rivalries have undermined the aspirations of the Palestinians for a state of their own. Since its foundation, Israel has mastered the art of using regional rivalries for its purpose of undermining the unity of the pro-Palestinian front. Since the Iranian revolution, Israel has played to anti-Iran and anti-Shia sentiments in the region and aided Arab autocrats to divert attention from its occupation of Palestinian lands. It has aligned itself with Arab Gulf states (and the United States) in an anti-Iran coalition, trumpeting the threat posed by the Islamic Republic and vowing to counterbalance it. The result is that the prospects for granting the Palestinians the right of self-determination and ending Israeli military occupation have stalled. There is no end in sight for alleviating the suffering of the Palestinian people.

The role of this geostrategic curse in sustaining political authoritarianism and hindering social and political progress should not be underestimated. A close look at the current constellation of regional and global politics points to a grim situation. There exists near consensus in the United States, Europe, and the international community on the need to preserve the regional status quo, a balance of power to which Western leaders have given birth and which they have nourished over the past decades. The civil wars in Syria, Libya, and Yemen and the instability in neighboring countries are cited as a cautionary tale against experimenting with change and democracy.

Russia's and China's greater engagement in the Middle East reinforces this reactionary trend of eschewing change. Middle Eastern autocrats could not be happier. They sell themselves to the United States and Western Europe as preservers of stability while warning about the destabilizing effects of promoting human rights, political participation, and the right to dissent. When they sense danger to their survival, Middle Eastern strongmen quickly recalibrate their policies and tone down the geopolitical rivalries. It is difficult to keep up with the ever-changing geostrategic regional chessboard.

Of course, this geostrategic curse is not destiny. The Iranian revolution in 1979, the Arab Spring uprisings in 2010–12, the Palestinian resistance to Israel's military occupation, as well as the subsequent wave of revolts that started in 2019, show clearly that people's agency has not yet been quelled and that it can overcome internal and external barriers. The challenge facing agents of change is to develop strategies to minimize the role of foreign stakeholders, which is easier said than done. But there is no denying that social and political progress will be difficult to institute without isolating and neutralizing geostrategic rivalries. A suitable regional context can help facilitate internal struggles for democracy. The reverse is also true.

The Road Not Taken

With this as a starting point, we follow the road not taken to see how the Middle East would look without the damaging effects of that momentous conflict, America's imperial ambitions in the first decades of the global Cold War, amplified over the years and felt intensely to this day. Key among those were the resurgence of political Islam and the spread of Sunni and Shia pan-Islamism in the Saudi and Iranian models. Both these factors are dominant features of the landscape today across North Africa and the Sahel, in Indonesia, and in large parts of South Asia. They are also found among Muslim communities in the United States, the United Kingdom, Australia, and other countries where the ideologies have spread to people raised outside these traditions who are willing to lay their lives on the line for the cause.

It is doubtful if the Six-Day War in June 1967 between Israel and its Arab neighbors would have happened if the United States had not decided to cut Nasser's wings and fully sided with Israel and anti-Nasser Muslim fundamentalists like the Saudi rulers. Key to understanding the implications of that war is grasping the fact that for many Arabs, the setback, as they call that conflict, was far more than a military defeat; it ruptured the public imagination and robbed Nasserist Egypt of its grandeur and nationalist symbol. The defeat dramatically setback pan-Arabism and reminded millions of Arabs of the lasting and humiliating legacy of European colonialism and U.S. informal imperialism as well. Nasser's defeat was portrayed by others as an act of punishment by God, who had forsaken Egyptians for embracing Nasser's secular illusions of progress and socialism, so far astray from the "right" path of what it meant to be an authentic Muslim in the modern world. Smoldering in the embers of war lay the Nasserist project of secular Arab nationalism, which gave

Saudi Arabia's pan-Islamism the opportunity to rise out of the ashes.

With America's backing, the religious right in the Arab world was ideally placed to fill the ideological vacuum left by Egypt's defeat and Nasser's untimely death of a heart attack in 1970. Nasser's successor, Anwar Sadat, enabled the shift to religious conservatism. Seeking to rid Egypt of the outsize legacy of Nasser and build his own legacy, Sadat allied himself with Saudi Arabia and allowed the religious right to till Egypt's fertile soil. Breaking with Nasser's semi-closed economy and foreign policy, Sadat opened the Egyptian economy to global finance and joined the Pax Americana in the region.

The Americans rewarded Sadat with financial aid and arms, and the U.S. media heaped praise on him as a historic leader and peace-maker. Ironically, unleashing these forces would prove to be Sadat's own undoing. His bloodstained uniform from that fateful 1981 military parade in Cairo, on display in the Library of Alexandria, tells the tale of the violent end to his eleven-year tenure by the Egyptian Islamic Jihad, a group that Ayman al-Zawahiri, late head of Al-Qaeda, was a member of at the time and would in 2001 merge with Al-Qaeda, a few months before 9/11. More than any other leader, Sadat unwittingly helped tilt the balance of social forces in favor of political Islam and pan-Islamism. His alliance with the Saudis came at a propitious moment, when the oil revolution in the mid-1970s bolstered the conservative kingdom's finances and soft power in the Arab-Islamic world. From Egypt to Afghanistan and beyond, the Saudi oil boom bankrolled the pan-Islamist resurgence that continues a half-century later. The rise of the religious right in the Arab lands coincided with the revolution in Iran in 1979, which was subsequently captured by the clerics. Pan-Islamism of both Sunni and Shia stripes, feeding on each other, spreads near and far.

With America's backing, Israel has since consolidated its control of all Palestinian territories, including east Jerusalem, the West Bank, and the Gaza Strip, and it has annexed Syria's Golan Heights. U.S. leaders frequently pay lip service to the proposed two-state solution framework for resolving the Israel-Palestine conflict—a Jewish state for Israelis and a Palestinian state for Palestinians. American policy makers have turned a blind eye to Israel's expanding colonial settlements and repression of the Palestinian people.

Almost 1 million Israeli settlers now live in occupied Palestinian territories. As the anointed leader of the free world, the United States has consistently disregarded the human rights of Palestinian Arabs and their aspirations to self-determination. Over time, because of these double standards, Arabs and Muslims have become convinced that the United States is complicit in the Palestinian predicament. Not only have the people of the region become deeply critical of U.S. foreign policy, but their attitudes toward democracy and liberalism have hardened as a consequence. It would not be an exaggeration to argue that America's backing of Israeli settler colonialism is key to the spread of anti-American sentiments in the Middle East as well as a contributor to a rise in extremism.

The latest example of this trend is President Joe Biden's response to Hamas's bloody attack on Israel on October 7, 2023, and the subsequent full-scale Israeli military onslaught on the Gaza strip. Saying that it would tie Israel's hands, Biden vetoed UN Security Council draft resolutions that called for a "humanitarian pause" and humanitarian ceasefire. As Israel bombarded Gaza, killing thousands of Palestinian civilians, including children, women, and the elderly, the Biden administration's unwavering support for Israel risks deepening and widening anti-Americanism in the Middle East and the Global South. American weapons used by Israel in Gaza have also triggered accusations of war crimes against the United States.[15]

It is worth asking: What if the United States had neither confronted Mossadegh, Nasser, and other "godless" socialist- and secular-leaning nationalist leaders in Syria, Iraq, and elsewhere during the global Cold War, nor backed acquiescent autocrats and Israeli settler colonialism and Islamic-dominated states and movements as it did in Iran, Saudi Arabia, and Pakistan? It is very likely that political Islam and supra-Islamism might not have emerged as the most potent ideology offering an alternative identity to nationalism and radical Arabism embodied in the secular nation-state. Religion would have been a far weaker tool for political mobilization, resulting in a vastly different political landscape. Had Egypt not been militarily crushed in 1967, the cascading events that followed might have been avoided. Sadat might not have aligned his country with Saudi Arabia, the United States might not have relied so heavily on Saudi Arabia and Israel, and the 9/11 attacks might never have happened.

These are not far-fetched or imaginary scenarios, but important themes grounded in historical fact and based on an understanding of real forces that have shaped the Middle East's destiny in the second half of the twentieth century. The lives spared and human progress secured expand further when we consider that if Sadat had not isolated Egypt from the rest of the Arab world in the 1970s, the consequences in Lebanon would have been profound. The subsequent inter-Arab rivalries converged with social and economic inequities in Lebanon which led to the country's implosion. Lebanon was a model of religious and ethnic tolerance that might have been nurtured, scaled up, and adopted elsewhere. Instead, the country became the scene for fifteen years of one of the most heartbreaking civil wars ever to befall the region. Rather than that tragedy, one might instead imagine a Lebanon that would have gradually shed its sectarian power sharing and replaced it with a constitutional contract based on citizenship.

The United States changed the course of history by trying to impose its new imperial vision and Cold War obsession with Soviet communism on the newly independent states in the Middle East and other regions. This trampled on the aspirations of indigenous nationalist leaders like Prime Minister Mossadegh in Iran and President Nasser in Egypt.

The Architects at Home and What They Could Have Built

Although labeled superpowers for their potency, the United States and Soviet Union were far from alone in driving the history of the Middle East. In reality, the leaders across the region were also responsible for the existing calamity; officials such as Mohammad Reza Pahlavi, the shah of Iran, Nasser, David Ben-Gurion, Golda Meir, Sadat, Hosni Mubarak, Saddam Hussein, and Hafez al-Assad all played their roles in causing the current predicament.

We can clearly see what would have happened if Nasser had not acted impulsively in May 1967, giving Israel a justification to preemptively attack Egypt a month later. We can easily imagine how Egypt would have progressed and developed its institutions if Nasser had tamped down his antidemocratic beliefs and tolerated peaceful political dissent. We understand what might have been if Nasser's successor, Sadat, had genuinely pursued self-sustaining and inclusive economic and political development rather than crony capitalism and flirting with religiosity and Islamism as a counterweight to secular ideologies. And we see how Egypt could have served as a model of open society for other Arab countries, thwarting the rise of political authoritarianism and political Islam as the dominant force in Arab politics. We could envision the Arab states succeeding in turning the League of Arab States into a regional organization such as the European Union if geostrategic rivalries had not intensified after the mid-1950s. An Arab Union might have been a global powerhouse able to rise above the intra-elite rivalries that have long paralyzed the league.

In Israel, we can witness what might have been if Prime Minister Ben-Gurion had agreed to international initiatives in the 1950s to reconcile with the Palestinians and the Arabs. Had he given up the dream of a greater Israel, Israelis and Palestinians might be living side by side in peace, a secure Israel fully integrated into an Arab neighborhood. The tragedies averted are incalculable, the financial savings astronomical, and the ramifications around the world profound, since the Israeli-Palestinian conflict has been used to justify radical movements from the Sahel in Africa to South Asia and beyond.

Meanwhile, in Iran, we can imagine what would have happened if the radical Islamists had not hijacked the revolution in 1979: Iran's role in fueling the spread of pan-Islamism might have been forestalled. Saddam Hussein's wars, including the ill-fated invasion of Kuwait in 1990, inflicted a national tragedy on Kuwaitis and Iraqis as well. His monstrous miscalculations led to the destruction of the Iraqi state and the pauperization of the Iraqi people.

Even if the 9/11 terrorist attacks had unfolded as they did, had President Bush not used them as a pretext for his global war on terror, the focus could have remained on the perpetrators who carried out the attacks. Bush escalated by invading and occupying Afghanistan and Iraq and destroying the states, not just the Taliban and the Saddam Hussein regimes. The consequences of the U.S.–led invasion and occupation of Afghanistan and Iraq are catastrophic for both countries and others as well.

It will take Iraq decades to recover from dismantling its institutions—as authoritarian as they were—and shattering the fragile coexistence among its diverse communities.

Although U.S. military forces withdrew from Afghanistan in 2021, officially ending the occupation, the Costs of War report notes that Afghans are "suffering and dying from war-related causes at higher rates than ever."[16] The irony is that the Taliban seized power in 2021, twenty years after their removal by the United States.

As the reader will see in the following pages, Bush's global war on terror follows a pattern in U.S. foreign policy toward the developing world that has been in place since the early decades of the global Cold War. Al-Qaeda was a child of the Cold War. The mass murder of Americans on 9/11, while morally indefensible, did have roots in cynical and catastrophic decisions by U.S. leaders. Instead of reflecting on how to prevent further bloodshed by rethinking their approach, they doubled down on failed policies, which led to disastrous consequences for people in the Middle East, North Africa, and Central Asia. Instead of cultivating the good-faith friends they might have made within and beyond the Middle East, they lashed out angrily at real and imagined enemies. By invading and occupying two Muslim countries—Afghanistan in 2001 and Iraq in 2003—the United States created conditions for the emergence of Al-Qaeda in Iraq in 2004 and its successor, the even more infamous Islamic State, in 2014.

President Bush might have left a different legacy in the Middle East. Instead of his search for phantom weapons of mass destruction in Iraq, he could have used 9/11 as a catalyst to reeducate Americans about the world and invest in a Marshall Plan for the Middle East. He could have realigned U.S. foreign policy by cultivating valuable allies in the Arab world while winning the hearts and minds of millions of Arabs and Muslims.

Given the far-reaching ramifications of events in both Iran and Egypt, as well as other incidents, we are left with the question of what might have transpired if the progressive nationalist visions of Mossadegh and Nasser had been allowed to run their natural course. Lessons learned can help provide a way forward.

CHAPTER TWO

A Portrait of Mossadegh

ORN TO A MOTHER descended from royalty and a father
serving as a high-level political official, Mohammad Mossadegh could have lived out his days in aimless comfort.
But more than luxury, his family cultivated within him a
passion for politics and the idea that his privileged status carried
with it a special duty toward the homeland. This influence cata-
pulted Mossadegh to the heights of power, the depths of injustice,
and the annals of history. He was a symbol of independence in his
home country and an inspiration to those seeking to throw off the
yoke of imperialism around the world. It was 1882 when Mossadegh entered the world and 1967 when he left it, changed forever
by his commitment to his country.

Often portrayed as a fallen hero and a secular saint, Mossadegh
held a naive and idealistic view of world politics that led him to
monstrously miscalculate and fall prey to internal and external enemies. He was caught in a fight that set the stage for a cascade of
tragic decisions by those bent on stopping him. Despite his stub-
born and romantic character, Mossadegh offered a constitutional
model of what Iran could have been—and yet could still be—if
Iranians were left to choose their own leaders, control their own
resources, and shape their own future. This portrait reexamines
and reconsiders the role that Mossadegh's vision could have played

in the rise of Iran as a constitutional power at peace with itself and the world.

Mossadegh's Origins

Before attaining this iconic status through ambition, courage, and sacrifice, Mossadegh was the son of Iran's minister of finance and, on his mother's side, the great-grandson of a prince belonging to the Qajar dynasty, which had ruled Iran since 1789. At the time of his birth, tensions between Iran and the colonial powers—namely, Britain and Russia—presaged the confrontations Mossadegh would endure at the cost of his life.

A decade before his birth, Mossadegh's forebears in the Qajar dynasty experienced increasing foreign intervention and domestic turmoil, which led in 1872 to the cancellation of an agreement between King Nassereddin Shah Qajar and a British entrepreneur, Baron Julius de Reuter (founder of the Reuters news agency). This pact would have effectively handed control of Iran's entire economic machine over to foreigners, mirroring the very interference and exploitation that Mossadegh spent his life opposing.[1] The imperialist vanguard and the former viceroy of India, Lord Curzon, described the concession, which never went into effect, as the most expansive grant ever made to one country over control of another country's resources.[2] This was at the meagre sum of £40,000 (around £5 million today).[3]

The incident helped precipitate Iran's Tobacco Rebellion, a nationwide boycott led in 1890 by merchants, intellectuals, and clergymen who forced the cash-strapped shah to cancel yet another concession, this time one that would have granted the United Kingdom a monopoly over Iranian tobacco. It was, effectively, Iran's first major nationalist movement: a "Persian awakening," unfolding as the backdrop to Mossadegh's childhood. During this momentous time, Iran experienced more interaction with Europe, the birth of new intellectual projects, and a proliferation of literature that generated a greater understanding of governance and law. As the aftermath of the rebellion gave a new lease on life to the intelligentsia and the wider civil society, government practices failed to keep pace with changing attitudes centered on independence. The Qajars ceded progressively more control to the Europeans in order to replenish their coffers—with a lasting impact. The British oil concession of 1909 gave birth to the Anglo-Iranian Oil Company (AIOC), which is the origin of the vastly influential and still-enduring monolith British Petroleum.[4]

Within this environment of changing popular perceptions, the future prime minister began to find his footing. Mossadegh was exposed to elite ideas and the Iranian bureaucratic framework from an early age. When his father died of cholera, his uncle received the title of tax collector in Khorasan province—a position Mossadegh would later occupy at just twelve years old. His early career continued to outpace his age so that at fifteen he was appointed chief of finance in Khorasan, again in honor of his father. There it appears that he earned admiration for his savvy and ability to navigate the court.

His precocious rise led Mossadegh, as an active supporter of Iran's Constitutional Revolution, to win election as a deputy to the newly inaugurated parliament the *Majlis*, in 1906, at the age of twenty-four—so young he failed to meet the required minimum age of thirty and could not assume his seat.[5] In 1921 the young Mossadegh, following in his father's footsteps, was appointed minister of finance. He earned his mother's disdain when he insisted on collecting her unpaid taxes.[6] While commanding the honorific "Mossadegh al-Saltaneh," later in life he preferred to be called Doctor in a tacit recognition that the aristocratic politics of his family and early life was less and less in tune with the democratic values he wanted to embrace. (It was a title, as we shall see, that he had earned.)[7]

Mossadegh might have been Western-educated and far more familiar with Western ways than the average Persian, but he was not in awe of everything Western—far from it.[8] The name *Mossadegh* itself is derived from a title that the shah had bestowed in recognition of the family's service.[9] Years later, when Iran adopted a national identity card system, Mohammad chose the surname Mossadegh, which means "true and authentic."

Loving—and Leaving—Iran

Mossadegh was not yet a transformative leader, but his constitutionalist sentiments were "always colored by traditional ideas of Muslim leadership, whereby the community chooses a man of outstanding

virtue—and follows him wherever he takes them."[10] Having received his early postings thanks to his family's connections, Mossadegh knew his ascent was seen, by modern political standards, as
illegitimate at best, and thievery at worst. But after all the fuel of
nepotism was spent, he continued to ascend on the strength of his
charisma; even his legendary melodramatic outbursts ultimately en-
deared him to many. From an early age, Mossadegh proved to be
competent, hardworking, and principled—skills and traits that facilitated his ascent and popularity. But mixed into this idealistic devo-
tion was also a naïveté that would ultimately result in his downfall.

Ever tied to the fate of his country, Mossadegh was transformed by the Constitutional Revolution, between 1905 and 1911,
aimed at enshrining the representation of the people and preventing the concentration of power in the shah's hands. Devoted to its
ideals, Mossadegh quickly gained fame as an incorruptible deputy
revered by many as a tireless defender of democracy and national
independence. The era was marked by public debates on political
and social demands, the formation of new parties, and the proliferation of print media, which saw the number of newspapers spike
from six on the eve of the revolution to more than ninety in the
following days.[11]

Intellectuals rushed to vocalize concepts that had long been
confined to conversations in the country's bathhouses and bazaars.
Now unable to be ignored, these concepts inspired the names of
many of the new publications, such as "awakening," "progress," and
"hope." The centuries-old hegemony of the Qajar dynasty was finally forced to give way to new institutions, new forms of expression, and a new social and political order—with Mossadegh at the
crossroads that would eventually become crosshairs. His heart was
with the dawn of a new era even as it was being opposed by a
cousin of his mother, King Nassereddin Shah Qajar, whose rule
lasted from 1848 until 1896.

By regional standards, the Iranian Constitutional Revolution
was a great leap forward. It advanced political development, promoted modernization, and transformed Iranian society, representing "the first direct encounter in modern Iran between traditional
Islamic culture and the West ... a movement of unprecedented
significance in Iran's modern history which embraced vast groups

of people from every social quarter, thus generating a heated debate between diverse ideologies."[12]

In other words, Iran was on course to embrace just the kind of pluralistic dialogue that the champions of democracy in London and Washington should have cheered. In those early years, Mossadegh was not afraid to speak truth to power. When the shah, aware of Mossadegh's links to the Constitutionalist movement, asked him in 1909 to convince the theologian and vanguard of the Constitutionalist movement, Seyyed Abdollah Bihbahani, to back his rule, Mossadegh retorted that Bihbahani was popular because he sold a product called Constitutionalism and that the shah would not need the support of Bihbahani if he did the same.[13]

Mossadegh's morality was ingrained and combative; if he believed his political projects had even the slightest chance of success, he would risk everything. His flight strategy was equally fine-tuned: in the face of a setback or perceived defeat, he did not shy away from retreating.[14]

When Mohammad Ali Shah launched a bloody bombardment of the Majlis in 1908 with mainly Russian support, Mossadegh faced a difficult choice: join the defense of the Majlis or honor his maternal ties to the ruling house.[15] He chose neither, opting instead for self-imposed exile.[16] Mossadegh's return was brief; the restoration of authoritarianism drove him out within a year. He feared that Mohammed Ali Shah had delivered a fatal blow to the Constitutional Revolution, concluded that Iran was not ready for democracy, and resigned to go study in Europe.[17]

A Persian in Paris

An Iranian newspaper article bemoaned the "depraved of Paris" just as Mossadegh arrived there to study at the prestigious École Libre des Sciences Politiques (also known as Sciences Po). Astutely aware of the taboo against Persian students frolicking in the "world capital of sin" in the name of education, Mossadegh eschewed even visiting the city's main attractions.[18] Belying the die-hard, progressive secularist he is sometimes portrayed as, his abstinence from this type of enjoyment gives a glimpse into the conservative ideas on which his beliefs and actions rested. Mossadegh's moral conviction was contrasted by his physical vulnerability. In Paris he experienced illnesses that would plague him throughout his life, as periodic flare-ups of ulcers and hemorrhaging forced him to lie down during lectures.[19] A respected physiologist in Paris ordered complete rest, but true to his bravado, Mossadegh ignored the command.

These conditions invariably became part of Mossadegh's persona. He was even known to faint during his characteristically impassioned speeches—as much from emotion as from any ailment. Perhaps one of the most dramatic and unorthodox politicians that Iran has ever known, Mossadegh conducted business in his pajamas and often wept publicly. When he later stepped onto the global stage, international foes ridiculed these unconventional aspects of his personality. In Iran, however, where age-old Shia religious practices involved outpourings of emotion unseen in the West, it was celebrated.[20]

Exhausted by work, he had a "complete collapse" in Paris and was forced to give up his studies just a year later and return to Iran. The pressure of having to adapt to an alien culture alongside the strains of holding an important state office, attending to a marriage, and expending great emotional energy and involvement on a revolutionary campaign back home simply became too much. His mental health was forever scarred by the burdens he felt in this period.[21] Mossadegh was so weak that when he changed trains at the Russian-Iranian border, he had to be ferried over in a wheelbarrow.[22]

Following his recovery, Mossadegh returned to Europe, this time with his young family, to study law in the small Swiss town of Neuchâtel. There he authored a thesis that included a deep engagement with shariah, or Islamic law. He advocated the introduction of Western-style jurisprudence to Iran, rather than imposing European institutions directly because "imitating Europe will be the spoliation of a country like Iran, for everything should be in proportion with the need."[23] Aligning himself with moderate cleric modernizers, and borrowing from his knowledge of European law, Mossadegh argued in favor of reforming and modernizing both public and private Islamic jurisprudence to keep pace with progress in society.[24]

Mossadegh developed these ideas as a break from the law-enshrined council of clerics that presaged the current Council of

Guardians in the Islamic Republic of Iran.[25] Ironically, during the Mossadegh era, there was no discussion of clerical oversight of parliament, and it would have remained a nonissue if Mossadegh had not been toppled—if only pluralism were allowed to flourish in Iran.[26] He found life in Switzerland slow and boring and told his children that they would return to their homeland.[27] "We are Iranian, and we are going to stay a short period in Europe and then go back to our country," he pledged.[28] His heart was back at home in Iran. By the age of thirty-two, Mossadegh became the first European-educated doctor of law in Iran.[29]

Oil and Iranian Sovereignty

Upon his return, Mossadegh ran as a member of parliament, first as a Moderate, and later as the Moderates' political rival, a Democrat, who spoke for the modern intelligentsia and steadfastly advocated the separation of mosque and state.[30]

During the Great War, he was appointed governor of Fars province in addition to serving for two years as the deputy of the Treasury. As the governor of Fars and later of the Iranian province of Azerbaijan, Mossadegh earned a reputation as a popular and effective administrator thanks to his productive dealings with the merchants and tribes. His impressive achievements in Fars included brokering peace between the tribes and restoring law and order in the province, which had been known for its lawlessness. One newspaper called him a symbol of "unity, consensus, and stability."[31] He even boasted of his popularity, at the same time acknowledging that he had governed well.

True to his anti-imperialist stance, Mossadegh refused to recognize British authority in Fars throughout his tenure. He championed the strict nonalignment policy of "negative equilibrium" aimed at ensuring independence from foreign domination. He argued that the country's political elite endangered Iran's very existence by "capitulating" to the Great Powers. And he warned that this led other powers to demand equal concessions, which further undermined Iran's national sovereignty.[32] For this reason, Mossadegh opposed basically all types of foreign concessions, well aware that in the nineteenth century, such concessions were often colonial in nature. He maintained this principled view toward accords with any power, whether the 1919 Anglo-Iranian Agreement, shipping rights in Lake Urmiyyeh, a proposed concession of northern Iranian oil to the Soviet Union, the 1933 oil concessions to the Anglo-Iranian Oil Company, or Caspian fishing rights to a Russian company.[33]

All these, he felt, were direct tests of Iran's sovereignty—especially the issue of oil.[34] His goal was to gain Iran's full political autonomy and sovereignty in order to use the country's resources for the benefit of its peoples.

Oil for Mossadegh was much more than a commodity, and Iranian control over it was an important, enduring, and invaluable symbol of national independence. As he would later put it, the "moral aspect" of oil nationalization was far more important than its "economic aspect."[35] His unwillingness or inability to strike a balance between an idealist's hopes and a realist's expectations would eventually doom his cause.

Defiant!

Mossadegh stubbornly defied those in power, even the authority that appointed him. He repeatedly rejected central government demands to toe the official line and instead opted to pursue a path he felt could further strengthen Iranian independence.

As early as the 1921 British-facilitated coup d'état that toppled the central government, Mossadegh refused to recognize the new authority. The administrator and bureaucrat was gradually evolving into a revolutionary statesman. So bold was his defiance that Mossadegh provoked a death threat.[36] Rather than caving, he stood by "his own moral impetus," resigned from his post as governor of Fars province, and fled from the central authorities, taking refuge with the nomads of western Iran.[37] Despite resigning from his post, he later reentered the halls of government, serving as minister of finance, minister of foreign affairs, and governor of the Azerbaijan province. But with each post, his concerted drive to eliminate corruption and establish national independence drew opposition.

By the time he reached those positions, Mossadegh had shed his youthful caution, developing an ambitious vision of democracy and solvent economy at home and, on the global stage, unconditional independence from the Great Powers. "He seemed to believe that every battle was worth fighting."[38] As a member of parliament in the Majlis in 1923, Mossadegh was one of only five, including nationalists and modernizers, who opposed ending the Qajar dynasty because of his ties to the dynasty and his fear that it could usher in a more autocratic order in the country.

Mossadegh had no personal quarrels with the future shah, Reza Pahlavi, but feared that monopolizing power in any one man's hands would lead to tyranny. Mossadegh remained in government as Reza Khan rose to power as the prime minister. But Reza Khan's appointment as shah in 1925 was a step too far for Mossadegh, who along with others criticized the autocracy and warned against establishing an absolute monarchy. Addressing parliament in October of that year, he boldly warned the deputies against giving one man too much power: "Today our country, after twenty years of widespread bloodshed, is about to enter a phase of retrogression. One and the same person as king, as Prime Minster, as Minister of War, as Commander-in-Chief? Even in Zanzibar no such state of affairs exists!"[39]

His warning, together with those of politicians and intellectuals, fell on deaf ears. On December 12, 1925, the Majlis declared Reza Shah the new monarch of Persia, making him the first shah of the Pahlavi dynasty. Mossadegh retired from politics in disgust. This was not a passive retreat, however. Mossadegh continued his opposition to the new regime, which itself threw its weight against him. He was forced into seclusion in his home in Ahmadabad, where he kept a small ivory statue of Gandhi. The Persian in pajamas took inspiration from the pacifist in a loincloth, part of a generation of Western-educated Iranians who returned home "to sell freedom to their compatriots."[40]

In a sudden and dramatic escalation, the shah had him arrested in 1940. Mossadegh was jailed in Birjand prison, a barren fortress in southern Khorasan. During his imprisonment, he sank to the depths of despair, reportedly twice trying to commit suicide, and was released a few months later thanks only to the intervention of Crown Prince Mohammad Reza.

Mohammad Reza, the twenty-two-year-old son of Reza Shah, was installed by Soviet and British troops in 1941 when they invaded

Iran and forced Reza Shah to abdicate. The newly crowned leader was young, inexperienced, and much more tolerant of dissent than his autocratic father. Iran enjoyed a political spring during the first decade of Mohammad Reza's reign, as exiled politicians and intellectuals returned home.

This climate of greater tolerance allowed Mossadegh to reengage in the political arena. He was again elected the first deputy for Tehran in the 1944 parliament, receiving the highest number of votes in the capital. His maiden decisive battle in the parliament aimed to advance the cause that shaped his life: he sponsored a law that banned the government from giving oil concessions to occupying foreign powers. In the process, he firmly reminded Iranians that the Pahlavis had "deprived [them] of their freedoms, stripped them of the right to elect [their own] deputies, . . . extended the oil concession by thirty-two years, and made millions out of [that] deal."[41] This indictment was as scathing as it was truthful.

The National Front

As nationalist sentiment grew, Mossadegh became a key organizer. In 1949 he set up the National Front, an alliance between secular nationalists and modernizing clerics, the latter led by Ayatollah Kashani. The National Front quickly became an influential force, gaining the largest representation in parliament and offering the first organized political platform to promote free and fair elections, freedom of the press, and an end to martial law.

His father's position in government during Qajar rule had allowed Mossadegh to witness firsthand the debates that eventually led to the Constitutional Revolution at the beginning of the century and with it the establishment of Iran's first parliament.[42] In many ways, Mossadegh took up where the Constitutional Revolution had left off before Reza Shah established the Pahlavi monarchy. These early experiences fomented his push for a more democratic and pluralistic system later in life. Mossadegh became a fervent proponent of representative democracy and fought hard to maintain the constitutional structure that had produced a contested political system and fair elections. As he put it: "Parliamentary elections must be free. It is not the task of parliamentarians to approve a new electoral law that conditions freedom of election. The attribution, to some government officials, of the power to select candidates for elections is an obvious violation of the constitution."[43]

Acting on his convictions, Mossadegh organized a protest against the premiership of Ahmad Qavam, fearing that he "intended to establish a one-party state."[44] And Mossadegh spoke against the postponement of the fifteenth Majlis elections, arguing that Iran should not be without a mandated parliament for a prolonged period.[45] In addition, he planned a series of reforms to strengthen the rights of women and workers. As the party's leader, Mossadegh went further by advocating a reform agenda based on three guidelines: first, constitutional revision and reinforcement of the parliament; second, revision of the law on freedom of expression and speech; and third, more guarantees for the members of parliament to be independent and to freely express their opinions.

He was adamant in his defense of democratic principles in his public declarations, as when he defined the duty of a deputy as representing the people. "If the shah does not like the MP to express his opinions, then the country should not even have a parliament," Mossadegh asserted. "So, if there is a parliament at this time, this means that members can freely express their opinions. The shah who, according to the constitution, is the first citizen of the country, must only reign and not govern."[46]

Nationalization of Oil: The Match That Lit the Wildfire

A staunch nationalist and anticolonialist who envisioned a truly independent Iran, Mossadegh had pleaded the case for oil nationalization and international political nonalignment since the early 1940s.[47] He repeatedly called for the end of concessions to Britain and Russia as well as engagement with "third powers," which at the time included the United States.[48]

Iran had been a de facto British protectorate since the onset of the twentieth century. Britain's majority stake in the Anglo-Iranian Oil Company ensured that the Royal Navy, the arrowhead of Britain's imperial power projection, ran without hindrance. Winston Churchill, first lord of the admiralty when Britain's navy converted to oil, spoke of Iran's oil reserves with his usual oratorial eloquence, describing it as "a prize from fairyland far beyond our brightest hopes."[49]

Bucking this history of exploitation, in October 1947 the Iranian parliament refused to grant oil concessions to the Soviet Union and pushed to regain control from Britain over Iran's southern oil resources. Under a 1933 agreement between the AIOC and Iran, Iran was promised a number of measures to protect it from fluctuations in oil prices, including a fixed rate of four shillings per ton as well as a minimum annual payment of £750,000 (around £60 million today). Iran's share of the company's global profits jumped from 16 to 20 percent, the workforce was to be "Persianized," and the AIOC committed to provide better pay for its laborers, chances for advancement, and improvements in the country's health, educational, communications, and logistical infrastructure.[50] Although the terms were better than before, the injustice was clear and, inevitably, the astronomical revenues that the AIOC enjoyed at the expense of the Iranian government thrust oil sovereignty to the top of the new constitutional parliament's political agenda. In truth, the AIOC undermined the promises in the 1933 concession and never built the roads, hospitals, and schools that it had committed to.

In contrast, in the same years, the American oil giant Aramco finalized a far more favorable fifty-fifty agreement with Saudi Arabia.[51] But in the heady moment when success seemed possible, optimism surged. A month after having put together a working coalition, Mossadegh was elected prime minister—winning nearly 90 percent of the votes in parliament.[52] As the leader of Iran, Mossadegh pushed for an independent judiciary, promoted free elections, and defended freedom of religion and political affiliations. He actively sought to modernize the country and lift it out of bondage in an orderly and peaceful way.

Lofty goals were not enough, however, to achieve these noble ends. Never seeking a revolution, Mossadegh lacked a strategic blueprint for his agenda and made tactical mistakes that alienated internal and external stakeholders. His vision, including leadership and the rousing of public sentiment, posed an existential threat not only to Britain's (and America's) national economic interests in Iran but ultimately to the shah himself. Mossadegh, along with others,

aimed to transform Iran into a constitutional monarchy, the first
of its kind in the Muslim world. A royalist speaker of the Majlis
voiced his exasperation in what amounts to unintended praise:

> Statecraft has degenerated into street politics. It appears that
> this country has nothing better to do than hold street meet-
> ings. We now have meetings here, there, and everywhere—
> meetings for this, that, and every occasion; meetings for
> university students, high school students, seven-year-olds,
> and even six-year-olds. I am sick and tired of these street
> meetings. . . . Is our prime minister a statesman or a mob
> leader? What type of prime minister says "I will speak to the
> people" every time he is faced with a political problem? I al-
> ways considered this man to be unsuitable for high office.
> But I never imagined, even in my worst nightmares, that an
> old man of seventy would turn into a rabble rouser. A man
> who surrounds the Majlis with mobs is nothing less than a
> public menace.[53]

After Mossadegh was appointed prime minister in 1951, he
made oil nationalization a key strategic objective to bolster Iran's
struggle for economic sovereignty and independence. His aim was
to use the oil resources to spearhead a massive development program and alleviate poverty.[54] Here a country's leader sought to use
the revenues from its resources to benefit its people. What would
seem to be a commonsense approach earned Mossadegh more ire
from several leaders who preferred to line their own pockets while
offering concessions to foreign powers at the expense of their
people—both in Iran and beyond. "The main reason that I agreed
to become prime minister in 1951 was to get the oil nationalization
done," he wrote, affirming Iran's right to own its revenues.[55] The
controversy surrounding the British oil concession granted in 1901
and modified in 1933 intensified and became inescapably linked
with Iranian domestic politics.[56]

Oil was far more than a commodity—it was a means to and
symbol of economic and political independence, and the United
Kingdom thus became a natural enemy for Mossadegh. Mossadegh's National Front championed the call for outright nationaliza-

tion when Britain refused to accede to its demands. In March 1951 the National Front organized a huge rally to advance the cause in Baharestan Square, facing the stately arched entrances to the historic parliament. On March 15, 1951, on the eve of the Iranian New Year, the nationalization bill received the senate's final approval, marking a seminal point in Iran's history.

One radio commentator offered a succinct analysis: "All of Iran's misery, wretchedness, lawlessness, and corruption over the last fifty years has been caused by oil and the extortions of the oil company."[57] Sadly, those words would continue to ring true for decades to come.

A Plot Thicker Than Oil: Britain's Plans to Oust Mossadegh

But to tell the story of Mossadegh's premiership and the issue of oil, we should step back to the dramatic events that preceded his appointment and revealed the high stakes regarding, international interest in, and global implications of Iran's domestic politics. This diversion will also shine a light on how the question of oil and foreign interests led to domestic violence and the assassination of Iranian Prime Minister Haj Ali Razmara, Mossadegh's predecessor.

Just 134 days before Mossadegh assumed the office of prime minister on July 19, the AIOC's iron grip on Iranian oil was dramatically disrupted by just eight grains of gunpowder and three bullets that took the life of a central player who had a more nuanced approach than Mossadegh's. The victim and scapegoat was Prime Minister Razmara, a former general who had put down nationalist uprisings in Iran's Kurdish and Azeri provinces in the mid-1940s. Razmara had been appointed prime minister in July 1950 by the shah under U.S. and British pressure, as he was seen as the path to ratify the Supplementary Oil Agreement aimed at derailing the nationalization of Iranian oil.[58]

Like Mossadegh in that he wanted independence, Razmara differed from him in attempting to achieve positive equilibrium, making concessions to both the Russians and the West, rather than to neither of them. Iran needed cash in order to provide full employment and raise living standards. This prompted Razmara to open trade with the Soviet Union for the first time since 1946 as well as to pursue negotiations to ratify the Supplementary Oil Agreement with London.[59] Arguably, Razmara was more cunning than Mossadegh. He wanted to use concessions to create a balance by pitting Russia, America, and the United Kingdom against each other. But in the process of trying to create a wider balance and opening the doors to the Soviet Union, Razmara pushed the conservative and powerful *bazaari*, the merchant class, closer to Mossadegh's National Front, helping ease the path for Mossadegh in his attempt to gain the premiership.[60]

Far from being merely a stooge, Razmara was the first Iranian prime minister to have his own independent power base. Yes, he had been picked by the British and Americans to serve and facilitate their interests—and to some extent he did—but he also directly disobeyed his Western partners on several occasions. Razmara disagreed with the top American adviser regarding Iran's Seven-Year Economic Plan. Razmara, who also thawed relations with the Soviets, suffered a downfall not for being a puppet but rather because of his ambitious plan to turn Iran into an independent actor. Instead of winning on all sides, he created enemies in all camps: the Soviets, Americans, and British as well as domestically between the center, right, and left. Razmara's personal ambitions clouded his vision of how to navigate internal and external alliances. And that paved the way for an equally ambitious and politically nearsighted leader: Mossadegh.[61]

Razmara's alienation of the bazaaris had pushed the National Front and the powerful, conservative group closer together. He was shot and killed on March 7, 1951, by a member of the fundamentalist Fadayan-e Islam in front of the Shah Mosque in the northern section of Tehran's Grand Bazaar. Mossadegh took some time to condemn Razmara's assassination, which raised questions about Mossadegh's intentions and damaged his reputation, and a few months later he was appointed prime minister, with no intentions of bargaining with the AIOC.

Mossadegh's decision to nationalize Iran's oil reserves quickly brought him into direct conflict with the British government, which owned a golden share of the AIOC. Its oil refinery in Abadan, in the country's southwest, was considered the "greatest single overseas enterprise in British commerce," which in 1950 brought Britain a staggering profit of £170 million (the equivalent of £6.9 billion today).[62] As a significant source of revenue to the battered British economy and an emblem of prestige for the declining British Empire, AIOC's oil refinery in Abadan provided Britain with the equivalent of America's Marshall Plan loans to London from 1948 to 1952.[63] It was also a model for the developing oil industries of other British protectorates, such as Iraq and Kuwait.

Britain pressed on with a sustained campaign to destabilize Mossadegh's government through a variety of tactics, including a global embargo on the sale of Iranian oil and even state-sanctioned sabotage against the major oil refinery in Abadan. Although the AIOC was a private company, its Iranian operation was Britain's single largest overseas investment. For both sides, the struggle went beyond a valuable resource to constitute a powerful symbol—for Iran, of its sovereignty and independence, and for Britain, of its fast-fading dominance and economic woes after a crippling World War II. British officials expressed a willingness to negotiate with Iran but were never genuinely prepared to accept nationalization. Over the ensuing months, Britain adopted a "three-track strategy" of legal maneuvers, economic sanctions, and covert political action designed to reestablish control over Iran's oil—either by coaxing Mossadegh into a favorable settlement or by removing him from power.[64]

With regard to the first of these stratagems, a negotiating team from the International Court of Justice was sent to Tehran to arbitrate the oil dispute. Despite repeated attempts at reaching a settlement over the coming months, Mossadegh rejected all proposals because they did not explicitly recognize Iran's legitimate ownership and control of its oil. From then on, Britain refused to negotiate directly with Mossadegh, relying instead on mediation by the International Court of Justice, the United Nations, and the United States.[65]

The decision to nationalize Iran's oil reserves at a time when the country lacked the means to adequately extract, market, and distribute oil was risky. Iran did not produce large enough quantities to disrupt the global oil markets; Saudi Arabia and Kuwait compensated effectively for the absence of Iranian oil. As a powerful cartel across the Middle East, the dominant "Seven Sisters" of the international oil industry—AIOC, Royal Dutch Shell, and the American five—controlled the extraction and supply of oil globally.[66] As an extension of the Western international economic order that emerged after World War II, the Seven Sisters, together with their governments, regarded stability in the energy sector as a necessary condition for containing Soviet communism and maintaining foreign investments worldwide.[67]

The embargo was starving Iran financially. True to form, Mossadegh viewed any economic losses as minor compared to the "ultimate prizes, oil and honor," along with independence.[68] In his memoirs, the proud nationalist declared that he challenged British power. "I managed to govern the country even though the Westerners were against us."[69]

Mossadegh's views on nationalization were deeply tied to his fundamental belief in unconditional independence from foreign domination. As a result, he "elevated national independence over everything else, turning it into an existential question that needed an answer before the other questions could even be asked. ... He would accept nothing but nationalization." This dogged persistence in fighting the nationalization battle drew admiration across the world. An adviser to President Harry Truman, the millionaire diplomat Averell Harriman, homed in particularly on Mossadegh's versatility, stating that the prime minister seemed able to transform himself easily from a "frail, decrepit shell of a man into a wily, vigorous adversary."[70]

Mossadegh suffered from chronic idealism sometimes bordering on naïveté. His disregard for Iran's geopolitical predicament would eventually prove his undoing.

Gaining Fame in America but Not Help

As Britain's decision to impose de facto sanctions on Iran increased pressure on the government, Mossadegh appealed to the United States for help. Like many other leaders of nations struggling for independence, Mossadegh had a benign view of America, contrasting it with the practitioners of European imperialism. Hoping to drive a wedge between the two Anglo-Saxon allies, Mossadegh gambled on the Truman administration's coming to Iran's rescue. This gamble was huge, the stakes enormous, and the result calamitous.

In October 1951 Mossadegh traveled to New York to personally defend Iran's right to nationalization at the United Nations Security Council as well as to get the Americans to help him reach a deal with the British. While in the United States, he met President Truman, Secretary of State Dean Acheson, and Undersecretary for Political Affairs George McGhee, whose background as a millionaire oil prospector served him well also in this engagement. Of all the characters in the saga, he ended up having rare insight into the doomed nature of Britain's imperial impulses. Mossadegh made a convincing case regarding Iran's right to nationalize the oil industry at the Security Council, which decided against British wishes to adjourn the debate until the International Court of Justice had given its verdict. He also made a strong impression on ordinary Americans, if not officials, who sympathized with the bedridden Persian patriot.

Gaining international stardom during this period earned Mossadegh *Time* magazine's Man of the Year in January 1952, under the title "He Oiled the Wheels of Chaos"—his second *Time* cover in less than a year.[71] The magazine cover was packed with Orientalist symbolism, racism, and fear: olive-pigmented fists punching through the sandy dunes of Egypt and Iran; oil wells proliferating around the Persian Gulf; and Mossadegh in the foreground, tight-lipped and with extraordinarily creepy skin.

Mossadegh's hopes that the Americans could deliver the British were misplaced, however. Hours spent in secret negotiations in which McGhee laid out the broad outlines of a deal proved fruitless; Secretary of State Acheson wrote that his British counterpart, Anthony Eden, said that the proposal was totally unacceptable. According to Acheson, the British feared that their elimination from Iranian oil production would have a destructive effect on all foreign concessions in the Middle East. McGhee worked hard to get Mossadegh's seal on a deal with Britain—and he warned his British counterparts that their attempt to maintain imperial hold was doomed to fail. Capturing the pulse of the anticolonial moment, McGhee urged his friends in the Foreign Office to set their relations with the Middle East "on a basis of equality" and convince these countries that they were being treated as "equals and part-ners." Unlike his cohorts in Washington and London, McGhee appreciated the strength, vitality, and legitimacy of the nationalist movements in Iran, Egypt, and beyond, seeing in them "examples of a much wider movement in men's minds."[72] But his was a lonely voice in Washington and London.

Although Truman's advisers were preoccupied with the communist threat and feared that Iran was a ripe target for a red takeover, they did act as peace brokers—yet not honest ones. They earnestly engaged Mossadegh in order to broker a deal between Iran and Britain and privately pressed their British allies to be flexible and accommodating toward a growing nationalist sentiment in the newly decolonized world. Truman officials had long taken issue with London for its unwillingness or inability to peacefully resolve the conflict with Iran over the nationalization of oil. State Department officials were originally unconvinced that Mossadegh's nationalization of Iran's oil reserves posed any immediate threat to U.S. attempts to curtail the spread of Soviet communism. Secretary of State Acheson went so far as to criticize the British for being "destructive and determined on a rule-or-ruin policy in Iran."[73] U.S. Ambassador to Tehran Loy Wesley Henderson wrote that Britain had simply "lost touch with events."[74]

Calls by Truman officials fell on deaf ears. In meetings in late 1952, Britain's MI6 startled their American counterparts with a plan for a joint paramilitary operation to oust Mossadegh.[75] Britain's plea for U.S. cooperation in the plan was met with a resounding "get over it" from the Truman administration. This did not stop London from planning and eventually convincing Washington to overthrow Mossadegh.

International developments such as the Chinese Communist Revolution, the Soviet development of an atomic bomb in 1949, and the Korean War in the early 1950s brought about a marked shift in U.S. strategy. The new policy shift introduced in the 1950 NSC-68 national security document weaponized the Cold War, turning the entire world, and not just Europe, into an America-Soviet battleground. The Truman and Eisenhower administrations, and particularly the latter, actively confronted assertive nationalist leaders in the developing world who pursued an independent path for their countries' economies and foreign policy.

With America sliding into this militaristic mood since the early 1950s, Mossadegh's fate was sealed. As early as 1951, Britain was devising plans for a solo military invasion of Iran—code-named Operation Buccaneer—which would have involved direct intervention by the Royal Navy, the Royal Air Force, and the British Army.[76] In a breathtakingly bold admission of their perceived entitlement, the conservative *Daily Express* argued bluntly: "If Britain gives in to the Persians, then the time is near when we give in to the Egyptians and hand to them the Suez Canal—and Sudan. If we bow to Tehran, we bow to Baghdad later."[77] Another conservative newspaper, the *Daily Mail*, urged the government to "do something about Persia before the rot spreads further."[78]

As Britain began to operationalize invasion plans, "three brigades of airborne troops were flown to the base at Shaiba in Iraq and the Persian Gulf squadron was strengthened by three frigates and four destroyers from the Mediterranean," according to the minutes of a British Cabinet meeting in July.[79] Only in September did Prime Minister Clement Attlee abandon the idea of a military invasion of Iran, citing pressure from the Truman administration, which warned its British ally in strong terms against using force.[80] In his address to the Cabinet, Attlee conceded that "in view of the attitude of the United States Government," he did not "think it would be expedient to use force to maintain the British staff in Abadan."[81]

At this stage, the Truman administration was still reluctant to use force to oust Mossadegh, fearing that naked gunboat diplomacy could trigger a blowback in the newly decolonized world. Truman officials had also aimed to convince Mossadegh to agree to a settlement that gave Iran a higher share of oil revenues but maintained international control of the industry. From the beginning of the crisis to the end, the U.S. government opposed Mossadegh's nationalization of oil because that would have created a precedent that threatened America's interest in an open global economy. The American-controlled world economic order in the postwar era "was to a large extent built on the control of oil."[82]

CHAPTER THREE

Saving Iran from Democracy

ANS OF THE JAMES BOND blockbuster franchise will recall that in *Quantum of Solace*, Agent 007 faced a villain who profited by bringing down governments and replacing them with those that would pay with natural resources for the privilege of power. Bond might have expected support from his U.K. masters in this endeavor or at least sympathy from Washington, the champion of democracy. Instead, the C.I.A. agent in charge threatens a junior who questions this approach, and the movie's British foreign secretary argues in favor of it. "The world's running out of oil," he asserts. "The Russians aren't playing ball, and the Americans and Chinese are dividing up what's left. 'Right or wrong' doesn't come into it."

Such naked disregard for principle might seem entirely in the realm of the imagination, but the actions of American and British intelligence operatives in Iran in 1953 reveal that this plotline is ripped from the headlines—or would have been if the contemporaneous reporting had been accurate. Instead, the 1953 coup against the legitimate leader of Iran, Mohammad Mossadegh, was fomented and carried out covertly; some U.S. newspapers and magazines even did the bidding of the agents who engineered it. These covert actions point to neo-imperial designs, challenging the official histories in Washington and London. Pulling back the curtain on this momentous event reveals more than a single frame in a film reel; here a pattern begins to appear. It was in Iran that craven, ignorant, and ruthless adventurers set the mold that would be replicated elsewhere, leaving a trail of unnecessary bloodshed, destabilizing whole countries in the service of greed and power, and running counter to the very principles of freedom and democracy that the Western powers claimed to defend.

By reconstructing the dramatic events that led to the overthrow of Mossadegh, this chapter tells the story of how the U.S. informal empire took shape in the Middle East and the broader developing world. If this seems a damning condemnation, these events at least deserve credit for inspiring Hollywood plotlines that earned millions at the box office. But the real-life costs were astronomical.

Churchill and Eisenhower: The C.I.A.–Led Coup

With the return of Winston Churchill to power in 1952 after spending six years in opposition, any hesitation regarding military intervention in Iran disappeared. Britain's position toward Mossadegh hardened as the former empire teetered on the brink of bankruptcy. The Americans sympathized with the agony of a close ally, Britain, which had gone from being the world's biggest creditor to its biggest debtor; its gold and dollar reserves were enough to cover just a few months of imports.[1]

U.S. Secretary of State Dean Acheson explicitly stated that "the cardinal purpose of British policy is not to prevent Iran from going Commie; the cardinal point is to preserve what they believe to be the last remaining bulwark of British solvency."[2] Acheson's comment reflected the fierce Anglo-American competition over control of Iran's vast petroleum resources, which Iran's scholar John Ghazvinian calls one of the great unspoken rivalries of the twentieth century.[3]

As I mentioned previously, the Truman administration would not back a military coup against a legitimate sitting prime minister in a sovereign nation, and it declined to carry out a joint covert operation with Britain to depose Mossadegh. Although sympathetic to their British ally's severe economic crisis and wanting to help, Truman officials appreciated the growing nationalist aspirations of

newly independent states, including Iran and Egypt, and did not
see an urgent need to oust Mossadegh. Truman, the first Cold War
president, a Democrat, attempted to broker a deal between Britain
and Iran that would ensure the financial lifeline of its ally.

Just as Winston Churchill brought a dramatic change to London, the election of the Republican Dwight D. Eisenhower in
November shifted the winds in Washington. Eisenhower was a
Cold Warrior who believed that America faced an "implacable
enemy whose avowed objective is world domination" and that
"long-standing American concepts of fair play must be reconsidered."[4] Eisenhower was an expansionist at heart, stocking up on
nuclear weapons and rejecting compromise, at the cost of peace, as
he did in South Vietnam. He combined "God and country" with
Wilson's international mission, creating a highly explosive cocktail
of American exceptionalism and adventurism.[5]

The convergence of the power shift in London and Washington doomed Mossadegh. Unlike his predecessor, Truman, who
aimed at containing communism, Eisenhower wanted to roll it
back. Ideologically and militarily, the Truman administration had
already weaponized the Cold War. His NSC-68 laid the building
blocks of fortress America, vastly increasing military expenditures,
pursuing the hydrogen bomb, and taking the lead in forming the
North Atlantic Treaty Organization, or NATO, a military alliance
of Western powers.[6] After Eisenhower became president, a cabinet
of Cold Warriors took charge of American foreign policy and felt
emboldened to intervene directly and indirectly in many theaters
worldwide. These Cold Warriors played empire.

The incoming secretary of state, John Foster Dulles, and his
younger brother, Allen, who was appointed director of the C.I.A.,
were even more extreme Cold War zealots than their boss. They
were the key figures behind the plot to oust Mossadegh, as
Churchill was incapacitated by a stroke when key decisions about
the upcoming coup were made. Neither needed any convincing
that Mossadegh was a dangerous madman pushing Iran into communist arms and that he must, therefore, be deposed. Eisenhower
Cold War proponents now saw Mossadegh as a spoiler: a recently
declassified C.I.A. document described him as one of the "most

mercurial, maddening, adroit and provocative leaders with whom [the United States and Britain] had ever dealt."[7]

God, Country, and Family: The Dulles Brothers

At the center of the growing forest of American imperialism was a family tree rooted in American government with two main branches in the persons of the Dulles brothers: John Foster Dulles, U.S. secretary of state from 1953 until 1959, and Allen Welsh Dulles, head of the C.I.A. from 1953 until 1961. The shadow they cast looms over American foreign policy to this day. Characterized by unapologetic disruption and military intervention in the internal affairs of newly independent states, this approach was fundamentally driven by anticommunism, the free market and open global economy, and a Christian sense of mission. Exploring the background of these two pivotal personalities not only adds color to the historical narrative but also sheds light on the ideological elements that contributed to shaping the burgeoning American empire in its formative years.

Marking the first time that two brothers led both America's overt foreign policy and its covert one, these two influential figures come from a family that includes two former U.S. secretaries of state and a long line of devout clergymen. The interweaving of diplomacy and the Christian faith was passed on, so to speak, with their mother's milk. Their father was a Presbyterian minister who required his sons to carry on a "rigorous and intensive religious life involving attendance at church three or four times a week and memorization of long passages from the Bible."[8] His father, their grandfather, was a Presbyterian missionary who had served in Madras, India, spreading the word of God.[9]

The Dulles brothers were raised in the Calvinist Church, which teaches that there is absolute good and absolute evil in the world, conferring on the believer responsibility for ensuring that good triumphs in the end. Seen through this lens, it is easy to understand why the Dulles brothers continuously sent American covert and overt agents to crush "fanatical nationalist leaders" and contain "evil" Soviet communism. The conviction of the clergy on their father's

side was matched on their mother's side by heavyweights in government with expertise in foreign policy. Their maternal grandfather,
John W. Foster, and Uncle Robert Lansing had both been secretaries
of state. A closer look at this history sheds further light on the gene-
alogy of America's imperial ambitions. Grandfather Dulles headed
the State Department the first time it deposed an established government, in 1893, when the United States helped overthrow the
Hawaiian monarchy and then annexed the territory five years later.[10]
Their Uncle Robert Lansing was involved in interventionist foreign
policy as secretary of state during Woodrow Wilson's presidency. If
there is a DNA marker for hegemonic neocolonialism, it has a spot
on the Dulleses' double helix.

On the surface, however, they were very different: John Foster
was modest and reserved, more a social outcast than a social but-
terfly, while Allen was outgoing, with fewer scruples and more
women. Building on the legacy of their antecedents, the Dulles
brothers easily bested the family record for foreign military interventions. They were proud of this heritage. In his fifth-floor office
at the State Department, John Foster Dulles hung pictures of his
relatives who had served before him as secretary of state.[11] He also
had a mismatched collection of books: the Bible, the *Federalist*, and
Stalin's *Problems of Leninism*. The first two were at the heart of his
family's values, and the third was on the opposite end of the spectrum, in tribute to the old dictum to keep your friends close but
your enemies closer.

The revulsion toward "godless communism" and sense of mission to obliterate it ran deep. Believing that everything in it flowed
from a godless premise, Dulles asserted that without God, "there is
no moral or natural law."[12] In his binary worldview of good versus
evil, he was convinced that the atheist Soviets were an evil threat
because they felt "a duty to extend this [atheist] system to all the
world."[13] This worldview was the paradigm driving U.S. foreign policy under their leadership and in the years since. Their influence was
so strong that the *New York Times* obituary pointed out that Dulles
was "undoubtedly the strongest personality of the Eisenhower Cabinet."[14] Dulles was committed to rolling back Soviet communism.[15]

Like his predecessor, the first Cold War president, Harry Truman, Eisenhower believed that the global struggle against Soviet

communism was also a religious war, referring, as early as 1950, to the Soviet Union as both "aggressive" and "godless."[16] But these Christians were not religious fanatics; they were cynical, hardcore realists whose Christian ideals never stood in their way of imposing their views on other people and establishing an "informal empire." What was good for America and American capitalism was good for God. Rolling back godless communism went hand in hand with opening the global economy to create opportunities for American financial and business interests. The Dulles brothers had paid allegiance to these values long before joining the Eisenhower administration. Both brothers had represented U.S. multinational corporations in cases involving international disputes. This is perhaps natural considering that they grew up breaking bread at the family lodge on Lake Ontario with great industrialists, supreme court justices, and presidents.[17] As an adult, it was perhaps only natural that John Foster Dulles would work at Sullivan and Cromwell, "the biggest, most powerful, most respected law firm in the world."[18] A crossroads of politics and industry, the firm cultivated relations with the most powerful public officials nationally and internationally.[19] The rewards were handsome, in terms not only of power but also of money; Dulles became the best-paid lawyer in the country, if not the whole world.[20]

For his part, Allen, or Allie, as he was known to his family, lead the C.I.A. during what has been called its "golden age," from 1953 to 1961, when the agency executed some of its most successful covert missions worldwide and flexed its real political influence.[21] During his tenure, Allen Dulles turned the C.I.A. into nothing less than a paramilitary apparatus that helped oust unfriendly governments and engaged in acts of sabotage and suppression of nationalist leaders in the developing world. He effectively sanctioned aggressive intervention by the C.I.A. and its officers. Like his older brother, Allen was an interventionist at heart who had authored two books advocating a more active and offensive role for the United States in the international arena. As I mentioned, Allen said that the anticolonial movement championed by the newly independent leaders like Mossadegh and Nasser represented an existential threat to Western civilization.

The Dulles brothers were able to experiment with new ways to subvert democracy, undermine the nationalization of natural resources beyond America's borders, and install puppet regimes. Their influence benefited from Eisenhower's deteriorating health, which included two heart attacks and a stroke, and his preference for the golf course over foreign policy.[22] It was Eisenhower's very cognizance of his fragile health that led him to create a team that could operate independently of his presence.[23] The Dulles brothers took full advantage of these conditions.

Ultimately, Eisenhower's preponderant worldview was mirrored by his cabinet, which would authorize the use of covert and overt military intervention while empowering the C.I.A. to subvert legitimate governments in the Middle East, Latin America, Asia, and beyond.[24] With the change of administration in the White House, Mossadegh's luck had run out. Since the 1930s, American leaders had recognized the strategic role of oil in powering the world economy. President Truman called oil "one of the greatest material prizes in world history."[25] In his book based on declassified U.S. documents, Ervand Abrahamian points out that the Eisenhower decision to oust Mossadegh was driven by the desire to control Iranian oil and not by the latter's intransigence.[26] Eisenhower officials began preparing contingency plans regarding a potential overthrow of Mossadegh as part of broader global effort to block Soviet expansionism and stop the nationalization of Iran's oil.[27]

Instead of seeing Mossadegh's actions as motivated by a quest for full national sovereignty, Washington's Cold War hard-liners labeled the Iranian leader a subversive communist proxy. The big prize for American foreign policy was the control of Iranian oil and replacing the British as the biggest stakeholder in the country.

Mossadegh's Strategic Miscalculation Backfires

Unaware that the United States had started plotting his removal, Mossadegh reportedly met with the U.S. ambassador to Iran and warned him that Tehran might develop friendlier relations with the Soviet Union if Washington did not commit to supporting the Iranian government. Mossadegh never wavered from his belief that the United States could act as an honest broker between Iran and Britain. His memoirs show a leader who was inexperienced in international affairs, believing that the Americans would not fall to

Britain's warmongering and collude with them to oust him. His warning was based on a strategic miscalculation aimed at driving a wedge between the two transatlantic allies.

Mossadegh was wrong on all counts. He failed to properly make sense of the situation and misjudged the right responses. His defiance and bold political tactics, such as threatening to build closer ties with the Soviet-backed Tudeh Party, reinforced the suspicion of him by Eisenhower's Cold War zealots.[28] Instead of seeing Mossadegh as an authentic leader who embodied Iranians' aspirations for independence, freedom, and modernization, the Americans saw him now as a communist stooge and opposed his state-led management of the economy. The die was cast for his downfall.

Mossadegh represented a new generation of postcolonial leaders who struggled to rid their countries of the legacy of imperialism and reclaim sovereignty, dignity, and pride for their people. Deeply suspicious of the great powers, these proud nationalists or freedom seekers had an organic relationship with their populations. Iranians saw Mossadegh as one of them, sharing their fears, hopes, and aspirations. If Mossadegh had succeeded in establishing a functioning representative democracy with popular backing, Iran could have evolved into a prosperous country at peace with itself and the world.

The Cold Warriors in Washington and London were more interested in having newly independent states join their informal empire and their anti-Soviet crusade than in allowing them to pursue a different path of development and full political autonomy. Mossadegh was a victim of this imperial mindset that opposed Third World nationalism and "neutralism," or nonalignment, as it was later called. Before the coup in 1953, the U.S. government had already concluded that "Iran's reversion to an attitude of neutrality" was not acceptable.[29]

Mossadegh faced a two-pronged and interrelated internal and external challenge. In addition to the gathering storm emanating from Washington and London, his National Front coalition at home weakened the prime minister further and hastened his ouster by British and American spies. Mossadegh, the "wily old master," as U.S. Ambassador to Iran Henderson described him, soon faced stiff resistance by coalition partners and allies who deserted him because he was, in their eyes, acting unconstitutionally. While the progressive wing of the National Front backed his program, the conservative religious branch led by Ayatollah Kashani, a charismatic political cleric, criticized his reforms as too liberal and un-Islamic. The National Front had always represented two divergent forces: a traditional middle class, the bazaaris, formed of small merchants and clerics; and a modern middle class, the intelligentsia, composed of secularly educated professionals. The clerics and religious conservatives esteemed Islam as a whole way of life and the shariah as the principal component of legitimate law. The intelligentsia was made up of graduates of secular state schools and held that religion should be separated from the state and that Western-educated technocrats were most qualified to lead the country forward. One side was conservative, religious, and mercantile, the other was forward looking, secular, and technocratic.[30]

Six major fault lines divided them: nationalization of large corporations, women's suffrage, land reform, the sale and drinking of alcohol, the appointment of anticlerical intellectuals to be ministers of justice and education, and the prospect of an alliance with the communist Tudeh Party.[31] Before long, these internal tensions and differences within the National Front became such that the clerical wing, headed by Kashani, withdrew, denouncing Mossadegh for having "betrayed Islam" and imposing a "socialist dictatorship."[32] An Iranian writer argues that these conservative clerics played a prominent role in Mossadegh's removal.[33]

If the split had been over only ideological rifts, it might not have been as insidious. But C.I.A. documents, declassified decades later, showed what many suspected. The C.I.A.'s Donald Wilber divulged that Iranian C.I.A. agents had posed as communists, mounting a sustained campaign of harassment against Islamic leaders, even going so far as to bomb a cleric's home in a bid to turn the country's religious community against Mossadegh.[34] U.S. "black" propaganda disseminated and orchestrated by the C.I.A. demonized Mossadegh and incited people against him.[35] Wilber, the officer in charge of psychological warfare at the C.I.A., boasted that his task was to "fan to fever pitch public opinion against Mossadegh."[36]

The men in charge of the C.I.A. propaganda and sabotage operation in Iran were graduates of Harvard, Princeton, and other Ivy League schools. Similarly, the team in charge of the British outfit were scholars at prestigious universities like Oxford and the London School of Economics. The C.I.A. planted stories that aimed at undermining Mossadegh's credibility, especially in the American media. Just before the C.I.A.–led coup in the summer of 1953, major American publications bought into the C.I.A. propaganda and trashed Mossadegh. The *New York Times* dubbed him a "dictator," and *Newsweek* asserted that he was facilitating a "communist takeover." *Time* went further, claiming that Mossadegh and Iran were "one of the worst calamities to the anti-communist world since the Red conquest of China."[37] Western correspondents in Iran even assisted the C.I.A. coup. A *New York Times* correspondent, Kennett Love, bragged about his role in speeding the final victory of the royalists by telling the coup commanders to storm Mossadegh's house as opposed to keeping their tanks idle at the radio station.

The C.I.A.'s clandestine sabotage tactics proved effective. The National Front splintered further, which severely diminished Mossadegh's popular base. The numbers told the story: on the first anniversary of the 1952 uprising, in July 1953, the National Front's rally attracted only 10,000 people, whereas the Tudeh Party's commemoration drew more than 100,000. Mossadegh's foes, including the royal court and religious forces, smelled blood and amped up the pressure on him. Mossadegh's political ideology was a long distance from Soviet communism. Far from a Russian sympathizer, he was a democrat with a profound belief in the rule of law, checks and balances, human rights, and economic justice for the people of Iran. His political objectives revolved around unconditional independence from foreign powers, democracy, and a solvent, frugal state.[38]

As a social democrat, he advocated state-managed intervention in the economy in order to modernize the country and lift its vulnerable people out of poverty. He passed land reforms that benefited the poor and introduced social security and rent controls to help the working class. He spearheaded initiatives for more equal wealth distribution, putting the military under civilian control and gradually empowering women despite clerical opposition.[39]

The growing internal and external opposition to his leadership forced Mossadegh to play into the hands of those claiming he was a dangerous commie. Attempting to strengthen his domestic constituency, he drew closer to the communists represented by the Tudeh Party. The result is that many of Mossadegh's backers recoiled and turned against him, including National Front members. The U.S. Cold War proponents had long feared the "danger of serious Tudeh infiltration of the National Front and the government bureaucracy," and they were increasingly alarmed that many elements of the Tudeh's political platform were being subsumed by Mossadegh himself.[40]

They did not care if "the [Tudeh] not only considered the National Front a rival but attacked its professed principles as well."[41] As I mentioned in the previous two chapters, by the early 1950s fears of communism's spread had reached a boiling point in the United States, where officials became deeply concerned that Iran might fall under the sway of the Soviet Union if its proxy Tudeh Party were to attain power. The fear of a communist takeover in Iran was a key motivating factor behind America's decision to oust Mossadegh. The irony is that the C.I.A.'s sabotage and propaganda tactics inside Iran drove Mossadegh closer to Tudeh, a tactical move, not ideological or strategic. Mossadegh's decision to nationalize the oil industry was as important as the specter of Iran's falling under communist influence in convincing the Americans to remove him from power.

Operation TP-AJAX

Soon after Eisenhower's inauguration in early 1953, the British pressed their American allies to force Mossadegh out, emphasizing the threat of a communist takeover at the hands of the Tudeh Party. This truth was plainly stated by no less credible a source than the C.I.A.'s former Iran analyst Richard Cottam, who conceded decades later: "The British understood the extent of paranoia in the country concerning communism. This was the day of Joe McCarthy, and the British consciously played on that fear in order to help persuade us to involve ourselves in the coup."[42]

Churchill preyed on this paranoia for Britain's economic gain, suggesting that the risk of a communist takeover did not arise "from the country's bad financial situation," which controlling its own oil might help rectify, but rather from Mossadegh's unwillingness "to check the growth of communist strength."[43] The British were "disposed to bring about a coup d'état in Iran" and hoped that they would be able to replace Mossadegh with a more "reliable" leader—meaning a subservient client. It was pitched, with barely veiled self-interest, as the "best chance to save Iran."[44]

The coup cannot be blamed solely on the British, however; no matter how hard they lobbied, this coup had the Stars and Stripes sewn all over it. The decision to overthrow Mossadegh was made in Washington, D.C., by Eisenhower's Cold Warriors, particularly the two Dulles brothers. Fixated on the global Cold War rivalry and control of Iran's oil, they did not tolerate policies of "neutralism" or unconditional independence. The truth was the first casualty in this effort. They manipulated existing evidence to execute their strategy.

As early as April 1948, the C.I.A. had produced an expansive report on Soviet policy toward Iran, claiming that Moscow intended to dominate the country by undermining the government's authority and expanding communist influence in the void that followed.[45] Then, in July 1949, the National Security Council produced its first major policy paper on Iran, reaffirming that Iran was "a continuing objective in the Soviet program of expansion."[46] As I mentioned, by 1950s the U.S. government was already gearing up to roll back Soviet communism and to tame nationalist leaders who dared to create state-directed economies and pursued an independent—or nonaligned, as it would soon be called—foreign policy.

Therefore, with a new administration in Washington, Allen Dulles, then deputy director of the C.I.A., agreed to Britain's offer of a joint U.S.–U.K. cooperative effort to oust Mossadegh.[47] A "take-no-prisoners" type, Allen Dulles was a notoriously stoic and ruthless figure who took the Soviet threat more seriously than most.[48] As early as March 1951, Allen Dulles had already begun to warn that Iran could be "lost to the West in the coming twelve months."[49] In May 1953 the C.I.A. sent Donald Wilber, a Princeton scholar who was an expert on Persian architecture, to Cyprus to draw up initial coup plans together with another key figure, Norman Darbyshire, the chief of Britain's MI6 in Iran.[50] Although the Cyprus meeting marked a seminal point in the buildup to the 1953 coup, there remained still a great deal of distrust between the two transatlantic allies. According to declassified C.I.A. documents, when the conversation at the meeting turned to the touchy subject of identifying their key agents inside Iran, the Americans lied about their best "assets," demonstrating little trust in their British partners.[51] In fact, the C.I.A.'s top brass was divided over whether the plan drawn up in Cyprus to oust Mossadegh could even work at all.

In the lead-up to the Cyprus meeting, Mossadegh's grand-nephew Mahmud Afshartus, an ardent supporter of the Iranian National Front who had been appointed police chief, was kidnapped, kept in a cave for forty-eight hours, and later murdered.[52] This assassination clearly aimed to undermine the perceived rule of law under Mossadegh, and General Fazallah Zahedi, the man picked to lead the coup by the Americans and British, was "strongly suspected of being a leader of this conspiracy."[53] Zahedi became wanted for the kidnapping and murder of Afshartus, but he was told by the speaker of the Majlis, Sayyed Kashani, "I have given orders that as long as your freedom has not been secured, you will be received with welcome here."[54] Mossadegh did not pursue him but instead allowed him to take sanctuary under the protection of Kashani. This was arguably another tactical blunder that would end up costing Mossadegh dearly, as it gave Zahedi a base from which to plan and orchestrate the coup. The C.I.A. team in Tehran repeatedly warned Washington that "the Shah would not act decisively against Mossadegh," adding that General Zahedi "appeared lacking in drive, energy and concrete plans."[55]

According to C.I.A. records, Allen Dulles, while planning the coup, relied heavily on advice from "experts" who shared his interventionist and aggressive stance, dismissing any intelligence that erred on the side of caution. For instance, Dulles and his Cold War cohorts ignored at least one C.I.A. report that pointed out the limits of U.S. resources in Iran, and another that concluded the Tudeh Party was incapable of usurping Mossadegh's government anytime soon.[56] By this stage, being firmly committed to getting rid of Mossadegh, the C.I.A.'s top brass cast aside anything deemed "incompatible with the planned covert political action" against him.[57]

After the ouster of Mossadegh and the installment of the pro-British General Zahedi as prime minister, the agreement stipulated that the latter would sign an oil agreement reversing the nationalization of the oil industry in return for further U.S. aid to Iran.[58] Mossadegh's plan to finance Iran with its own resources for the benefit of the people was dashed. The C.I.A. tentatively pressed on, disseminating "gray propaganda," bribing journalists and politicians, and planting incriminating and hostile articles about Mossadegh in the local press.[59] At the same time, a C.I.A. telegram to President Eisenhower from March 1953 shows that the agency had already begun assembling weapons and ammunition for use by tribal leaders in Iran's south, in case "the North should go Communist."[60] The C.I.A. telegram also acknowledged suspicions that Britain had been doing the same, despite their steadfast denials. The coup makers would rather watch Iran plummet into civil war than see Mossadegh stay in power.

In early June 1953 the C.I.A. and MI6 met again, this time in Beirut, to kick-start the covert operation. Soon after, the chief of the C.I.A.'s Near East and Africa Division, Kermit Roosevelt, grandson of President Theodore Roosevelt, slipped back into Tehran and took charge of the operation. He would go on to play a crucial and autonomous role in the coup. Despite being the C.I.A.'s Middle East expert, Roosevelt spoke neither Persian nor Arabic. He had previously served in Cairo under the Office of Strategic Services (O.S.S.), the C.I.A.'s World War II predecessor, before participating in the Allied invasion of Italy.[61] Kermit Roosevelt's experience in the region amounted mainly to travels in the Levant and Iran, but in a characteristically arrogant flourish of unearned self-confidence, he wrote his first book, *Arabs, Oil, and History*, in which he argued for the pressing need to reform Arab society. After joining the C.I.A. in 1950, he was tasked first and foremost with curbing the spread of Soviet communism as the Cold War intensified.

After returning to Iran in the summer of 1953, Roosevelt began amalgamating preexisting British intelligence networks with his own. His efforts to destabilize Mossadegh's government focused primarily on manipulating public opinion and paying off rioters to demand the prime minister's resignation. As part of a concerted attempt to pressure the shah into dismissing Mossadegh, Roosevelt also had himself smuggled into the Marble Palace, the shah's residence, for secretive midnight talks. According to declassified C.I.A. documents, the U.S. intelligence agency exerted a great deal of pressure on the shah to sign the royal decrees, or *firmans*, ordering Mossadegh's removal because "it would be easier for him to sign the papers required of him than it would be to refuse." On July 11, 1953, President Eisenhower finally signed off on the coup operation, named Operation TP-AJAX by the C.I.A., to depose Mossadegh.[62]

A Botched Coup Attempt

The first coup attempt backfired massively and almost led to the dissolution of the Pahlavi dynasty. It was arguably Mossadegh's insistence on law and order and an unwillingness to enact martial law to rid the country of the conspiratorial elements in the wake of the failed coup that led to his downfall. While his idealism is admirable, it is also a reflection of the many miscalculations he made throughout his career—miscalculations that would cost Iran dearly.

The planning for the coup initially stalled reportedly because of the shah's "unwillingness to take any initiative" against Mossadegh.[63] This was not because he had any qualms about letting foreign powers interfere in his country, but only because he was unsure about taking the risk. Unlike his father, Reza Shah, the current shah was indecisive, irresolute, and spineless. He was also concerned about the likelihood of domestic instability if he unilaterally removed a legitimately elected prime minister. U.S. Ambassador Henderson at one point even suggested replacing the shah if he continued to be uncooperative.[64]

American and British officials were more eager to oust a legitimate prime minister than the shah himself. Sensing his uneasiness, the C.I.A. and MI6 reportedly dispatched officers to France to locate Princess Ashraf, the Shah's twin sister. She was brought back to Tehran from gambling at the casinos in Deauville, Normandy, in the hope that she could convince her brother to sign the royal decrees.[65] The plan called for the shah to remain steadfast as the C.I.A. and MI6 stirred up chaos on the streets, and for him to issue then the decrees dismissing Mossadegh and replacing him with

General Zahedi. The C.I.A. never intended to replace Mossadegh with the shah, pointing out that he was "vacillating, hesitating and indecisive" and that he "lacks guts." From the U.S. viewpoint, Zahedi was obedient and agreeable. Roosevelt settled on Zahedi after reading a C.I.A. profile that described him as "competent, energetic, aggressive and patriotic," conveniently ignoring his lack of a popular mandate and his having been a Nazi sympathizer during World War II.[66]

Initially, the C.I.A. plan backfired. The return of Princess Ashraf to Iran sparked a wave of protests by Mossadegh supporters and enraged the shah, who refused even to see her at first. There are also reports that Mossadegh, knowing what might be afoot, personally prevented her from seeing her brother.[67] It was only when a staff member at the palace, another British agent, intervened, according to declassified C.I.A. documents, that the shah agreed to meet his sister in late July.[68] The princess informed her brother of the news that the C.I.A. had enlisted the shah's longtime friend General H. Norman Schwarzkopf as part of Operation TP-AJAX to oust Mossadegh. The father of the commander of the 1991 Gulf War, this Schwarzkopf was the former head of the U.S. Gendarme Mission to Iran during World War II. He assured the C.I.A. leadership that "he was sure he could get the required cooperation."[69]

In early August 1953, the C.I.A. intensified its plotting against Mossadegh. To stoke anticommunist furor among the religious establishment, Iranian operatives posing as Tudeh members threatened Muslim leaders with "savage punishment if they opposed Mossadegh."[70] In other words, peace joined truth among the operation's casualties. To reinforce the impact of the threats and violence, British and American intelligence agencies expanded their propaganda campaign. One example was the bribing of a leading newspaper owner with a personal loan of $45,000 (by today's standards, ten times as much) to enlist the news outlet as a pro-shah and anti-Mossadegh mouthpiece. The C.I.A.'s efforts were not enough to convince the shah to sign the agency's written decrees to replace Mossadegh with General Zahedi. During a meeting with General Schwarzkopf, the shah, having reportedly convinced himself that his residence was bugged, "led the general into the grand ballroom, pulled a small table to its exact centre," and demanded that they discuss matters there instead. Roosevelt cited this meeting in concluding that the shah was a "wimp."[71]

Discerning the mounting plot against him, Mossadegh moved swiftly to cement his power by calling for a vote in the first week of August to dissolve the Majlis. He won 99.9 percent of the vote, though it was widely alleged that the polling was rigged in his favor, arguably another chink in the moral armor of Mossadegh. Given Mossadegh's long-standing championship of fair democratic practices, the vote-rigging in the Majlis backfired, furnishing "an issue on which Mossadegh could be relentlessly attacked" by C.I.A.–backed propaganda news outlets.[72] On August 4 President Eisenhower accused Mossadegh of moving toward "getting rid of his parliament, and of course he was in that move supported by the Communist party of Iran." The shah refused to seize this window of opportunity, telling Roosevelt that "he was not an adventurer, and hence, could not take the chances of one."[73]

The C.I.A. then sent an Iranian agent to inform the shah that Roosevelt "would leave in complete disgust unless the Shah took action within a few days." Upon hearing the ultimatum, the shah finally conceded and signed the decrees on August 13, 1953. Word soon spread among royalist officers backing General Zahedi that the shah had agreed to a military coup. These royalist officers had been secretly plotting for months to destabilize the Mossadegh government by supplying weapons to rebellious tribes and establishing contact with prominent dissidents from the National Front, particularly Kashani.[74]

The first coup attempt proved to be a total disaster, however, forcing the shah to flee, first to Baghdad and then to Italy. Tipped off by the Tudeh's military network, Mossadegh's chief of staff, General Taghi Riahi, learned of the plot just hours before its execution. He swiftly arrested the pro-shah officers dispatched to seize the prime minister at home. The next morning, radio stations across Tehran blared the news that a coup plot had failed, and Mossadegh appeared panicked as he attempted to strengthen his hold on the army and key security installations.[75]

As chaos unfolded on Tehran's streets, C.I.A. officers inside the U.S. embassy confided that they had "no way of knowing what was happening," according to recently declassified C.I.A. documents.

Roosevelt took it on himself to personally venture out onto the streets in search of General Zahedi, whom he found in hiding just north of Tehran. Against the odds, the two men agreed to press on with the plot to oust Mossadegh, believing they could turn the tide so long as they were able to spread the news that the shah had signed the two decrees installing Zahedi as prime minister. C.I.A. documents note that the agency arranged for this news to be disseminated in some Tehran papers, but the propaganda initiative quickly faltered because most of the C.I.A.'s Iranian agents either had been jailed or were on the run, and they could not find a printing press left unwatched by pro-Mossadegh forces. As the situation worsened, crowds of supporters of both Mossadegh and the Tudeh Party soon poured into the streets, destroying royalist statues and taking over municipal buildings in a number of provincial towns. The past turned out to be prologue when the same scenes unfolded twenty-six years later during the Iranian revolution in 1979.

Then, though, the shah assumed his days as king of Iran were finished and told U.S. diplomats in Baghdad that "he would be looking for work." He even considered whether America might be a nice place to raise a family.[76] Officials in Washington saw failure looming and wanted to pull the plug on the operation entirely.[77] The C.I.A. headquarters reportedly cabled the Tehran station urging Roosevelt to cease operations and leave immediately. Some say Roosevelt ignored his bosses' orders, but this is a dubious claim that inflates his own importance. Either way, C.I.A. operatives in Iran acted lawlessly and recklessly, treating the country as if it were the Wild West. Dispensing loads of cash, Roosevelt's team, together with MI6 British operatives, bribed street thugs, politicians, tribal leaders, army officers, and reporters in order to sully Mossadegh's reputation and engineer a perfect storm against him.

A Shambolic Model for the Future

Eisenhower's policy toward Iran was shambolic, lacking a strategic vision and concern for the welfare of the Iranian people. However deserving of criticism, his policy was driven by strategic calculation, as he punished assertive nationalist leaders who pursued independence and refused to open their economies to global finance and join America's alliance against Soviet communism. The Eisen-hower administration went against Mossadegh with eyes open, aiming to rid Iran of a leader who nationalized oil, a key resource for the world economy, and who allowed a communist party to exist and even established an internal coalition with it.

By deposing Mossadegh in the early years of the global Cold War, Eisenhower was drawing a line in the sand for like-minded nationalist leaders who would cross at their own peril. Eisenhower Cold War proponents pressed potential freedom seekers or post-imperial leaders like Mossadegh and Egyptian President Nasser with a classic "you are either with us or against us." It was not only a matter of choosing American ideology; they also had to sign over a degree of independence and sovereignty.

The operations against Mossadegh became a template for fre-quent U.S. direct and indirect interventions in the developing world in the 1950s, 1960s, 1970s, and 1980s. The importance of the C.I.A.–sponsored coup in Iran lies in the lingering effect it had on America's perception of itself and its ability to construct its new imperial order regardless of opposition. Franklin Delano Roosevelt is often credited with the famous line "He may be a son of a bitch, but he's our son of a bitch" in describing a dictator, and whether the quote is apocryphal or accurate, its lasting legacy reflects how well it described an immoral (and imperial) strain of U.S. foreign policy that got its start in the post–World War II years in Iran.

After the first failed coup attempt, U.S. Ambassador Hender-son promised Mossadegh aid if he reestablished law and order. Mossadegh, in turn, instructed the army to step in and clear the streets. It was another strategic mistake: Mossadegh used the mili-tary, a disloyal force, to rid the streets of protestors who were his main source of power.[78] Although Mossadegh survived the first putsch, he did not go far enough to reassert control and purge the renegades plotting against him, particularly those in the security services. Far from imposing curfews and carrying out a widespread campaign of repression against his foes, he counseled his ministers against controlling the media and attempted to return the country to normalcy. Right up until his last day as a prime minister, Mossa-degh respected the rule of law and eschewed abusing his authority against the coup plotters. As some of his close advisers pressed him hard to have them executed—part response to the past, part deterrence against future attempts—Mossadegh insisted that the law must take its course.[79]

The terrible irony is that playing by the rules ensured Mossadegh's overthrow. At this critical juncture, he made a fatal mistake. Lulled by the arrest of the bulk of the coup plotters and aware that the shah had fled Iran, Mossadegh recalled troops stationed around the city to their barracks. The same night, the C.I.A. smuggled General Zahedi and his entourage into the U.S. embassy compound "in the bottom of cars and in closed jeeps." They convened a new "council of war" inside the embassy and quickly decided on a counterattack, sending a leading cleric from Tehran to the city of Qom to mobilize support for a holy war against communism.[80] Using travel papers forged by the C.I.A., leading royalist officers were also sent to provincial military barracks to persuade commanders to join the coup.[81]

These plans were foiled by the shah when he left Baghdad for Rome. Upon learning of his departure, newspapers supporting Mossadegh boldly exclaimed that the Pahlavi dynasty was history.

Saving Iran from Democracy

Like the villain in a horror movie who appears dead at a moment of calm just before resurfacing, the C.I.A., when the coup was seemingly over, effected a sudden shift on the streets of Tehran. From its war room in the U.S. embassy, the agency continued to spread propaganda that served to suddenly shift the mood on the streets of Tehran. As dawn broke on August 19, Tehran awoke to headlines in pro-shah papers that finally published his long-awaited decrees. Before long, raucous crowds were building in the streets calling for Mossadegh's ouster.

The C.I.A., so often dismissing the ability of the Iranian people to determine their future, strained to give them credit for the act that it had poured money, weapons, and misinformation into fomenting. In a history written at the time, the agency claimed that the Iranian people "needed only leadership," deflecting responsibility for the coup that had opposed popular will and been imposed from without. All leadership came from the C.I.A. and MI6, which manned the front lines in providing operational, logistical, and material backing for the coup. U.S. spies incited anti-Mossadegh sentiments throughout the country, organized mobs, and bribed influential individuals in the security services, the press, and the political and religious establishment. They even pressured the shah to violate Iran's constitutional arrangement and depose Mossadegh. One journalist who was among the agency's most important assets in Iran led a crowd toward the parliament building, "inciting people to set fire to the offices of a newspaper owned by Dr. Mossadegh's foreign minister." Another Iranian C.I.A. agent reportedly led a procession to sack the offices of pro-Tudeh papers.[82] Key C.I.A. operatives conceded that the protests they organized against Mossadegh were merely tools in the agency's broader plan. "That mob that came into north Tehran and was decisive in the overthrow was a mercenary mob. It had no ideology and that mob was paid with American dollars," Richard Cottam, the former C.I.A. Iran analyst, conceded.[83]

Events were moving so fast that, even by their own admission, C.I.A. operatives struggled to keep up. An Iranian colonel involved in the previous coup attempt suddenly appeared outside parliament with a tank, while hundreds of now-disbanded Imperial Guard soldiers seized trucks and directed protestors. Within hours, the central telegraph office had fallen, and cables were sent to the provinces urging them to revolt against Mossadegh. Before long, the Ministry of Foreign Affairs and Tehran's police headquarters had also been seized. The pro-shah protestors also captured Tehran Radio—arguably the biggest prize of them all—just as it was half-way through a program on cotton prices.[84]

Roosevelt swiftly got General Zahedi out of hiding and arranged for him to be driven by tank to the radio station, where he addressed the nation live on air. As tanks rolled down the streets of Iran, thousands of armed thugs attempted to storm Mossadegh's residence. This crowd included police; soldiers of the armed customs guards, the army, the air force, and the Imperial Guard; teams of the "Devotees of the Shah"; and tank squadrons.[85] More than just an uncoordinated lynching, it was a full-blown military siege. After three attempts to storm Mossadegh's house, the assembled units finally succeeded, only four hours after Radio Tehran had fallen to the coup makers.[86]

That fateful night, more than the prime minister's home was reduced to ash—so, too, were the last remnants of Iranian democracy. Mossadegh initially escaped but, realizing that resistance was futile, ordered the police to stop defending him and asked his companions to leave the government building. Ever defiant, Mossadegh wanted to stay put and be either arrested or killed. His supporters insisted that he take his chances by hiding in a neighbor's house. In the afternoon, Mossadegh climbed the wall of the house together with his companions and hid for the night. But the following day, Mossadegh decided to surrender to the army and asked his assistant to inform General Zahedi. Before this could happen, a team of detectives found the prime minister lying on a mattress in an upstairs room. They took him by car to the police headquarters.

The C.I.A.: More Royalist Than the King

"We were all smiles now. . . . Warmth and friendship filled the room," Kermit Roosevelt later wrote about the moment he raised a glass to the new leader of Iran, Shah Mohammed Reza Pahlavi.

Roosevelt's memoirs came out on the eve of the Islamic revolution in 1979—quite poignant timing considering that his actions, which aimed at installing a subservient U.S. ally, ultimately had the opposite effect. Even the title of his book, *Countercoup*, amounted to misinformation. In it, he wrote that the shah was overcome with emotion. " 'I owe my throne to God, my people, my army—and to you!' By 'you' he meant me *and* the two countries—Great Britain and the United States—I was representing. We were all heroes," proclaimed Roosevelt, without even a hint of irony, regret, or reflection.[87]

According to declassified C.I.A. documents, the agency operatives had surprised themselves, describing what "seemed to be a bad joke," in view of the depression that still hung on from the day before and exulting that the moment "should never have ended. For it carried with it such a sense of excitement, of satisfaction and of jubilation that it is doubtful whether any other can come up to it."[88] This account hides the chaos that unfolded on the U.S. side. The Tehran C.I.A. station reportedly sent only two telegrams during the entire day of the coup; Roosevelt later stated that if he had told his bosses what was going on, "London and Washington would have thought they were crazy and told them to stop immediately."[89]

Roosevelt's own story paints a picture of the C.I.A. crew in Tehran as intoxicated with the Great Powers game, running a criminally thuggish racket designed to remove a legitimate leader regardless of the consequences. In their fervor to depose Mossadegh, Roosevelt and his crew were "more royalist than the king." The shah was more cautious and shrewder than the C.I.A. operatives, who could not have cared less if Iran descended into either civil strife or monarchical dictatorship. According to Roosevelt, the coup had cost less than $100,000.[90] As had been agreed beforehand, the C.I.A. swiftly transferred to Zahedi the funds that were left over from the covert operation, about $1 million to be followed later by an emergency grant of $45 million.[91] As part of U.S. strategy, the bribe was intended to push Zahedi into quickly confirming a new oil agreement that served both U.S. and British interests. And Zahedi did deliver, granting U.S. corporations 40 percent of Iran's oil production and a dominant position for nearly a quarter century in a pivotal Middle Eastern state bordering the Soviet Union.[92]

In appreciation of Roosevelt's exploits, in 1954 President Eisenhower secretly awarded him the National Security Medal and praised him for the coup's having saved Britain from bankruptcy. Roosevelt's account is very hard to believe, however. He claims that when he met Churchill on his way back to the United States, the old statesman had told him, "If I had been but a few years younger, I would have loved nothing better than to have served under your command in this great venture!"[93] When the shah returned home from exile, he praised what he called a bloodless and heroic people's revolution that had succeeded in protecting the monarchy.[94] President Eisenhower subsequently informed the American people that Iranians had "saved the day" because of "their profound love for their monarchy," and, most important, because of their "revulsion against communism."[95]

Both Eisenhower's and the shah's tales of what happened were designed for public consumption, but they were hardly historical truth. Caught in the victor's moment, Eisenhower and the shah failed to appreciate the long-term consequences for Iran and the world of deposing a transformative leader who had been legitimately elected. It was a short, pyrrhic victory. The spirit of Mossadegh would live on, coming to haunt the shah and U.S.–Iranian relations till today.

The new shah regime and the armed forces swiftly set about dismantling Mossadegh's social network and cracking down on the opposition. Although the majority of National Front leaders received comparatively lenient treatment (most faced prison terms no longer than five years), the Tudeh Party's members suffered the brunt of a brutal clampdown. Over the next four years, the security forces executed forty party officials, tortured to death fourteen more, sentenced two hundred to life imprisonment, and arrested more than three thousand of the rank and file.[96]

The shah, with the help of British and U.S. intelligence services, had finally cemented his power. Mossadegh, together with any sliver of constitutional opposition, had been relegated to the history books. With Mossadegh out and the shah in, political life in Iran underwent a metamorphosis. The country lost not just an exceptional leader with a deep commitment to democracy and constitutionalism, but also a pluralistic system based on the rule of law and the will of the people.

The 1953 coup and the consolidation of the shah's power was a turning point in Iran's modern history. Oil was denationalized, civil society was suffocated, the political opposition was crushed, and the press was silenced. Iran remained a commodity-dependent economy without any real productive sectors, and U.S. military and foreign aid to the shah quadrupled. These momentous events set Iran on the path of political authoritarianism in a way that inevitably shaped the revolution of 1979, in which progressive and democratic forces arrived weakened and undermined.

Although the country has been locked in that trajectory ever since, Iranians have shown that they can and will break this vicious cycle of tyranny. Remembering their proud history, their homegrown leaders, and their principled resistance is critical to understanding not just the problems but the possibilities that Iran possesses. And this way of looking at Iranian history helps us better understand the unquenchable thirst for democracy of this people and see the connections between the struggles of the 1950s and those of today. By acknowledging Iranians' struggle for freedom, dignity, and justice, it becomes possible to help form a progressive and enlightened vision for the future and chart a course—an independent course, free of foreign interests, interference, and meddling—to realize it.

CHAPTER FOUR

From the Cusp of Democracy to the Abyss of Absolute Monarchy

G OOD AND EVIL. Right and wrong. Batman and Joker. Understanding history through binaries never does justice to the nuances and intricacies of reality. This is a story of the aftermath of the C.I.A.–led coup that ousted Mossadegh and of the shah's gradual descent into absolute political authoritarianism. Few leaders, if any, sit on the throne for decades without eventually suffering from illusions of grandeur or toxic entitlement. This is not simply a story about the principled Mossadegh, who portended dignity and prosperity for Iran, and the shah, enamored of violent crackdowns, torture, and suppression of democratic values all while suffering from a serious God complex and voracious greed. The shah was not born evil, nor did he set a course for megalomania as soon as he became king. Rather, it was decades of a slow descent into authoritarianism, backed by America and sealed by his political success of maneuvering Iran through the 1973 oil crisis, that turned the country into a police state and a pivotal regional power. After all, Mossadegh had a princely background, but he struggled for democracy and stood tall for independence.

Now picture them on different sides of a divide. Where does the United States plant its flag, that red, white, and blue banner that supposedly stands for freedom? If only Washington had backed instead of ousted Mossadegh, decades of suffering, repression, and bloodshed could have been prevented in Iran. And if that were not enough of a missed opportunity, consider the wider implications: had the Cold Warriors not enforced, backed, and persuaded the shah to support the ouster of Mossadegh in 1953, Tehran—and perhaps the entire region, where for better or worse Iran has always been an influential force—could have tacked toward a peaceful and prosperous future rather than veering ahead on its current, perpetually insecure, conflict-torn, and authoritarian trajectory.

This alternative trajectory is worth reflecting on in the reimagination of the Middle East. The United States did more than passively side against Mossadegh and for the shah; it ousted the former and installed the latter. The question is not whether this was a cataclysmic mistake but how to fix it. There is a way, and it begins with a reconstruction of the recent history of the Middle East.

Authoritarianism under American Tutelage

Although the shah did not start out thinking he would do so, he succumbed to the temptation of absolute power. To gain and maintain absolute power, he needed the support of the United States. So, where Mossadegh struggled to lead his country to real independence, the shah deepened Iran's dependency on the new rising Western superpower that, far from modeling the love of democracy it pretended to espouse, chose to trample the will of the people in a dirty deal for power.

The path that led the shah to office was not one of straightforward, blind ambition. As I pointed out in the previous chapter, C.I.A. conspirators in Tehran in 1953 portrayed the shah as cowardly, indecisive, and reluctant to authorize the removal of Mossadegh from office. These U.S. operatives called on their political bosses in Washington to pressure the shah to stiffen his resolve against Mossadegh. This fact shows a young and wobbly shah in the early 1950s, far from thirsty for power at all costs, as he would eventually become.

In the 1960s and 1970s, the shah felt free to dispense with constitutional checks and balances and build an absolute monarchy.

Although Mossadegh was at the time in solitary confinement in a military prison in central Tehran, his influence could not be contained in his jail cell; it would reverberate through time and space, still affecting actions today. Far from incinerating the memory and legacy of Mossadegh to ashes, the violent overthrow of the first fully legitimate prime minister turned him into a legend. Contrasting his fealty to independence, it tattooed onto the image of the monarchy the permanent mark of the imperial Western powers—the United States and the United Kingdom.

The coup and its aftermath triggered the destruction of the progressive nationalist coalition led and nourished by Mossadegh, but the aftershocks reverberated with the Pahlavi dynasty until its very last days. If the results in Iran were tragic, the ramifications for the United States were also spectacularly counterproductive. The overthrow of Mossadegh jettisoned a potentially positive model for the region and paved the way for the eventual emergence and spread of radical and revolutionary ideologies like Marxism and Islamism.

I argue that there is a connection between the shah's reversing Mossadegh's popular reforms and nationalization of oil, crushing all political dissent, and pursuing economic policies that widened social inequalities and gave momentum to the Islamic clerics who seized power in 1979. The U.S. government knowingly chose an autocratic political system in Iran that ensured compliance with American wishes. Up to the end of the shah's rule, in 1979, U.S. foreign policy nurtured his authoritarian streak and helped him build a repressive police state. Mohammad Reza Shah tied his political fate to America, which replaced colonialist Britain as the dominant actor in post-Mossadegh Iran.

Whereas Mossadegh sought to take ownership of Iran's oil and invest the resources to develop and modernize the country for the benefit of the people, the shah allowed Western companies to control the Iranian oil industry. A year after Mossadegh's overthrow, the shah bowed to U.S. pressure and signed the Consortium Agreement in 1954, which granted Western oil companies, including AIOC, 40 percent ownership of Iran's oil reserves. This predictable action came after the Eisenhower administration made its support for the shah conditional on Iran's signing an oil agreement, effectively abandoning nationalization. Iran and the United States agreed that the contract would last twenty-five years; it would expire just a few months before the Iranian revolution of 1979.[1] Doing away with Mossadegh's nationalization of the oil industry, the Consortium Agreement privileged U.S.–owned companies over Britain's Anglo-Iranian, marking a seminal pivot in Iranian foreign policy.[2]

In his sweeping and thought-provoking book, *America and Iran*, John Ghazvinian tells the story of what he calls "one of the great unspoken rivalries of the twentieth century: the competition between the United States and Great Britain for Iran's vast petroleum bounty."[3] Similarly, James Barr, in *Lords of the Desert*, an impressively well-researched book, argues that the American-British coup against Mossadegh was an exceptional joint venture. Throughout World War II and after, the two Anglo allies competed fiercely for control of the Middle East's petroleum and resources.[4] In a way, the C.I.A.–led coup against Mossadegh effected regime change in Tehran along with the international realignment of the country as the United States replaced Great Britain as the dominant economic and political master there.

On the surface, this fulfilled Washington's nakedly cynical aims for the coup against Mossadegh: controlling Iran's oil and bringing the country to the U.S. side of its struggle against Soviet communism. In the long term, the putsch backfired, setting the stage for disaster for the United States on both fronts: control of resources and international security. Immediately after Mossadegh's ouster, Eisenhower officials breathed a sigh of relief, believing that the coup had given the United States a "second chance" to save Iran from the scourge of communism, according to Secretary of State Dulles. Promising emergency aid pending an oil agreement, the Americans would now tighten their grip on the country and prop up the shah's regime by helping him lay the foundations of a police state.

Before the dust settled on the streets in Tehran, the U.S. ambassador to Iran, Loy Henderson, recommended to the shah that he presides over an "undemocratic independent Iran," meaning an authoritarian regime under Western tutelage.[5] In other words, the shah was not the only one selling out his principles; the highest

U.S. representative to Iran had no compunction about blatantly advocating authoritarian rule. The shah obliged. In December 1953, Eisenhower's vice president, Richard Nixon, visited the shah to formalize the new relationship and put the presidential seal on it. Vehement protests accompanied Nixon's visit, and three students were killed on what came to be known as "Student Day," still marked annually by students with organizing and demonstrations.

Like a seesaw sinking to the wrong side of history, the shah's popularity plummeted among the Iranian people and rose in equal measure with the government of the United States. He became "one of America's most trusted Cold War allies."[6] A 1957 U.S. State Department report praised the shah for his "growing maturity" and no longer needing "to seek advice at every turn," as a previous 1951 profile of him had derisively concluded.[7] In contrast to the jubilant celebrations that followed Mossadegh's decision to nationalize oil in March 1951, the shah's decision to effectively cede Iran's sovereignty and control of its hydrocarbon resources to foreigners was detested by most of the country. Parliamentarians, academics, and religious leaders publicly criticized what they saw as a retreat from everything Mossadegh had done to attain Iran's economic and political independence.

Although Iran did benefit economically from the end of the British embargo and an uptick in oil revenue after the signing of the Consortium Agreement, the political and economic costs far outweighed the benefits over time. According to Fuad Rouhani, an adviser in the consortium talks and later first head of the Organization of the Petroleum Exporting Countries (OPEC), the cost to Iran from the shah's oil concessions would amount to $412 million, which, adjusted for inflation, is $4.55 billion today. This was far greater than the publicized compensation meted out to Iran.[8]

A Paranoid Ally

Domestically, the removal of Mossadegh radically changed social and political life in Iran. In many ways, Mohammad Reza Shah picked up after the 1953 coup where his father had left off—fulfilling his dream of constructing a top-down expansive authoritarian state.[9] Rising oil revenues allowed the shah to monopolize power and secure his rule.

Following the 1954 Consortium Agreement, Iran became the world's fourth-largest oil producer and the second-largest exporter.[10] Corruption, cronyism, and patronage rose sharply as Iran gained increasing oil revenues and U.S. loans.

Rather than invest the oil revenue to create a productive and diverse economy, the shah spent a big chunk of the money on expanding Iran's military and security forces. From 1954 to 1977, the military budget grew twelvefold, and its share of the annual budget increased from 24 to 35 percent—from $60 million in 1954 to an astonishing $5.5 billion by 1973.[11] Seeing the shah as the guardian of American interests in the Gulf region, U.S. officials buttressed his power by pumping in massive amounts of economic and military aid, including an upfront emergency grant of $68 million immediately after the 1953 coup and an additional $1.2 billion over the next decade.

In 1957 the United States also helped Iran launch its own nuclear program as part of President Eisenhower's "Atoms for Peace" initiative. In 1967 the United States went even further and provided Iran with weapons-grade uranium and a nuclear reactor of its own, and this close nuclear collaboration lasted right up until the fateful start of Iran's 1979 revolution. This is an astonishing fact to contemplate from today's perspective on the Iran nuclear issue, which is widely perceived to trace its origins to clerics seeking the game-changing weapon in 1988 at the end of the Iran-Iraq war. They can claim no such glory; it was Eisenhower Cold War officials who first started Iran's nuclear program and deserve a share of credit for the foreign policy mess that ensued.

The U.S.–Iranian relationship under the shah was not all fun, games, and nuclear ambitions. Reza Shah's dependence on the United States for survival left him paranoid that the C.I.A. was plotting to unseat him—the very agency that had helped reinstate him as a monarch in August 1953. In matters of romance, they say the partner who cheats with you will cheat on you, and the shah was in a similar bind, having gotten in bed with a power that demonstrated through its very relationship with him that it had no fealty to legitimacy. The shah resented America's infidelity, complaining that it treated him like a "concubine" rather than a "wife."[12] This played out on February 27, 1958, when a failed military coup against the shah led to a major crisis in U.S.–Iranian relations. As U.S. State Department records confirm, word soon got out that associates of General Valiollah Gharani, the driver behind the coup, had reportedly held meetings with U.S. diplomats in Athens in the months beforehand.[13]

Although there occurred no rupture in U.S.–Iranian relations, the shah suspected that the United States was not as committed to the defense of his regime as it had previously affirmed. He lamented that the Americans did not join the Baghdad Pact regional military alliance, even though they had conceived the idea, and did not provide his country with "guarantees," as they had with NATO member states.[14] To protect his flank, in January 1959 the shah began negotiating a nonaggression pact with the Soviet Union, something he argued was necessary given this perceived lack of U.S. support.[15] U.S. officials demanded that the shah suspend the talks with Moscow.[16] When he quickly complied, the Russians tagged him as an American puppet and called for his overthrow.[17] Soviet-Iranian negotiations suggest that tensions existed beneath the surface of the shah's close patron-client relationship with the United States.[18]

America's contempt for democracy in Iran came back to its own shores, damaging democracy at home. The shah's mistrust of the American government led him to contribute money to the Nixon campaign in the 1960 U.S. presidential election.[19] Washington's interventionism in Iran eventually created reverberations in America's own domestic political life. And though Nixon lost to John F. Kennedy, the shah's funding of Nixon's presidential campaign demonstrates one of many ways in which American democracy was tarnished as a direct cause of its leaders' hawkish Cold War foreign policy. The American undermining of Iranian democracy was a two-way street, and the frequent, deadly traffic pileups came at a cost to the two countries' people, though the cost to the Iranians was much dearer.

A Nightmare Come to Life: SAVAK—the Shah's Secret Police

To augment his control and silence opposition, the shah established a new intelligence agency or secret police force in 1957: the infamous SAVAK. Once again, the contrast between Mossadegh's and the shah's vision for Iran came into sharp focus. Where Mossadegh had tried to promote transparency and the rule of law, the Shah's covert state-building project was helped by both the U.S. Federal Bureau Investigation (F.B.I.) and Israel's secret service, the Mossad.

According to declassified C.I.A. documents, the United States sent an army colonel who worked for the C.I.A. to Iran immediately following the coup to assist in creating the shah's secret police force.[20] Two years on, the colonel was replaced with a permanent team of five career C.I.A. officers, each with a broad range of specializations ranging from covert operations to counterintelligence. Among these was Major General Herbert Norman Schwarzkopf, the very same conspirator who had proved so instrumental in the 1953 coup. He was to train "virtually all of the first generation of SAVAK personnel."[21] The secret police force terrorized the public and instilled fear. It was estimated that one of every 450 male Iranians was a SAVAK informer. There were even rumors that one in ten Iranians was a SAVAK informer, and although this number was probably inflated, it reflected the perceived sense of SAVAK's omnipresence.[22]

Headed by General Nematollah Nasseri, SAVAK gripped everyday life for all. The organization censored the media, screened applicants for government and academic jobs, and used brutal methods of torture and summary executions against anyone who fell afoul of the shah's oppressive autocratic rule. In the words of Robert Graham, a British journalist for the *Financial Times* in Tehran, SAVAK was the shah's "eyes and ears, and where necessary, his iron fist."[23]

Already in 1954, three years before SAVAK was officially established, the police identified and arrested a sizable group of officers with links to the communist Tudeh Party.[24]

The violent post-coup repression drove the number of industrial strikes down from seventy-nine in 1953 to seven in 1954 and three in 1955. Public protests were then a thing of the past, and the right to peacefully demonstrate was quashed with violence. As Manuchehr Eqbal declared after assuming the role of prime minister in April 1957, "I have a personal distaste for this word 'strike.' It is a term introduced into our language by the Tudeh Party. As long as I am premier, I don't want to hear of any strikes."[25] The shah also amended the constitution to cement his control of the government, investing himself with the authority to appoint prime ministers and officials he considered loyal to top posts. Of the eight men who headed cabinets from 1953 until 1977, all but two were his personal favorites.[26]

One of the exceptions, General Zahedi, who had been hand-picked by American and British intelligence agencies to carry out the 1953 coup against Mossadegh, was exiled to Switzerland after only twenty months as prime minister. The British ambassador reported at the time that the shah wanted to let everyone know who was in charge by deposing Zahedi during a parliamentary recess.[27] One prime minister even introduced himself to the parliament as the sovereign's "slave."[28] The shah personally presided over weekly cabinet meetings, deterring any parliamentarian from daring to speak out. If only the walls could speak, they might have cried; this posture stood in stark contrast to Mossadegh's, whose reform agenda of 1949 pushed for and later implemented guarantees for members of parliament to be independent and freely express their opinions. The shah also personally assigned deputies their party affiliation.

In stark contrast to the vibrant pre-coup political environment, during this period the Majlis was formed of two major blocs—aptly coined by many as the "yes" and the "yes, sir" parties. The shah's power and control had extended into all aspects of the political process, turning the concept of parliamentary democracy into a farce. Mossadegh's vision of a parliamentary monarchy mutated into an absolute monarchy under the U.S.–backed Reza Shah. The C.I.A.–led coup against Mossadegh shaped the destiny of Iran for decades to come.

The New "Great Civilization" and the Personality Cult

Capitalizing on the proceeds of the oil boom, Mohammad Reza Shah boldly and foolishly declared the birth of his new Great Civilization. Iran's future would be greater than its past ever had been, harking back to the time of the ancient Achaemenid, Parthian, and Sassanid empires, the shah stated. He even claimed that the country would soon surpass Europe in wealth and status. Even the shah's Western allies pointed out that he had become drunk on power, obsessed with "Napoleonic illusions of grandeur."

The shah imagined the Iranian monarchy as the binding force of society and its backbone. The move "Toward the Great Civilization" —the title of the shah's book published originally in Persian in 1977—was not just about modern and social reforms but about preserving and protecting the essence of Iranian national identity, which according to Pahlavism could not exist without the monarchy. As the shah stated: "In Iranian culture, the Iranian monarchy means the political and geographic unity of Iran in addition to the special national identity and all those unchangeable values which this national identity has brought forth. For this reason no fundamental change is possible in this country unless it is in tune with the fundamental principles of the monarchical system."[29]

Ultimately, this imperial nationalist narrative assumes that the monarchy is the spirit of the Iranian national identity, on the basis of historically incorrect as well as fabricated "facts," which led a contemporary U.S. Treasury official to describe the shah as a "nut case."[30] Nut case or not, however, the shah's move was not only fueled by one man's narcissistic personality. It was a meticulously planned, ideological project designed by the ruling elite to preserve privileges and as much power as possible, in a political climate where pressure from below was challenging their grip on power.[31]

As part of this grandiose rebirth, Mohammad Reza Shah enacted far-reaching modernizing reforms in the hope that they would induce structural changes in Iranian society and bolster his rule. His modernization program created "oligarchic species of industrialization, with the landless poor becoming a new urban working class—fodder for Marxists and Islamists alike."[32] The White Revolution launched in 1963 had the stated aim of preventing a much-feared "Red Revolution."[33]

The shah publicly advertised the White Revolution as a step toward modernization, but in reality it was just as much politically designed to weaken the influence of the bazaaris, the Shia clerics, and other traditional classes whose influence challenged the status quo. To create a new power base among the peasants and the working class, the White Revolution focused on land reform.[34] This is clear when we examine the details of the plan: it limited landlords to one village and transferred excess land to sharecroppers granted tenancy rights. As might be expected, the plan's aims did not match the real results, and, for instance, landlords passed the control of villages to their close relatives.[35] Overall, though, these land reforms were transformative, diminishing the power of the feudal class, ridding Iran completely of terms such as notables (*fudal*, *a'yan*), aristocracy (*ashraf*), and large landlords (*omdeh malek*).[36] For the first time in Iran's history, 1.5 million peasant families who had effectively been slaves under the feudal system could own the lands they worked.[37]

The shah's reforms went beyond rural areas. His social programs generated a boom in the number of literates and a boost in public health. Kindergarten enrolment increased by more than twenty-fold and college enrollment rates spiked from nearly 25,000 to more than 145,000. Beyond changes in quantity, there were shifts in quality. The curriculum was redesigned to undercut clerical control over education. Iran established a Literacy Corps, like that in socialist Cuba, which raised the literacy rate from just over a quarter of the population to more than two-fifths. Health-care initiatives more than quadrupled the number of doctors and medical clinics and doubled the number of nurses and hospital beds.[38]

These initiatives, combined with drives to end famine and childhood epidemics, resulted in rapid population growth in Iran, from nearly 19 million people in 1956 to about 34 million by 1976. The White Revolution also helped address the concerns of women as well as gender imbalances in society. It granted women the right to vote and to run for elected office. And the 1967 Family Protection Law restricted men's power to get a divorce or take multiple wives; it also raised the marriage age to fifteen.[39] At the same time, the shah drummed up five-year plans to catalyze Iran's industrial revolution, pushing for the country to become a competitive industrial power. These plans improved port facilities, expanded the Trans-Iranian Railway, and helped pave the main highways connecting Tehran to the provinces.[40]

Le Monde drew parallels between France's industrial revolution and the shah's push for entrepreneurs to "enrich themselves" with the aid of low-interest loans and tax exemptions in order to bolster the private sector.[41] According to Ervand Abrahamian, one of the world's leading historians of Iran, from 1953 until 1975 the number of small factories increased from 1,500 to more than 7,000; medium-sized factories from 300 to more than 800; and large factories, employing more than 500 workers, from fewer than 100 to more than 150.[42]

The shah's limited economic and social liberalization was not matched by political liberalization. Far from it: he tightened his grip on political life and unleashed his fearsome security forces against critics and dissidents. Immediately after the removal of Mossadegh, Mohammad Reza Shah and General Zahedi, the new prime minister, imprisoned thousands and summarily executed dozens of Mossadegh's supporters. The reign of terror persisted in the following years. Elections were rigged. Dissidents were tortured. Protestors were drilled with bullet holes.[43] Mohammad Reza Shah's chokehold on the country became progressively more overt, as did his need to invent himself as a cult icon. A U.S. embassy dispatch at the time portrays a classic dictator's megalomania: "The Shah's picture is everywhere. The beginning of all film showings in public theaters presents the Shah in various regal poses accompanied by the strains of the National Anthem. ... The monarch also actively extends his influence to all phases of social affairs. ... There is hardly any activity or vocation in which the Shah or members of his family or his closest friends do not have a direct or at least a symbolic involvement."[44]

Mohammad Reza Shah, who was both contemptuous of Mossadegh-style democratic politics and proud of his own autocratic rule, bluntly stated in 1961 that the Iranians were not ready for democracy: "When Iranians learn to behave like Swedes, I will behave like the King of Sweden."[45] This was perhaps the most pronounced striking contrast with Mossadegh, who believed above all in the potential of his country's people, never denigrating them as somehow less than Europeans. The shah had once claimed to take a two-party system seriously, declaring: "If I were a dictator rather than a constitutional monarch, then I might be tempted to sponsor a single dominant party such as Hitler organized."[46] But he showed his true colors in 1975, abolishing the two-party system entirely, replacing it with a one-party state under the Rastakhiz, or

Resurgence, Party. He justified his despotic action by shamelessly asserting: "We must straighten out Iranians' ranks. To do so, we divide them into two categories: those who believe in Monarchy, the Constitution, and the [White Revolution] and those who don't. . . . Such an individual belongs to an Iranian prison, or if he desires he can leave the country tomorrow, without even paying exit fees; he can go anywhere he likes, because he is not Iranian, he has no nation, and his activities are illegal and punishable according to the law."[47] Patriots were defined by whether they were in the monarchy camp, and those who rejected the shah's autocratic rule were deemed traitors and sent to prison or forced into exile.

Paving the Way for the Islamization of the Political Sphere

The shah's reforms backfired completely, intensifying social tensions and opposition to his repressive rule. Instead of winning the peasants' hearts and minds, land reform produced large numbers of independent farmers and landless laborers, collectively a "loose political cannon," according to Abrahamian, with no innate loyalty to the shah.[48] The combined size of the intelligentsia and urban working class—traditionally the most serious challenge to the shah's father—had now more than quadrupled.[49] Their resentment of the monarchy was exacerbated by the fact that they had been systematically stripped of political parties, trade unions, independent newspapers, and other organizations that channeled their interests and concerns.

The unintended consequences of the shah's social reforms weakened his hold on the country. Abrahamian notes: "The White Revolution had been designed to preempt a Red Revolution. Instead, it paved the way for an Islamic Revolution."[50] The road to an Islamic revolution was not as straightforward, however. Before June 1977, Ayatollah Khomeini was not the country's main opposition force. Instead, a figure sharing similarities with Mossadegh, Ali Shariati, could have been a real contender to lead Iran after the revolution. Like Mossadegh, he had a Ph.D. from Europe (University of Sorbonne) and was even a member of the National Front party that Mossadegh had founded. Shariati, an intellectual who

taught and wrote on history, sociology of religion, politics, literature, psychology, and philosophy, borrowed ideas from different
cultural fountains, forming "an eclectic synthesis of non-Muslim
and non-Iranian ideas, including socialism, Marxism, existential-
ism, the writings of certain Third World theorists, and esoteric
themes and metaphors from the Perso-Islamic mystic tradition
of Sufis."[51] His worldview was a form of Shia nationalism, which
believed that the core of Shiism was the overthrow of repressive
governments.[52]

Shariati was part of a group of Global South intellectual activists
who championed the rights of colonized people in their struggle for
emancipation and freedom. While studying in Paris, Shariati became
involved with the Algerian liberation movement against French imperialism. Rivaling Mossadegh as a nationalist and Khomeini as a
theologist, Shariati subsequently earned the honor of "the most popular mentor of Islamic radicalism in modern Iran."[53] His premature
death at age forty-three on June 18, 1977, and his lack of a political
party or network, however, meant that there was no organization or
person to carry on his ideas. He had the potential of being the revolutionary leader whom protestors chanted for during the Iranian
Revolution in 1979, and his rising popularity suggested that Iran had
space and thirst for a forward-looking leader like him.

My point is that there was nothing inevitable about the Islamization of the Iranian revolution. Khomeini deliberately appropriated Shariati's leftist ideas in order to cement and broaden his
popularity because without "the decisive support of non-Islamic organizations, secular intellectuals, and political forces on the ground,
the creation of a theocratic regime in Iran and its consolidation
could not have been realized."[54]

The White Revolution may have modernized Iran—but that
cannot be examined in a vacuum; it must be considered alongside
the failure of some land reform policies, the democratic deficit,
jackbooted repression, and opposition to reform from the clergy
and the petite bourgeoisie. Ultimately, these, and not just the effort
by the Islamists, caused the downfall of the shah and, with him, the
Pahlavi dynasty in 1979.[55]

From 1953 onward, religious activism gained momentum in
Iran—even if not all activism was religious—while the Pahlavi mon-

archy's symbolic brand of nationalism never conquered the masses. The post-coup social tensions, together with the shah's attempt to undermine the opposition's privileges through the White Revolution, inflamed political radicalism among the intelligentsia, the urban working class, and the religious establishment, or *ulama*.[56] The late 1950s saw the birth of a new generation of Islamic intellectuals, or *Roshanfekr-e Dini*, including prominent representatives such as Jalal-e Al-e Ahmad, Mehdi Bazargan, Ali Shariati, Morteza Motahhari, and Abolhassan Bani-Sadr. Inspired by Quranic principles and a revolutionary interpretation of Islam, this generation of Islamic intellectuals sought to mobilize the masses in opposition to the shah and his imperialist Western masters.[57]

These intellectuals, some more conventionally Islamic than others, had an enormous influence on shaping public opinion not just through their lectures in universities and cultural centers, but also in the work they produced. One of the major outlets in which they disseminated their ideas was the Islamic Cultural Centre (*Hosseinie-ye Ershad*) in the heart of Tehran. Islamic intellectuals like Ali Shariati and Morteza Motahhari had enough space to organize speaking engagements about political Islam. Members of the lower middle class, students, and young social and political activists flocked to the movement. They believed in a hybrid version of Islam that borrowed from other cultural sources—as long as these were in line with Islamic values—as well as an Islamic system of governance that could guarantee social justice, equality, and freedom from imperial powers.[58]

By contrast, the ability of secular opposition to organize and expand was limited. The security services targeted the secular opposition while keeping a distance from religious institutions. The state's crackdown constrained the ability of secularists to effectively build grassroots organizations throughout the country.[59] Two factors help explain the weakness of the secular opposition. First, the clergy's connection to the wealthy and powerful bazaari class in society provided them with the economic means to thrive. Second, the Americans aided the shah's "rule of terror" through a multitude of repressive tools that silenced freedom of speech and suffocated nonreligious activism by the late 1960s.[60]

Ironically, the shah tolerated the Islamists' propaganda while clamping down on the communists and the so-called Mossaddeqi, whom he perceived as a bigger threat to his rule. Over the years, the social space was dominated by a combination of political ideologies, particularly leftism, Marxism, Islamism, and Third-Worldism. Radical ideologies, including political Islam, established a strong foothold in the country, offering the population a better model than the shah's repressive strongman rule.[61]

Ayatollah Khomeini and the Radicalization of the Clergy

Khomeini stood out by directing his ideology not to Iran's young intelligentsia, as Shariati and others did, but predominantly toward the ulama itself, in the form of clerical populism. Khomeini, who gained his leadership role in the early 1960s, initially followed tradition by accepting the monarchy—but gradually he changed his mind and taught that Muslims had a sacred duty to destroy it.[62] Khomeini preached that the monarchy itself was a pagan (*taqut*) remnant from the age of polytheism (*sherk*) and therefore fundamentally irreconcilable with Islam.[63]

The White Revolution both precipitated and exacerbated this shift in the ulama's stance toward the monarchy. The powerful Shia ulama saw many of the program's "Westernizing" initiatives as dangerous, spreading what they called Westoxication (*gharbzadegi*), a term coined by Al-e Ahmad. Khomeini shrewdly popularized these concepts, accusing the West of waging a frontal "attack on Islam" itself.[64] Critics of the shah from the right and the left, including the Shia ulama, believed that the hasty attempt at modernization involved "Western" customs and standards that were uprooting Iranian cultural and religious identity and reducing the country to a puppet of the West and a passive market for Western goods. Ultimately, one of the long-term effects of the White Revolution was facilitating the rise of Khomeini's political stardom and the radicalization of his thought. Once Khomeini openly opposed the shah, people from all different walks of life—from hard-liners to moderates, bazaaris to peasants—saw him as a leader.[65]

Seeking to seize the moment, on January 22, 1963, Khomeini issued a strongly worded declaration denouncing the shah's White Revolution and called on the country's religious establishment to boycott it. Opportunistically mimicking leftist critics, Khomeini vehemently condemned the shah for supporting Israel at the expense of Palestinian Muslims, aligning with the West in the Cold War, pouring endless resources into the bloated military, failing to bring basic services to the villages while creating huge shantytowns in the cities, and bankrupting the bazaars by failing to protect them from foreign capital and entrepreneurs.[66]

Following Khomeini's speech, the shah traveled in an armored column to Qom and delivered a harsh sermon attacking the ulama, a show of force that ignited already bubbling tensions with Iran's clerics.[67] Khomeini was not deterred. A few months later, on the holy day of Ashura, Khomeini called the shah a "wretched, miserable man" in an impassioned sermon.[68] Khomeini was arrested just two days later on the shah's orders, which sparked three days of deadly rioting. In some instances, the police threw students to their deaths from high buildings. In his memoirs published after the 1979 Iranian revolution, Khomeini claimed that the army had "slaughtered no less than 15,000," probably a grossly exaggerated number.[69] Supporters of the clerical regime in Tehran view the fateful "15 Khordad" riots (a reference to the Iranian calendar) in 1963 as sowing the seeds for the social protest movement that eventually seized power in the 1979 revolution. By destroying Iran's secular progressive opposition, including nationalists and socialists, the shah inadvertently replaced it with a radical religious opposition that "proved in the long run to be far more lethal."[70]

Mohammad Reza Shah released Khomeini from house arrest in April 1964 and sent him into exile in Turkey that November, but this exile did little to stifle his growing influence inside Iran. Khomeini was exiled because he had questioned the diplomatic immunity given to American soldiers and diplomats on Iranian soil.[71] Even after his exile, however, Khomeini continued to receive substantial donations from Iranian supporters.[72] In September 1965 he traveled to Iraq, where he would spend the next thirteen years developing his theory of Islamic government, or *Hokumat-e Eslami*.[73] Tensions at the time between Iraq and Iran allowed Khomeini to establish an Iranian opposition radio station broadcasting calls on the public to resist the shah's tyranny.[74] By the end of the 1960s, Khomeini began giving lectures and disseminating material on the concept of *Vilayat-e Faqīh*, which stipulates that Islam gives an Islamic jurist (*faqīh*) guardianship over the people. This concept, "the guardianship of the jurist," was Khomeini's most influential and foundational contribution and subsequently became the defining idea at the heart of clerical rule after 1979. In October 1978, after pressure exerted by the shah on Iraqi President Saddam Hussein, Khomeini left Iraq for Neauphle-le-Château, about twenty-five miles west of Paris. Far from curtailing Khomeini's influence, the exile to France raised his international profile.[75] Eventually, Khomeini would launch the revolution from a sleepy French village.

The Shah's (Apparent) Peak of Power

Iran was one of the founding members of OPEC, alongside Iraq, Kuwait, Venezuela, and Saudi Arabia. When the Arab states deployed the "oil weapon" in 1973 to aid the effort in the 1973 Arab-Israeli Yom Kippur War, oil prices increased exponentially. The result was that Iran's oil income rose almost fourfold between 1973–74, from $4.6 billion, and 1975, to a staggering $17.8 billion. The country experienced unprecedented economic growth of 33 percent in 1973, 40 percent in 1974, and 50 percent in 1975.[76] Not only had Iran's oil revenue taken off to the moon, but the shah had also positioned himself as a powerful actor within OPEC, playing his cards right in a time of chaos.

Praise was coming in from right, left, and center as the oil shock crippled Western economies and turned Iran into an economic tiger. Western leaders scrambled to please the Middle Eastern oil producers. In one instance, as the shah was descending from the ski slopes in St. Moritz, in an apparent role reversal, he was greeted and paid homage to by the British chancellor of Exchequer, Anthony Barber, and Trade Secretary Peter Walker. This was sweet music to the shah's ears and ego, and he in turn promised them both 5 million tons of oil for £100 million of British goods.[77]

The shah felt that his country was on a path to equaling the Western states he was so in awe of. His reputation as a charlatan and a bon vivant with more time for royal leisure than responsibility was fading, and instead of jokes about his incompetence or playboy attitude came jokes about his almighty influence: "Bankers joked that when the Shah sneezed, Wall Street caught a cold."[78] In 1975 both the British prime minister and French president requested $1 billion loans from the shah, which he granted.[79] The tables had seemingly turned, and Persia's once quasi-colonial masters were now requesting support from the Great Civilizational leader. This episode stoked the shah's ego and helped him grow from a simple narcissist with power into a megalomaniac—a tendency that deepened throughout the 1970s. He claimed to have received "messages" and "visions" from God himself, boasting in one interview, "I am accompanied by a force that others can't see. My mystical force. And then I get messages. Religious messages."[80]

In another instance, when one of his obsequious imperial courtiers suggested nominating him for the Nobel Peace Prize, he replied, "If they beg us, we might accept."[81] Notwithstanding the skyrocketing oil revenue, the share of manufacturing in the economy remained around 10 percent of the GDP, very low compared to that in the industrialized nations. The shah also neglected agriculture, which turned Iran into a food importer.[82]

It was not just on the economic front that Iran was forging ahead. A year before the oil crisis in 1973, the shah got the United States to designate him as the sheriff of the Gulf. Up until 1971, when the British withdrew their troops from the Gulf, the area had been in London's sphere of influence and ruled by semi-independent Arab sheikdoms under the Pax Britannica. London had actively sought to create a balance of power between Iran and Saudi Arabia, which would ensure that neither of the two Gulf states ever became powerful enough to achieve regional hegemony while deterring other great powers from intervention there.[83]

The situation changed on May 31, 1972, however, during President Richard Nixon's state visit to Iran when he uttered the famous words "protect me."[84] This was a reference to the Nixon Doctrine, which bestowed more defensive responsibilities on its regional clients. The shah welcomed the Nixon Doctrine and convinced his American counterpart to remove all bans on weapon exports to Tehran, which he did. The result is that the United States increased arms transfers to Iran by more than fivefold, from $103.6 million in 1970 to $552.7 million annually in the first half of the 1970s.[85] The shah succeeded in getting Nixon and his influential Secretary of

State Henry Kissinger to drop the policy of equilibrium that Britain had maintained in the Gulf in favor of backing Iran as the regional heavyweight.[86]

America's tilt toward the shah effectively made Iran one of its most important Global South partners, thus further encouraging his Icarus-like journey to the sun. The historian Roham Alvandi asserts that the Nixon Doctrine and the subsequent vast arms sales to Iran "supposedly fueled the shah's megalomania and contributed to the 1979 Iranian Revolution and the subsequent Tehran hostage crisis."[87]

In late 1975 the shah's Resurgence Party declared all-out war against Iran's clergy, denouncing them as "black medieval reactionaries" while simultaneously portraying the shah as a "spiritual" leader in his own right.[88] The shah also replaced the Muslim religious calendar with a new imperial system that allocated 2,500 years for the presumed length of the Iranian monarchy and another 35 years for the shah himself. Iran jumped almost overnight from the Muslim year 1355 to the imperial year 2535. His moves against Iran's religious establishment extended to sending special investigators to scrutinize clerics' sermons and expanding Iran's Literacy Corps so that peasants could be taught about "true Islam."[89] As a newspaper close to the country's religious establishment noted, the shah's actions were a bid to "nationalize" religion.[90] But this was more than his attempt at Machiavellian power politics; it also reflected his intoxication with power and his epic self-delusion.

And then it all came together—the delusions of grandeur, the megalomania, the tyrannical self-indulgence—in one giant party. Unashamedly billed as "the most expensive party ever," the shah played host to his own 2,500-year celebration of the Persian Empire. If he hoped to project power, the shah failed miserably, like the unpopular kid hosting an opulent dance only to be shunned as a wallflower. Instead of cementing the shah's rule, it fueled the growing popular opposition to his reign; Khomeini referred to it as "the Devil's Party." The three-day bash and feast were held in 1971 amid the ruins of Persepolis, the ancient capital of the Persian Empire. The esteemed guests, who included the U.S. vice president, French prime minister, and Yugoslav leader Josip Tito, required VIP housing, so the shah erected fifty luxury apartments in a star pattern around a fountain. Nicknamed the "Golden City," the complex took more than a year and more than thirty-seven kilometers of silk to build. The apartments were all shaped like tents and had been designed by Maison Jansen, the world's first international design firm, whose credits included designing the White House Red Room for John F. Kennedy. "Billion-Dollar Camping" blared the headline of the Swiss *Schweizer Illustrierte.*

At what was supposed to be a celebration of the Persian Empire, the food and other touches paid more homage to European (more specifically French) tradition, in large part because the shah was deeply Francophile. Catering was provided by Maxim's, the most prestigious restaurant of the mid-twentieth century. So prioritized was the shah's fête, Maxim's had to close down its restaurant in Paris for two weeks in preparation for the extravagant banquet. The uniforms for the Persian court were created by the French designer Lanvin, and the dinnerware was all French Limoges porcelain. In one of the grimmest symbols of this doomed affair, the shah had even imported 50,000 songbirds from Europe—and all died three days later in the desert climate. Also flown in from Paris were eighteen tons of food, from beef to parsley to lamb to chives. The one ingredient not imported from France was the alleged 150 kilograms of beluga caviar procured locally. Iran's caviar was the most expensive in the world, at a price of $7,000 to $10,000 per kilo. In addition to serving the magnum of Château Lafite Rothschild, vintage 1945, the shah had imported 410 crates filled with 2,500 bottles of Champagne, 1,000 bottles of Bordeaux and 1,000 bottles of Burgundy, all delivered to a purpose-built cellar in Persepolis. All in all, the *haram*, or forbidden, bottles of wine, the multitude of foreign (French) suppliers, and the lavish abundance of luxury at a party that had been more French than Iranian did not sit well with the clergymen, the growing urban working class, or the nationalists. Rather than re-creating the Iranian national identity around the monarchy as a central figure in it, the shah had only exposed the inequalities and foreign influence that constituted his rule.[91]

Like the Persepolis debacle, the establishment of the Resurgence Party in 1975 unequivocally weakened the shah's regime, though it had been intended to cement his hold on the country. By angering both the bazaaris and the clergy, the regime in effect "undercut the few frail bridges that had existed in the past between itself and traditional society."[92] The regime's attempts to monopolize social institutions deprived local actors of viable means of representation to channel their grievances in the political arena. It helped draw much of the opposition toward the religious establishment, which was seen as the last bulwark against the shah's despotism. The clerics were vocal in their opposition to the shah's one-party state system; the main seminary in Qom suspended sermons in protest.[93]

Religious leaders issued fatwas declaring the Resurgence Party unconstitutional, and Khomeini stated that the party was explicitly designed to destroy both Iran and Islam.[94] The SAVAK swiftly arrested Khomeini's associates (many of whom would play a leading role in the 1979 revolution), something that deepened resentment against the shah's autocratic rule.[95] The religious opposition steadily gained momentum owing to the clergy-baazaris connection and the economic power derived from this relationship, coupled with the important role of religion in Iranian society.[96]

The Blowback

Contextualizing the rising tensions between the ulama and the shah, Ali Mirsepassi, a keen observer of Iran, views the ouster of Mossadegh as a rupture that created a political vacuum filled mainly by political Islam:

> The crisis and decline of secular and democratic institutions [after the 1953 Mossadegh coup] resulted in a political vacuum in the country, and provided an ideal opportunity for the forces of political Islam to organize themselves and mobilize the population on their own behalf. In the absence of any formal institution or organization of political dissent, the Islamicists took advantage of the existing religio-traditional institutions to organize themselves and promote their political agenda, and mobilized the disenchanted Iranians against the regime. The Iranians, who could hardly identify themselves with the ideals of the Pahlavi state, embraced the populist Shi'i ideology as a source of self-

empowerment and national identity. The Shi'i clergy became the leaders of the movement by offering a religious
populist ideology as a safe haven to the masses. ... In this
context one can say that the anti-Shah movement was actually delivered to Khomeini and his political movement.
There was no contesting force or opposition [particularly
secular opposition] to challenge political Islam or to avail
itself to the people.[97]

The physical proximity of the mosque and bazaar in Iranian
towns reinforced the two groups' ties and increased the awareness
of each other's activities.[98] Paying one's religious alms and maintaining a good relationship with the ulama—the guardians of
Islam—signaled piety and was therefore helpful in maintaining
respect and even business success in the bazaar community.[99]
Moreover, when confronting the shah, particularly with regard to
his support for the "grand bourgeois" or foreign investors, the bazaaris recognized that they "needed the canopy of the ulama's protection."[100] At the same time, the mass support of the bazaaris was
vital to solidifying the religious establishment's power base. These
mutually beneficial ties led the bazaaris and the ulama to share a
plethora of commonalities in their worldview. Much like the
ulama, the bazaar community resented the shah's promotion of a
Western secular lifestyle, particularly that of the more privileged
grand bourgeois. This culture clash manifested itself in daily interactions with unveiled and often "provocatively clad" middle-class
and upper-class women and the increasing competition with Westerners in the country's business sphere. The influx of Western foreign capital and secular lifestyles and ideas cemented the alliance
between the ulama and the bazaaris and their opposition to the
shah's Westernization.

The quashing of the constitutional process in 1953 triggered a
chain of events that ultimately led to the revolutionary events in the
1970s. The suspension of democracy allowed radical ideologies like
pan-Islamism and Marxism to flourish at the expense of liberal
nationalism, constitutionalism, and democracy. The coup against
Mossadegh was therefore a key watershed in contemporary Iranian
history and the country's collective memory. There is near consensus

among the intelligentsia in Iran that the overthrow of Mossadegh was a turning point that instigated a "blowback"—a term ironically coined by the C.I.A. in the wake of that fateful night.[101] "Possibilities of blowback against the United States should always be in the back of the minds of all CIA officers involved in this type of operation," noted an internal C.I.A. lessons-learned report in 1954 about Mossadegh's fall. "Few, if any, operations are as explosive as this type," added the report.[102]

The reverberations of that fateful night are still felt in Iran more than seven decades later. It laid the groundwork for anti-Western sentiments in the Persian country, and for the spread of pan-Islamism within its borders and across the entire region.[103] The blowback is exactly what happened in 1979, even though there was no visible line between Operation TP-AJAX, which deposed Mossadegh, and the Islamic revolution. The 1953 coup and its aftermath left deep psychological trauma at the core of Iranian society, and America was held responsible for the destruction of parliamentary democracy. The list of grievances against America and its client the shah is long. It includes the bloody suppression of secular nationalist opposition to the creation of the ruthless SAVAK secret police, and the granting of favorable oil concessions to the Western powers, particularly the United States. The mullahs effectively weaponized Iranians' grievances, turning anti–U.S. sentiments into the raison d'être of their Islamic revolution.

Mossadegh was and continues to be an iconic figure in Iranians' political imagination. Leftists view his removal as a tragedy, diverting Iranian history and arresting its social and political progress. Although the left accuses the Americans and British of facilitating the putsch against Mossadegh, they first and foremost blame the shah. In contrast, the Islamists say the Americans are the culprits, and the British to a lesser extent, avoiding going into specifics because clerical leaders had backed the shah against Mossadegh in 1953. In fact, Ayatollah Khomeini was one of those religious leaders who strongly opposed Mossadegh. Years later, Khomeini was interviewed about Mossadegh, and he famously remarked that "Mosadegh will be slapped; and it was not long before he was slapped; had he survived, he would have slapped Islam," adding that Mossadegh "was not a

Muslim," a comment that reflected emerging postrevolutionary tensions between Islamists and secularists in Iran.[104]

Nevertheless, postrevolutionary Iranians still debate the responsibility of the internal and external actors in the coup that toppled Mossadegh, which signifies the staying power of this historical leader in the nation's imagination. For example, when the youth use a symbol against the Islamic Republic, they often flag Mossadegh's photo, an emblem of resistance, legality, and democracy. Surmising the effects that the coup has had on the public imagination in deeply personal terms, an Iranian academic aptly wrote:

> We knew that the shah owed his throne to the likes of Kermit [Roosevelt]. But we also knew ... that we owe to the Kermits of the world our tortured past: years of being forced as students to stand in the hot sun of Tehran in lines, waving his majesty's picture or flag as his entourage passed by in fast moving, shiny, big black cars with darkened-glass windows; years of being forced to rise and stay standing in every public event, ... years of being hushed by our parents, fearful of being arrested, if we uttered a critical word about his majesty's government or his American advisors ... and ... years of trying to prove to the American people that the 1953 CIA coup was not a fig-leaf of our imagination or a conspiracy theory, that it indeed happened and that they, whether they like it or not, have a certain culpability in what their government does around the world.[105]

CHAPTER FIVE

What Did the Overthrow of Mossadegh Mean for Iran and the Middle East?

W HAT IS IT ABOUT Mossadegh that makes him so important for Iranians even today as well as for the Middle East and the world? To begin with, statesmen with such a commitment to their nation and its people do not come around very often. It requires the perfect combination of position and circumstance, leadership, and will power for these individuals to be able to capture the imaginations of a diverse population like Iran's. Mossadegh rose to prominence immediately after the formal end of imperialism, a period when Iranians were beginning to imagine the path not taken, a future free of foreign domination and meddling, a future as a proud, independent, and prosperous nation. He was the first Middle Eastern leader to try to build a modern nation on the basis of collective and individual liberty.[1] If Mossadegh had been allowed to lay out the foundation of a democratic nation-state and put its economy on a dynamic path, Iran's seeds of freedom could have fertilized neighboring states' soil.

A Transformative Leader

Just before his removal from power, Mossadegh was not an all-popular, undeniably unifying figure. But political rivalry and in-fighting are common traits of healthy parliamentary politics, and Iran's was no exception. A large part of Mossadegh's popularity within Iran rested on his principled opposition to imperialism, es-pecially British policy in Iran and the question of ownership of oil. According to the Iran scholar James Bill: "For many in Iran, the raising of the national flag showed the world that the country had finally gained true independence. Oil nationalization was for Iran what national independence was for many former colonies in Africa, Asia, Latin America, and the Caribbean."[2]

This is a core theme in the political identity of the developing world, and Mossadegh effectively tapped into this long-standing demand of Iranian nationalist forces. Thus, Mossadegh's story had resonance far beyond Iran because it took place during the age of decolonization, a formative moment in world affairs. Though Iran had not been formally colonized, it faced the same core challenges as other countries in the Global South, trials that defined their mo-dernity and which were rooted in the struggle for political and economic independence.

Among the generation of post-independence, anticolonial lead-ers who sought a clean break with Western imperial tutelage, Mossadegh was a pioneer and a trailblazer. A contemporary of Gamal Abdel Nasser of Egypt, Jawaharlal Nehru of India, Kwame Nkrumah of Ghana, and Sukarno of Indonesia, Mossadegh defined the Iranian struggle as an extension of a global struggle for human liberty and equality. He fell on his sword defending the dignity and honor of the Iranian people and the aspirations of newly freed peo-ple everywhere. In his first address to the United Nations Security Council, in New York on October 15, 1952, Mossadegh defended Iran's nationalization of its oil, saying that World War II had "changed the map of the world." He reminded fellow delegates to the world body that "hundreds of millions of Asian people, after centuries of colonial exploitation, have now gained their indepen-dence and freedom. It is gratifying to see that the European powers have respected the legitimate aspirations of the peoples of India,

Pakistan, and Indonesia, and others who have struggled for the right to enter the family of nations on terms of freedom and complete equality. . . . Iran demands that right."³

Mossadegh's call for freedom and independence echoed not only in the halls of the United Nations but also on the streets in Cairo, New Delhi, Islamabad, Belgrade, and beyond. Indian Prime Minister Jawaharlal Nehru and other non-Western leaders had already declared their support for the Iranian nationalists. His universal ideals were an inspiration to a generation of anti-imperial leaders and activists who followed in his footsteps. He laid the foundation for the global anticolonial movement that would meet in Bandung, Indonesia, in 1955, just a couple of years after his removal. Mossadegh's ideas were enshrined in the Non-Aligned Movement, which was formally established in Belgrade in 1961. He coined the term *negative equilibrium* to define his neutralism; the goals were to avoid being embroiled in the global Cold War between the United States and the Soviet Union and to ensure "the national independence, sovereignty, territorial integrity and security of non-aligned countries," which Mossadegh had championed and for which he had lost his premiership and freedom.⁴

As has been seen so often in the modern Middle East and the decolonized countries, when indigenous leaders try to free their nations from the clutches of economic dependency and colonial control, the Western powers stop at nothing to remove them from power—Emir Faisal in Syria, Mossadegh in Iran, Nasser in Egypt, and the list goes on.

Oil as a Symbol of Freedom

In Iran's struggle for freedom, the nationalization of oil was the bone of contention. But for Mossadegh, the struggle for oil was a symbol of the country's struggle for sovereignty and the way to development and the eradication of poverty. Oil was synonymous with full political and economic autonomy and honor. "For Mossadegh, the nation's oil represented life, hope, freedom."⁵

The prime minister had earned the trust and affection of the Iranian people with his dogged pursuit of nationalization. Nationalization united Iranians of all ideological and political persuasions:

women donated wedding rings and civil servants handed back some of their pay to support the effort. Setting an example for his nation, the prime minister declined to draw a salary and paid his own expenses when representing Iran abroad. At least 95 percent of Iranians backed Mossadegh's nationalization of oil, Henry Grady, the U.S. ambassador to Iran in 1950–51, conceded.[6]

Equally important, Mossadegh was engaged in building a free, democratic, and modernized nation-state that could have been at peace with itself and the world. The liberal principles that Mossadegh practiced—and not just advocated—like respect for the rule of law, transparency, and accountability, and the primacy he placed on the interests of common Iranians, offered an alternative and progressive path for Iran. For example, the prime minister brought the military under civilian control and retired corrupt and hostile army officers. He strengthened the separation of powers, putting the judiciary in charge of judicial appointments instead of the government. And for the first time, women were enfranchised when the Mossadegh administration held the first provincial elections where women could vote.

All of Mossadegh's liberal reforms, however, did little to assuage American fears of a communist takeover: "Iran is [a] sick country," U.S. Ambassador to Tehran Henderson wrote, "and [Mossadegh] is one of its most sick leaders."[7] As his biographer de Bellaigue noted: "His enemies called him a malignant, negative personality, but his vision was broad and progressive and had ripened over a lifetime. From his actions as prime minister and his long-established beliefs, it is possible to conjecture the Iran he might have made."[8] This alternative progressive path would have been beset by difficulties and obstacles, but it probably would have been far closer to being optimal.[9]

Mossadegh faced significant internal challenges stemming from the diversity of the country's population, the collapse of the tacit alliance between politicized clerics and the National Front, and the weakening of the very notion of what it meant to be Persian. Iran was still a very poor country and still in the early phases of modernization—something Mossadegh himself conceded, in a meeting with U.S. Secretary of State Dean Acheson in 1951.[10] For some constituencies Mossadegh became iconic, but his reign was always challenged, even when he assumed the highest political office in the country.

Mossadegh and the Shah: A Study in Contrasts

Not only did the shah and Mossadegh represent completely different political systems, but the vast gulf between their visions and ideals manifested itself in their being, body, and doing. Mossadegh was a transformative leader with the potential to begin bridging the gaps between the Iranian people (the nation) and the state. Wearing his emotions on his sleeve, he spoke to the people from the heart, unafraid to show emotion, even crying during speeches. A practicing Muslim, humanist, and pacifist, he eschewed the use of violence and extrajudicial means against his political foes, a quality that proved to be his undoing.

On the other end of the spectrum of humanity lay the shah. In his earlier years, he showed potential for democratic openings and more political liberties. After the 1953 coup that overthrew Mossadegh, however, he slowly and steadily began his descent into authoritarianism, ultimately transforming himself into an autocratic leader who placed his own interests—and not those of the people—at the heart of the state. The distance between the people and the state was fundamental to the Iranian identity, stated the shah. Iran was to him a kingdom of kings and servants, and in 1967 he officially changed his title from shah to shahanshah (king of kings), which the Qajars had originally used during a lavish coronation (and presaging other megalomaniacal leaders such as Muammar Qaddafi, the self-proclaimed "king of kings of Africa").

U.S. and British politicians fed into the shah's inflated ego. "Our Middle East Charles de Gaulle," opined the British ambassador to Saudi Arabia, William Morris.[11] In his later years, the shah's delusions of grandeur turned chronic. In an interview with *Der Spiegel* in 1974, he painted a futuristic picture of Iran's cities a decade thence: cars would run on electricity, and industry would be so automated that people would have up to three weekly vacation days.[12] Where Mossadegh rested confidently in his own vulnerability, the shah was an insecure, power-projecting man who attempted to show strength in direct proportion to his actual fragility. The shah was all too aware that his Pahlavi dynasty was fairly new; it was not from a royal bloodline, its power having been born in a military coup. Threatened by his parvenu royal status, he spent large sums in a bid to gain recognition from more established royal houses.[13]

In 1968 Ambassador Morris, the same who had compared the shah to de Gaulle, pointed out his insecurity regarding the authenticity of his royal status, calling him "the son of the illiterate Persian sergeant, self-consciously masquerading as heir to the 3,000 years old Achaemenid monarchy."[14] Although the Pahlavis were not of royal blood, having seized power in a military coup replacing the eighteenth-century Qajar dynasty, the irony is that it was the British who convinced the shah's father, Reza Khan Pahlavi, who originally intended to turn Iran into a republic like Turkey, to drop that idea in favor of taking the crown for himself.[15] Far from being comfortable in his person, he wore elevator shoes to appear taller and more imposing.[16]

By contrast, Mossadegh preferred substance over style and an honest, unvarnished presentation of himself, even when he was in tears. It is no wonder that the local press dubbed him Iran's Gandhi.[17] One of Mossadegh's first acts after coming to power was to end the tradition of forcing a fawning press by ordering the police chief not to pursue any newspaper editor for insulting the prime minister. "Let them write what they want!" And so, the press heaped abuse on him, the likes of which no Iranian head of government ever faced before or since.

In comparison, the shah not only established SAVAK but also frequently and brutally cracked down against suspected political opposition and dissidents—using methods of torture both plentiful and obscene when trying to extract information from suspects: "nail extractions; snakes (favored for use with women); electrical shocks with cattle prods, often into the rectum; cigarette burns; sitting on hot grills; acid dripped into nostrils; near-drownings; mock executions; and an electric chair with a large metal mask to muffle screams while amplifying them for the victim. . . . Prisoners were also humiliated by being raped, urinated on, and forced to stand naked."[18]

Most of the torture took place within prisons. In another twist on the benefit of American imports, the shah erected four maximum-security prisons based on U.S. models.[19] Once again, Iran looked to the United States to optimize its tools of repression. Evin Prison was the most notorious of the four. Ever since its completion in 1972, it has been the primary destination for the incarceration, torture, and execution of political prisoners, a practice the Iranian theocrats amplified after 1979. Evin Prison has also been dubbed "Iran's Bastille," famous for being so harsh that it made other prisons look relaxing.[20] The purpose-built block 209 for political prisoners was and is still ironically referred to as "Evin University" for the high proportion of intellectuals held there. It was also the scene of a symbolic riot and prison fire on October 15, 2022, in solidarity with the large-scale nationwide protests against the Islamic Republic after the killing of Mahsa (Zhina) Amini, a twenty-two-year-old woman who died in a hospital in Tehran after being arrested by the morality police for not wearing a hijab; the riot resulted in eight deaths and more than sixty prisoners wounded.

Under the shah, prisoners at Evin could spend no more than two hours a day in the courtyard. They were forced to wear blindfolds outside their cells, even when they were taken to interrogation. They had no reading room and already censored government newspapers were even further censored for them. There were no trees, gardens, or flowers; in the words of one inmate, there was "nothing but iron and steel."[21] The prison had several basement interrogation (read: torture) chambers along with its own courtroom and execution yard. The latter was used for extrajudicial vengeance killings, on orders from the highest political level: the shah.[22]

In contrast, decades earlier Mossadegh had delivered a powerful speech in parliament denouncing the "madhouse" of the Iranian incarceration system. He was moved to take this position after visiting a jail administered by police, which, compared to Evin, would have been a "place of rest." Mossadegh even went so far as to taste the broth the prisoners were served for lunch, the quality of which only amped his fury. He urged the other members of parliament to legislate to "get these people out of jail."[23]

Mossadegh's commitment to the rule of law was manifested in his battles against state infringement on the separation of powers and his resignation from a government position. He set high standards for integrity, honesty, and civic sense. One of his first acts as prime minister was to ask his older son, Ahmad, to resign as deputy minister of roads. And Mossadegh refused financial aid for his grandson, who was studying in Geneva, even though every Iranian student abroad was entitled to it. He barely shared the same planet as the shah, who threw himself the "world's most expensive party" in Persepolis in 1971. Starting with his family, Mossadegh set an example for the nation about transparency and good governance. He eschewed the chance to have the State pay family travel expenses when representing Iran abroad and reportedly donated his earnings to the law library at the University of Tehran.[24]

In other words, he was precisely the type of individual who had at heart the same values that the West claims to promote and should have earned its support. Instead, the Western-backed 1953 coup denied Iranians their right to self-determination and freedom from foreign control. U.S. officials prioritized Iran's "security" over democracy and naturally favored subservient despots like the shah, who did America's bidding.[25]

The result is that Iran's state development continues, decades after the coup, along the path of autocracy, clientelism, and a commodity-dependent economy. Lacking domestic legitimacy, the shah resorted to repression and divide-and-rule tactics, tearing the fabric of society. History has proven that these tactics, in the long run, can only backfire. People eventually, inevitably throw off the yoke of injustice. Ultimately Mossadegh was brought down by the sinister machinations of the United States and Britain, particularly the Eisenhower administration, which was fixated on both the communist threat and the control of oil supplies. The colossally destructive decision to overthrow Mossadegh was to Washington just another chess move in its global effort to block Soviet expansionism and to tame assertive nationalists.[26]

Had the United States not been solely motivated by controlling oil and rolling back Soviet communism, Iran could have developed a durable form of legitimate governance and an inclusive economy with reverberations across the region. If Iran had been allowed to travel on this path, the country could have been appreciated and rewarded as a source of inspiration rather than feared and punished as a threat to the region's stability. Iran could have developed into a stable liberal democracy with a prosperous economy. It could have also been a beacon for other countries in the Islamic world and beyond. Imagine that.

The Scars Left by the 1953 Coup

The 1953 coup did not just remove a progressive leader from power; it also stunted Iran's liberalization and economic development. A lot that has happened in the country since then can be traced to that tipping point. There was nothing inevitable or predestined about the descent of Iran into repression and political and religious autocracy. In his earlier years, the shah was not always happy with his father's use of an iron fist, referring to him as "one of the most frightening men."[27]

America's push and encouragement were decisive in hardening the shah's soft authoritarianism. There is overwhelming evidence that the coup ruptured political life in Iran, triggering a cascade of crises that radically altered the country's trajectory. This flash point set the stage for the 1979 revolution, inadvertently contributed to the rise of pan-Islamism, and weakened secular politics. It undermined the forces of liberal democracy, enhancing the appeal of Shia supra-Islamisn—still a marginal current at the time—and laid the foundation for deep-seated anti-Americanism.[28]

In a way, the 1953 coup is the Persian equivalent of what the historian Elizabeth Thompson calls the Western "theft" of Arab democracy, referring to the post–World War I events in Syria. Colonial France and Britain crushed the nascent democratic experiment led by Emir Faisal.[29] After these developments, few people could believe any longer that the West's proclaimed values of freedom and democracy applied to the people of the Middle East too. Seventy years after the coup, the C.I.A. has for the first time acknowledged that its role in overthrowing Mossadegh and cementing the rule of the shah was undemocratic. Far from affirming the impact and legacy of C.I.A. interventions in Iran and beyond, its spokesperson Walter Trosin claimed (citing the agency's historians) that the majority of the C.I.A.'s clandestine activities in its history "bolstered" popularly elected governments. "We should acknowledge, though, that this is, therefore, a really significant exception to that rule," Trosin remarked about the 1953 Iran coup.[30]

Anti-American sentiment was by no means just a remnant of the coup itself; it is a noxious seed nurtured by successive U.S. administrations in the decades since. After crippling Iranian democracy, they continued to doubt the country's capacity for self-governance, along with Iranian competence in general, hinting again at another covert regime change: "What they lack is the capacity for sustained, dynamic effort," wrote Robert Komer, an adviser to President Kennedy, in October 1962. "They don't have what it takes to run a country themselves."[31] He failed to note that this is axiomatic for Iranians—indeed for any people—who never had the chance to determine their own future. Iranians of all political stripes and persuasions, even those strongly critical of the Islamic Republic, view the current crisis in U.S.–Iran relations through the prism of the past, not least the seminal events of the early 1950s, the C.I.A.–led coup, the toppling of Mossadegh, and the strong support for the shah by successive U.S. administrations.[32]

Taking stock of this toxic legacy is a first step in resolving the dangerous standoff between the United States (and the Western powers in general) and Iran that has endured for more than four decades. Coming to terms with history can bring about healing and reconciliation between warring peoples and nations. There is hardly any recognition among Americans of the scars that the ouster of Mossadegh left on the Iranian popular consciousness or their country's complicity with Reza Shah's crimes against his people. U.S. leaders have not taken responsibility for their government's destructive backing of the shah, let alone admitted their role in arresting Iran's political development at a formative moment in its history. There were gestures, however. In a diplomatic overture to the Iranian government in March 2000, Secretary of State Madeleine Albright publicly admitted that the United States "played a significant role" in orchestrating the 1953 overthrow of Mossadegh, and she said this was "clearly a setback for Iran's political development."[33]

With the exception of Albright's half-apology and the acknowledgment by President Barack Obama, in passing, of America's involvement in the coup, there has been zero recognition by top U.S. officials of the pain and loss caused by the coup.[34]

The United States also has offered no apology to the Iranian people for actively supporting the shah's security forces, particularly the SAVAK, which terrorized the population. There have been calls for reflection from the mainstream media, including a recent *New York Times* editorial stating that U.S. leaders need to acknowledge history and the ways in which their own policies have contributed to the current crisis.[35]

For example, Iran's nuclear program dates back to the 1960s, when the United States supplied the shah with a nuclear research reactor and subsequently commended his ambitions to build twenty civilian nuclear reactors and train the first cadre of Iranian nuclear scientists. After Iran's clerics seized power in 1979, Supreme Leader Ayatollah Ruhollah Khomeini declared nuclear power to be "un-Islamic" and stopped the nuclear program. Iran's nuclear program was not revived until 1984, after the invasion by Iraqi President Saddam Hussein, who had a nuclear weapons program of his own. The bloody eight-year war with Iraq killed approximately 200,000 Iranians, including many who died a horrible death from chemical weapons used by Saddam. Iranians have never forgiven the United States for siding with Saddam Hussein and for shielding him from liability internationally.

As President Ronald Reagan's special envoy to the Middle East, Donald Rumsfeld became a conduit for extending American intelligence and military aid to Iraq as well as opposing European efforts to have Saddam Hussein held accountable by the Security Council for his use of gas and chemical weapons.[36] Washington did this all while Oliver North was covertly selling missiles to Iran to fund an illegal war in Nicaragua, on another Cold War front. Instead of educating Americans about their government's past meddling in Iran's internal affairs, U.S. politicians and the media continuously offer the public a binary narrative that depicts Iran as a rogue state that threatens America's interests worldwide.[37] Iran's ruling clerics hate America, the U.S. public is told, implying that Iran's rulers hate freedom and liberty and that the clash between the two countries is about values and Americans' way of life rather than genuine historical, political, and ideological differences and grievances. This dominant U.S. narrative perpetuates misunderstanding, fear, and conflict.

As the multiple waves of large-scale social protests in Iran show, the clerics are not angels—quite the opposite. They are as repressive and antidemocratic as Reza Shah ever was. But the story of the

Islamic Republic of Iran can't be told without excavating the full historical record of the C.I.A.–led coup that removed the country's first fully legitimate leader from office in 1953. That landmark event and its aftermath bequeathed Iran's repressive institutions developed jointly by the shah and the United States, such as Evin Prison. America's subsequent full-throated embrace of Mohammad Reza Shah roiled Iranians and soured their attitudes toward the United States. Many of them have neither forgotten nor fully forgiven the United States for subverting Iran's sovereignty and democratic development trajectory.[38]

This view is evident in the reaction to the hostage crisis precipitated on November 4, 1979, when a group of revolutionary Iranian students stormed the U.S. embassy in Tehran and seized sixty-six hostages, mostly diplomats. Americans saw this as a "declaration of war" by a foreign government emulating a "terrorist," as the *New York Times* described it in an editorial two days later.[39] Throughout their 444 days of captivity, the hostages' plight gripped the American imagination. U.S. politicians and commentators demonized Iran and its clerics as savage, barbaric, and irrational. Lost in the fog of the crisis and the suffering of the hostages was any informed and reflective discussion of the possible blowback against the United States that the C.I.A. itself warned of less than a year after deposing Mossadegh.

If the American memory was short, the Iranian one was long. In fact, one of the proclaimed aims, if not the most important aim, of seizing the U.S. hostages was to avert another C.I.A. coup against the Iranian revolution. The hostage takers were deliberately crueler toward the C.I.A. agents they managed to capture in the embassy takeover than they were toward the civilian diplomats. One C.I.A. agent said the hostage takers regarded him and his teammates as surrogates for the agency's past; "unable to punish those involved in the 1953 coup, the Iranians took out their anger on us."[40] While the immediate trigger for detaining the U.S. diplomats was President Jimmy Carter's decision to admit the shah to the United States for cancer treatment, the hostage takers were motivated by a feeling of historic injustice and the search for payback for all the wrongs that the U.S. government had perpetrated against the Iranian people.

By severing relations with the United States, the revolutionary students were making a clean break from Iran's past. They sought to expel the United States from their country and regain full political autonomy—the same goal, with vastly different means, that Mossadegh had regarding Britain in the early 1950s. Mossadegh belonged to a generation of nationalists after World War II who saw Britain as a malignant force in their country's internal affairs and, by contrast, viewed America as a force for good.[41] His worldview had had echoes in the past. Russia's and Great Britain's interventions in Iranian domestic affairs from the mid-nineteenth to the early twentieth centuries encouraged Iranian officials to seek a countervailing third power.

For four decades Iranian leaders tried to attract American interest in their country.[42] The hard labor paid off, and eventually the bonds were strengthened between the youthful Western republic and the Persian dynasty, although Washington never fully immersed itself in Iranian affairs at the time. Favor for American influence and allyship with Iran grew only when the United States became the sole foreign power to back Iran's participation in the post–World War I Paris Peace Conference. In that same year, the Americans openly contested the Iranian-English treaty of 1919, whose contents ostensibly turned Iran into a quasi-independent state and de facto British protectorate.[43]

The peak of American efforts to pull Tehran toward its sphere of influence came when the United States pressured the Soviet Union to pull out of Azerbaijan following World War II. U.S. intervention, along with that by its Western allies, had directly salvaged Iran's territorial integrity and demonstrated to both the Soviet Union and Great Britain that the Persian Gulf was no longer their exclusive sphere of influence. It is no wonder then that historically Iranians trusted the Americans and relied on them to counterbalance the British and Russians. Suspicious of and tired of British subjugation and Russian threats, Iranian leaders, including Mossadegh, had been willing to cooperate with the United States in a mutually beneficial relationship that was based on respect for the country's sovereignty and independence.

The C.I.A.–led coup that ousted Mossadegh put an end to the long U.S.–Iranian honeymoon. The Iranian students who seized the American hostages in 1979 transferred their visceral hostility from Britain to the United States. Ayatollah Khomeini gave voice to the revolutionary students by calling America "the great Satan" and Great Britain its "evil" ally.[44] C.I.A. architects and their bosses reaped what they had sown in 1953.

Against this backdrop, a qualification is in order. In the last few years, thousands of critical new documents have been declassified—in both the United States and Iran—that show that C.I.A. officials were briefing the Iranian government right up until October 1979. The declassified documents also show that in 1979 the Carter administration played an important role in facilitating the rise of clerical rule in Tehran. Before the hostage crisis that began that year, Carter officials tried hard to befriend Khomeini and his reactionary faction. For them, it did not matter which autocrat ruled over Iran, as long as the revolution did not veer to the left. After all, America had supported religious activism and fundamentalism on the other side of the Persian Gulf, in Saudi Arabia, for decades, and was about to do the same in Afghanistan. But this attempt was without success, as the clergy were deeply suspicious of—even hostile toward—America.[45]

U.S.–Iran: Walking on a Knife's Edge

America and Iran are still caught in a deadly embrace, unwilling to come to terms with the past and reconcile. The poison of the 1953 U.S.–backed coup and the subsequent shoring up of the shah continue to circulate in Iran, just as the poison of the hostage crisis does in the United States.[46] These perceived injuries and wrongs can't be swept under the rug; they must be directly addressed.

The stakes are life and death. Over the past four decades, the United States and Iran have more than once come close to military blows, with potentially devastating consequences for international peace and security as well as countless lives. Despite their denial, Republican administrations seek regime change in Tehran. Under Donald Trump, the United States engaged in war by other means, imposing some of the most punishing economic sanctions on the Islamic Republic. Many of Trump's closest foreign policy advisers openly called for regime change. Iranian leaders rightly accused the

United States of waging economic warfare against their country, trying to bleed the economy and force the clerics to surrender. The costs of economic and financial sanctions on the state and society in Iran cannot be overstated. They caused a tenfold increase in inflation, drove mass unemployment, increased poverty, and heightened social tensions. For example, the number of Iranians living in absolute poverty has doubled to 25 million, according to an internal study by the Institute for Social Security Research.[47]

All this has occurred in a country blessed with natural wealth. Trump's decision to assassinate Major General Qassim Suleimani, Iran's top security and intelligence commander, in January 2020 amounted to a U.S. declaration of war against Iran, according to a United Nations expert investigating summary executions.[48] The targeted killing of Suleimani, the Quds force commander and second-most powerful leader in Iran, after Ayatollah Ali Khamenei, brought the two countries to the brink of all-out military confrontation.[49] Iran retaliated by firing missiles at two U.S. military bases in Iraq, injuring more than one hundred American soldiers in early January 2020. Less than a week after Suleimani's death, Iran accidentally shot down a Ukrainian passenger plane leaving Tehran, tragically killing all on board.[50]

A U.S.–Iran war would certainly have had drastic and far-reaching consequences that could ripple violently throughout the Middle East and the world.[51] Nearly a year later, Israel reportedly assassinated Iran's top nuclear scientist, Mohsen Fakhrizadeh, in an ambush on his car in Absard, some fifty miles from Tehran. Three American officials told the *New York Times* that Israel was behind the attack. Although the widely read newspaper shied away from saying that the United States may have known about the operation in advance, it acknowledged that the United States and Israel are the closest of allies and have long shared intelligence on Iran.[52] John Brennan, who had been the C.I.A. director under Barack Obama, called the killing a "criminal" and "highly reckless" act that "risks lethal retaliation & a new round of regional conflict." "Such an act of state-sponsored terrorism would be a flagrant violation of international law & encourage more governments to carry out lethal attacks against foreign officials," Brennan tweeted, urging Iran to resist the temptation to strike back.[53]

The fact that a former head of the C.I.A. warned that acts of "state-sponsored terrorism" like the killings of Suleimani and Fakhrizadeh could trigger all-out war between the United States and Iran should motivate leaders of both countries to avoid the unthinkable.

Amid this grim picture of intransigence and historical amnesia, evidence has recently emerged pointing to half-hearted efforts by the United States and Iran to come to terms with each other at the onset of the Islamic revolution. As I have mentioned, U.S. documents declassified in the last few years show that before the hostage crisis of 1979–81, the United States tried to befriend the new clerical regime. Similarly, Khomeini, while in Paris and soon after returning to Tehran in 1979, sought good relations with the United States.[54] A rapprochement never happened for reasons that can be debated, among them the existence of a volatile revolutionary situation in Tehran.

Since the early 1980s, the clerical regime has helped found and finance paramilitary Shia groups in several Arab countries to advance Iran's strategic interests and export their Islamic revolution throughout the region. This created tensions between Tehran and Washington. Largely for this reason, the Western powers (overtly if not always covertly) backed Saddam Hussein during the Iraq-Iran war. Iranians saw this as proof of U.S. intentions to reverse the Islamic revolution. Even when Saddam Hussein used chemical weapons in the 1980s, the United States did nothing to condemn him or hold him accountable at the time—a fact Iranians repeatedly bring up to highlight Western double standards on human rights.

Iran has developed a long list of powerful allies and proxies from Lebanon to Yemen, to Iraq, to Syria. In the last, strongman Bashar al-Assad extinguished the flame of a peaceful uprising in 2011 with a bloodbath that continues to this day. Iran's human rights record is dismal, surpassing Saudi Arabia in its number of death sentence executions every year, according to the most recent report from Amnesty International. It is already not a pretty picture, and the 2021 election of Ebrahim Raisi, a hard-liner, has already exacerbated these trends, especially state repression at home, as exemplified by a massive wave of demonstrations following the killing of Mahsa Amini while in the custody of Iran's

morality police. Protests have taken place cyclically in the past decades, but this most recent wave has been described as the biggest
threat from below to the clerical establishment. Women have been
at the forefront of this movement and have been able to mobilize
across cultural, ethnic, and class lines. It is not surprising that this
movement has gained a mass character precisely when the most reactionary wing of the clergy has returned to power, dashing hopes
for internal reforms.

According to the sociologist Asef Bayat, this movement is the
culmination of a process that started with the protests of 2009, 2017,
and 2019, and that now is able to bring together "the urban middle
class, the middle-class poor, slum dwellers and people with different
ethnic identities—Kurds, Fars, Azeri Turks and Baluchis."[55] The
clerical establishment has responded to the biggest challenge facing
its rule in decades by violently repressing the protestors.

Nevertheless, Iran is not simply a rogue state that challenges
American interests in the Middle East. It is an extension of a great
Persian civilization. Regardless of who rules Iran, a secular democracy or a religious theocracy, Iranian leaders see their country as a
pivotal regional power deserving respect from the international
community and with a sphere of influence extending across large
parts of the Arab world. This expansive foreign policy doctrine has
been a defining feature of Iran's regional strategy since the 1960s.
It long predates the Islamic revolution and will probably outlast it.

The shah also pursued a muscular and grandiose regional policy, as does the current clerical regime. It is now forgotten that the
shah started the nuclear program, anointed himself the sheriff of
the Gulf with U.S. blessings, occupied three Emirati islands, and
frequently interfered in the internal affairs of nearby states such as
Yemen and Iraq. Unlike the shah, the clerics have spread their influence far and wide by using soft and hard power tactics, while eschewing direct military intervention (Syria is the exception to the
rule). America embraced the shah as its policeman in the Gulf and
rewarded him with advanced weapons, later applying punishing
sanctions against the clerics and treating them like pariahs.

There is a way out of this vicious cycle of hatred and conflict.
We saw this during the second term of President Barack Obama.
Serious diplomacy was prioritized. Under Obama and Iranian Pres-

ident Hassan Rouhani, deescalation replaced escalation. The 2015 signing of the nuclear deal known as the Joint Comprehensive Plan of Action (JCPOA) opened a window of opportunity. It was widely celebrated around the world. Donald Trump's election in 2016 put an end to this moment of optimism. He firmly shut the door with his disruptive and aggressive policies, asserting that Iran used the economic dividends to further its expansive regional policies and invest in its missile arsenal. With the Biden administration in power, opportunities for deescalation with Iran include the revival of the nuclear deal, which has not materialized.

The greater challenge facing both powers is to imagine a new relationship, one based on reconciliation, forgiveness, and cooperation. It is not wishful thinking to imagine a nuclear-weapon-free Middle East and a regional security architecture that takes into consideration the security needs of all the key countries in the Middle East. For this to happen, far-sighted and visionary leadership will be needed in both Tehran and Washington. And although such leadership has been in short supply so far, it can be tapped through a frank confrontation of the past and a realistic look ahead to the future.

As this reconstruction of the history of Iran shows, the fateful overthrow of Mossadegh in 1953 established a pattern in U.S.–Iranian relations that has proven hard to counter. If America had given a chance to Mossadegh's democratic experiment, the history of Iran—and, perhaps, the Middle East—might have followed a different path, to pluralism and prosperity. The prognosis, however, does not look good. With hardliners firmly entrenched in Tehran and the possibility of the Republican Party recapturing the White House in 2024, there is much to be concerned about.

CHAPTER SIX

Nasser

The Pan-Arab Icon

B REAKING A PATTERN THAT has endured for scores of years is no easy feat, but Gamal Abdel Nasser managed to achieve it, becoming the first leader of Egypt to rise from the masses and become the president of the republic.[1] While Nasser was anti-democratic and tolerated no dissent, the charismatic figure also captured the hearts of Arabs across the region and among the diaspora. An enduring symbol of Arab unity, Nasser continues to inspire those seeking dignity, which was his primary rallying cry. The contexts may have changed, and opinions about his imprint are still hotly debated, but the range of his influence remains unquestionably vast.

To understand how Nasser came to achieve this historical stature, it is necessary to understand his background, follow him through childhood, grasp the influences that shaped him, and appreciate all this in the context of the forces he witnessed, experienced, and bled for when he put his own life on the line in the service of a cause. His literary influences, fallen comrades, and even the personal interests that strengthened his political hand are all detailed in this examination of the man whose portrait still hangs in cafés from Baghdad to Brooklyn and beyond.

Leader of Egypt, a symbol of the dignity of the Arab world, Nasser ascended to power on a fast trajectory from young military officer to the top of the political ladder following the July 23, 1952, coup d'état by the Free Officers. Like Mossadegh, Nasser prioritized the expulsion of British forces, favoring modernization and aiming to lift millions of people out of poverty, but the two men also had stark differences. Nasser lacked Mossadegh's cosmopolitan upbringing and—most significantly—his belief in democracy and the rule of law. A middle-class product of the anticolonial era, Nasser was part of an early generation of postcolonial leaders who aimed to rid their countries of the legacy of imperial control and empower their peoples. As a top-down autocrat, Nasser was in a hurry to remake Egypt and transform it into a power to be reckoned with.

Nasser: Larger Than Life

Views of Gamal Abdel Nasser within and beyond Egypt vary widely, but all agree he was the most consequential of all modern Egyptian leaders. Larger than life, as much myth as he was man, Nasser still animates the imagination of many Egyptians and Arabs. Perhaps there is no more poignant symbol of this than the images of his portrait held aloft by protestors in 2011 in Cairo's Tahrir Square as well as in other Arab countries. Pictures of Nasser formed part of the collage of the millions of vibrant Egyptians demanding an end to the rusty, corrupt regime of Hosni Mubarak and a free, just, and dignified life for themselves and their children.

At six foot two—unusually tall among his peers—with intense dark eyes and scars from military battle in the 1948 Palestine War, Nasser embodied as much an action hero as the political colossus he would become. Nasser's continued resonance comes despite a number of blemishes on his record. He became progressively more authoritarian and caused the Egyptian army's defeat and humiliation in the June 1967 Six-Day War with Israel. His most ardent followers still blame General Abdel Hakim Amer, head of the Egyptian army, for being asleep at the wheel when Israel attacked on June 5, 1967, or fault America for having a hidden hand in Israel's obliteration of the Egyptian air force. No less than the Arab world's grandest diva, Umm Kulthum—so beloved in Egypt and the Middle East that she was also known as "the Fourth Pyramid"—sang, "Stay, you're our only hope," after Nasser resigned.[2]

Despite the obvious flaws, millions of Egyptians rose out of abject poverty and gained middle-class status under his leadership. Khaled Mohieddin, a friend of Nasser and a leading Free Officer who participated in the 1952 coup that ousted the pro-British monarchy, told me these Egyptians have a sense of appreciation and loyalty that blinds them to Nasser's faults.[3] Such deeply felt affection makes sense when we consider that Nasser rose from among his people. His rallying cry—"Raise your head, my brother, you are an Egyptian" (later expanded to "you are an Arab")—resonated in the national consciousness.

The indignities of colonial rule from the 1880s to the 1950s left deep scars; the despicable subjugation through a false superiority was propagated by leaders such as Lord Cromer, British consul general and the de facto leader of Egypt's finances and government from 1883 to 1907. His words are so derisive they would border on parody were they not so destructive: "Orientals cannot walk on either a road or a pavement (their disordered minds fail to understand what the clever European grasps immediately, that roads and pavements are made for walking); Orientals are inveterate liars, they are lethargic and suspicious, and in everything oppose the clarity, directness, and nobility of the Anglo-Saxon race."[4]

This type of colonial and racist thinking motivated Nasser and his comrades to oust Britain from Egypt. Numerous Egyptians have spoken passionately about how Nasser boosted their morale and instilled the sense that dignity is more valuable than gold. He repeatedly reminded the Great Powers that they must respect the dignity of Egyptians, inheritors of a great civilization. As his biographer Anthony Nutting noted, Nasser considered dignity to be "the very first principle of Egyptian and Arab nationalism" and observed that "dignity required independence and independence required the final and total elimination of all foreign occupation and interference."[5]

Beginning in the 1950s and continuing until he died from a heart attack in 1970, Nasser nationalized private industries and banks, starting with "Egyptianizing" foreign holdings after the 1956 Suez War; limited land ownership; and disinherited both the old privileged classes and foreigners who controlled the country's wealth. Speaking to members of the generation that benefited from his rule, I heard such phrases as, "I am middle class thanks to Nasser's policies," or "Nasser's educational reforms made me the professional I am today." The merits of Nasser's policies can be—and certainly are—extensively debated, but no one can dispute the fact that he engineered a social revolution that transformed the lives of millions of Egyptians, modernizing the country and leveling the social playing field. So popular was he that of the 35 million people in Egypt at the time of his death, fully one in seven attended his funeral.[6] On that October day mourning cries and ceremonial gunshots were heard all across the Arab world.

Critics and supporters alike saw Nasser's rise as the end of an era marked by the ascent of semisecular Arab nationalists in the Middle East. Like Iran's Mossadegh, Nasser belonged to a generation of postcolonial leaders who did not see any contradiction between being semisecular nationalists and pious Muslims. Both were practicing Muslims who informally accepted some sort of separation between mosque and state. But where Mossadegh was humble and unafraid to appear vulnerable, Nasser projected power and authority. A rousing public orator, he was both ambitious and authoritarian, aiming to be an unrivaled leader beyond his country's borders to the entire Arab world.

The two leaders arrived in power from vastly different origins and took radically different approaches. Unlike Mossadegh, Nasser was not a product of privilege; rather, he endured a long struggle to climb the social and political ladder. Unlike Mossadegh, he used an iron fist against his opponents. He emerged from humble beginnings and is believed to have died poor, leaving his wife and four children dependent on state support. As a postcolonial leader, Nasser was determined to do even more than achieve independence for Egypt and all Arabs; he led the Non-Aligned Movement across the Global South, along with such towering figures as Tito in Yugoslavia, Sukarno in Indonesia, Nehru in India, and Nkrumah in Ghana. He also played a key role in supporting national liberation and anti-apartheid movements in Africa and in establishing the Organization for African Unity, now known as the African Union.

The Upbringing of a True Egyptian

Nasser was beloved by the Egyptians for being one of them: a man of the people. He was the first leader for millennia to hold this distinction, though General Mohamed Naguib had briefly done so from 1952 until 1954. Previous rulers read like a Who's Who of history's great invaders, from Greece's Alexander the Great's conquest to the Damascus-centered Ummayad Caliphate, to the Kurdish ruler Saladin, to the Turkic Mamluk Sultanate, to the Ottoman conquest, to French Napoleonic colonization, to the Albanian dynasty of Muhammad Ali Pasha, not to mention the British invasion and domination of Egypt from 1882 until the early 1950s. In contrast to these foreigners, Nasser was a return to Egypt, perceived by some to embody a reborn pharaoh emerging from the fertile soil of the Nile Delta.

"All his life, Nasser lived and acted like a commoner and died almost penniless," Nasser's confidant and official chronicler, Mohamed Hassanein Heikal, said. "No other Egyptian leader has captured the heart of the people like Nasser did."[7] Whereas Mossadegh descended from a noble line, Nasser spent most of his life eating, breathing, and being raised like the vast majority of Egyptians. His father, a postal clerk, earned just enough for "the bare necessities of life" but, thanks to having married the daughter of a better-off coal merchant, had the benefit of income from her family business that afforded Nasser a good education.[8] His family moved often, inadvertently exposing Nasser to the abject poverty and inequity suffered by millions.

Adding to the insight he gained about class, Nasser had a broad perspective on faith, having attended both religious and secular schools. From ages seven to nine, he went to Beni Mur qur'anic school, performing so remarkably that the school's sheikh singled him out in front of the other kids as exemplary.[9] Nasser's faith in Islam, like Mossadegh's, ran deep without ever becoming confused with politics, though after Egypt's defeat in the June 1967 war, Nasser used religious expressions to explain the defeat. Sent to live with his paternal uncle in a working-class neighborhood in Cairo, Nasser attended school near the al-Azhar Mosque, the oldest religious and higher educational Muslim institution in the world. These "colourful surroundings, where jewelers, goldsmiths, tinkers

and carpenters made and sold their goods in small shops lining a
maze of noisy narrow streets," formed the soil to nourish the boy
who was widely viewed as intellectually gifted.[10]

After his father joined the postal service in Alexandria, Nasser
subsequently moved there and attended the Ras el-Tin High
School, which first nurtured nationalist feelings in him. When he
was a young teen, Nasser protested alongside other students against
the Sidqi government for abolishing the 1923 constitution and replacing it with a more authoritarian document. Nasser recalled his
battle against the brute force of the state:

> While crossing the Manshiya Square in Alexandria, I no-
> ticed clashes between some demonstrating students and the
> police, I did not hesitate: I immediately joined the demon-
> strators not knowing anything about the cause of demon-
> stration for I found no reason to ask. . . . I was struck by a
> blow on the head by a police baton followed by another
> blow until I fell down. All drenched in blood, I was driven
> to prison along with a group of students who failed to es-
> cape. It was at the police station, while receiving treatment
> for my head injuries, that I learned that the demonstration
> was an anti-government protest led by the "Masr El-Fatah"
> (Young Egypt) society.[11]

It was a society Nasser would soon join and then quickly leave
after realizing that "in spite of their lofty claims they achieved
nothing substantial."[12] He acknowledged having flirted with a host
of political parties and organizations that shared as their main goal
ridding Egypt of foreign interference. But Nasser never considered
joining the Communist Party because of two major conflicts between communism and his own beliefs:

> The first of these being that at heart Communism is atheist
> and I have always been a true Moslem with an unshakeable
> belief in a Higher Power which is God who controls our
> destiny. It is impossible for a person to be a true Moslem
> and a true Communist. The other obstacle was my aware-
> ness that Communism necessarily meant that there would

be a form of control exerted by the international Communist Parties; this too was something I completely rejected.
My colleagues and I struggled long and hard to wrestle
the power away from the feudal classes and shatter foreign
control over Egypt so our country could achieve the genuine independence it so badly needed and, therefore, the
mere hint of foreign control was something I could not
accept.[13]

Nasser had an early role model in one of his paternal uncles who
had been jailed for political agitation during World War II. Morally
alert and adamantly opposed to unfair and unjust situations, he once
joked that the only conditions he had ever accepted were those of
his wife's brother when asking for her hand for marriage.[14]

When he was fifteen, Nasser's political belief system started to
form, and he became head of a students' activist organization,
which prompted his high school to alert his father, who sent him
away to stay with his uncle in Cairo.[15] His activism was only fueled
by clashes with the police and a visceral hatred for British imperial
rule. In Cairo, Nasser studied at El-Nahda Secondary School, de-
vouring, above all, the subject of history and reading beyond the set
syllabus to learn about the great figures of the past. Nasser's favorite icon was Julius Caesar—notably, the one who had first invaded
Britain.[16]

Nasser was influenced by classics like *A Tale of Two Cities* by
Charles Dickens and *Les Misérables* by Victor Hugo, both pro-
foundly antiauthoritarian works. And Nasser offered his own
glimpse of literature's influence on his thinking in an essay he wrote
as a student on Voltaire, praising the author for his independence of
thought.[17] Living close to the National Library, Nasser channeled
his animosity toward the British into reading voraciously in both
Arabic and English, consuming nonfiction books and serious peri-
odicals, as well as fiction and poetry.[18] A romantic idealist, Nasser
may well have sensed that one day he might be just the man to expel
colonial Britain from his homeland. In high school, Nasser also
acted in school plays, acquiring oratory skills that would later advance his political career.[19] He came to appreciate staged events and
ultimately imbued his grand speeches with theatrical undertones

that captivated Voice of the Arabs radio service listeners. His appreciation for the drama did not stop in school; his wife recalled Nasser's ongoing love of cinema. Nasser was eager to educate himself not because of his background, but despite it.

Nasser entered the world at the precise moment that Egypt was breaking away from its colonial overlord. Nasser was born just before the revolution against British occupation began in 1919, and his earliest years coincided with a gathering vision of Egypt as an indivisible community. It was a time of national unity as movement against the British united Egyptians from all walks of life. The urban-rural divide dissolved as a new political class emerged.[20] From early on Nasser gained a sense of oneness and commonality as well as a deeply held sentiment that British domination and interference marked the biggest threat to this organic political community.

As a teen and young adult in the 1930s and 1940s, Nasser bore witness to the severe economic crisis that gripped Egypt. Antigovernment strikes brought civil unrest. Like others of his generation, Nasser came into contact with student organizations, socialist groups, revolutionaries, and the Muslim Brothers. Several of them would come together in 1935, united in their call to restore the 1923 constitution, which adopted a parliamentary representative system based on the separation of powers and cooperation among authorities.[21] At the time—Nasser was seventeen—he wrote to a friend to express his growing frustration with the political establishment. "The situation today is critical; Egypt is in a precarious state," he cautioned, before lamenting the dying nationalist spirit of Mustafa Kamil: "Mustafa Kamil said, 'If my heart were to move from left to right, or the pyramids were to change their place, or the Nile were to change its course, I would never abandon my principles.' This is but a long prelude to an even longer struggle; we have frequently spoken of a great action that would bring dramatic change to the nation and awaken it from its slumber. However, nothing has been done yet."[22]

This letter was also notable for its inclusion of a reference to the loss of *al-karama*, the term Nasser used to express what he held most dear: dignity. Ultimately his populist appeal would rest on his defense of the nation on this front above all others.[23] It touched such a deep chord in the Arab soul that it transcended Nasser's time and place. For example, the 2010–12 Arab Spring protests were peppered with references to al-karama; the mostly young people in the streets were denouncing corrupt, often pro-Western rulers in monarchies and republics across the Arab world. If young Nasser was busy with street politics, by comparison, Mossadegh, when he was seventeen, filled the Qajar dynasty coffers in his role as tax collector.

In 1937 Nasser was accepted to the Abasseya Military College, from which he graduated as a second lieutenant in 1938. Other alumni include Anwar Sadat, who got to know Nasser while they were serving in the infantry.[24] Their relationship would prove consequential for Egypt and the region. As a military officer, Nasser started gaining influence within the institution he believed could end the British presence in Egypt, according to his fellow army comrade and friend Khaled Mohieddin.[25] His co-recruits recalled a highly politicized young man deeply appalled at the British for their control of the Egyptian military and political domination of the country. In 1941 Nasser started a two-year military posting in Sudan, where he witnessed firsthand how Britain sought to increase its rule in Sudan at the expense of Cairo. Nasser "could not but feel slighted by the continued British rejection of Egypt's claim to sole sovereignty in the Sudan which had been voiced by the first prophet of modern Egyptian nationalism, Mustafa Kamil," observed Anthony Nutting.[26]

Early in his political career, Nasser believed that political independence could coexist with the monarchy and so steadfastly committed himself to the goal of an independent Egypt ruled by King Farouk. Nutting persuasively argues that "far from being directed against the throne, [Nasser's] initial object was, so he subsequently told me, to try to put some stuffing into the King and, by creating a militant opposition within the army, to strengthen Farouk's resistance to further encroachment on Egypt's sovereignty."[27] Nasser saw the monarch as "for better or worse, the symbol of Egypt's nationhood."[28] His real qualms were with the British, not with his own countrymen, as had been the case since his early teens, his confidant Heikal told me.[29]

Egypt Is Humiliated by the U.K. and Israel, and Nasser Is Radicalized

Two key developments contributed to Nasser's transition from a relatively conservative politics as a young man to a more radical view. His thinking altered dramatically when, in 1942, Britain rolled its tanks to the royal palace in a bid to impose its chosen prime minister on the king. And Nasser was personally deeply affected by the cataclysm of the 1948 Palestine War.[30]

In 1942, as part of the Third Reich's North Africa campaign, when the Panzer tanks of the German "Desert Fox" Erwin Rommel were approaching Egypt, the British feared that King Farouk and Prime Minister Ali Maher would welcome the Germans to Egypt to free themselves from British control. Consequently, on February 4, 1942, the British ambassador to Egypt, Lord Miles Lampson, stormed into the court of King Farouk, allegedly calling him a "boy" and demanding that he replace Ali Maher with the anti-Nazi and quasi-liberal nationalist politician Mustafa Al-Nahhas.[31] Through the palace windows King Farouk could see an entire British battalion laying siege to his home. Threatened with arrest, the king acquiesced to the British ultimatum.

Outrage spread across Egypt. Nasser was among those who chafed against the British for their unrelenting resolve to control Egypt. The palace siege sparked the first open discussion of revolution among Nasser and his military comrades.[32] Britain's humiliation of the king and Egypt led Nasser to realize that "there is a dignity to be defended."[33] While despising London's actions, Nasser also regretted that the king gave in to British pressures just to defend his throne. On the other hand, Nasser appreciated its mobilizing effect on the Egyptian military when the officers "started talking about sacrifice and dignity instead of women and amusement."[34]

Nasser's close friend Khaled Mohieddin recalled that Britain's humiliation of King Farouk and the nation was a game changer for Egypt's proud officers: "We were determined to free Egypt of the clutches of British imperialism and build a new egalitarian society."[35] Nasser drew the conclusion that political change requires force—a view eschewed by Mossadegh, who held fast to the principles of nonviolence even through the most severe tests.[36]

The perspective Nasser gained from the 1942 palace siege was cemented when he fought in the 1948 Palestine War. The catastrophe, or *Nakba*, as it came to be known, was dismal for Nasser, the junior officers' corps, Egyptians across the country, and Arabs across the region. Arab armies had been defeated, Palestinians expelled en masse, and the land itself lost along with the battle. Nasser was among the troops who experienced the consequences of their leadership's poor decisions and even worse military equipment that left them exposed before the irregular armed Jewish troops. These officers drew a clear conclusion: any response demanded a revolutionary approach. No longer could they tolerate what they perceived to be a corrupt political establishment that put its selfish interests above its own citizens, national dignity, and the fight against Zionist aggression.

For those Egyptians aiming to throw off London's imperial yoke, the Nakba was a seminal event that galvanized them toward also ousting the quasi-liberal political system in Cairo. Nasser noted bluntly in his autobiography that it became a personal mission and strategic priority to "save the homeland" from the grip of "wolves"—a sentiment that presciently spoke for many young army officers in Egypt, Iraq, Syria, and beyond.[37] Nasser was so personally and deeply affected that he recorded his sense of loss and betrayal in his memoirs: "In the tragedy which we witnessed in Palestine, the nightmare continued for six long and dark years. . . . There is a criminal who should be held accountable for the defeat. . . . The army did not commit the crime of Palestine but someone else did. . . . We suffered from a destructive lack of information. . . . The night of 20 May [1948] was the most depressing of all my entire life as I was in the Gaza military hospital surrounded with beds of soldiers injured on the battlefield."[38]

Mohamed Hassanein Heikal, Nasser's chronicler who knew him from those days in Palestine, noted that he saw the war as being about the strategic territory linking Egypt with Syria and the Red Sea with the Mediterranean.[39] Nasser credited his experience in Palestine with convincing him that there was an umbilical cord between Egypt and neighboring Arab countries. The bitterness of the Palestine conflict moved Nasser to commit to Arab nationalist principles and abandon his previous brief flirtation with the Muslim Brothers.

The Palestine War revealed the shortcomings of the Arab military campaign, which suffered from a lack of coordination among the different Arab military contingents sent—often reluctantly by kings and emirs—to assist the Palestinians in their struggle against the Zionists. It took a heavy toll, and though the Arab armies did manage to push the Israelis back, any momentum was soon lost. Arab leaders agreed to a twenty-eight-day truce, which the Israelis used to buy arms from Czechoslovakia. Then the Zionist commander and future Israeli prime minister Yitzhak Rabin said that without those purchases, "it is very doubtful whether we would have been able to conduct the war."[40] After the truce, the Arabs lost the edge in terms of firepower and soon botched the war, allowing the Israelis to seize more Palestinian land.

Returning home in September 1948, Nasser brought with him a blood-stained shirt and handkerchief and told his wife that he had been wounded by a bullet that hit a few centimeters from his heart.[41] The stained clothes were kept as a grim reminder of his brush with death and defeat. He saw imperialism behind the uprooting and displacement of the Palestinians, blaming the old regime in Egypt and neighboring countries for their complicity in the Arab defeat.[42] In prioritizing the challenge ahead, Nasser sought first to defeat the "near" enemy, namely, the king and the British occupier, and then, boosted by this victory, to go on to tackle the "far" enemy, namely, Israel.

The coup plans that Nasser would eventually execute in 1952 germinated during a siege he endured for over four months from 1948 to 1949 in the Palestinian village of Falluja, near Gaza.[43] Nasser's contemporaries also recounted how he came to believe that the military was society's strongest institution to lead the overthrow of the old regime and the creation of an independent nation-state. Here, too, Nasser's journey differed radically from Mossadegh's, who spent his life battling political opponents peacefully and openly in public, while eschewing violence, even at his own risk. The predicament Nasser identified was shared across the Arab world, as was a sense of common destiny. The Palestine War imbued in him a deep appreciation of Egypt's strong ties with its Arab neighbors.

In his autobiography, *The Philosophy of the Revolution*, Nasser describes their solidarity in a common cause: "When the Palestine crisis loomed on the horizon, I was firmly convinced that the fighting there was not fighting on foreign territory. Nor was it inspired by sentiment. It was duty imposed by self-defense. After the siege and the battles in Palestine, I came home with the whole region in my mind one complete whole. The events that followed confirmed this belief in me. . . . An event may happen in Cairo today; it is repeated in Damascus, Beirut, Amman or any other place tomorrow."[44]

Nasser wrote movingly of the peoples of the pan-Arab nation: "We have suffered the same hardships, lived the same crises; and when we fell prostrate under the spikes of the horses of conquerors, they lay with us."[45] And while his emotions were authentic, they were also strategic; like most gifted politicians, Nasser could deploy sentimental touchstones at key moments to pull heartstrings and amass support. He did this to great effect during the late 1940s and early 1950s.

The Palestinian historian Walid Khalidi notes that Nasserism was an "attitude of mind" that was at the same time radical and conservative, not a fixed ideology.[46] It was radical because Nasser wanted to achieve real independence at all costs in a country that had been ruled by foreigners for millennia, and conservative because it had to happen on Arab, not universal and liberal, grounds. As I mentioned previously, Nasser fiercely rejected communism because he did not see Marxism as compatible with Arab traditions and beliefs.

Both Mossadegh and Nasser saw the United States as a potential force for good, in contrast to the imperial powers in Europe. Both leaders would be sorely disappointed by Washington's squandering of this goodwill.[47] The United States was aware of the potential for allyship—but the Cold Warriors in Washington "missed the memo," literally. That "memo" came in the form of a report by the King-Crane Commission, which had been sent to the Arab countries by President Woodrow Wilson in 1919 following World War I and returned with a positive assessment of Arab orientation toward the United States. The favorable consideration is not that surprising when viewed through the lens of imperialism: Arabs could well relate to America's struggle for independence from Britain. And the United States had a clean slate since, unlike imperial Europe, it had never ruled Arab and Muslim lands. American missionaries and travelers left a decidedly more constructive mark by setting up universities, schools, and hospitals.

It would be difficult to overstate the cost of this missed opportunity. Mossadegh and Nasser both placed faith in America that never paid off, but from different perspectives. Where Nasser was a pan-Arabist, Mossadegh had no transnational ideal. On one level, this could be explained by the different groups they represented; Arabs were dominant in the Middle East and North Africa while the myriad Iranian ethnicities were more heterogeneous. But on a deeper level, the disparity stemmed from differences in temperament between the two men, and those could be traced to their respective upbringings. Those born with less can be hungrier than those born into power. The two shared the aim of breaking Britain's grip on their sovereignty and societies, but Nasser had a vision and role for Egypt beyond its national borders, whereas Mossadegh did not have something similar for Iran.

The Free Officers Movement and the Black Saturday

Nasser's home in Heliopolis was a secret meeting base for the newly set up Free Officers Movement, an underground network of dissident army men joining forces to overthrow the Egyptian monarchy. Nasser was its driving force and quickly rose in the ranks.[48] In 1949 he formed a coordinating committee and a year later became the committee's head. In her memoirs, Nasser's wife gives a glimpse of his role:

> Visitors came constantly, most of them officers who spent some time with Gamal and then left; others—one or two— would stay late into the night, talking in low, muted tones. Some nights there would be a knock on the door after we had gone to bed and Gamal would rise and see his guest into the salon where they would talk for a while; some stayed till dawn. Some nights he had more than one visitor

and on other nights he would get dressed and go out with the caller, even though the house had retired to bed. This was how it was.[49]

The Free Officers Movement was an umbrella organization for different voices all united against their common enemy: imperialism and the Egyptian system enabling it. They were mainly middle-class, mostly lower-ranked, hardworking men who had made it into the military academy because of the post-1936, albeit limited, meritocratic openings in the institution.[50] The underground movement was one of many contemporary nationalist groups at a time of rapid change: urbanization was on the rise, radical and subversive ideas were seeping down to the masses, and radical groups such as the Muslim Brotherhood, the Socialist Party, and the Communist Democratic Movement for National Liberation (HDTW) were gaining momentum.

The full story of the Free Officers Movement goes far beyond the remit of this study.[51] Suffice it to say that Nasser's leading role in the formation and development of this underground network had a lasting effect on him. This was clear in the fact that long after becoming one of the most powerful leaders in the Middle East, Nasser often suspected that domestic foes—the Muslim Brothers and estranged former army comrades—were colluding with foreign powers, particularly the United States and the Saudis, to destroy his regime.[52] Nasser had a deeply suspicious and secretive temperament that fed his autocratic tendencies and led him to clamp down on the opposition. Nasser's paranoid bunker mentality can also be seen in the fact that he even proposed setting up an underground paramilitary organization in the 1960s to sniff out internal enemies—as if Egypt's sprawling security apparatus were not effective enough with the use of their coercive methods—according to his official in charge of the ideological indoctrination of youth, Abd al-Ghaffar Shukr.[53]

Nasser and the Free Officers needed a spark to ignite their revolution. That catalyst came on January 26, 1952 (later referred to as Black Saturday), when Cairo went up in smoke, heralding the coming of a new political era in Egypt and neighboring Arab lands. First, the Opera Casino in Cairo's central Opera Square was set on fire. Next was the turn of the Shepheard's Hotel, one of the country's and world's foremost hotels. From there it was a downward spiral of destruction, looting, arson, and death until late in the night, when the Egyptian military quelled the rioters. From the ashes and smoke rose the protestors' clear rallying cry: no foreign influence or interference in Egypt. The attack was directed toward the cosmopolitan and liberal heart of Egypt, patrons of imperial Britain and foreign capital, and more than 750 stores were destroyed.[54] The damage to British and foreign property totaled £3.4 million.[55] The human toll was heavy. More than fifty Egyptians and nine Britons died and more than five hundred people were wounded.

Not only did the flames incinerate the bodies of Egyptians and foreigners, but they also destroyed the tiny bit of legitimacy left by the monarchy as well as the traditional political factions of Egypt. Cairo was highly flammable because the British had proverbially doused it in gasoline the day before with a humiliating attack on the Egyptian auxiliary police force in Ismailia, in the British Canal Zone. That zone itself was one of the pillars of imperial power in Britain's Middle East and Africa strategy and was granted to the British following a 1936 Anglo-Egyptian treaty. It symbolized humiliation and imperial domination to the Egyptians. Nationalist police officers had facilitated the Free Officers Movement's launching of *fedayeen*, martyrs, against British troops in the Canal Zone. The British had tracked them down to the police station in Ismailia. British Brigadier Kenneth Exham, commander of the forces of the Canal Zone, had on the morning of January 25 ordered the Ismailia police force to vacate the Canal Zone and hand over the fedayeen. The request was turned down by both the Ismailia governorate and Interior Minister Fouad Serageddin; their defiance was the last remaining representation of anything that resembled Egyptian authority in the Canal Zone. Brigadier Exham moved swiftly and surrounded the police with a force outnumbering them 10 to 1 and armed with vastly superior firepower, giving them an ultimatum: surrender or face the consequences. The Egyptian police stood their ground but lost fifty killed by the British, who imprisoned all the survivors.

King Farouk's attempts at damage control did little more than expose his hunger for power at the cost of even more popular support. Martial law was introduced, parliament was dissolved, and the Wafd government, which had won more than 70 percent of the votes in the 1950 election, was dismissed. Curfews from six in the morning to six at night were mandatory; exemptions were allowed only for security forces. King Farouk also tapped his loyal stooge Ali Maher Pasha to replace the Wafd Party's leader, Mustafa Al-Nahhas. Order had collapsed, and along with it fell public trust in the British-backed Egyptian government.[56]

Over the course of roughly half a year, starting with Black Saturday and the 1952 coup, the country changed prime ministers four times. Ali Maher Pasha lasted for 35 days before being replaced by Ahmed Naguib el-Hilaly, who, in turn, lasted 122 days before Hussein Sirri Pasha's 20-day premiership, which then Hilaly reheld for one day before the coup on July 23. As King Farouk's grip on power became more tenuous, the Free Officers Movement prepared to strike a fatal blow against the old regime at a moment's notice. Their plans gained sudden urgency in late May 1952, when Nasser got word that King Farouk knew of the coup plans—even down to the names of some of the Free Officers, whom he would soon move to arrest. Anticipating a crackdown, Nasser gave a trusted comrade and a friend, Zakaria Mohieddin (a cousin of Khaled Mohieddin), the responsibility to hasten the D-Day of the military coup.

As Zakaria Mohieddin was vetting which army officers were loyal to the movement, Nasser identified the ideal figurehead for the revolution: Mohamed Naguib, easily one of the military's most popular men, who, in turn, boosted the Free Officers' popularity by joining them. He had a distinguished military background, having been wounded three times in Palestine, as well as doctoral and law degrees. A known war hero, Naguib burnished his credentials by turning down King Farouk's offer of the post of minister of war as part of the monarch's attempt to bolster his image after Black Saturday. In what amounted to a reprise of his popularity in the army, Naguib, secretly supported by the Free Officers, bested the candidate of King Farouk, Major General Hussein Serry Amer, in the elections for the presidency of the Army Officers Club on December 31, 1951. Nasser knew that while he'd risen in the ranks and made a name for himself, Naguib, with his greater seniority and prestige, would command the respect of the more experienced military officers. The scene was set.

Given that Nasser did not officially or publicly look like the leader of the coup, those close to him were unaware of his ultimate aim. His friend Khaled Mohieddin told me that from the beginning Nasser had been maneuvering to use the movement as a springboard to becoming the sole leader of Egypt. "Nasser had had a grand design to be the leader of a new Egypt. We only knew this immediately after the revolution."[57]

The Bloodless Revolution

Nasser and his comrades could not have asked for a better stroke of luck than the Cairo burning that cremated the last remaining trust in the monarchy. On the morning of July 23, 1952, Egyptians woke up to the sound of a new political era. From their radios, Anwar Sadat heralded the tidings, but the words were scripted by Nasser: "Egypt has passed through a critical period in her recent history characterized by bribery, mischief, and the absence of governmental stability. . . . Accordingly, we have undertaken to clean ourselves up [in the army] and have appointed to command us men from within the army whom we trust in their ability, their character and their patriotism. It is certain that all Egypt will meet this news with enthusiasm and will welcome it."[58] Chance, skill, and fortuitous conditions merged on the night of the coup to reshape Egypt's future and, along with it, the Arab world as a whole.

The coup began in Cairo, then moved to Alexandria. The takeover of the capital involved occupying key bridges, the Post Telephone and Telegraph Building, radio stations, and the army headquarters. Military planes circled above. Nasser, dressed in civilian clothes to avoid detection, drove from location to location across Cairo ensuring that everything was going as planned. At hour zero, Anwar Sadat, famously kept in the dark, was at the movies with his wife. In another cinematic move, Free Officer Muhammad al-Gizawi used his acting skills to impersonate his commanding officer, who was under arrest. Answering several calls from the commander in chief of the army, Muhammad al-Gizawi pretended to be his superior and denied any extraordinary troop movement.[59] By three o'clock in the morning, the Free Officers had taken control of Cairo, and Nasser summoned Naguib to the army headquarters. Four hours later Sadat read out the declaration written by Nasser. The coup was a success, and even a virtually bloodless one: only two soldiers had died. After Black Saturday, the Free Officers capitalized on the public discontent and published their Six Principles:

1. Ending colonialism, including the British army stationed in the Suez Canal Zone, and punishment of the Egyptian traitors who had supported it
2. Ending feudalism
3. Ending political influence through wealth
4. Reestablishing social equality and ending economic exploitation and despotism
5. Aiming to build a powerful army
6. The creation of a healthy, democratic atmosphere[60]

The Six Point Program was vague because the Free Officers were a heterogeneous group mainly bound together by opposition to imperial Britain and its constant intervention in Egypt's internal affairs as well as frustration with quasi sovereignty, royal cronyism, and corruption. Democracy was at the bottom of their list of priorities. Neither Nasser nor his comrades were liberal democrats.

According to Khaled Mohieddin, Nasser was "antidemocratic"; his priorities were "the consolidation of the revolution, expelling British influence of Egypt, and sitting on top of a bourgeoise-reformist autocratic system."[61] Here is where Nasser diverges completely from Mossadegh. Nasser never even pretended to be a democrat. From the beginning to the end of his rule, Nasser repeatedly stated that democracy is a luxury that Egyptians cannot afford. He claimed that external powers and the wealthy classes could subvert the electoral process by purchasing votes and spreading misinformation.[62] In short, Nasser believed that Egyptians would not be ready for parliamentary democracy until their basic needs were met. The lack of substance of the Six Principles demonstrates that the Free Officers did not look past the goal of overthrowing the monarchy. Nasser and his army comrades had not given much thought to leadership or governance. They knew only that they wanted to expel British influence from Egypt and prioritize economic and social development over liberal democracy.

The British lit the spark for the revolution with the 1936 reforms, which ultimately began the end of London's influence and that of the monarchy. A product of the Anglo-Egyptian treaty of the same year, the reform called for Britain to withdraw its troops, keep the auxiliary force of 10,000 in the Suez Canal Zone with a view to guarding the Suez Canal's security and freedom of navigation, and help Egypt build its own military capable of defending the nation without British aid. The reforms conceived of a military based more on merit than on nobility and status. In this way, the British unwittingly allowed members of the nationalist middle class or petite bourgeoisie, like Nasser, to gain access to the military—and they ultimately used that access to take back their nation.

On the eve of the coup, Egyptians generally shared the belief that parliamentary politics was a sham designed to enable the rich to get richer and the British to preserve the status quo. Several decades of parliamentary elections had kept Egypt's destiny firmly in the hands of the British. This was the perfect soil for nurturing alternative approaches to politics. The widely held disillusion with a nationalist elite that had failed to come up with a unifying social, political, and economic project for the country's future paved the way for the rise of semifascists as well as authoritarian and paramilitary groups in the 1930s and 1940s.

Nasser and the Free Officers Movement leveraged the power of widespread popular dissatisfaction with the status quo to achieve a total transformation of the political system. The failures of the old regime's quasi liberalism as well as the damage to its reputation sustained from being dominated by a foreign power pushed Egypt's new leaders, particularly Nasser, to look for answers not in the near past but in their own culture and history. The loss of Palestine to the Zionists was a major cause for many of Nasser's generation in Egypt and in the neighboring Arab states to blame the old ruling classes for failing to improve the well-being of the people and to protect national security.

Nasser and the Birth of the Authoritarian State

Although the Free Officers held no brief for the values of the old regime, they paid lip service to democratic rule. Their figurehead, Naguib, stressed that the coup had been executed to "purge the Army and the country of traitors and corrupt people and to restore constitutional life."[63] After forcing King Farouk to abdicate and sending him into exile, on July 31 Naguib promised that "all political affairs are in the hands of the government and will be conducted in a constitutional manner."[64]

Yet the early pronouncements of the Free Officers diverged dramatically from their subsequent policies. Lofty goals quickly fell victim to a power struggle among former military comrades who lacked commitment to parliamentary democracy. The devolution from constitutionalism to authoritarianism only intensified thanks to Washington's stance. By isolating Nasser and attempting to undermine his regime in the second half of the 1950s, America reinforced autocratic tendencies in Cairo and deepened the military's role in the country's internal affairs.

The repercussions still reverberate. Egypt's military now dominates almost every aspect of life in the country. To say it is politically independent from the state would be an understatement; more accurately, the state is politically dependent on the military. The bare numbers give a sense of how dominant the military is in Egypt: since the coup in 1952, Egypt has had only one year and 342 days of nonmilitary presidents, and for 339 of those days it was ruled by a civilian interim president handpicked by General Abdel Fattah el-Sisi in 2013. Economically, the military operates like a corporation with its own factories, hospitals, supermarkets, and hotels. It even owns 51 percent of the Administrative Capital for Urban Development, which has the main responsibility for building Egypt's $45 billion New Administrative Capital thirty-five kilometers east of Cairo. The military is exempt from various state taxes and is often favored for government contracts.

Nasser had no issue with Egypt turning into a military state ruled by a military elite. The Egyptian leader wittingly or unwittingly institutionalized and legitimatized the role of the army in Egyptian and Arab political life. He popularized the rule of the

man on horseback, which became the dominant model in neighboring Arab states. This failure to advance political progress and an
open society were, fortunately for Egyptians, not repeated in the
social realm. Nasser achieved a measure of economic development
and reduced poverty. His initial social and economic policies
turned many excluded and otherwise marginalized people into a
sizable middle class grateful to Nasser for having lifted them up.

The Free Officers elevated their coup to a revolution with
the 1952 land redistribution program that limited landholders to
two hundred acres, set a minimum wage for agricultural workers,
capped the cost of renting land, and facilitated agricultural cooper-
atives to cut costs on fertilizer, pesticides, and transport. It gave everyday Egyptians a taste of social justice and, along with it, credit
to the Free Officers for breaking the bitter injustice of the old regime. Nasser aimed to empower the roughly 16 million landless
peasants and give dignity to the people.[65] In an even more radical
move, in November 1953 the state confiscated wealth from people
connected to the now-abolished royal family, after the republic was
declared on June 18, 1953.[66]

The Free Officers' decision-making arm, the Revolutionary
Command Council, knew it would be risky to forfeit the support of
the other political parties and organizations. But for Nasser, it would
be out of the question. The stage was set for a two-pronged confrontation: one between the Free Officers and the pre-1952 political
forces, including the liberal Wafd Party, the left, and the Muslim
Brothers, and the other among the Free Officers themselves.

Soon after the revolution, the Free Officers vied against each
other for power and dominance. The movement split along two
wings—Naguib versus Nasser. On January 16, 1953, the Free Officers banned all parties, except, temporarily, the Communist Party
and the Muslim Brothers, and declared a three-year transitional period under the rule of the Revolutionary Command Council. Naguib
argued against the military's monopolization, but he also showed autocratic tendencies. He had no clear democratic vision for Egypt
emerging from the monarchy and backed the suppression of political
parties and independent voices. He wanted to preserve the old order
by reforming and modernizing it, whereas Nasser sought to annihi-
late the old regime and upend social classes. Naguib, a conservative

senior officer, was pitted against Nasser, a shrewd, ambitious junior officer. The desire for power, not ideology, fueled their rivalry. In the struggle that soon turned violent, Naguib would prove no match for Nasser's will power and blind ambition.[67]

Egypt: The American Key to the Middle East

The coup in Egypt unseated one of the West's closest allies, but the State Department still issued a statement of goodwill toward the new regime, simply because the Free Officers posed no threat to U.S. interests in the Middle East.[68] Egypt's closing the door on the influence of the United Kingdom opened a window, so to speak, that the United States could enter. That is why when Nasser ascended to power, he saw Washington as a potentially rich source of assistance with Egypt's industrialization and independence, putting the Brits in their place by offsetting them.

It will become clear in the analysis that follows how earnestly Nasser approached the United States in a sincere attempt to engage on constructive terms. From 1952 to 1955, he asked only that Egypt remain free and independent, enjoying rights that Americans fought to achieve for themselves roughly two centuries before. Instead of seizing the opportunity to profit in terms of stability, trade, and human progress, the Cold War hawks rejected these overtures, presenting only an ultimatum: our way or the highway. Either Nasser would join America's Pax Americana and its global alliance against Soviet communism or be ostracized and penalized.

This was not a policy mistake or miscalculation on the part of the Cold War proponents but, rather, a deliberate offensive strategy designed to force newly decolonized countries to take America's side in the struggle for world hegemony.

Both Nasser and Mossadegh were caught in this trap. With little wiggle room, they pursued nonaligned foreign policies that, because of the rigid ideologues in Washington, inevitably put them in direct confrontation with the United States. In a pattern that continued from Mossadegh, America squandered the opportunity to cultivate Nasser—beloved in Egypt and across the Arab world—as a valuable ally and instead turned him toward the socialist camp. If the United States could have accepted nonalignment at face value, understanding it was not against the United States, Washington might have forged ties that would have effectively changed the political trajectory of U.S.–Egypt relations and the Middle East as a whole. Instead, as the following chapter shows, the Cold Warriors lost Egypt, a pivotal regional state that could have been an anchor of prosperity and stability and a driver of peace across the region.

Although the picture of Nasser's record is mixed, his better qualities could have been harnessed in the service of national progress for Egypt, regional advances for the Middle East, and greater global stability. Reconstructing this history will excavate lost opportunities while pointing toward a new paradigm that draws on those lessons to demonstrate the possibilities for a new future.

CHAPTER SEVEN

Nasser in "Little Hollywood"

Losing Egypt, Losing the Peace

A NY GRADE SCHOOL STUDENT is taught that it is better to make a friend than an enemy, but this basic childhood lesson was completely forgotten by the Cold Warriors, who in Egypt, as in Iran, repulsed a potential ally in Nasser.[1] This move spoiled Washington-Cairo relations for a couple of decades but, worse than that, tarnished America's image in the eyes of the Egyptian people for much longer. Rather than understanding and cultivating the proud nationalist leading a country that had recently broken free from centuries of foreign domination, the new superpower suffocated Nasser, never allowing him to enjoy an independent foreign and economic policy. The concerted U.S. attempts to draw him and his Free Officer comrades into Pax Americana failed to budge Nasser from his determination to achieve full political autonomy and his principled commitment to nonalignment.

America's Chance with Egypt

Buoyed by Egypt's newly won independence and with the memory of British dominion all too fresh, Egypt was a poor candidate for a superpower to drag to one side of a bipolar world. This powerful, strategic country offered instead a prime opportunity for a super-power to draw it into a friendly partnership that was based on mutual gains—if only the hawks in Washington could have heeded their own Cairo envoys' advice to do this. America's myopic view of Nasser's quest for independence—seen as anti-American rather than pro-Egyptian and pro-Arab—was worse than unproductive; it was counterproductive. The intended goal of the Cold Warriors to head off Soviet influence backfired so badly that it actually created an opportunity for Moscow.

None of this would have happened with a bit of foresight, a touch of sensitivity to the local culture, and a hint of understanding of the larger context, particularly of Nasser's pursuit of development and modernization.

Above all, officials in Washington showed a breathtaking failure to grasp that a longing for sovereignty and independence and a resolve to achieve national dignity are universal. If only these Cold War die-hards had credited Egypt's leader for his effort to throw off the colonial yoke anywhere near as much as they celebrated the Founding Fathers of the American republic for doing the same, common ground might have been forged. But Nasser's legitimate aspirations were not treated as though they deserved respect equal to those exercised in the history of the United States, and this unequal treatment ultimately led to an unsustainable imbalance. It needn't have been so.

Nasser and the Free Officers initially looked to America as a potential ally in their bid for independence, sharing a romantic view held by many Afro-Asian people. That worldview shattered with the emergence, from the ashes of World War II, of the United States as a superpower. The fact of its dominance was not the source of this mistrust, which stemmed, rather, from the hegemon's "with-us-or-against-us" mentality. Forced to choose, many formerly colonized peoples eschewed the one issuing the ultimatum. The countries targeted in this ideological gambit were not themselves, first and foremost, concerned with grandiose ideologies.

Like Mossadegh, Nasser took power with a full domestic agenda. Millions of his citizens in Egypt lived in poverty; there was a desperate need for modernization, social justice, and industrialization.

Nasser, the son of one member of the lower middle-class *fellahin*, was especially conscious that these groups lived in abject conditions. He looked to America to help him rise to this epic challenge and secure the means to develop the land of the Nile. For three solid years starting in 1952, Nasser aimed for a friendly relationship with America. While deftly avoiding getting caught up in the superpowers' rivalry, he showed a clear preference for American over Soviet friendship while insisting that Egypt not be used as just another pawn on the U.S. Cold War chessboard.

Starting with the Bandung Afro-Asian Summit Conference in 1955, where Nasser himself, for the first time, acquired international exposure and recognition as a leader of independent Egypt, he favored nonalignment, engaging with both sides to the extent that it benefited Egypt as well as pursuing state-directed development. The myopic vision of the hawks in Washington could not see this in perspective; it appeared to them as nothing less than a provocation. The same lack of compunction that enabled the United States to depose Mossadegh prevailed in Egypt when it came to removing Nasser from power, but the tactics differed. Instead of a plot to overthrow him, Washington sought to completely undercut him with a humiliating blow. The net effects? America turned Nasser from a likely friend to a galvanizing foe.

To the degree that Nasser's immense popularity echoed across the region, so, too, did a commensurate negative view of America among Arabs that reverberates to this day. The result was that the balance of power that the U.S. hawks wanted so badly to shift in their favor was to tip the scales in favor of the Soviets, who, thanks also to Washington's mistakes, were making headway throughout the increasingly decolonized Global South.

The Free Officer and America: A Promising Beginning

Nasser and Mossadegh shared the hope that the United States would not turn into an imperial power, but instead would act consistently to uphold its ideals of democracy and human rights while respecting the sovereignty of other nations as enshrined in the United Nations Charter.

Nasser was primed by the media to be predisposed toward hoping for the best from America. For about a year after the 1952 coup, he would hang out at the U.S. embassy in Cairo. Decades before Joseph Nye wrote *Soft Power*, that very approach, rather than military might, could have worked to sway Nasser, who was a genuine fan of American culture, particularly the cinema. This was attested to by William Lakeland, a young political officer at Washington's Cairo embassy, who recalled passing many evenings with Nasser in its canteen enjoying films starring Esther Williams.[2] At the time, Egypt had the world's third-largest film industry, but Nasser still loved a good Hollywood production.

Of course, interests overlapped beyond the silver screen. Americans and Egyptians both stood to benefit from a solid working relationship. From Nasser's perspective, a close relationship between Egypt and America could speed progress toward his country's independence and help end the legacy of Britain's imperial presence there.

The Americans only stood to gain from a close relationship with the most populous and culturally influential Arab country; that much should have been obvious.

There was cause for hope in those early years. Certainly the coup in Egypt may have unseated one of America's closest allies— the British—but the American State Department still issued a statement of good wishes to the new regime.[3] The Americans themselves, according to a subsequently declassified memorandum from Alta F. Fowler of the Office of Near Eastern Affairs to the Officer in Charge of Egypt and Anglo-Egyptian Sudan Affairs, did not believe that there were any communist elements involved in the coup. "There is apparently little or no Communist influence in the army, and there have been no evidence of Communist elements at work in this latest upheaval," he wrote.[4]

Even before the coup—two days before, to be precise—the American assistant military attaché, David Evans, told a Free Officer, Ali Sabri, "If you are not Communist then go for it."[5] The Free Officers held the belief that the Americans would work as a bulwark against a potential British intervention, and for that reason they gave Washington advance notice.[6]

In fact, from their early days in power, Nasser and the Free Offi-cers had established good relations with the Americans through their embassy in Cairo.[7] After the coup, Nasser and Lakeland spoke at length about the future of the U.S.–Egyptian partnership. Receptive to American advice and backing, Nasser saw the United States as a potential partner to help Egypt expand its economy. America was viewed as a progressive model of modernity in contrast to colonial Britain and France, which stood for imperial domination. The Free Officers hoped the United States would professionalize the poorly equipped Egyptian army while providing aid, investment, and eco-nomic assistance. The cultural memory of U.S.–Egyptian military cooperation in the nineteenth century was ingrained in the officers' minds. In the mid-1800s, a group of fifty U.S. ex-Confederate and Union soldiers had come to Egypt to help with the modernization of the Egyptian army, providing training and building schools, includ-ing a military academy modeled on New York's West Point. Other Free Officers made confidential undertakings to American diplo-mats, and these, coupled with Nasser's assurances, prompted the U.S. ambassador to Cairo, Jefferson Caffrey, to characterize the political philosophy of the new Egyptian regime as "anti-Communist and relatively pro-Western."[8]

This assessment was confirmed by my own research. Having personally interviewed Free Officers over the years, I saw an emerg-ing portrait of the coup plotters as mainly middle-class and lower middle-class young men who were socially conservative and enam-ored with capitalism. Very few Free Officers were either socialist or communist, and any who had such leanings were gradually pushed to the margins after being expelled from executive authority or sent abroad to serve as military attachés in Egypt's embassies.

On the other side of the equation, the dominant view within the Free Officers' executive decision-making body, the Revolutionary Command Council, was that the communist bloc had little to offer Egypt, which desperately needed investment, aid, and technical training and expertise. Communism raised suspicions on its own for the petit bourgeois army officers, who feared it could polarize Egypt's working class.[9] During the first two years after the revolu-tion, Nasser and his comrades never seriously considered seeking Soviet support. Going further in August 1952, they violently cracked down on a socialist-inspired strike of over 10,000 workers in the Nile Delta. That incident was the first real crisis faced by the new Egyptian government. It highlighted the danger that the organized subaltern classes could pose to their rule—and they used it as an occasion to demonstrate their power in response.

On the Soviet side, these feelings were reciprocated. At first, Joseph Stalin and his advisers regarded the coup d'état in Cairo with suspicion; they saw it as an extension of Anglo-American rivalry in the Middle East or as a covert U.S. plot to abort a genuinely popular revolution. The coup was, to them, "just another one of those military take-overs [they also] had become accustomed to in South America."[10] The most prominent Russian analyst on Egypt, L. N. Vatolina, called the Cairo revolutionaries "madly reactionary, terrorist, anti-democratic, demagogic."[11] Soviet media repeatedly mocked Nasser as a "fascist lackey of the West," accusing him of treason and urging an uprising in Egypt against the Free Officers.[12]

Clearly, there was at first no love lost between the Free Officers, who were interested in U.S. aid and diplomatic backing, and Soviet communism, which perceived them as ideologically pro-Western.

Independence and Internal Power Struggles

Consensus among officials in Washington was based on the understanding that Egypt was strategically crucial. That is why in March 1953 a National Security Council directive called for the United States to deepen its ties with Egypt as a "key" country.[13] The disconnect between those intentions and later actions stemmed from an ideological divide between policy makers in Washington who relied on rigid, abstract thinking and U.S. diplomats in Cairo who understood the realities on the ground.

This chasm reflected fissures between Nasser and Naguib. The Free Officers had internal struggles and autocratic tendencies that started emerging soon after the revolution. As early as January 1953, they banned all other parties (save the Muslim Brotherhood and the communists, though the latter had conveniently been banned by the old regime) and declared that the Revolutionary

Command Council would rule for a three-year transitional period. This frustrated Naguib, who felt the military's role should be to protect those in power, not to hold power. Naguib, who did not want radical change, aimed instead to rid Egypt of corruption without undertaking structural reforms. With his desire to maintain and improve the old political parties, Naguib was the kind of man the Americans could use.

In contrast, Nasser wanted a full break from the past and dignity for all Egyptians. Though at first he didn't see revolutionary change, Nasser steadfastly aimed for domestic progress as well as freedom from foreign interference. But the Free Officers had no desire to alienate themselves from the world, especially not from the United States. A week after the coup, Prime Minister Ali Maher changed the Company Law of 1947 so that foreign capital could control a majority share of limited companies, effectively allowing foreigners to be majority stakeholders. In other words, he opened the market for Egyptian commodities. In his first address to the people following the coup, Naguib assured foreigners in Egypt that "their interests, their lives, their property and their money will be safe and that the Army holds itself responsible for them."[14] He subsequently granted long-term visas to foreigners and instructed visa and port authorities to be hospitable toward them.[15]

Neither these words nor these actions sufficed to convince the Eisenhower administration to give aid or arms to Egypt. Advised by the Dulles brothers, Eisenhower made all conditional on Egypt's taking the U.S. side in the global struggle against Soviet communism and on its normalizing relations with Israel. As I mentioned earlier, U.S. Secretary of State John Foster Dulles and his brother Allen Dulles, director of the Central Intelligence Agency, came from a politically powerful and religiously strict family. Fixated on the Soviet Union, they saw the global Cold War as more than a superpower rivalry in a bipolar word; to them, it was a spiritual battle between God and godlessness. This reflected their family tree, which had a potent mix of religious and political influence. And their time in power coincided with the first time in American political history that overt and covert foreign policy was ruled by two brothers. The Cold War lens for them was not so much a pair of glasses through which to view the world as a congenital cataract that clouded their perception of everything.

Unable to see regional complexities or local dynamics, they were rigid in their myopic Cold War view. Reports from diplomats stationed in Cairo, were, to the Dulles brothers, mere background noise. They maintained an uncompromising stance rather than listening thoughtfully to the advice of the diplomats in the field who were far more knowledgeable about the situation. The Dulles brothers turned a deaf ear to recommendations by those diplomats that the Americans co-opt Nasser through economic aid and arms sales to the Free Officers.

At the same time, Nasser had to fight a battle within the ranks of the Free Officers—especially with Naguib, who had, within eight weeks of the coup, sent the Americans an almost fawning four-point plan for their future bilateral relations: "1. The military is completely on the side of the United States and unalterably opposed to communism. 2. Its first problem is 'Selling US to Egypt's public' and educating Egyptians in the dangers of communism. 3. To 'sell' the United States to Egypt's people, it needs 'military supplies and financial assistance' from the United States. 4. In exchange the government is prepared to make secret commitments to long-term objectives including MEDO [Middle East Defense Organization] and or partnership with the United States."[16]

The Americans were intrigued by the offer of joining MEDO, given that they saw the Middle East as Europe's southern flank that was also vital to the energy security of their allies. They foresaw a potential Soviet foothold in the region as an extra bridgehead to launch an attack and cut off NATO countries from critical oil supplies.[17]

The positions of the older and more conservative Naguib, who had made promises of joining the American alliance, and the younger and more passionate Nasser, who kept rejecting it on the grounds of maintaining Egyptian sovereignty and independence, were irreconcilable. At the same time, the two leaders were inexorably linked; Nasser had to take account of Naguib, who had allied himself with the Muslim Brotherhood and was popular in the streets. And with Naguib safely in place, the American hopes of MEDO stayed alive.

Nasser: Becoming a Martyr without Dying

There was sound logic to the approach taken by Nasser, who, having thrown off the British yoke, did not want to replace it with an American one. He wanted one alliance only: an Arab one.[18] At the same time, Nasser, pro-American and anticommunist, was ready to cooperate with Washington in many areas, including peace talks with Israel. His reason for rejecting the American anticommunist alliance mirrored his reason for rejecting communism in his younger years: the shots were being called outside his homeland. Nasser was a straightforward Egyptian nationalist willing to cooperate with the United States, but the C.I.A., out of touch with reality, mistook this approach as evidence that they could push him onto the Pax Americana bandwagon.

Classified by the C.I.A. as an "asset," Nasser was not and would never be Washington's puppet.[19] U.S. diplomats in Cairo saw his interactions with them immediately after the coup as evidence that the young Egyptian leader was disposed to America's vision, which he initially was. But what they failed to see was that Nasser would never compromise Egyptian sovereignty and independence. As we saw in the previous chapter, Nasser (and his comrades) prioritized full political autonomy and freedom from foreign domination and control.

In 1953, making his first visit to the Middle East in his capacity as secretary of state, John Foster Dulles tried convincing Nasser to join the anticommunist alliance. Nasser offered a sound analogy: the Soviet Union "never occupied our territory . . . but the British have been here for seventy years. How can I go to my people and tell them I am disregarding a killer with a pistol sixty miles from me at the Suez Canal to worry about somebody who is holding a knife a thousand miles away?"[20] Nasser was uninterested in defense pacts, observing that within them, "small nations . . . cannot stand on an equal footing with big powers."[21] And, with striking prescience, Nasser said he regarded the participation of the major powers in organizing the defense of the region as "masked imperialism."[22]

While Nasser was fearful of compromising Egypt's fledgling independence and made clear that he would not take sides in the global Cold War rivalry, Naguib kept alive the idea of Egypt's joining MEDO. But there was more to the Nasser-Naguib dynamic than meets the eye. It was a power struggle over the control of the state. Nasser was in a hurry to replace Naguib as the top leader.

In an event so dramatic that it would change the political tides in a matter of hours, Nasser gained the upper hand. On October 26, 1954, he took to the radio airwaves to tell the Arab world about his successful negotiation of the British withdrawal from the Canal Zone. Suddenly, a shot rang out. Seven others followed. The airwaves went silent. Listeners feared the worst. Some wailed in agony. But just as citizens panicked that he was dead, Nasser's voice broke the radio silence with a passionate appeal to the hearts of the Egyptian people, inspired by his courage, selflessness, and dedication to their shared patriotism. "Let them kill me; it does not concern me so long as I have instilled pride, honor, and freedom in you. If Gamal Abdel Nasser should die, each of you shall be Gamal Abdel Nasser. . . . Gamal Abdel Nasser is of you and from you and he is willing to sacrifice his life for the nation."[23]

Nasser's spontaneous act was a stroke of political genius. His words resonated in Egypt and throughout the Arab world. And they signaled a psychological turning point in how he communicated with the people. Nasser had found his voice, which would soon ring out down the decades and across the Middle East. Before the assassination attempt, he had not connected with ordinary Egyptians on a personal or emotional level. Naguib was more popular and endearing to the public than Nasser. All that changed after that fateful afternoon, when a violent event humanized the young colonel in Egyptians' eyes. From then on, Nasser would harness the power of colloquial Egyptian Arabic to great effect, winning hearts and minds.

The assassination attempt was a defining moment in the rise of Nasser's popularity in Egypt and neighboring Arab countries. Nasser survived martyrdom, living to bear the fruits that the status conferred. Not one to miss an opportunity, he spent his newfound windfall of political capital on a massive clampdown against real and imagined enemies, signalling a robust authoritarian rule. Because he had been attacked by a Muslim Brotherhood member, Nasser arrested thousands of Muslim Brothers, but also communists and officers loyal to Naguib. As for Naguib, he was tossed into house arrest. Nasser had finally fulfilled his dream of becoming the undisputed leader of the new Egypt.

. With Naguib out of the picture, there was no way Egypt would join an anticommunist, Western-led alliance. Sensing this, the Dulles brothers incubated a new approach.

The Baghdad Pact: The Honeymoon Is Over

The Dulles brothers were not the only ones sensing the change in the winds. By mid-1955, Nasser realized that the Cold War–obsessed Americans allowed no chance for a mutually beneficial relationship based on respect for Egypt's neutrality.

Like Mossadegh, Nasser reaped nothing from his trust in Washington. His overtures were evidenced in his actions, including risking political suicide by taking part in secret American-encouraged peace talks with Israel, and agreeing to American proposed water-sharing agreements among Jordan, Egypt, and Israel.[24] For the Americans, however, anything short of joining an anticommunist regional alliance would never earn their trust and aid. The result zoomed out to the wider Middle East; John Foster Dulles looked to the East—to Iraq, whose capital would that year ultimately lend its name to a new Anglo-American-sponsored defense pact.[25]

Nasser was effectively undermined. His goal had been to eschew the anticommunist alliance and avoid involvement in the global Cold War, but he suspected the Baghdad Pact threatened to expose Arab countries to Western governments' intervention in their internal affairs. His suspicions were later confirmed. The pact also undermined Nasser's status as the Arab world's greatest leader. Should Syria, Jordan, Lebanon, and other countries join, Egypt would be left isolated with no means of procuring arms while facing Israel alone.[26]

Even worse, from Nasser's perspective, any U.S.–led pact compromised Egypt's bargaining position in the still-unresolved Suez dispute with Britain as well as in the Israeli-Palestinian conflict.[27] Further inflaming the situation, a Cold War flare-up could provoke a Soviet reaction against Arab countries.[28] The Baghdad Pact triggered fierce geostrategic rivalries and was the initial shot that ignited the Arab cold war, pitting Arab against Arab. Ironically, the pact had a lasting impact on inter-Arab relationships while being by most accounts the most inefficient alliance of the global Cold War.[29]

Nasser's worldview underwent a dramatic shift on February 28, 1955, when Israel launched a crushing attack on Egyptian troops in Gaza. The toll in human life was grave—scores were killed and injured—and beyond that, the attack pulled back the curtain on the Egyptian military's weakness. Only four days had passed since the signing of the Baghdad Pact. The proximity of these two events linked them in the mind of Nasser, who viewed the Baghdad Pact and the Israeli attack as two means to the same end: a neocolonial conspiracy to destroy his regime and to reassert Western control over the entire Arab world.[30] Through this lens, Israel was seen as an instrument of Western imperialism in the region.[31]

The combustible combination of the Baghdad Pact and the Israeli raid prompted Nasser to contemplate what had previously been unthinkable: turning to the Soviet Union to obtain arms. This followed three years of the Free Officers going to great lengths to purchase arms from the United States. Multiple calls on Washington to provide Egypt with defensive weapons went unanswered. Egypt's army post in Gaza was in ruins, and the Free Officers were pressuring Nasser to recalibrate the power balance with Israel by pursuing alternative routes of arms procurement—from the communists, if necessary, despite the fact that they viewed that ideology as a threat to their regime. Nasser appealed to Dulles's emissary, George Allen, saying that it would be futile to build schools, hospitals, and irrigation dams without the ability to defend them. But the Americans refused to provide Egypt with badly needed defensive arms, forcing Nasser to reevaluate his country's relations with Washington and turn to Moscow for help. In Nasser's words: "Our need to acquire arms became linked with the task of defining our identity on the international stage."[32]

Nasser strategically timed his decision to get Soviet arms with the nonalignment conference in Bandung, Indonesia, in April 1955. There he asked Chinese Premier Zhou Enlai to explore with Moscow officials the possibility of their selling arms to Egypt. Moscow eagerly stepped in. To Nasser's surprise, the Russians responded promptly and positively, even agreeing to deferred payment in Egyptian cotton and rice. They indicated a willingness to help Egypt with industrial projects, a step toward breaking the Western monopoly in the Middle East and beyond.[33]

The Bandung conference bolstered Nasser's international standing. He resonated strongly with the Afro-Asian bloc, calling for real independence, economic fairness, and freedom from imperialism.[34] By playing a key role in the establishment of the Non-Aligned Movement, Nasser actively participated in the attempt at world making, a rejection of the emerging bipolar global order. Even with promises of a Russian arms deal, Nasser, holding out hope for the United States to change its mind, reached out to the Eisenhower administration for a last round of talks. At a meeting on May 22, 1955, Nasser informed the U.S. ambassador to Egypt, Henry Byroade, of the Russian arms offer, which came to be known as the Czech Arms Deal. Byroade had arrived at the meeting after repeatedly urging his superiors in Washington to be more sensitive and accommodating toward the nationalist government in Cairo, and he left it all the more determined to impress on his bosses the need to take Nasser's threat seriously. In this effort, Byroade emphasized the far-reaching implications to U.S. interests if Egypt got arms from the Soviet Union.[35]

Dulles never replied to Byroade's urgent report, miscalculating in spectacular fashion that Nasser was bluffing and the Russians would not sell arms to Egypt. When the United States refused to sell arms to Nasser, he accepted the Soviet offer. "For us it was a matter of life and death, and we had no choice," he explained.[36] There had been no substantial gain from three years of flirting with the U.S., and the honeymoon was over. Nasser's belief in the U.S. lay in tatters. Secret peace talks with Israel had also failed. Israeli leaders David Ben-Gurion and Moshe Dayan increased the number of Israel Defense Forces' raids into the Gaza Strip. Nasser was not only pressured; he felt humiliated, perhaps one of the worst feelings to be experienced by a man who had based a large part of his career prioritizing Egyptian and Arab "dignity." He needed a tangible win to show his population, a payoff for his steadfast belief in the Americans—and had none.

Pushing Nasser Away

The U.S. Cold Warriors were shocked by Nasser's decision, but, rather than seek common ground, they became intransigent, turning the screws, pressuring him to unilaterally rescind the arms deal.

The Eisenhower administration employed intimidation tactics, financial pressure, and the threat of regional encirclement in a bid to get Nasser to stand down. This had the opposite effect. Rather than making him compliant, Washington's strategy emboldened Nasser and drove him to build closer ties with the socialist bloc.

The infamous Kermit Roosevelt, then head of the Middle East section of the C.I.A., was dispatched to meet Nasser and force him to abandon the newly signed arms deal with Moscow. Roosevelt duly read Nasser the riot act, informing him that the arms deal was a heavy blow to Dulles's policy of containment of Soviet communism. Claiming that Nasser's arms deal with the Soviets would undermine the military balance between the two superpowers, the envoy went so far as to threaten Nasser with the breaking of diplomatic relations, the imposition of an economic blockade, and other "severe" consequences against Egypt if he didn't abrogate the deal.[37] This represented a gross misreading of the Egyptian leader's character. Rather than addressing Nasser's fears and concerns, Roosevelt threatened him with the very thing he could tolerate least: more humiliation and submission. Roosevelt's hubris was not born in a vacuum; it was nurtured by the recent successful C.I.A. coups against Mossadegh in August 1953 and Guatemala's President Jacobo Árbenz in June 1954.

According to Abdel-Latif al-Baghdadi, a comrade of his who attended the meeting, Nasser told Roosevelt that Egypt was free to pursue a foreign policy that served the country's national interests. Reminding Roosevelt that the colonial era was over, Nasser bluntly warned that current U.S. policy "would force us to fight you in the region even if we had to go underground."[38] Unlike Mossadegh in 1953, Nasser had consolidated his power by 1955, purging the country of political dissidents and strengthening his control over the army, making it impossible for Kermit Roosevelt and the C.I.A. to use the same playbook that had worked to oust Mossadegh and Árbenz from power against Nasser.

This strong stand resonated powerfully, all the way to Washington. The Dulles brothers pulled back from punitive measures, fearing they might push him closer to the Soviets. U.S. intelligence agencies warned that a confrontation against Nasser could endanger the position of the Western powers throughout the Middle

East.[39] Dulles, whose hotheaded, rigid attitude had created the crisis, nevertheless concurred, making no secret of the greed for "black gold" at the heart of U.S. strategy: "We should not allow developments to take this direction because Middle East oil was important not only to NATO but to the Western world." As for the global Cold War rivalry, always uppermost in Dulles's mind, he observed that "Egypt as a neutralist would be more tolerable than as a Communist satellite."[40]

Reciprocating the American decision not to escalate, Nasser reassured U.S. officials that the arms deal was merely a commercial transaction with no political strings attached. In a message delivered to Washington by the Egyptian ambassador, Ahmed Hussein, Nasser emphasized Egypt's commitment to an independent, nonaligned foreign policy and made it clear that he was determined to prevent communist influence from spreading in the region. This was consistent with the philosophy held also by Sukarno, Tito, and Nehru. They shared a genuine commitment to avoiding entanglement in the East-West rivalry. Deeply suspicious of communism, Nasser never loosened his iron grip on his country's domestic communists. As he had affirmed, the Soviet-Egyptian arms deal was transactional, not ideological, simply signaling Egypt's agency and dignity.

Like Mossadegh, Nasser was willing to go down fighting to assert his country's independence and freedom to choose its own dynamic path. According to Anwar al-Sadat, Nasser's fellow Free Officer, the armament issue was "one of life and death for us."[41] The arms deal solidified Nasser's popularity in Egypt, in the Arab neighborhood, and throughout the decolonized world, elevating him to the status of an international political icon. The deal was hailed by Egyptians and Arabs as a "bold assertion of independence from Western tutelage, and as a highly effective move toward overcoming Israel's military superiority."[42]

U.S. officials concluded that Nasser was becoming more confident in pursuing his objectives in the region.[43] Yet U.S. intelligence reports said nothing about repeated Egyptian requests for American weapons, which, unanswered, ultimately pushed Nasser to purchase arms from the socialist bloc. Despite the attempt by Washington and Cairo to deescalate, the Soviet-Egyptian weapons deal further

ruptured U.S.–Egyptian relations while breaking the Western monopoly on arms supply to the Middle East.

These events as well as the Baghdad Pact prompted Nasser to
shift his focus from a predominantly domestic agenda to an international one. Egypt thus deepened its engagement in inter-Arab
affairs and realigned its external relations.[44] A chain reaction ensued, ultimately causing a complete breakdown in relations between Washington and Cairo. This state of affairs was epitomized
by the Aswan Dam affair.[45]

The Aswan Dam: A Rupture in U.S.–Egyptian Relations

Eisenhower officials now saw Egypt as the rising power in Arab
politics and Nasser as a tough and disruptive actor to be reckoned
with. Rather than confronting the Egyptian leader, they decided to
co-opt him and try to buy him off.

In December 1955, the United States, together with Britain
and the World Bank, offered nearly $70 million in aid to Egypt to
help in the construction of the Aswan High Dam on the Nile
River.[46] This massive development project aimed to contain the
cycle of floods and droughts that had caused devastation to Egypt
for millennia. It was critical to Nasser and his comrades, who saw it
as a way to prove an independent Egypt could develop and modernize on its own terms. The Free Officers were keen to build the
dam with Western technical aid as a way to reaffirm that Cairo was
neither taking sides in the Cold War nor depending on Russia for
aid. Nasser, who had spent much of his political capital, along with
national funds, presented the Aswan Dam to the Egyptian people
as a symbol of the new era of modernization he was ushering in.

The Aswan Dam aid, like the arms deal, was predicated by the
Eisenhower administration on Nasser's signing a peace treaty with
Israel and joining America's global struggle against the Soviet
Union.[47] Nasser rejected these conditions because they constrained
his freedom to act regionally and internationally while letting Washington dictate terms that threatened unfettered Egyptian sovereignty. America's meddling in inter-Arab affairs and the Arab-Israeli
conflict were deeply resented by Nasser and his comrades.[48] Bilateral
peace with Israel not only would equal political suicide and probably

literal death, but could lead to further assassination attempts against Nasser, as would later happen to Anwar Sadat. Moreover, previous secret talks between Egypt and Israel, with U.S. mediation, did not yield positive results.

Nasser told a reporter for the *Economist* that American officials were exploiting Egypt's need for a loan to build the Aswan Dam in order to pressure him to sign a peace deal with Israel, and that the United States' condition of normalizing relations with Israel for economic assistance was unacceptable.[49] Like Mossadegh, Nasser prioritized full political autonomy despite huge costs to his nation and his own political survival. Both belonged to a new generation of postcolonial nationalist leaders who aspired to pursue a neutral foreign policy and state-directed development as opposed to an open, laissez-faire economy.

The .Eisenhower administration resented Nasser's decision to sabotage its design for an Arab-Israeli diplomatic settlement, which could have ushered in a regional security pact against the Soviet Union. U.S.–Egyptian relations were further frayed by Nasser's refusal to stop buying additional arms from the socialist bloc and his constant attacks on the Baghdad Pact. American officials ascribed Nasser's refusal to his growing sense of power, which they saw as having been gained from his association with communist Russia, and his ambition to be the sole leader of the Arab world. Eisenhower said Nasser was becoming not only more arrogant—a euphemism for unwilling to do what U.S. officials told him to do—but also a disruptive influence in the region, poisoning friendly relations between the United States and other Arab states. Nasser disrupted America's plans to establish regional hegemony and secure its energy resources. The greatest fear of Eisenhower and Dulles was that Nasser's policies had opened the door to Soviet communism in the Middle East and, unless reversed, this situation could lead to a "major catastrophe." They recommended decisive action against Egypt to stop Nasser from "disregarding the interests of Western Europe and the United States in the Middle East region."[50]

Negotiations on the dam were repeatedly postponed and U.S. aid to Egypt was cut. At the same time, Eisenhower aimed to "build up King Saud as a figure of sufficient prestige to offset Nasser" and bring about a split between Egypt and Saudi Arabia.

To counter the revolutionary young colonel, the Cold War warriors hoped to gather an anti-Nasser Arab coalition of conservative Arab states like Saudi Arabia, Iraq, Jordan, and Lebanon. As Dulles said, Washington, in close collaboration with Great Britain, aimed to compel Nasser to change his tune.[51]

Nasser: Pushing Back Harder

Alarmed by the rupture Washington's Cold War proponents caused with Egypt, U.S. ambassador Byroade wrote a dissenting memo to the State Department warning against demonizing the Egyptian leader or blaming Nasser personally for America's problems in the region.[52]

Byroade's rebuttal of the prevailing imperial mindset sheds light on the big divide in U.S. foreign policy between diplomats in the field and Cold War hawks in Washington, highlighting the contradictions of U.S. policy toward both Egypt and the other newly independent states in the Global South. Byroade's report helps show why Washington's informal empire builders lost Egypt in the mid-1950s and turned Nasser from a potential friend to a bitter foe. These Cold War warriors confused the rising currents of nationalism that swept the decolonized lands after World War II with communism and misjudged how easily Nasser could mobilize those currents in the pursuit of his interests. This experienced U.S. diplomat repeatedly cautioned his superiors against underestimating Nasser, who, like Mossadegh, would and could never compromise on the question of independence.[53]

Byroade was a lone dissenting voice in the Eisenhower administration. Bolstered by the success of toppling Mossadegh in Iran and Árbenz in Guatemala, Washington chose to confront Nasser and force him to join Pax Americana. Nasser fought back and remained popular both within and beyond Egypt's borders. At the same time, he expanded his military, economic, and political ties with the socialist camp, going so far as to do what for Washington was unthinkable: recognize communist China in May 1956 in order to circumvent any agreement by the two superpowers to deny him arms. At the time, China was not a member of the United Nations, so Nasser reasoned that it could provide Egypt with weapons even if the UN imposed an arms embargo on the region. Nasser's recognition of China also served to help assert his independence and push back against Western efforts to isolate him.[54]

Eisenhower and Dulles refused to believe Nasser's political neutrality, instead viewing his actions as a "slap in the face of the United States." Many Americans believed that "Nasser had made a bargain with the Devil with the hope of developing his own power and establishing an empire stretching from the Persian Gulf to the Atlantic Ocean," Dulles told the Egyptian ambassador to Washington. Eisenhower officials agreed that Egypt was playing East against West by blackmailing both and even joining the anti–U.S. camp. Deciding that Nasser's "interference" in world politics must be punished, Dulles rescinded the Western aid package totaling nearly $70 million to build the Aswan Dam, well aware of its significance to the Egyptian leader.[55] Eugene Black, president of the International Bank for Reconstruction and Development (IBRD), said Dulles believed that preventing the dam's construction would mean "the end of Nasser."[56]

Credible U.S. voices warned that the Soviet Union would be prepared to finance the Aswan Dam, but Dulles wrote to Eisenhower that Nasser was bluffing by pretending to have received an offer from Moscow. Dulles easily convinced the U.S. foreign policy establishment to back his decision to weaken Nasser. There was a near consensus among U.S. officials that Nasser's policies undermined the West because he was establishing diplomatic relations with China, collaborating with the socialist bloc, and refusing to normalize relations with Israel.[57] By portraying the young Egyptian leader as a dangerous troublemaker who had given Soviet communism an opening in the Middle East, Eisenhower turned Nasser into U.S. public enemy number one.

Dulles: Making Matters Worse

Rather than heed the warnings of Ambassador Byroade by accepting the idea of neutralism and nonalignment championed by Nasser, Washington officials took their frustration at his criticism out on the ambassador himself. In June 1956 Dulles informed Byroade of the president's decision to relocate him to South Africa—a clear signal that Washington was toughening its policy toward Egypt. The following month, Secretary of State John Foster Dulles publicly revoked the offer of aid to Egypt. Britain also announced the withdrawal of its offer to assist Egypt in building the dam, adding up to collective Western punishment of Nasser.[58]

The mid-1950s thus shaped up to be a pivotal era for the Middle East, one marked by two key flash points: the overthrow of Iranian Prime Minister Mossadegh in 1953 and the overt attempt to undermine Nasser's grip on power. As I will show, the C.I.A. also had been plotting to overthrow the Syrian government and replace it with a pro–U.S. regime, creating more political instability and chaos in Damascus. Regional solidarity and cooperation among local states were sacrificed at the altar of superpower imperial ambitions. America's decision to roll back Soviet communism and to tame assertive Third World nationalists like Nasser opened a chasm in regional politics, pitting Arab against Arab. Nasser, with good reason fearful of a U.S. bounty on his head, retaliated by attacking pro-Western Arab rulers who had joined America's regional defense pacts. His decision to challenge America's hegemony in the Middle East led to the 1956 Suez Crisis and ultimately to the destruction of his army in the Six-Day War with Israel in June 1967.

Seen through this lens, the U.S.–Egyptian confrontation in the mid-1950s can be understood as an inciting incident that caused a cascading series of crises in the Middle East, dramatically altering the regional balance of power and the internal balance of social forces within countries across the region. The effects reverberate today in their impact on inter-Arab relations, Arab-Israeli relations, and the deepening of political authoritarianism in the region. These deleterious outcomes can be traced to a Cold War U.S. perspective that was so fixated on rolling back Soviet communism and promoting liberal capitalism that it failed to see, let alone understand, local impulses for independence and sovereignty, viewing them instead—mistakenly—as crypto-communism and opposition to the American vision of an open global economy.

The approach taken by a handful of insular yet powerful officials in Washington in response to efforts by both Iran and Egypt to embark on their own paths set the mold for the crises still unfolding today. The lessons of those events are critical to the new reconstruction of contemporary Middle Eastern history and politics as well as our understanding of what really went wrong in the region.

CHAPTER EIGHT

The Suez Crisis

THE DRAMA, INTRIGUE, and sheer scope of the Aswan Dam project were unlike anything Nasser had experienced—but its monumental significance would soon be overtaken by events that took a much higher toll—in political capital, international relations, and human bloodshed. The minefield that Nasser traversed next included turncoat allies, a treasure that was Egypt's birthright, and plotting so worthy of a spy thriller that would have been entertaining if confined to a movie.

Instead, the explosive events left shrapnel in the international body politic that has yet to be removed. The damage spread so far because the Eisenhower administration's response to the Suez Crisis spawned events that would set the stage for U.S. misadventures in the Middle East to be replicated far beyond the region, as became evident when the Eisenhower Doctrine evolved into an imperial enterprise unmoored even from the Cold War warriors' guiding principle of anticommunism. The Eisenhower Doctrine was as much about taming defiant nationalist leaders like Nasser as about rolling back Soviet communism. The seeds for this noxious global approach were sown during the Suez Crisis, which was inextricably linked with Washington's maneuvers to bring "the end of Nasser" by withdrawing aid for the Aswan Dam. During that time, friends of Egypt might have sought to forestall it, but instead, Cairo's enemies moved in for the kill.

Nationalizing the Canal

The Suez Canal is one of the most strategic waterways on the planet. It is the sole sea route for goods traveling from the east to the west, and vice versa, without an expensive and time-consuming detour around the Horn of Africa that adds 5,000 nautical miles to the journey. It was also the scene of one of the momentous turning points in history when the United States exchanged a wealth of political goodwill and the possibility for a chance to buttress its dominant position in the global Cold War rivalry and the developing world. The Cold Warriors had grossly underestimated the powerful drive of newly independent peoples and countries toward sovereignty and dignity.

But if they overlooked the yearning pulsing in hearts across the world, Nasser was keenly attuned to it. And he harnessed the power of this sentiment, so deeply embedded in his own conviction, to set in motion events that would result in the waning of European imperialism and the waxing of U.S. dominance. Nasser's leadership inspired formerly colonized peoples around the world— and their admiration meant commensurate outrage at the injustices perpetrated against him. After being pushed toward the Russians by the intransigent Cold War mindset that gripped the Dulles brothers and others in Washington, Nasser knew the withdrawal of aid for the Aswan Dam constituted "an attack on the regime and an invitation to the people of Egypt to bring it down."[1]

Awareness dawned on the Free Officers that what influence they commanded could not endure forever. Compelled to act decisively and quickly to maintain their credibility and save their regime, Nasser obtained Russian aid for the Aswan Dam at 2 percent interest. This meant that he had to prepare to pay back the Russian loan, which would leave Egypt in need of funds. And to do that, Nasser could see only one way forward: nationalizing the Suez Canal Company. He did so on July 26, 1956.[2] This step had historical importance and impact on the region that was comparable to Mossadegh's nationalization of the oil industry in 1953 as an assertion of national independence. But like Mossadegh's nationalization of Iran's oil, Nasser's nationalization of the Suez Canal would not go unanswered. The consequences were dire: the tripartite invasion of Egypt by Britain, France, and Israel almost escalated into a nuclear standoff between the two rival superpowers.

Nasser saw beyond the reaction to breaking developments, viewing Egypt's nationalization of the Suez Canal as an opportunity to mark the end of imperial practices of ultimatum and gun diplomacy not just in Egypt but in the wider Arab world. Heralding a new era of dignity and full political autonomy for Arab states, Nasser declared: "Our reply today is that we will not allow the domination of force and the dollar."[3]

In his landmark nationalization speech, Nasser criticized Western imperialism for its attempt to thwart Egyptian sovereignty. He reminded Egyptians of their traumatic "political occupation through economic occupation" and of the importance of regaining control over water for achieving economic sovereignty. Nasser also reiterated his resolve to pursue a nonaligned foreign policy. Condemning the U.S. refusal to assist in financing the Aswan Dam, Nasser disputed Dulles's claim that Egypt's economy was unsound. He framed this position as a conspiracy to discredit Egypt as punishment for its legitimately independent international relations. Revenues from nationalizing the Suez Canal Company, Nasser said, would enable Egypt to build the dam without reliance on U.S. aid.[4] Like Mossadegh in his nationalization of oil, Nasser wanted to use the revenues from the Suez Canal Company to benefit his people. Egyptians of all political stripes cheered for the dismantling of the last bastion of foreign domination and control, which turned Nasser into an Egyptian mythical hero, according to Anwar Sadat, then a Free Officer and a member of the Revolutionary Command Council that ruled Egypt between 1952 and 1956.[5]

But Nasser's heroism was appreciated beyond the borders of Egypt; he was an Arab hero and a Third World hero. His act of defiance at the height of the 1950s Cold War put Egypt at the helm of the global movement as it broke the chains of the past. The rise in Nasser's profile brought an increase in his size as a target of the hawks in Washington. They saw his defiance as more than a problem with Egypt: rather, as a potential inspiration that could drive

similar actions by nationalists in other parts of the developing
world. It was not lost on U.S. intelligence that ordinary Arabs
looked up to Nasser as a role model.[6] Cold War proponents in
both Washington and London, looking at the region from the outside in, saw the nationalization of oil and the Suez Canal as an extension of the Cold War rivalry with communist Russia.

   Nasser, unlike Mossadegh, who relied heavily on the United
States to counterbalance Britain, appreciated the value of building
a coalition of sympathetic Arab allies along with the wider Afro-
Asian bloc. He believed that the Non-Aligned Movement—which
had not existed during Mossadegh's time but had become a major
global force since the 1955 Bandung Conference—could restrain
the aggressive tendencies of the Western powers. Like Mossadegh,
in interviews and speeches Nasser saw and explained the Suez dispute as part of a greater struggle between the Great Powers and
newly decolonized states.[7] He and his comrades perceived that
Britain and France were searching for a pretext to invade Egypt,
overthrow him, and reverse the nationalization of the canal, formerly controlled by an Anglo-French concessionary company.
They knew that the French and British position on the use of military force was far more aggressive than the American position. The
Free Officers saw the headlines: the Korean War was a very fresh,
very painful memory in the mind of the Americans. It would be
hard at any time to stomach press coverage of American soldiers
returning from another campaign in caskets draped in flags—much
more so with the presidential race fast approaching.[8]

   As Mossadegh had before him, Nasser appealed to America's
sense of justice and fairness and actively distanced himself from the
Soviet Union in the hopes that the United States could restrain
British Prime Minister Anthony Eden and French Prime Minister
Guy Mollet from launching an invasion. The United States hoped
for the same. Leaders in Washington did not acknowledge for a
moment that their actions had triggered the Suez Crisis. Their
approach had, from the start, been consistent with Eisenhower's
stated aims: "We must adopt a firm policy but at the same time not
jeopardize our long-term posture by precipitate action."[9] Dulles,
too, wanted to downplay the use of force. To restrain the NATO
partners and to advance a policy that would achieve a stable and

efficient administration of the canal, Eisenhower sent Deputy Under-Secretary Robert Murphy to London and Secretary of State Dulles to Europe to impress on Eden and Mollet the need to resolve the crisis peacefully.[10]

On the Egyptian side, Nasser was at pains to emphasize that the canal's nationalization had nothing to do with the Cold War; it was simply about modernizing Egypt. The Free Officers repeatedly went to great lengths to convince the United States of this position. Nasser did his part, meeting, just a few days after nationalization, with the new U.S. ambassador to Egypt, Raymond Hare, to offer reassurances that "the canal would remain open and be efficiently operated."[11] Nasser followed this the next day with an official statement affirming Egypt's determination to honor all its obligations regarding freedom of navigation in the Suez Canal. This pledge served to address one of the Eisenhower administration's major concerns and constituted a deliberate effort to halt the march toward war. Nasser aimed to gain time while mobilizing world public opinion and striving for a peaceful resolution to the Suez Crisis.[12]

Both Eisenhower and Dulles wanted to cut Nasser down to size without resorting to military means. In Dulles's language, offering a promise to his European counterparts, Nasser should be made to "disgorge" what he had swallowed by internationalizing the Suez Canal Company.[13] This echoed a tactic employed by Washington against Mossadegh during negotiations on the nationalization of Iranian oil as a ploy to maintain British control over it. Of course, it also failed to acknowledge that what Nasser had "swallowed" was, in fact, the fruit of his own land.

The U.S. position on the Suez Crisis would not be a one-off; it would come to be a defining feature of the Eisenhower administration and its successors. The chief motivation was to avoid any risk of a regionwide conflict that would threaten the West's access to oil. Prioritizing petroleum, Eisenhower said the British Cabinet's decision to use force to confront Nasser represented outdated thinking. Eisenhower was aware of Western dependence on Arab oil, U.S. officials confirmed, and he feared that hostilities in the Middle East would jeopardize Western access to this vital source of energy.[14]

The U.S. president cautioned that military action would alienate the Arab and Muslim world and endanger the supply of oil to
the West. Eisenhower and Dulles were outspoken in advising their
British allies that war would spell disaster for Western interests in
Asia and Africa—not only because the dynamic would shift away
from them but because it would shift toward the Soviet Union,
creating a vacuum that communism could fill. Eisenhower warned
his allies that using force unilaterally would wreak far-reaching
consequences in the region and around the world. "The American
reaction would be severe and the great areas of the world would
share that reaction," the president emphasized.[15]

The Crisis

The United States and its European allies may have disagreed about
the use of force, but they shared an antipathy to Nasser that animated a desire to drive him out of power. No amount of effort by
Nasser to clarify that Egypt's position that nonalignment and friendliness with the United States were not mutually exclusive seemed to
penetrate the obdurate thinking in Washington. In a long policy
memo, a special aide to Dulles, Francis Russell, wrote that Nasser
aimed to merge "the emotions and resources of the entire Middle
East and Africa into a single onslaught against Western civilization."[16] This extreme hyperbole belied the fact that Nasser's ultimate
aim reflected the same yearning for independence the American
Founding Fathers had sought from their own colonial overlords—
the British—in the eighteenth century.

The Eisenhower Cold Warriors wanted to get rid of Nasser as
much as the French and British did, but they disagreed on how.
Americans feared that war would only help elevate Nasser's influence on the Arab stage, raising his standing as the leader of Arab
nationalism. To avert that outcome, Dulles prevailed on his recalci-
trant French and British allies to join in a plan to set up an international regime that would manage and control the Suez Canal
Company, starting by calling for a conference for maritime states
in London in August 1956.[17]

The success of this scheme hinged on Nasser's willingness to
accept an international regime of control and supervision. It echoed

the 1953 U.S. attempt to convince Mossadegh to accept an international board to supervise Iran's oil sector. Dulles's proposal met
with complete failure. Nasser rejected the Suez Canal Users' Association, along with all other forms of international supervision,
bluntly calling them "collective imperialism in regulated forms."
He was not prepared for what happened next, dismissing a warning
from the Saudi king about a possible Anglo-French-Israeli attack to
seize the canal and depose him. To Nasser, collusion with Israel
would amount to political suicide for Britain and France in Arab
lands. The proper forum for settling the crisis was the United Nations, and to Nasser this was also the ideal venue, since Egypt,
under international law, would retain ownership of the canal.[18]

The prevailing view of this sequence of events is that Nasser
brilliantly snatched a political victory out of the jaws of a military
defeat. Published testimony builds the narrative that before, during, and after the Suez Crisis, Nasser and his comrades calculated
the pros and cons of all scenarios and proceeded deliberately on
the basis of strategic considerations. My reading differs dramatically from this celebratory story. Over the last three decades, I conducted interviews with Egyptian officials, including close friends
and colleagues of Nasser, and concluded that their actions were not
so much calculated as taken on the spur of the moment, based less
on planning than on a strong belief in the righteousness of their
cause.

Like Mossadegh, Nasser was willing to go down fighting to
affirm his people's dignity, freedom, and inalienable right to control their natural resources. The decisions by both Mossadegh and
Nasser—quite apart from their strategic ramifications for local and
global politics—must be understood on the psychological-
emotional and moral levels. Like Mossadegh, Nasser underestimated the depth of Eden's innate hatred of him and his resolve to
wipe Nasser out along with all he had built and stood for.

The Free Officers' coup that toppled the pro-British monarchy
in 1952 was driven by a desire to stop Britain's constant interference
in the internal affairs of Egypt. Acting on their convictions, they
sabotaged British interests in the region. They targeted Britain on
ideological grounds, along with pro-British Arab rulers, including
the Hashemite monarchies in Iraq and Jordan. Eden understood

that Nasser represented a threat to the British presence in the Middle East, and he agreed that removing the Egyptian leader would be best.[19] Writing to Eisenhower, the British premier baldly stated that among his top priorities was Nasser's removal and the installation of a pro-Western government in Cairo.[20] The British minister for foreign affairs, Anthony Nutting, saw the coast as clear: "Now at last [Eden] had found a pretext to launch an all-out campaign of political, economic and military pressures on Egypt and to destroy forever Nasser's image as the leader of Arab nationalism."[21]

Eden himself said in an emergency meeting of the Cabinet that "Nasser must not be allowed to get away with it," and he told Eisenhower that he was prepared to use force to bring Nasser to his senses.[22] He planned to use the playbook that had worked against Mossadegh when London insisted on maintaining control of Iran's oil and urged the United States to oust him.

Considering Nasser to be a greater threat to the West than Mossadegh had been, Eden pressed the case. The Americans stood firm in being against using force in the Suez Crisis.

For his part, Mollet wanted to punish Nasser for supporting Algerian nationalists fighting for independence from colonial France. That dynamic was also a key driver of the growing relationship between Israel and France.[23]

But although they dusted off the Mossadegh playbook, they failed to update it. The C.I.A.–led covert operation against Mossadegh had benefited by exploiting divisions within the Iranian body politic and the security forces. In Egypt, army officers were in full control by 1956, and, as an army man, Nasser did not share Mossadegh's disavowal of political violence. Adding to the equation, the world had undergone significant transformations since the coup against Mossadegh. The emergence of the nonaligned movement, driven in large part by Nasser himself, created an anticolonial third force in international affairs, offering a route for him to acquire arms and aid from the socialist bloc and become a more formidable power.

The Eisenhower Cold Warriors heard loud and clear the Soviet warnings of "severe consequences" if Britain and France attacked Egypt.[24] U.S. officials communicated their opposition to an armed strike against Egypt publicly and privately. Eisenhower told a press conference in September 1956 that if France and Britain attacked, the United States would "not go to war." But Eden was unmoved both because of his personal and imperial concerns and also—according to Nutting—because he resented Dulles's patronizing attitude. So Eden kept Washington in the dark about the secret tripartite plot to invade Egypt.[25]

The Plot

For three months after Nasser's nationalization of the Suez Canal, Israel, the United Kingdom, and France schemed about their response. Eden preferred the military option from the outset, seeking only a justification to execute it while deceiving both his own population and the rest of the world. Only days after Nasser nationalized the Suez Canal, on July 26, Eden sent the order for plans to invade Egypt.[26]

This reflected Eden's myopic delusion of Britain's status in the post–World War II order. He had attended the aristocratic institutions that churned out elites and studied "Oriental languages," which made him an Orientalist of the kind Edward Said so well described, romanticizing while patronizingly othering these people, relying on studies that sought to belittle and control the Arabs, not understanding them on their own terms. For example, Eden attributed rivalries for the Arab world between Egypt and Iraq to "the age-old rivalry of Nile and Euphrates."[27]

Sadly, this false narrative persists today in the form of Western officials who fail to see contemporary contexts, neglect to look below the surface level, and instead affix all blame on supposed ancient sectarian hatreds such as the Sunni-Shia divide. Tellingly, Eden was present in 1916 when Lord Mark Sykes enlisted Arab dominions in Ottoman lands against their overlord—efforts that culminated in the notorious Sykes-Picot Agreement (1916), essentially the colonial division of the Middle East between Great Britain and France.[28] He sought to justify an Anglo-French intervention by blaming Egypt's inability to navigate ships through the canal, one of the most important waterways in the world. A recently declassified top-secret annex from the C.I.A. from September 1956 noted strong indications of a pending military intervention and said its likelihood "would increase in the event of provocation such as an interruption of the flow of traffic through the Suez Canal."[29]

Eden tried to provoke Nasser by green-lighting the Suez Canal Company's withdrawal of its shipping pilots from the Suez Canal on September 14, 1956, to create a pretext for an invasion. Aiming to humiliate Nasser, Eden arrogantly gambled that the Egyptian pilots would fail to maintain the smooth flow of navigation through the canal, showing the world that backward Egypt was dependent on Western technological capacity.[30] It was an immense challenge for Nasser, who called, encouraged, and motivated the Suez Canal Company staff every day during this period. Before the foreign pilots left, there had been three hundred of them ensuring that everything ran smoothly in the canal, but Nasser had only three dozen Egyptian pilots, many of them trainees. They were assisted by forty-one Russian pilots, in addition to the many Greek pilots who voluntarily agreed to stay.[31]

Working themselves to exhaustion, the understaffed team rose to the challenge. For three days starting on September 16, more than one hundred ships transited the canal.[32] Nasser invited the foreign press to see how Egypt had managed. The media reported that contrary to the predictions of London and Paris, Egypt was fully capable of governing its own land and resources. Adding to the volatility of the situation was Eden's addiction to amphetamines, which he had started taking to deal with the effects of a botched operation in 1953 that had damaged his bile duct. Having what amounted to a speed freak leading a risky military intervention did not bode well. Eden's resulting sleep deprivation only added to the irrationality of the British goal, shared also by the French: to control the canal, not just ensure the traffic through it was smooth.[33] France and the United Kingdom knew full well that they could not just invade Egypt without a just cause. So they invented one.

The Protocol of Sèvres—The World's Most Famous Secret

On October 22, 1956, a golden autumn day in Sèvres, in the Western suburbs of Paris, British, French, and Israeli government representatives met behind a thick veil of secrecy in a private villa.

Adding to the mythology of the moment, the owners were a family that had supported the French resistance movement by, among other things, lending the villa as a resistance base during World War II.[34] This could have fed the sense of those gathering against Nasser that theirs was a just cause and not a ploy for material control and geostrategic dominance. That was one way to spin it.

For this disparate group of allies to join forces required a binding agent, and that was France, which had grown closer to Israel because of Nasser's support for the Algerian liberation struggle, and by the mid-1950s France was Israel's biggest arms supplier. On October 14, French General Maurice Challe and acting foreign minister Albert Gazier visited Eden at Chequers, the British prime minister's stately and bucolic country manor, where they cooked up the plan for Israel to attack Egypt as an excuse for a British and French invasion. Nutting, who was there, said Eden reacted with "glee."[35] Two days later, in Paris, France's Prime Minister Guy Mollet suggested this idea to Israel's Prime Minister Ben-Gurion, who rejected it because he distrusted the British. Fearing for the viability of the plan, Mollet aimed to build confidence between Israel and the United Kingdom. Toward this end, he brought Ben-Gurion and a group of close aides to Sèvres on the luxurious French presidential D4 plane.[36]

The British had not yet arrived when the first meeting was held on October 22. Ben-Gurion, flanked by senior defense officials Moshe Dayan and Shimon Peres, laid out his master plan for the Middle East: dividing Jordan between Israel and Iraq, expanding Israel north up to the Litani River, annexing a large Lebanese Shia population, and in turn increasing Lebanon's relative share of Christians. He also proposed that the Suez Canal be turned into an international zone and that the Gulf of Aqaba come under Israeli control. The precondition for this scenario was the removal of Nasser. Mordechai Bar-On, who was present at the meeting on Israel's side, called this plan embarrassing and "more fitted to the kind of imperial discussions which took place at the end of the Great War following the dismemberment of the Ottoman Empire. It was totally out of place in the international realities since the Second World War."[37]

The plan was indeed a blatant imperial grand design comparable to the Sykes-Picot Agreement, but it is important to note that

Israel did eventually occupy the West Bank in 1967 and southern Lebanon between 1982 and 2000—with disastrous and deadly consequences still causing suffering to this day. When the British delegation arrived that evening, led by Foreign Secretary Selwyn Lloyd, they brought a message that upset the Israelis: the United Kingdom said Israeli troops would have to be alone on the ground for seventy-two hours before the French and British would intervene, in response to an ultimatum given to the two parties. Ben-Gurion had several reasons to reject this. Israel did not want to be exposed for seventy-two hours to Egyptian aerial bombardment, and an ultimatum would paint Israel as the aggressor. Ben-Gurion worried that Lloyd would not keep in mind the interests of the French and Israelis, who both relied on the British air force to strike Egyptian airfields.[38] Time equaled strategic advantage: with each passing hour that Britain waited to deploy air assets, the threat of Egyptian bombardments against Israel increased. Yet on October 24 these men all signed a document designed to deceive the world.

Released in 1996, the document became arguably the most famous smoking gun from the Cold War. More than just a plot to foment war, the Sèvres Protocol embodied the toxic imperial mindset; it contained grand designs for reengineering the region, whispers of oil, and, most important, naked deceit. Israel's collusion with formerly colonial Britain and France reinforced a widely held belief among Arabs that Israel was an imperial outpost planted by the West in the region. Beyond even the lies to the peoples of the region, the tripartite allies lied to their own countrymen. These are the same essential dynamics at play in the covert coup against Mossadegh. For its part, the United States condemned the Suez War but not the playbook that triggered it, following the same moves in different contexts as the years went on. The supposed paragons of democracy had proven to be as ruthless, self-serving, and unprincipled as any dictatorship.

The Invasion

In contrast to the covert coup against Mossadegh, Britain, France, and Israel engaged in an overt invasion of a sovereign country in order to seize the Suez Canal and topple the Egyptian regime. The operation was an abject failure. Their policy objectives, far from being achieved, were pushed further out of sight: sunken ships obstructed the canal and forced it to remain closed for a year. As for Nasser, his resistance consolidated and expanded his regional influence. Britain and France lost international status, becoming secondary powers on the world stage. The colonial stench around the tripartite invasion of Egypt reeked across the world. Peoples in lands that had been British or French colonies were especially sensitive to this foul odor. Eden and Mollet's joint military venture proved the limits of imperial hubris. The invasion of Egypt was almost universally condemned. Allies and foes alike were shocked. Nasser stood his ground against Israel and the two biggest imperial powers, which helped burnish his image as an Arab and Third-World hero.

In yet another sign that his anti-imperial stance was not to be confused with an anti-American one, Nasser turned for help to the United States, not the Soviet Union. He sent a message through U.S. Ambassador to Egypt Raymond Hare to Eisenhower "requesting United States support against Anglo-French aggression." Nasser's willingness to receive U.S. military assistance marked the first time that he had ever requested it from anyone, and he said he reached this decision after careful deliberation on what was, for Egypt, a matter of life and death.[39] Nasser's message to the United States was consistent with his careful walk across the fine line between the two rival global blocs. Egypt's ties to the Soviet Union were practical, made possible thanks only to Nikita Khrushchev's pragmatic leadership and the Soviet departure from a strictly ideological foreign policy.[40]

Nasser was right to bet on the United States, which had opposed the tripartite invasion. The Eisenhower administration immediately took the matter to the UN Security Council. Britain and France exercised their vetoes, killing a draft resolution that would have called for an immediate ceasefire and Israeli withdrawal. And, upon learning the extent of the Anglo-French-Israeli collusion, Washington cranked up the pressure on its allies to stop the invasion.[41] The Eisenhower administration imposed economic and military sanctions against Israel on October 31, 1956. And the president himself gave strict orders to the State Department that Israel should understand that American domestic politics would not come into play: "We should handle our affairs exactly as though we did not have a Jew in America. The welfare and best interests of our country were to be the sole criteria on which we operated."[42]

The United States also imposed punishing economic sanctions on Britain and France, and this at a time when British oil and sterling reserves were in a precarious state. Eisenhower said the two countries would have to address their own energy problems or—in his rather macabre words—"boil in their own oil, so to speak." Dulles predicted they would cave quickly to U.S. demands.[43] Turning the screws, the Eisenhower administration refused to alleviate their fuel shortage, allowing the pound sterling to depreciate.[44]

In Cairo, Nasser energized his people with a rousing call after Friday prayers on November 2 at the al-Azhar Mosque: "We will fight from house to house, from village to village. We will fight and never surrender. We will rather fight than live humiliated." Students of history hear in this resolve an echo of Churchill's "We shall fight on the beaches" speech during World War II. Ironically, the English were now on the side that was threatening freedom and independence, not defending it. And where Churchill's posh intonation reminded citizens of his elite status, Nasser spoke in a pure colloquial Cairene dialect, reaching even people in the slums both with the substance of what he said and with the style in which he said it.[45]

Four days later, Eden and Mollet were forced to surrender to U.S. economic pressure by agreeing to an immediate ceasefire and troop withdrawal. Israel followed suit two days later and withdrew from some, but not all, of the territory it had occupied, relenting only after Eisenhower threatened "far-reaching effects upon Israel's relations throughout the world." The Israeli Foreign Minister at the time, Golda Meir, conceded that "the whole world was against us."[46] By January 1957 Eden was losing in the court of public opinion, finding himself described in headlines as "a Lonely Man and a Sick Man."[47]

The Price of the Suez Crisis

The Suez Crisis had killed Eden's career. His attempts to emulate Churchill by turning Nasser into Hitler had backfired. The Soviets, busy quelling the Hungarian revolution, played a limited role with a belated intervention, waiting until November 5, 1956, to issue their threat to smash the aggressors and restore peace in the Middle East. Pictures of the rubble and tanks in Budapest were a vivid reminder of Soviet military might as well as its willingness to exert force. As a result, Western officials read Moscow's threat as evidence of a possible Soviet ballistic missile attack. But the Soviet remarks came only after the Americans had forced a surrender.[48]

The Americans clearly were not motivated by sympathy for Nasser but, rather, by their own fear of losing control of Middle Eastern oil. U.S. officials also feared that the invasion of Egypt would offer Khrushchev the chance to seize the mantle of world leadership as a champion of the rights of newly independent states; they were keen to check Soviet influence by reasserting America's leadership in opposition to its allies' invasion.[49]

A favorite saying in the developing world during the Cold War was "When the elephants fight, the grass suffers. When the elephants make love, the grass still suffers." But in this case, the U.S.–Soviet global rivalry allowed Nasser to trample his own way to political victory. Eisenhower and Dulles sought to disassociate themselves from the European powers' openly imperialist policies. In Eisenhower's words, America faced the question: "How could we possibly support Britain and France if in doing so we lose the whole Arab world?"[50] He and Dulles agreed that the United States should have sole dominance over the Western alliance in the international system.

Confirming America's dominance, the Suez Crisis marked the formal end of classical colonialism. In the place of colonial powers, the United States—and to a lesser extent the Soviet Union—shaped the international order that has lasted till the present. It was a transformative change in the international balance of power, marking the consolidation of Pax Americana.

Nasser emerged as the hero of the Arabs with the responsibility to build a coalition of Arab states that could maximize his bargaining power regionally and internationally. The Suez Crisis fueled the passions of the pan-Arab nationalist movement, creating a lethal threat to the pro-Western conservative Arab rulers. By participating in the 1956 Suez War, Israel markedly escalated Arab-Israeli hostilities, which then became the defining feature of the

Middle East, setting in motion a cascading series of cataclysms: geopolitical rivalries, perpetual conflict, and a regional arms race that siphoned resources from economic development. All this came at the cost of countless lives and untold thwarted societal progress.

The Suez Crisis and its aftermath inspired newly decolonized people around the world to hope for success in standing up to the Great Powers. Africans, Latin Americans, and Asians saw Egypt defy its former colonial master, and they realized they could potentially rise up and triumph. Suez psychologically boosted oppressed nations. It spelled out how to bring down the age of colonial domination and gun diplomacy.

Though the Eisenhower administration opposed the invasion, it still contributed to the Suez Crisis. By trying to weaken Nasser by withdrawing the U.S. offer to finance the Aswan Dam, Eisenhower set the stage for Nasser to nationalize the canal. In the absence of that, the Suez Crisis might never have occurred. Regional and local change often affects global change—but this lesson was lost on the Great Powers, which raised the risk of nuclear peril during the global Cold War.[51]

All hopes for amicable U.S.–Egyptian relations in the early 1950s crashed on the altar of America's imperial ambitions and its opposition to Third World nationalists like Mossadegh and Nasser. A different story could have been written by America. Had it taken an anticolonial stance, Washington could have benefited from Nasser's skill in staying nonaligned as the world lurched toward bipolarity. Although he had extended a hand of friendship to the Americans, they were not willing to shake it on an equal basis. This unbalanced relationship could never be accepted by the Egyptian leader, whose country had just thrown off a millennia-old yoke of foreign rule. For Nasser, independence and sovereignty were nonnegotiable.

Here again, Washington forgot the history lessons it had written into the books. Although Egypt and the United States share this historical experience at the core identity of their republics, the Eisenhower Cold Warriors squandered the potential for common ground. The price was steep: for this failure of vision from Washington, the United States faced a Soviet foothold in the Middle East, the diminishment of key U.S. allies, and the loss of Nasser, now an even more influential leader who had cemented his autocratic rule. The resulting new dynamics generated more conflict, bloodshed, and chaos for decades to come. Had it only been courageous enough to put democratic values, freedom, and dignity for the Arab peoples, including the Palestinians, above coerced imperial interests, the United States would have reaped enormous benefits, which in turn would have benefited the region and the world.

The 1956 invasion of Egypt was followed by the Six-Day War between Israel and Egypt in June 1967, a turning point in the decline of Nasser's Arabism and the resurgence of pan-Islamism led and financed by the Saudis. The regional balance of power and dominant ideologies in the Middle East tilted toward the religious far right and far left, radically altering the trajectory of societies in the Arab and Muslim world and beyond. While there is no straightforward, uninterrupted line in this history, clearly the U.S. Cold Warriors' offensive policies against Nasser in the 1950s sowed the seeds for future turmoil in the Middle East.

Egypt and Reality Reloaded

At this propitious moment in history, the misguided, deadly, and self-destructive U.S. anticommunist, antinationalist stance took shape in Egypt as nowhere else. Ultimately, the Eisenhower administration's frenzy of paranoia framed this civilizational country, which declared itself proudly unaligned, as a nascent Soviet client state. And rather than lure the influential young Egyptian leader with friendship and aid, U.S. leaders first punished and then resolved to oust Nasser.

The drama played out in Cairo, but the depth, breadth, and reach of the implications extended much further. Washington's posture toward Egypt soon calcified its position toward a host of countries around the world. And this hegemonic stance was taken even when America was not threatened. The bald eagle didn't need to battle the black bear for the United States to take up an ideological conflict. Eventually, capitalism would win—but not before the Eisenhower Doctrine set the stage for destructive policies that would cost untold human life in the Middle East, South Asia, Latin America, and Southern Africa while diverting precious resources from meeting the pressing needs of the people of the United States whom the government was elected to serve. Even if the tripartite invasion of Egypt in 1956 had removed Nasser from power, the Middle East arguably would have followed the same course. Like Mossadegh, Nasser represented a new generation of postcolonial leaders seeking independence and dignity for their people. British and French domination was opposed, even hated, throughout the region, which had reached a point of no return. If Nasser were unseated, another Nasser could have taken his place.

The one factor that could have dramatically altered the destiny of Egypt and the region was the behavior of the United States, as a newly emergent superpower with political capital to spare in the form of trust by the formerly colonized states. This was squandered because the American government never wanted to understand Egypt on Egyptian terms. With open eyes, the Cold War advocates could have easily forestalled Nasser's turn to communist Russia for aid and arms, and the United States would not have become a nemesis across the Middle East.

Although U.S. policies never dealt a fatal blow against Nasser, they amounted to relentless pressure throughout his tenure. The outcome in Egypt differed from what happened in Iran, but the net effect in both was more internal despotism and long-term regional instability. As Nasser's leadership was defeated, so was secular nationalism in the Arab world. What rose in its place was Saudi Arabia's pan-Islamism. As the 1970s progressed, puritanical Islam and neoliberal elites fueled by the Saudi oil revolution swept across Arab lands until inequality and political Islam reigned supreme across the Arab world.

The Suez Crisis could have provided a window for rapprochement between the United States and Egypt. Nasser and his comrades acknowledged that Washington—not Moscow—had played a decisive role in forcing the invaders to withdraw from Egyptian territory. In their first meeting after the war, Nasser pointed this out to his cabinet.[52]

Hoping to reconcile U.S.–Egyptian relations, Nasser sought to ease American worries by again emphasizing that the nonalignment policy was purely defensive. He told U.S. Ambassador Hare directly that Washington could rest assured that when it came to communist activities in the region, Egypt would maintain its long-held stance against foreign domination, including that from communist Russia. "I don't trust any big power," Nasser declared, a statement wholly consistent with his attachment to nonalignment.[53] In plain terms, he said: "A United States steering an independent course should have no special difficulty in reaching an understanding with Egypt and other Arab states."[54] He was not against the United States, only for Egypt.

CHAPTER NINE

Frustrating Nasser's
Arab Nationalism

I F NASSER NEEDED REASONS to hold fast to his mistrust of world powers, the Eisenhower administration handed them to him. The Suez Crisis had prompted U.S. officials to further isolate Nasser.[1] Eisenhower couldn't have been clearer when he said bluntly, "We regard Nasser as an evil influence." Dulles went so far as to say he wished the British had toppled Nasser before withdrawing from Suez. To Washington hard-liners, Nasser was nothing but a Soviet pawn. They feared he would clear the path for communism to gain a foothold in the Middle East.[2] Ironically, if the Russians were indebted to anyone for gaining influence in the region it was the United States, which had for more than three years obdurately rejected Nasser's reassurances, requests for aid, and attempts at forging better relations.

The Eisenhower Doctrine

The United States continued along its destructive path as far as relations with Egypt were concerned, moving away from repair and toward confrontation. Considering Nasser a source of regional instability, Washington suspended assistance while boosting his regional rivals.[3] The president himself codified this on January 5,

1957, at a joint session of Congress, where he articulated what came to be known as the Eisenhower Doctrine. Stressing the importance of the Middle East to the United States, he warned of the threat of communism encroaching on the region. He proposed a resolution that green-lit authorization for the president to intervene militarily if any communist-controlled regime attacked any country in the Middle East or beyond.[4]

This vision was not only damaging—it was understated. The Eisenhower Doctrine would ultimately become a pretext for much more nefarious, covert, and expanded military interventions. Anticommunism was ultimately beside the point. And not only did the Eisenhower Doctrine result in mission creep in terms of mandates, it also meant the spread of military intervention geographically far beyond the borders of the Middle East. Ideologically as well as geostrategically, the Eisenhower Doctrine departed from its origins quickly and with enduring consequences.

In short, the doctrine led to U.S. interventions anywhere in the world where America's interests, often defined through the lens of corporate profit, were threatened, at the expense of the freedom and lives not only of peoples beyond the borders of the United States, but also of those living within them. This was the first American foreign policy doctrine for the Middle East, and it marked a deepening of American involvement in the region, where the United States came to replace colonial Britain as the dominant informal imperial power.

Nasser and other Arab nationalists understood that the Eisenhower Doctrine was more a reboot of imperialism than a measure against communism. Nasser spelled out his concerns to U.S. Ambassador Hare, pointing out that Eisenhower's proposal failed to address Arab countries' pressing needs for economic development and political independence, as well as a resolution to the Palestine question. At the same time, the lesson Nasser drew from the Suez Crisis was that there was no real Soviet threat to regional security, but that Britain, France, and Israel were the real enemies. Nasser saw Eisenhower's new doctrine as an imperial baton passed on to the United States from Britain and France.[5] And to Nasser, the baton would now double as a shield, hiding the motivations of Cold Warriors when they intervened in the internal affairs of Arab countries under the guise of fighting Soviet communism.

Indeed, the Eisenhower Doctrine codified an anti-Nasser regional policy that the United States had pursued since 1955. And it achieved its aim of sowing divisions within Arab ranks, triggering a fierce Arab cold war. States and societies were ravaged by geopolitical rivalries while inter-Arab competition undermined trust and the prospect of fruitful cooperation and trade. Conservative monarchies were propped up by America in Saudi Arabia, Iraq, Jordan, Lebanon, Libya, and Tunisia. Thanks to Eisenhower, the Saudis were put in the lead because he believed that King Saud, the custodian of the Two Holy Mosques in Islam, could represent a spiritual counterweight to dampen Nasser's charisma. Eisenhower noted that King Saud "professed anti-Communism, and he enjoyed, on religious ground, a high standing among all Arab nations."[6] Nasser's secular nationalism, by this logic, could not compete with a Pax Islamica under Saud's leadership.

The U.S. decision to ally with pan-Islamism against secular nationalists and "godless Communists" characterized its foreign policy from the late 1950s until the end of the Cold War in 1989. America's partnership with the Afghan mujahedeen against the Soviet invaders in the 1980s was not the exception but the result of a long-term strategy. Billions of American dollars were pumped into Islamist groups, dramatically altering the balance of power in the region and beyond. The landmines they laid—metaphorically and also literally—continue to detonate to this day. While radical nationalists had no inhibitions about dealing with the socialist bloc, pan-Islamists opposed the atheist and communist East more than they did the imperialist West.

This generated an unlikely alliance among Washington's Cold War proponents, the Saudis, the Pakistanis, and other Islamists in the Middle East and across the newly decolonized world. The Eisenhower Doctrine targeted first and foremost Nasser's Arab nationalist project, which the United States viewed as a threat to its vital economic national interests in the region. The result was a toxic inter-Arab rivalry whose aftershocks still reverberate across the region and around the world today. This geostrategic curse took its greatest toll on countries that had just embarked on their journey of freedom and development after being emancipated from imperial rule. At the tender moment when state building was in its infancy, the global Cold War converged with an Arab cold war, as scholars would call it.⁷ This convergence was to undermine progress just when newly independent Arab countries needed time, space, and freedom from foreign intervention in their internal affairs.

The effects were ruinous. From the Baghdad Pact in 1955 to the Arab Spring uprisings in 2010–12, geostrategic rivalries have allowed strongmen and their regional and global patrons to maintain the stagnant status quo. The narrative that these conflicts date back to "ancient hatreds" falls apart when compared to contemporary German-French relations, so friendly now after centuries of fighting.

Egypt and Iran, possessing vast human resources and early modernization efforts, could have inspired other regional countries, leading the way in establishing the rule of law, state institutions, and productive industrialization. Instead, they became more militarized and despotic, marked by domestic patron-client relationships that deepened inequalities and abused the trust of millions of people. The devastating effects were not felt only in the region. America's support for pan-Islamists in the Middle East served to create a pool of young, marginalized, jobless, and angry men ripe for the picking by extremist organizations.

All this unfolded against the backdrop of socioeconomic inequalities that were exacerbated by geostrategic rivalries. These were among the noxious roots of deadly terrorist attacks by militant groups in the United States decades later. More generally, the U.S. military was dragged into the region without a clear exit plan, a move that cost trillions of dollars and the even heavier price of countless American, European, Arab, and Muslim lives. The Eisenhower Doctrine provided the cover for the United States to engage in trench warfare against Nasser and other secular nationalists in Syria, Iraq, and elsewhere. Nasser clamped down on Egyptian communists and socialists and fought efforts by Iraqi and Syrian communists to gain power. If America's Cold Warriors had any genuine interest in preventing the communist influence from spreading in Arab lands, Nasser, relentless in his opposition to Arab communist parties, would have been their man.

Syria: Graveyard of C.I.A.–Sponsored Coups

A clear example of how U.S. policy went awry early on can be seen in Syria. Eisenhower's Cold Warriors attached special importance to the country at a sensitive time in its political progression. In 1949 Syria became the first Arab state whose leadership was overthrown with C.I.A. assistance.[8]

Like so much else in U.S.–Middle Eastern relations, things didn't have to be this way. Syria and America were on track to develop a healthy bilateral relationship in the early years of Syrian independence. Syrian nationalists appreciated the United States for helping them expel French colonialists from the country in 1946, when Syria effectively became the first fully independent state of all the European Arab colonies.[9] And that help was not lost on other Arab nationalists, who saw the value of Washington's role as a counterweight to colonial powers. There was a solid foundation of mutual interest and respect on which to build U.S.–Syrian relations.

Yet this promising beginning was soon sabotaged by the C.I.A.'s covert meddling in Syria's internal affairs. No surprise, then, that U.S.–Syrian relations quickly deteriorated after the newly decolonized country gained independence. One of the earliest points of contention was the American recognition of the United Nations Partition Plan for Palestine in 1947. In response, the Syrian parliament continuously blocked any legislation that would ratify the American-owned Aramco's plans to build the Trans-Arabian Pipeline—an ambitious infrastructural project stretching all the way from Saudi Arabia to Lebanon, which would expedite the process of transporting energy to Europe, then recovering after World War II. The pipeline was set to cross the Syrian Golan Heights on its way to the Lebanese port of Sidon, thanks to successful lobbying by Aramco together with the U.S. State Department for rights of passage from Saudi Arabia, Jordan, and Lebanon.[10] Only concessions from Syria were needed to make these ambitious plans a reality. There was another point of friction that kept Syrian legislators from approving the Aramco oil pipeline: Syria's northernmost province, Hatay, which France had ceded to Turkey at the beginning of World War II. The United States was not sympathetic to

Syria's irredentist claims on Hatay, again because of Turkey's strategic importance in the Cold War chessboard.[11]

By May 1948, negotiations on making Syria the terminus for Saudi oil had broken down after America had recognized the State of Israel. Secretary of State George Marshall told the U.S. ambassador in Saudi Arabia, J. Rives Childs, that the decision would guarantee "continued refusal [of the] Syrian Government to grant concession [for the Trans-Arabian Pipeline]."[12] In late 1948, long before the C.I.A.–led coup in Iran and even before the Soviet Union had tested its first atomic weapon, the agency prepared to overthrow the Syrian government.[13]

In just three years, U.S. policy toward Syria had radically shifted from supporting its independence from France to seeking an overthrow of the government of this newly independent state. On November 30, 1948, in the midst of nationwide anti-American and anti-Israeli rallies, Stephen Meade, a C.I.A. Middle East specialist, secretly met with Husni al-Za'im, a Syrian colonel of Kurdish origin. This was their first of six meetings to discuss the possibility of an "army supported dictatorship" backed by the United States.[14] The aim was to overthrow the two-time popularly elected Shukri al-Quwatli in favor of a convicted swindler, Colonel Za'im.[15]

The Americans were all too aware of Colonel Za'im's incompetence. Meade described him as a "Banana Republic dictator type" but endorsed him because of his "strong anti-Soviet attitude."[16] And unlike Quwatli, Colonel Za'im was willing to recognize Israel, according to Meade. The situation intensified around mid-March 1949, when Colonel Za'im made clear to the Americans that he sought resources to "provoke and abet internal disturbances" in Syria.[17] The gasoline had its desired effect on the fire, which Colonel Za'im watched grow for about a fortnight. When the temperature was high enough, he executed the coup, overthrowing Quwatli and suspending the constitution. So much for the United States standing for government by the people and for the rule of law. But when those fell in Syria, Washington achieved what was a higher-priority objective: the elimination of any obstacle preventing the Trans-Arabian Pipeline from crossing Syrian territory. The balance sheet weighed heavy losses for the long term against the interest of short-range gain. Washington traded Syria's nascent democracy.

To Meade's satisfaction, Za'im delivered. Within two weeks of the coup, he reported having arrested four hundred communists. He was also ready to approve the pipeline project with the condition that America recognized his putschist regime.[18] Less than a month after the coup, U.S. Ambassador James Keeley presented his credentials in Damascus, rewarding Za'im for making good on his promises. Za'im continued to let Washington pull the strings on his puppet regime, quickly resuming peace talks with Israel and planning to resettle a quarter million Palestinian refugees in the Jazirah Valley.[19] The transit agreement with Aramco for the Trans-Arabian Pipeline was ratified by May 1949. All the while, he cracked down on the left, banned the Communist Party, renounced all claims on Hatay, and even signed an armistice with Israel.[20]

At the time, friendliness to Israel amounted to political suicide—not only metaphorically, as evidenced by the fact that King Abdullah I of Jordan was shot dead for alleged collusion with Israel just two years later. Za'im opted for American patronage and protection in return for blind loyalty. Or so it seemed. Eventually, he would pay the price for his open defiance of Syrian public opinion. In less than five months, Za'im's fellow army officers sent him to the notorious French-built Mezzeh prison. Ultimately, he was executed.

The C.I.A.'s assistance in overthrowing Quwatli created a dangerous precedent in the newly decolonized country that foreshadowed new interventions. Power was now up for grabs in Syria, the fragile democracy was completely shattered, and any officer with enough military status and political savvy was a potential contender to rule. Za'im's ouster and execution in December 1948 were followed by another military coup. Syria joined a club of instability, lining up with Thailand, Paraguay, Bangladesh, and Vietnam as the only other countries to have experienced three coups in a year. As of this writing, as Syria suffers through more than a decade of war, the question "What might have been?" rings with an implied scathing critique.

At the time of the Eisenhower administration, Syria was still a critical transit route for Persian Gulf oil to the Mediterranean. Both the Iraqi Petroleum Pipeline and the Saudi Trans-Arabian Pipeline (then the world's largest oil pipeline system) transported their oil through Syria in the 1950s.[21] In addition to its strategic location, Syria had also been an intellectual hub for radical ideologies such as Arab nationalism, socialism, and communism. Syria was the birthplace of another, Ba'athism, a socialist pan-Arab ideology that would later go on to dominate two of the longest-reigning and most powerful Arab regimes in the region. Syria also boasted the Arab world's most active Communist Party.[22]

From independence in 1946 to the merger with Egypt in the United Arab Republic in 1958, Syria had ten different "revolving-door governments," so named because they didn't last long enough to steer the country in a pro-Western, pro-Arab, or pro-Soviet direction.[23] In his memoirs, Eisenhower said this cocktail in Syria of domestic instability, lack of strong government, and potent nationalist and communist ideological currents was a recipe for a communist takeover—conveniently ignoring the C.I.A.'s role in the early destabilization of the country: "[Syria] was far more vulnerable to Communist penetration than was Egypt. In Egypt, where one strong man prevailed, Colonel Nasser was able to deal with Communists and accept their aid with some degree of safety simply because he demanded that all Soviet operations be conducted through himself. In Syria, where a weak man was in charge of the government, the Soviet penetration bypassed the government and dealt directly with the various agencies, the army, the foreign ministry and the political parties."[24] The perception of a gathering storm in Damascus—in Eisenhower's words, "Syria was considered ripe to be plucked at any time"—added urgency to the efforts of those who wanted an intervention there.[25]

In March 1956 the British MI6 devised a plan for overthrowing the Syrian government code-named Operation Straggle.[26] This plan to infiltrate Syria centered on funding a pro-Iraqi party, the *Parti Populaire Syrien* (PPS), to stir up the masses while using the paramilitary arm of the right-wing Syrian Social Nationalist Party, based in Lebanon, to help support the uprising. That era in the Middle East was characterized by youth formations that galvanized supporters in street parades and sports rallies designed to attract students and activists. Though they might have had relatively benign origins, they eventually metastasized into pressure groups whose political power was exceeded only by the military's.[27]

Britain found its anticommunist coup point man in Syria in the person of a pro-Iraqi Christian named Mikhail Ilyan. A cofounder of the National Bloc Party, he had fought for independence and served as foreign minister in Iraq.[28] After some initial hesitation, the Americans joined the British coup plot in the late summer of 1956. Secretary of State John Foster Dulles publicly denied any support for a coup in Syria but endorsed it privately in meetings with Eisenhower.[29] Washington provided Ilyan with $140,000 to buy the cooperation of Syrian army officers in taking control of Syria's major cities and radio communications. The preparations made and money spent were at best a dress rehearsal for future operations; ultimately the coup had to be aborted when the Suez Crisis broke out and Ilyan said the Israeli aggression against Egypt would undermine the planned putsch in Syria.[30]

Operation Wappen and Harassment of the Syrians

Emboldened by their successful coups in Iran in 1953 and Guatemala in 1954, the Cold Warriors in Washington were not going to let extenuating circumstances affect the preparations for a coup against the Syrian government. In 1957, with an initiative codenamed Operation Wappen, the C.I.A. upped the ante and increased their coup budget more than twenty-fold, from $140,000 to $3,000,000 (equivalent to $30 million today), to bribe Syrian army officers and have them oust the government.[31]

To their credit, the Syrians could not all be bought. Despite the C.I.A.'s pouring relatively large sums of money into the operation, as it grew so did the numbers of people aware of the plans, and among them were Syrian military officers who did not support the American adventure. Several of them took the initiative to foil it, informing Syria's head of intelligence, Colonel Abdel Hamid al-Sarraj, of the plans. They even provided the names of those C.I.A. contacts pulling the strings: Francis Jeton, Howard E. Stone, and Robert Molloy.[32]

Though the agency had been successful in engineering coups in Iran and Guatemala, it had difficulty achieving its aims in Syria. This, however, did not dissuade the Cold Warriors, who only seemed to have more incentive to direct the destiny of Syria because of its ability to evade manipulation by Washington. Syria was like the unconquered maiden who was all the more attractive for being unavailable. That attitude is fairly harmless when a much-rejected high schooler keeps trying to get the popular girl as his prom date, but when a superpower keeps trying to overthrow a government, it's fantastically damaging. John Foster Dulles never explicitly asked Turkey to intervene militarily in Syria, but when he signed a sixteen-point telegram to Ankara, he left the possibility distinctly open. The message was subtle but the subtext was clear: Dulles gave an implicit green light to Turkey's military intervention in Syria.[33]

In a sign that the message was received loud and clear, Ankara boosted its troops on the Syrian border from 32,000 to 50,000 while carrying out military maneuvers there to pressure Syria against moving toward Soviet communism.[34] America played Turkey as its proxy in the bid to weaken Damascus. Syria suffered its share of instability but still managed to thwart not one but two U.S.- and British-led coups in those years. Rather than dissuade Washington and London from plotting the fate of the Syrian people, their respective intelligence agencies—the C.I.A. and MI6—created a third secret Anglo-American Working Group with a mandate to bring down the Syrian government. In a sign of their seriousness, the C.I.A. put in charge Kermit Roosevelt, their most aggressive operative, who had, as we have seen, been central to carrying out the 1953 coup against Iranian Prime Minister Mohammad Mossadegh.[35]

Code-named the Preferred Plan and launched on September 18, 1957, this plot had as its goal stoking civil unrest and fabricating a casus belli for Iraq, aided by Jordan, with Turkey ready as a backup in case more firepower was needed to invade Syria and topple its government. The plan called for assassinating Colonel Sarraj, head of military intelligence; Khalid Bakdash, leader of the Syrian Communist Party; and Afif al-Bizri, army chief of staff. In this effort, the C.I.A. drew on similar blueprints used for the Guatemalan coup in 1954: "In order to facilitate the action of liberative forces, reduce the capabilities of the Syrian regime to organize and direct its military actions, to hold losses and destruction to a minimum, and to bring about desired results in the shortest possible time, a special effort should be made to eliminate certain key individuals. Their removal should be accomplished early in the course of the uprising and intervention and in the light of circumstances existing at the time. Those who should be eliminated are Sarraj, Bizri, and Khalid Bakdash."[36]

Sarraj, a Kurd who was at the same time a staunch Arab nationalist, was the most powerful of the three on the hit list. He had served as one of the first army officers after Syria gained independence from France in 1946. Thanks to the close links he maintained with the Egyptian intelligence service, by the age of thirty-five he was the most powerful figure in the military, and he would ascend to vice president of the United Arab Republic after its creation in 1958.[37] He was targeted by the C.I.A. for more than his influence; the agency put a target on his back the moment he played a key role in foiling and exposing Operation Straggle. That was the moment he was transformed into a popular figure while—and by—costing the reputation of the C.I.A. and U.S. foreign policy.[38]

The C.I.A. came to stand not just for the cynical, calculating, and sinister side of American foreign policy but also for its brooding vengefulness. Instead of understanding why a newly independent state like Syria, free from foreign political domination for the first time in centuries, wanted to maintain its sovereign integrity, the Cold Warriors sought to exact vengeance against the spoiler of their coup plot that aimed to diminish Syrian independence. The Preferred Plan went beyond assassinating these officials, envisioning psychological warfare, and using overt and covert propaganda to demonize the Syrian regime at home and abroad while countering the country's own messaging.[39] The C.I.A. plotters had learned well in Iran and Guatemala that the propaganda war was at least as important as the boots on the ground; "at least as" implies "if not more so."

As had become its habit, the C.I.A. sought to foment internal unrest and weaken the security institutions with its by-then-familiar tactic of arming paramilitary groups. The planners believed that for the coup to succeed, the peoples, militaries, and governments of Jordan and Iraq must believe that Syria threatened their security.[40] Playing the long game and with an eye to international attention, the C.I.A. also planned sabotage and incidents on Syria's border with Iraq and Jordan so that the respective governments of these neighboring countries could invoke their right of self-defense under Article 51 of the United Nations Charter. This would serve to facilitate a global green light for them to depose the government in Damascus.

The plan might have gone forward but for a regional intervention that prevented chaos. On September 25, 1957, King Saud of Saudi Arabia went on a mediation mission to Damascus for talks with representatives of Syria and Iraq. Baghdad's envoys started to backtrack, and though King Hussein of Jordan was still ready to intervene in Syria, Iraq's participation was essential to implementing the plan. Turkey presented no alternative because of its history of colonization when it ruled the Ottoman Empire. The United States knew enough not to turn to a former imperial power to win the hearts and minds of Arabs. From Egypt, Nasser further foiled the C.I.A.–led plan by sending a contingent of his troops to Syria's main seaport on October 13 to counter Turkish forces massing on the Syrian border.

Syria raised the issue of Turkey's buildup of troops on its borders in discussions at the United Nations, where Damascus received support for its position from the Soviet Union.[41] In fact, it was Moscow that ultimately helped resolve the Turkey-Syria border crisis. With that, the Preferred Plan met its end, becoming the third C.I.A. plot in three years to be thwarted before it became operational.

The Cold Warriors lost big in Syria. Their misguided approach only served to disprove the fears that Arab nationalists in Egypt and Syria posed a "communist threat." Rather than undermining regional solidarity, the United States succeeded only in giving Nasser the chance to help safeguard Syria's independence with support from Egyptian troops while stopping both superpowers from intervening in the country's internal affairs. This bolstered Nasser's standing and boosted his popularity as an iconic leader of the Arab world. By the second half of the 1950s, tensions intensified between Moscow and Cairo because Nasser opposed the growing communist influence in Syria.[42]

U.S. officials, though they had no fondness for Nasser, did concede that he dealt a blow to communist influence in Syria.[43] Still, in a plainly self-defeating move, the United States ignored the clear fact that nationalists and communists were rivals with clashing agendas. Mossadegh, Nasser, Sarraj, and other anticolonial leaders did not trust Marxists, working together only when they needed to

join forces against common internal and external threats. Nationalists and leftists had a shaky alliance that faltered often and turned
violent in the late 1950s. But the C.I.A. conspirators and their
bosses cared less about these nuances and complexities of Arab politics than about compliance with their imperial design to confront
Soviet communism and to promote an open global economy,
which eclipsed all else in their line of sight. Viewing them as the
enemy amounted to a self-fulfilling prophecy that brought rivals
together for a common cause. The failure of C.I.A. covert plans in
Syria in 1957 didn't stop Washington from acting with impunity in
the Middle East and other regions.

The Anglo-American Working Group set a pattern that would
continue for decades by institutionalizing coordinated covert action
between MI6 and the C.I.A. The Americans and the British used
this template three months later in Indonesia during the Indonesian
Outer Island Rebellion.[44] Lessons learned by the C.I.A. from Iran
and Guatemala were applied not only to Syria but also later to other
countries, veering way beyond its original intelligence-gathering
mandate into carrying out paramilitary activities around the world.
In the Middle East, where it all began, the C.I.A. precipitated a
downward spiral where intended goals receded further in the distance as misguided efforts strengthened the Soviet hand. In the process, they violated the very principles that the United States was
supposedly defending with all this meddling and bloodshed: self-
determination, freedom, and the rule of law.

Lebanon: Opening Pandora's Box

The setback in Syria, rather than offering lessons in restraint, unleashed a determined effort to apply the Eisenhower Doctrine with
even greater zeal in a bid to redeem past mistakes and recover lost
ground.

Nowhere was this more incongruous than on July 15, 1958, a
normal day in the life of Lebanon, which started like any other hot
summer day in the Lebanese capital of Beirut. Families flocked to
the beach for the sea breeze and recreational sun. In a shocking
and unprecedented moment, the scene turned surreal, heralded by

the swell of waves caused not by any move of Mother Nature but by the most man-made of horrors: combat transport ships sent by the U.S. Navy with 1,700 American soldiers aboard. Deepening the nightmare scenario, they were backed by seventy warships with nuclear capabilities in the distance.[45]

There could be no more asymmetrical theater: placid swimmers and sunbathers on one side and locked and loaded U.S. soldiers on the other. In addition to holding a distinct place in history for its farcical absence of proportion, this event also set a dubious precedent, marking the first American direct military intervention in the Middle East. President Eisenhower, in green-lighting Operation Blue Bat and the subsequent invasion of Lebanon, declared with what would turn out to be a gross understatement, "We are opening a Pandora's Box."[46]

In addition to being a bizarre entry in the annals of military history, Operation Blue Bat marked a clear departure from previous moves by Washington, as those had involved only C.I.A. covert action and subversion. The aim had been to demonstrate that the Eisenhower Doctrine had teeth, but these teeth devoured U.S. interests along with regional stability. Ostensibly designed to preserve the rule of Lebanese President Camille Chamoun, viewed by the United States as "openly anti-communist" and "our friend," the intervention backfired completely.[47]

Chamoun, a Maronite Christian from the most powerful political group in multicultural Lebanon, was so pro-Western, so anti-Nasser, that he stood as the lone ruler in the Middle East to publicly support the Eisenhower Doctrine. The instability roiling Lebanon today has many causes, but one of its roots is certainly this openly pro–U.S. stance in the 1950s, which intensified a brewing internal crisis. Two months before the beach landing, as the country was preparing for presidential elections, bullets silenced a leading Chamoun critic. The assassination on May 8, 1958, of Nasib Al Matni, editor of *Al Telegraf,* intensified ideological and sectarian tensions. Violence spread across Lebanon. Other countries were drawn in, specifically the United Arab Republic, then only three months old, which provided materiel and personnel to pan-Arabist elements attempting to force Chamoun out.

Lebanon raised the issue in the United Nations Security Council on May 22, 1958. Some two weeks later, the council passed a resolution that aimed "to ensure that there [was] no legal infiltration of personnel or supply of arms or other material across the Lebanese borders" and sent three representatives, including UN Secretary General Dag Hammarskjöld, on a fact-finding mission to the area.[48] The Eisenhower administration sidestepped the council resolution and justified its military intervention in Lebanon by saying that Chamoun had invited Washington's actions. Two weeks after the initial landing, the number of American troops more than tripled, from 3,000 to 10,000.[49]

President Eisenhower and his senior advisers initially rejected Chamoun's request for U.S. military intervention. Their minds did not change because of the situation in Lebanon but, rather, because of the July revolution in Iraq, where one of the most pro-Western regimes in the Middle East was toppled.[50] Although it seems impossible, Chamoun in his loyalty was so off the charts that even the hard-liner's hard-liner, Secretary of State John Foster Dulles, thought he was too loyal to the Western camp to enjoy respect. Chamoun had adopted "an extreme pro-Western policy," Dulles said, even at one time suggesting that he change it.[51]

It was not long after the U.S. military beach landing that Eisenhower officials came to view Chamoun as a liability—to the degree that they took the rare step of opting for someone less pro-Western, namely, military chief Fouad Chehab. While exacerbating political tensions in Lebanon, Washington had no concern for the mess it created.[52] Displaying breathtaking disregard for the country's people, John Foster Dulles said Lebanon was "not very important in itself."[53] He even acknowledged that far from solving the problems at stake, the intervention "in fact, . . . may make them worse."[54]

The Cold Warriors had strayed far from their original mission, veering so badly off course that they lost sight of their bête noire, communism, which had been replaced by an obsession over Nasser and the rising Arab nationalist forces. Washington had seen the brutal murder of its ally Iraqi Prime Minister Nuri al-Said, who publicly supported U.S. regional defense pacts in the early 1950s, and, fearing the fall of other pro-Western Middle Eastern regimes, intervened militarily in Lebanon to prevent the defeat of the Chamoun forces and prevent Nasser from gaining more influence in the region.

The imagined consequences of inaction were described at an important meeting among officials from the Department of Defense, the State Department, and the C.I.A. The scenario began with Nasser, unchecked, holding the mantle of hegemony in the Arab world. That, in turn, would put at risk America's military bases in the region. Following this, U.S. influence would wane, and, along with it, Washington's credibility globally.[55] This nightmare scenario put the flaws of the Eisenhower Doctrine on steroids and caused nothing but damage to Lebanon, America's influence in the region, and its credibility in the world. Of course, those pulling the strings in Washington perceived a link between Nasser and the Soviet Union, and this justified in their minds intervention and animated in their hearts the ache for a response. To them, the transactional nature of Nasser's relationship with Moscow—a by-product of the Cold War warriors' own rigid, zero-sum approach—meant he had refused their with-us-or-against-us ultimatum and by default must be stopped. In contrast to the shah of Iran, who did America's bidding in the region, Nasser was assertive and a troublemaker. The Americans sought to tame Nasser and cut his wings.

Rather than letting the region govern itself and progress on its own, the Eisenhower administration actively intervened, internationalizing local rivalries and exporting the global Cold War to the area with an astonishing lack of understanding of or curiosity about the region's culture or people. This is another instance that makes painfully clear the fact that if, instead of confronting Nasser and trying to cut him to size, the United States had developed a working relationship with the charismatic and popular Egyptian leader, that might have had transformative effects on a region that has since become a source of instability around the world.

If the Cold Warriors got into Lebanon because of their own distorted understanding of Nasser, they got out thanks to his pragmatism and realism, which furnished a face-saving escape from a messy and dangerous situation. The Egyptian leader helped engineer a compromise settlement that ended civil strife in Lebanon. Washington was ready to use the good offices of the United Nations but tripped on the same Cold War stumbling block that in the

era froze all meaningful negotiations in a stalemate: the superpower
veto on the UN Security Council, this time exercised by the Soviet
Union. It fell to Nasser to actively support a solution by means of a
regional framework achieved after he convinced his Lebanese allies
to compromise by allowing Chamoun to complete his presidential
term, which concluded on September 22, 1958, and Chehab to succeed him.[56]

The many ironies coursing through and resulting from Operation Blue Bat, not to mention all the fallout, were lost on Eisenhower administration officials, who considered it a success because
they had secured the free flow of oil from the Gulf while recon-
firming the U.S.–U.K. special relationship. The body count was
low; only one American serviceman lost his life, and the troops
were back home by Christmas.[57] But to view this moment in a bub-
ble is to lose sight of the waves of subsequent deadly instability. In
his memoirs, Eisenhower recalls how "the operation in Lebanon
demonstrated the ability of the United States to react swiftly with
conventional armed forces to meet small-scale, or 'brush fire' situations" in the Global South.[58] Though the U.S. operation may have
been cheap, quick, and clean, Eisenhower would have been more
accurate to stick to his original "Pandora's Box" metaphor.

America's Lebanon intervention, like the C.I.A. coup in Iran,
weakened another institutional check on the ability of U.S. presidents to wage wars abroad, expanding executive power at the expense of democracy. The American people were denied a public
debate about the human, legal, moral, and political costs of the war.
Against the plans of the much-revered Founders of the United
States, neither the electorate nor even their congressional representatives had a say in Eisenhower's decision to dispatch troops to
Lebanon. The decision by the Cold War proponents to intervene
militarily in Lebanon had opened a Pandora's Box while creating a
precedent—some would say blueprint—for subsequent entanglements in the Middle East and beyond. America's ability to achieve
positive political change through military might was a fantasy, as
Lebanon's crisis had been resolved not by American military intervention but, rather, by a combination of regional diplomacy and
successful mediation among warring Lebanese factions.[59]

Nasser's Geostrategic Curse

This should have been a lesson—if only the Cold Warriors could have seen it: empower Arab leaders and diplomatically coordinate with them to fix their own problems. So simple and yet completely missed by Washington, which powered forward headlong in the opposite direction. This early chapter in postwar U.S. foreign policy set the stage for America to deepen and expand its overt and covert intervention outside the Middle East to developing nations around the world. Eisenhower bequeathed a dangerous legacy that his successors would carry out far less successfully and far more catastrophically in Vietnam, Afghanistan, Iraq, and elsewhere.

The impact and legacy of the Cold War continue to influence Washington's militaristic approach to questions of war and peace in the world. President Barack Obama described the United States as a nation on a "perpetual wartime footing." In a commencement address at the U.S. Military Academy at West Point in 2014, Obama, a self-declared realist, acknowledged the lingering U.S. tendency since the beginning of the Cold War to shoot first and ask questions later: "Since World War II, some of our most costly mistakes came not from our restraint, but from our willingness to rush into military adventures without thinking through the consequences—without building international support and legitimacy for our action; without leveling with the American people about the sacrifices required. Tough talk often draws headlines, but war rarely conforms to slogans."[60]

Fast forward ten years, and Obama's vice president, Joe Biden, is the current president of the United States. Not unlike his Cold Warrior predecessors, Biden has pursued a militaristic foreign policy and partnered with autocrats in the Middle East and beyond. Obama's sobering advice seems to be lost on Joe Biden, especially in the context of the Israel-Gaza war of 2023, where he stands accused of complicity with Israel's war crimes and ethnic cleansing of Palestinians.

The Cold Warriors justified American intervention abroad in terms of the global struggle against Soviet communism, but their direct targets were mainly nationalist leaders like Mossadegh and Nasser who hoped to free their countries from domination by the

Great Powers, and who refused to join the reconfigured Anglo-American informal empires. These American policy makers obdurately associated Iranian and Arab nationalism with communism, squandering a historical opportunity to build relations with newly independent states on the basis of common interests, trust, and respect for the sovereignty and dignity of decolonized peoples. These interventions also sullied America's reputation with the Arab-Islamic world at the grassroots level.

The damage did not stop there. The taste for military interference caught on in America like that for spices by colonizers before it, and the United States began a pattern of intervening in countries around the world, often for no ideology more thought-out than paving the way for corporate interests and global finance to prevail. Leaving aside the untold devastation they left, this also made the world less safe, less prosperous, and less well developed for American citizens themselves to enjoy.

The American and British Cold War proponents ignored Nasser's efforts to allay fears of communist penetration of the Arab world and were unimpressed by his prudence in the Syrian and Lebanese crises in 1957 and 1958. Above all, they resented his independent streak and his ambition to make Egypt the unrivaled leader of the Arab world. He was demonized by British and American officials, even at times compared to Hitler. The Eisenhower Doctrine embodied their desire to cripple Nasser to the point where he became irrelevant to the broader politics and economics of the region.

On the whole, U.S. policy toward Nasser was hostile and combative. Even though U.S. officials acknowledged that he got rid of the communist menace in Syria, they deemed the United Arab Republic—the merger between Egypt and Syria in 1958—as "contrary to our interests."[61] No amount of effort to disabuse the Cold Warriors of this myth could change minds; Washington saw the expansion of Egyptian power to Syria as a boon to "anti-Western and particularly anti-American tendencies in the Middle East and Africa." Should Nasser gain sole control over Middle East oil flowing to Europe, they worried he would be able "to exert pressure upon the U.S. and other Western powers."[62]

Obviously, confronting Nasser failed, but instead of facing and dealing with this reality, U.S. officials dissembled, behaving one way in public and another behind closed doors. Assistant Secretary of State for Near Eastern Affairs William Rountree called for preserving America's strategic goal of isolating Nasser from the rest of the Arab world while pretending to come to terms with him. In a word, the United States chose to lie its way to its policy goals. Rountree baldly stated that convincing the Egyptian leader of U.S. goodwill could weaken Soviet-Egyptian ties. To prop up their deceit, American officials relaxed economic sanctions, eased some trade restrictions, and took other minor, largely cosmetic steps to create the illusion of support for Egypt.[63]

This naive American approach underestimated Nasser's mistrust of the United States and his determination to promote Egyptian national interests. He forged on, trying to expand his influence in neighboring Arab lands, and locked horns with both Washington's Cold War proponents and pro-Western Arab rulers. The intra-Arab cold war intensified, pitting Nasser and his Arab nationalist allies against the pro-Western conservative monarchies. This led Egypt to squander precious resources battling its Arab rivals. Like Mossadegh, Nasser was a patriot, but Mossadegh had no potential for greater regional leadership since there were no other Persian states in the Middle East. Nasser, on the other hand, became gripped by regional ambition.

He had initially focused on improving the well-being of Egyptians, but the Baghdad Pact, the Suez War, and the Eisenhower Doctrine caused a shift in Nasser's priorities from the domestic to the regional and international. He recognized the massive potential of radio and funded Voice of the Arabs, one of the first and most prominent transnational Arabic-language radios. Nasser was able to use this outlet as his mouthpiece, thereby cementing Egypt's position as a discursive powerhouse.

Going on the offensive, Nasser appealed directly to the Arab people, galvanizing masses in Iraq, northern Yemen, and the Maghreb to rise up to "Arab reaction" and to rulers who did Washington's bidding. He had taken the bait set by the United States, draining domestic resources to engage Egypt in costly regional affairs. Seeing its effectiveness, the United States amped up pressure on Nasser and his nationalist allies while propping up his conservative Arab rivals. For more than a decade starting in 1958, the intra-Arab cold war escalated into a civil war as Arabs slaughtered each other in Iraq, Syria, Yemen, Jordan, Lebanon, and beyond. The Americans may not have ousted Nasser in one stroke (as they had with Mossadegh), but their relentless pressure forced him to overextend his limited resources.

Nasser had agency. He could have chosen his battles carefully, avoiding entanglement in reputationally, politically, and economically costly inter-Arab and intra-Arab affairs. He could have focused more on the home front—but he chose not to. The merger of Syria with Egypt in 1958 marked a decisive turning point in cementing Nasser as the Arab world's most popular leader—and that made him drunk with power. The same ideological purity that had made him a man of the people became his downfall. Expectations were too high, resources too scarce, and challenges too great for Nasser to succeed. As his regional power and influence grew, so did the resistance he faced from like-minded Arab nationalists in Iraq and Syria, not to mention the usual suspects—pro-Western monarchies, the U.S. Cold Warriors, and Israel.

Egypt, neither militarily strong nor wealthy, could not afford so many enemies. Regional clashes intensified to the point where U.S. officials feared their pro-Western allies in Iraq, Saudi Arabia, and Jordan could not survive. The Arab cold war increasingly destabilized the region. The Americans were unable to wrest the microphone from Nasser. But despite his popularity, Nasser faced financial and military ruin.

Unlike Mossadegh, who had little leeway to avoid the coup that sealed his fate, Nasser made decisions that embroiled Egypt in intense geopolitical rivalries. Pitting Egypt against Washington and its regional proxies in a protracted rivalry drained the country's economy and diverted precious resources away from economic development. Overextended and outsmarted by the United States and Israel, Nasser sleepwalked into the June 1967 war, which delivered the final blow to him and to Egypt's standing in the region. Infighting within Nasser's Arab nationalist front made him vulnerable to attacks from Syrian and Iraqi nationalists, generating paranoia that clouded his decision making.

As a result of Nasser's own actions, the same Arab nationalists who had offered Syria to Nasser on a silver platter in 1958 revolted against him and seceded from the union in 1961. That was to be expected; instead of respecting the United Arab Republic as a unified Arab state, he treated Syria as just another Egyptian province. This amounted to a failure to demonstrate how Arab unity would look in practice, leaving intact the same state borders that divided the Arab nationalist camp. Nasser did let former Ba'ath Party members in Syria maintain prominent political positions but never allowed them to rise to a level equal to Egyptian officials. And by the time the UAR was about a year old, he purged the majority of established Syrian politicians of their power. That was provocation enough, and Nasser added fuel to the fire by appointing instead his close friend—an incompetent and corrupt Egyptian military officer, Abdel Hakim Amer—as the ruler of Syria. The optics were insulting and the consequences even worse. Amer's heavy-handed tactics alienated people across the spectrum, turning them against the first pan-Arab unity experiment. In the end, as history shows, Nasser lost Syria.

Fearing for the security of his own regime, Nasser monopolized power and enforced single-party rule. His insecurity complex and paranoia sparked the suppression of all dissent and the slow climb to absolute political authoritarianism. By further nationalizing the economy, he cemented his grip on the state, and he launched a campaign of even heavier censorship of all print and broadcast media. When he should have been taking stock of what went wrong in Syria, Nasser doubled down and went on the offensive, carrying the banner of revolution from Egypt into neighboring Arab states. He made his position clear in a clarion call for revolutionary action. "Every village, factory, faculty and school, every council of professional syndicates, every man and woman, youth and child in this country should be turned into a lively and fertile revolutionary cell," he said in an address to the nation in October 1961.[64] Nasser told associates he aimed to "manufacture" a revolution at home in order to avoid the trap of bureaucratization and restore damage to his prestige caused by the UAR's breakup.[65]

I spoke to some of Nasser's close aides, who expressed the view that he became more radicalized and even "reckless" after the dissolution of the UAR, asserting that Egypt's humiliating defeat in the 1967 June war with Israel could be traced to that 1961 tragic episode.[66] For example, Nasser accused Saudi Arabia (and the United States) of financing and meddling in the union's breakup. In 1962 he saw an opportunity in a coup d'état in Yemen by a group of army officers against the traditional royalist regime to punish Saudi Arabia for its hostile role in Syria. When the ousted Imam Mohammad al-Badr fled to Saudi Arabia, where he rallied support from Saudi Arabia and northern tribes to defeat the army officers, the situation quickly deteriorated and turned into war. Nasser provided diplomatic and military support to the republicans. He faced a coalition of Yemeni royalists, Saudi Arabia, Jordan, Israel, and Great Britain.

From 1963 to 1967—in what became an Arab hot war—Nasser sent 70,000 Egyptian soldiers to kill and be killed in the Yemeni civil war. The Egyptian army performed well on the battlefield but paid a heavy price. Although the republicans eventually won three years after Egypt pulled out, Nasser had become bogged down in Yemen, which turned into Egypt's Vietnam, leaving the Egyptian military demoralized and spent. Entangled in a faraway conflict on the southern tip of the Arabian Peninsula, Egypt became vulnerable to attack, and that arrived with Israel's decisive victory in the Six-Day War in June 1967.

Led by the same shambolic Abdel Hakim Amer who had been appointed in Syria, the Egyptian military lacked leadership, motivation, and a coherent structure and was no match for the Israeli army. The end of the Egyptian-Syrian union in 1961 signaled the crumbling of Nasser's secular nationalist project; his defeat in the Six-Day War was the death blow. The United States did not play a direct role in Nasser's fall, despite his accusations that it colluded with Israel in the war, but its indirect role was undeniable: since the mid-1950s the American Cold Warriors had plotted hard to cripple him. Physically, he survived until 1970, when he died of a heart attack, but politically, he was done in by 1967, having succumbed to American and Israeli pressure and coercion and the inter-Arab civil war.

Looking back on the history of missteps by all players is essential to understanding how we as a world have arrived at such a sorry state in U.S.–Middle East relations. We review these events not to "cry over spilled milk," as the expression goes, but, so to speak, to churn fresh milk that can be enjoyed in all forms on both sides. Although major world religions find a crossroads in the Middle East, it takes no divine power—only human solidarity and understanding—to resolve the problems there. And that starts with an understanding of our collective common humanity.

CHAPTER TEN

What Have Egypt and the Arab World Lost by the Defeat of Nasser's Secular Nationalism?

F ROM THE MID-1950s till his death in 1970, U.S. officials worked hard to defeat Nasser. They finally succeeded by helping Israel deliver a shattering blow in the 1967 war that caused detriment to Egypt, to the Middle East, and to long-term Western interests, including national security losses on all sides. A core theme of this book is that the offensive policies of U.S. Cold War officials toward Egypt's Nasser in the 1950s sowed the seeds of the subsequent turmoil that roiled the Middle East.

No, I have not misread Nasser and do not exonerate him for turning Egypt into a dictatorship and suppressing any form of political dissent. Unlike Mossadegh, Nasser was not a democrat. But like Mossadegh, he was a developmentalist genuinely concerned about improving the dismal social and economic conditions under which most Egyptians lived, and he made strides in this direction. Nasser was not an ideologue, neither a Marxist nor a liberal democrat. He was an Egyptian nationalist who believed that the question of political independence from the West is critical to the question of development in the Arab world.

As for the question of democracy, it might have emerged in Egypt later on, as it did in South Korea and Taiwan, after the creation of a middle class and greater human development progress. As the sociologist S. N. Eisenstadt argues, modernizing societies like Egypt have their own specific journeys of modernity that have refuted the homogenizing and hegemonic assumptions of the Western program of modernity. Eisenstadt cautions against viewing the contemporary world, including the question of democracy, through the lens of the West's cultural program of modernity. He shows that developing countries have a multiplicity of ideological and institutional patterns that differ from those of the West.[1] The argument is worth contemplating and stating. The process of democratization and liberalization in Muslim-dominated societies cannot be unlinked from debates about the legacy of imperialism and the normative role of religion in government.[2]

Furthermore, it is worth mentioning that the Western states' own road to democracy had not been linear or peaceful—far from it. It had been blood-soaked, evolving over centuries and taking many forms.[3] There has also been democratic backsliding in many Western countries in the past two decades, including the United States

It is tempting to ask: What if America had listened to the hopes, concerns, and fears of postcolonial leaders who were protective of their independence and eager to gain full sovereignty and develop their countries? Nasser, the first Egyptian from a working-class background to lead his country, was positively disposed toward America and desired to build close relations with it after being dominated by Britain. He wanted to develop his country and lift the masses out of poverty with a strong developmentalist state, but he by no means wanted to build a communist society. In wooing Egypt, America could have gained a pivotal partner, not a client, in the heart of the Middle East. But the record shows that the United States wants clients, not partners, in the Middle East.

There is no straightforward causal link between the overthrow of Mohammed Mossadegh and the confrontation with Nasser in the 1950s and subsequent events. Rather, America's imperial impulse, arrogance, and aggressive actions in the early years of the global Cold War set off a chain of reactions and counterreactions that radically altered the direction of the region and the world. America's imperial outreach and militarism has persisted long after the end of the Cold War with devastating consequences in the Middle East. History is a chronicle of watersheds and turning points. The flash points in the Middle East during this era created geopolitical and social tsunamis whose repercussions reverberated near and wide and continue to haunt the Middle East today.

Peace with Israel

There was nothing inevitable about the escalation of the Arab-Israeli conflict in the late 1950s and 1960s. Nasser's original concerns were development and improving the well-being of millions of Egyptians, especially the *fellahin*, or peasants, who eked out a subsistence living. He eschewed confrontation and prioritized bread-and-butter issues. Like most Arabs, he viewed Israel as a colonial settler state, but his first priority was implementing economic and social reforms to solve Egypt's internal problems.

The relationship between Egypt and Israel soured because of America's refusal to provide Nasser with defensive weapons while France armed Israel to the teeth.[4] Responding to Israel's growing military might and aggression, Nasser had to seek arms from the Soviet Union, especially after repeated entreaties to Washington failed. The U.S. Cold Warriors underestimated Nasser's independent streak, losing Egypt and, with it, Middle East peace. Egypt was the culture capital of the Arab world, not just a geostrategic heavyweight. When Nasser rose to power, Egypt had the world's third-largest film industry, and Cairo was famously named "the Hollywood of the Middle East." Voice of the Arabs was the most prominent transnational Arab radio channel of the era, which was very influential among Arabs of all persuasions. Egyptian writers, artists, and educators nourished the minds of millions of people across the region. Nasser was not just the leader of the most militarily powerful and populous Arab country but the most popular of all Arab leaders.

Nasser was receptive to reaching a peaceful solution to the Arab-Israeli conflict that was based on United Nations principles as long as legitimate Palestinian rights were addressed. Far from being a warmonger, Nasser showed a certain moderation in regional and international affairs. There is every reason to believe that, with Egypt on board, the Palestinians and the other Arab states could have sat down with Israel and negotiated a just and lasting peace treaty.

At the time, America's leaders were less fettered by domestic politics and private interest lobbying groups when it came to dealing with Israel, and the United States could have been an honest broker bridging the Arab-Israeli divide. This was before the 1967 and 1973 wars made the Israeli-Palestinian conflict intractable. Both Arab and Israeli sides were led by secular and progressive nationalists, which made concessions easier. Today the religious far-right, which dominates in Israel, considers all the land sacred and thus nonnegotiable. Expanding Jewish settlements on the West Bank and occupied east Jerusalem have almost wrecked the proposed two-state framework and, with it, prosepcts for Israeli-Palestinian peace. This is a recipe for endless wars between Israel and its Palestinian and Arab neighbors.

Back then, Israeli leaders might not have been able to resist American pressure to negotiate. Israel had yet to develop a special relationship with America, so it was more vulnerable militarily and diplomatically. Conditions might have been ripe to strike a real deal of the century—not Trump's fake one—between Arabs and Israelis, paving the way for regional peace and stability.

Democratization also suffered. The Arab-Israeli conflict deepened political authoritarianism in some Arab countries by forcing Nasser and other Arab leaders to focus on security and regime survival over building state institutions that could have gradually managed political participation and power sharing. It gave the perfect excuse to strongmen such as Syria's Hafez al-Assad, Iraq's Saddam Hussein, Libya's Muammar Qaddafi, Sudan's Omar al-Bashir, and Iran's Ayatollah Khomeini to build up their police states and militarize their counties and the region. Israel also became a divisive issue in inter-Arab relations, intensifying the Arab cold war between two rival radical and conservative camps. Arab rulers outbid each other on Palestine in an attempt to gain popularity at home, which led to catastrophic decisions that harmed both the Palestine cause and Arab unity and security.

Israel's ongoing persecution of the Palestinians also poisoned Arab and Muslim perceptions of the Western states, sowing the seeds of nationalist and occasionally leftist, and as well as religious, radicalization and triggering a backlash against America. As I mentioned, the increasing anti-American sentiment in Arab and Muslim societies is organically linked to the escalation of Arab-Israeli hostilities and the consolidation of Israel's colonialization of Palestinian lands and its subsequent occupation of Egyptian, Syrian, and Jordanian territories. At a minimum, war could have been averted. If the United States had been a friend of both Egypt and Israel, the Six-Day War in June 1967 could have been prevented through robust diplomacy because Washington wouldn't allow two allies to go to war against each other.

The hoped-for peace dividends after the end of European imperialism in the 1940s never materialized. Instead, conflict, militarism, and economic mismanagement bankrupted Middle Eastern countries such as Egypt, Syria, and Iraq.

The Geostrategic Curse

The global Cold War played out on Middle Eastern streets and embroiled regional actors in endless rivalries and conflicts that weakened postcolonial states and drained their limited resources. Rather than building a strong, healthy, and equal relationship with Nasser, the U.S. Cold War warriors chose confrontation over compromise and dogmatism over pragmatism. In this sense, independence from colonial rule after World War II did not herald freedom, peace, and prosperity. Caught in the fierce rivalry between the two superpowers, newly emancipated Middle Eastern states faced a stark choice: join either the U.S.–led camp or the Soviet bloc. They were not allowed to be fully free and pursue a nonaligned foreign policy. Mossadegh and Nasser learned this at great cost.

For example, the United States set up a pan-Islamist dominated anti-Nasser Arab bloc led by Saudi Arabia in order to isolate and contain him. Nasser retaliated by targeting pro-Western Arab rulers and building another Arab bloc under his leadership. The result is that instead of focusing on state building, economic development, and gaining the trust of citizens and advancing political legitimacy, Arab rulers spent vast sums of money on augmenting their security forces and consolidating power. The civil wars in both

Yemen and Lebanon in the 1960s and the 1970s, respectively, could have been avoided or at least mitigated if inter-Arab rivalries had not heated up. Inter-Arab trade would have also increased substantially (much more than the paltry 10 percent of global trade that it now represents, and the Arabs might have succeeded in establishing more effective regional institutions.

Tellingly, it was American—not Soviet—animosity that paved the way for Soviet influence in the region and intensified geostrategic rivalries. After Nasser's refusal to join America's anticommunist crusade in the mid-1950s, the U.S. Cold Warriors confronted him and bled him by a million cuts, pushed him toward the socialist camp, and created an opening for the Soviet Union in the region.

The Eisenhower administration propped up fundamentalist Saudi Arabia as a counterweight to Nasser's semi-secular Arab nationalism. The choice to support Saudi Arabia politically and provide it with unconditional security guarantees allowed the kingdom to widely spread its pan-Islamist interpretation of Islam with long-term and far-reaching consequences on most of the Muslim world. Washington played a critical role in the emergence of these ideologies. The Six-Day War dealt a heavy blow to secular-leaning nationalists led by Nasser, whereas conservative religious activists like the Muslim Brothers, who were marginal to the politics of the region, received a new lease on life. The humiliation of the most powerful Arab power by a Jewish state was widely seen by many Muslims as God's revenge against secular Arab leaders who had forsaken God for godless ideologies like socialism and nationalism.

The 1967 war was a catalyst for conservative religious groups and pan-Islamists to gain new momentum across the Middle East. The dramatist and novelist Tawfiq al-Hakim poetically captured the sentiment of both the Arab elites and everyday citizens who were deeply and painfully jolted by "the nightmare of the defeat."[5] The ultraconservative pan-Islamist version of political Islam might not have dominated the regional landscape if the United States had not forged an unholy alliance with religiously conservative states and movements and if the Six-Day War had not occurred.

The post-independence surge of optimism that swept the region in the early 1950s was not rewarded with results but rather dashed by events. As feelings of hope and buoyancy receded, the region's peoples felt a bleak sense of loss and failure. The power-lessness that then took root in the public consciousness plays out tragically still, as we can see in the disenchantment of huge swathes of the population as well as the ability of extremist ideologies like those of Al-Qaeda and the Islamic State to capture support.

If the 1967 June war had not occurred, the October 1973 Arab-Israeli confrontation would not have occurred, either. And as a result, there might have been no Arab oil embargo, which caused skyrocketing oil prices, an inflationary crisis in the Western econo-mies, and significant effects on the global economy, all clearly demonstrating the links between the Middle East and the rest of the world.

Israel's occupation of the Palestinian territories after the 1967 war remains today the biggest obstacle to peace. Moreover, that fateful decision pushed new waves of Palestinian refugees to find shelter in neighboring countries and contributed to the destabiliza-tion of Lebanon. The subsequent Lebanese civil war in 1975, a confrontation that lasted for fifteen years and almost destroyed this beautiful, small, multicultural mosaic, might have never happened if Lebanon had been part of a peaceful and cooperative region and not surrounded by bullies intent on a zero-sum game.

If the Six-Day War had not shattered the Arab state system, Lebanon—the Arab world's center in terms of religious, ethnic, and social diversity and coexistence—might have avoided all-out civil strife. Lebanon and the region's destiny could have been radi-cally different. Peace dividends would have generated opportunity and prosperity. Hope would have replaced despair. The Middle East might not have imploded.

This alternative rosy picture is neither illusionary nor far-fetched. There is a thread that runs through the Middle East's tortured history from the mid-1950s till the mid-1970s. In the Middle East, everything is interconnected with everything else. History cannot be compartmentalized, segmented, and trivialized. This reconstruction of Egypt's modern history is worth consider-ing because it is empirically based and is taken for granted by the people of the region.

Beyond Egypt

Arguably, if the Eisenhower administration had accepted Nasser's nonalignment and provided developmental assistance, the United States could have won Egypt and peace in the region as well. As the most pivotal Arab country, Egypt could have been at peace with its neighbors and the world and more prosperous. With its focus on the home front, Egypt could have, over time, resembled South Korea or Japan in economic growth and vibrancy and perhaps even approximated Singapore's and Malaysia's illiberal democracies.

Like Mossadegh, Nasser prioritized development and industrialization. At the beginning of the 1950s, Egypt, Iraq, Lebanon, and other countries in the Middle East had median incomes similar to those of the Four Asian Tigers: Taiwan, Singapore, Hong Kong, and South Korea.[6] Egypt, like these East Asian countries, could have been part of a wealthy high-tech industrialized club. As an economic (non–oil producing) powerhouse, Egypt could have fueled growth in neighboring Arab countries and helped create the "Four Arab Tigers" (or perhaps they would have been dubbed "Falcons") with Iraq, Syria, and Lebanon. The Four Arab Tigers could have been as economically prosperous as their Asian counterparts—if not more so—given their proximity and cultural affinity to the world's biggest oil producers, their large populations, and their links to the European market. The comparison with South Korea is the most interesting. With a median income similar to Egypt's, South Korea was also under authoritarian rule, but economic development under American protection allowed the gradual growth of civil society and a vibrant middle class and set the basis for democracy to flourish by the mid-1980s.

Egypt was arguably the first non-Western country to begin its modernization and industrialization in the nineteenth century, decades before Japan.[7] Conscious of the need to catch up with Europe's technological superiority, Egypt's ruler Muhammad Ali (1805–1849) turned the country into a regional economic powerhouse linking the European, African, and Middle Eastern markets. Under his leadership, Egypt became an authority to be reckoned with. He modernized the armed forces along European lines, installed a centralized bureaucracy, reorganized the administration and the landholdings, and industrialized the country. Muhammad Ali sent training missions to Europe and replaced the fragmented Mamluk armed units with a standing national army consisting of Egyptian peasants, which at its peak counted 130,000 soldiers. He introduced the use of civil registers and statistics on a systematic scale to ensure that taxation and conscription ran smoothly.

Egypt was divided into ten administrative regions, each with its own governor responsible for law and order, conscription, and taxation. And at the core of this system were middle-level bureaucrats who were hired on the basis of merit (although the top government officials were still picked on the basis of kinship and relation to the ruling family). The goal was to centralize the country, in what we in modern terms would call state building. In other words, Muhammad Ali broadened the population's human capital, one of the key factors in Japan's miraculous economic revival after World War II. He changed the work patterns of peasants and upgraded Egyptian agriculture from one of sustenance to a cotton-exporting economy. The profits from the cotton exports were invested in textile factories, which then fed into the modernization of the military and development of infant industries, first by producing military uniforms as part of the modernization of the armed forces, and later by fabricating other textile goods.

Egypt under Muhammad Ali became so successful that he almost captured Istanbul, the heart of the Ottoman Empire. Intervention by the European powers rescued the Ottoman sultan from defeat not once but twice. Though Muhammad Ali's successors were unable to carry on his legacy, running up the country's debt with their lavish lifestyles and fixation on cotton, Muhammad Ali's reign is a testament to two important developments: first and foremost, Egypt's societal fabric had been centralized for centuries, which allowed for easier economic takeoff. Second, its historical role and geostrategic position—its location as the land link between Asia and Africa, its access to the Mediterranean economies, and its proximity to European markets—were just as strong a launching pad for economic growth in the nineteenth century as they would be in the twentieth.

Muhammad Ali's successors, however, were unable to continue their state-building project. Egypt's modernization attempt in the

nineteenth century was squashed by expansionist European powers. Driven by imperial economic interests and a militant foreign
policy, Britain invaded and occupied Egypt in 1882.[8] It took Egypt
more than seventy years to regain its independence. Nasser and his
Free Officers comrades were determined to right the wrongs of
British imperialism and industrialize the country. Yet Nasser's
twentieth-century modernization attempt met a fate somehow
similar to those of his nineteenth-century predecessors.

Of course, there is much more to the failed economic development in Egypt and Arab countries than the geostrategic rivalries,
imperialism, wars, and civil strife. Massive economic mismanagement and systemic corruption are key contributing factors. But
corruption exists everywhere; the costs of militarization, securitiza-
tion, and armed confrontation heavily weighed down the nascent
postcolonial economies of the Middle East and brought them to
the ground.

There is no guarantee that had U.S. policy been different,
Egypt would have developed successfully. The point of this book is
to theorize on possible alternative pathways that could have resulted had the international or regional context been different and
more conducive to development.

What Egypt and the Region Lost

Although no democrat, Nasser was a unifying and inspirational
leader in Egypt. Like Iran, a prosperous and strong Egypt at peace
with itself, its regional environment, and the world could have
been the rock the Arab world could have leaned on. To many people in Egypt and the Arab world, Nasser was a figure who genuinely wanted dignity for the man on the street. He was a man of
the people, authentic and in touch with the grassroots sentiments
of the streets. A stable and sovereign Egypt could have laid the
foundation for a stable and sovereign Arab world, and perhaps for
pluralism in the future. This was of course a foundation that came
with certain prerequisites: dignity, independence and territorial
sovereignty, and nonalignment.

Nasser struggled to gain full sovereignty and economic independence. But rather than building on this solid ground, the United

States decided to chip away at it, sometimes even for childish reasons such as the baseless, personal hatreds of the Eisenhower Cold War proponents. Or sometimes it was because of their simplistic black-and-white understandings of international relations that lacked any appreciation for the internal and regional context and the sordid experience Egypt had had with European powers in the nineteenth and early twentieth centuries.

American diplomats in Cairo had known better and had cautioned their seniors in Washington about the pitfalls of seeing Nasser through a global Cold War lens. As I mentioned in chapter 7, the U.S. ambassador to Egypt, Henry Byroade, repeatedly pointed out that Nasser, a man of his times, was a nonaligned leader and a champion of anticolonialism in the Global South. Byroade warned against focusing on Nasser's personality and failing to account for powerful currents like nationalism, nonalignment, and the desire for independence. Clearly aware of the internecine dynamics in the U.S. government, Byroade advised his superiors against accepting at face value intelligence reports about Nasser's destabilizing policies.

Byroade noted that the clash between U.S. and Egyptian interests could simply be explained by factors such as U.S. Cold War politics' lack of appeal to Nasser and his cohorts, who were motivated by local concerns such as opposition to colonialism, Western defence pacts, Israel, and adverse trade agreements. The U.S. ambassador noted that America's difficulties in the Middle East were not "primarily due to an ideological clash between our brand of democracy and Communism." The real threat, he said, stemmed from economic hardships and lack of development. The expansion of Russian influence in the Arab world, noted Byroade, came down to trade and commerce; Egypt's lack of hard currency made the subsidization of Russian trade highly attractive in such circumstances. For U.S. policy to succeed, it had to consider local concerns and fears, emphasized Byroade, who understood that Washington's confrontational and aggressive approach was counterproductive, especially given the fact that Nasser would not submit to pressure.[9]

If only the Cold Warriors in Washington had listened to the informed analysis of their ambassadors in the region, U.S.–Middle Eastern relations could have been built on better foundations, not on sand. Instead, as I argued previously, the Eisenhower administration played a pivotal role in radically transforming U.S. relations with two key Middle Eastern countries, Iran and Egypt, and the history of the region itself.

The Eisenhower years, from 1953 to 1961, weaponized the global Cold War, and its offensive and aggressive actions in the Middle East became the norm and model for future administrations. The language of force and the threat of force and the use of force, coupled with economic sanctions, have become defining features of U.S. foreign policy toward the region ever since. The disastrous U.S. war on terror and the invasions and occupation of Afghanistan in 2001 and Iraq in 2003 are cases in point.

A chain of events that started in the early 1950s influenced the region's political and economic development. Today's grim situation in the Middle East could have been very different if instead of seeing the world in black and white, good and evil, America had been willing to tolerate other states that did not see eye to eye with it on every foreign policy issue and economic system. There was no reason to enforce ideological uniformity on countries that had different national priorities, different historical experiences, and were at different development stages from the United States. A more flexible and dynamic approach could have been more effective in co-opting newly decolonized states and their leaders who had been naturally disposed to the young rising Western superpower.

Iran's Mossadegh and Egypt's Nasser had looked to America for support and friendship. For Nasser, as for many leaders coming to power in the wake of decolonization, multiparty democracy was not a priority. Countries impoverished by decades of colonial pillages saw modernization of their societies by building a strong developmental state as the best way to lift millions out of their misery. In their opinion, democracy might have waited. Surely, democracy had waited for a long time in the West, as the historian Mark Mazower notes, inventing and reinventing itself through war and other forms of social upheaval.[10]

Nasser knew that the C.I.A. had used domestic opposition in countries like Iran, Guatemala, and Congo to carry out regime change. He correctly feared that the 1956 Anglo-French-Israeli invasion of Egypt was designed to get rid of him. Similarly, the U.S.–backed Bay of Pigs invasion of Cuba against Fidel Castro in April

1961 reinforced a tendency among postcolonial leaders to build authoritarian police states and to justify their choice by blaming foreign plots against them.

A different Middle East could have emerged if Washington's Cold Warriors had not driven the nationalists Mossadegh and Nasser off the cliff. America could have reflected on its own history and birth from revolution and resistance against British colonialism and recognized common aspirations and parallels with postcolonial states in the Middle East and the Global South in general. These nascent and fragile states were struggling for self-determination, independence, and dignity, just as America's George Washington and his followers had two hundred years earlier. At peace with themselves and genuinely independent, Iran and Egypt could have become successful models of political and economic development in the region, stabilizing forces in an area that had been given a new postcolonial life.

While a different Middle East might not have been an oasis of democracy, it could have been more peaceful, stable, prosperous, and tolerant. Perhaps the social and economic conditions needed for future democratic transition could have been created by a more forward-looking and progressive American foreign policy. The region would not have been plagued by political authoritarianism and violence and revolution as it is today. The Middle East economies could have resembled, to a lesser degree, those of the stunningly successful Four Asian Tigers. Economic growth and prosperity would have reduced domestic instability and interstate conflict. A large middle class would have steered the region toward active political participation and an open society. Political authoritarianism might not have grown deep roots in Middle Eastern soil.

At a minimum, the situation would not have been economically and politically grim and bleak. Young men and women could not have been so desperate to flee their homes to distant lands in the hope of a better life. Economic opportunities could have taken the wind out of the sail of revolutionaries and extremists. Hope would have replaced despair. A true grasp of the motivations and madness that animated the misguided actions of the 1950s, leaving wounds that remain open today, will shed light on the path out of the quagmire.

There is no inevitability about conflict in, among, or with the countries of the Middle East—not ancient hatreds, religious differences, or some chaos inherent to the region. These and other false roots of division and violence only mask the truth. Far from being caused by some mystifying "oriental" (or even "Abrahamic") tendency toward entropy, the simple fact is that greed, arrogance, and a thirst for power and control of the region's resources are mainly to blame. And the clear lesson is that far from achieving any material gain, status, or influence, these drivers only lead to costs: in human progress, prosperity, peace, and life.

Analyzing this history of intrigue, secret alliances, devastating betrayals, and sudden reversals of fortune is more than cinematic in its scope; it is a guide to what went wrong and where we have been, and the map to a better future.

CHAPTER ELEVEN

From Iran to Guatemala

The Fabrication of a Communist Threat

THE SUCCESS OF THE C.I.A. coup against Iran's legitimately elected leader, Mohammad Mossadegh, cemented President Eisenhower's trust in the spy agency's ability to catalyze regime change overseas.[1] The C.I.A.'s previous covert forays in Italy, Syria, Ukraine, and Albania in the late 1940s had neither the ambition nor the impact of its ouster of Mossadegh in August 1953. That was the game changer that altered the course of Iran's contemporary history; its repercussions continue to haunt us today. The 1949 C.I.A.–sponsored coup in Syria might have been successful, but that country was not nearly as geostrategically important as Iran by any metric: population size, wealth, natural resources, or developmental potential. Italy was important, but there the agency engaged mainly in mounting a disinformation campaign and financing conservative parties in parliament. Similarly, the C.I.A.'s attempt to intervene militarily in Albania was one of the Cold War's best-kept secrets—and for good reason, since it was a failure that resulted in the execution of more than three hundred of its covert agents there.

Riding a wave of confidence from its success in Iran, the Eisenhower administration outsourced U.S. foreign policy to the C.I.A., which, in turn, embarked on a campaign of assassination and terror against nationalist leaders who were perceived as a threat to U.S. interests. The Cold Warriors wanted to tame assertive nationalists who were viewed as less than 100 percent loyal to the West, who showed an independent streak in the international arena, and who pursued economic development that was not completely wide open to the kind of exploitation that calls to mind the *Open Veins of Latin America*, the vivid title chosen by the Uruguayan writer Eduardo Galeano for his seminal book.[2]

The Global Strategy of Eisenhower's Cold War Warriors

Enforcing loyalty to American foreign policy and its open global economy doctrine, the C.I.A. executed the wishes of President Eisenhower and his Cold Warriors' cabinet. The Eisenhower administration pursued an offensive realist foreign policy strategy: sabotage, assassination, military intervention, and subversion of democratic processes were in the C.I.A.'s toolkit.

Far from constructing the foundations for democracy, these instruments only stoked sectarian tensions and sowed chaos in newly independent nations. After Iran, the Cold Warriors roamed the map, from Guatemala to Syria, from Indonesia to Cuba, from Cambodia to the Republic of Congo, the Dominican Republic, Brazil, Chile, Iraq, and beyond. Down the decades they went, landing in the 1960s through the 1970s in Vietnam, where they precipitated the most catastrophic military engagement in modern U.S. history, which resulted in untold casualties and trauma while destabilizing large parts of Southeast Asia. Heavy financial and human losses never diminished the enthusiasm of the Cold Warriors for assassination, coercion, and covert action to effect regime change. They targeted leaders called "fanatical"—often for the offense of standing up for the interests of their peoples against foreign interference and exploitation—leaders like Mohammad Mossadegh, Gamal Abdel Nasser, Guatemalan President Jacobo Árbenz, and the Syrian Shukri al-Quwatli.

Originating during the Cold War and rationalized by it, this political posture persisted even after the fall of the Berlin Wall in 1989, when Egypt and the Gulf countries jumped on Washington's bandwagon. Washington's interference persevered through the Gulf War in 1990–91 and its invasion and occupation of Afghanistan in 2001 and Iraq in 2003. Those events demonstrated America's determination to dominate the Middle East and control its petroleum with no regard for international law or the wishes of the people of the region.[3] Certainly, beyond geographical location, Iraq's Saddam Hussein the dictator and Iran's Mohammad Mossadegh the democrat had little in common, but both were toppled because they challenged American-Western hegemony in the region.

The intensity and persistence of Western (and foreign) intervention in the Middle East as a legacy of the global Cold War is a central thesis of this book. From the colonial moment to the Cold War and post–Cold War period, the Middle East has never been left alone to chart its own development. The region's black gold, raw commodities, strategic waterways, markets, and surplus cash from oil sales have proved too tempting for Western powers to resist. This toxic legacy crushed nascent pluralistic experiments and propped up autocrats throughout the region, altering the political trajectory of the region and laying the foundation for authoritarianism.

America's Cold Warriors weaponized the threat of Soviet communism against nationalist leaders like Mossadegh and Nasser, who pursued state-directed economic development and a nonaligned foreign policy as well. These postcolonial leaders sparked America's wrath by daring to challenge Western corporate interests and moving —sometimes because they were pushed by all-or-nothing dictates from the neocolonialists—to socialism.

Reconsidering this aspect of the global Cold War shines a bright and revealing light on how Western powers shattered newly decolonized states' early hopes for political autonomy and economic independence. The economy, society, and governance in vast parts of the Global South were significantly weakened by spiraling geostrategic rivalries and deepening authoritarianism.

It is time to zoom out for a moment, to see the Middle East as one region in the world. Yes, it has had more than its share of foreign intervention, but its experience is not unique. The icy flames of the Cold War conflagration spread to other regions as well. The activities of the United States were waged through multiple battles on multiple fronts in what amounted to a global war designed to roll back Soviet communism and secure the dominance of liberal capitalism. It was only a year following the ouster of Mossadegh when Guatemalan President Jacobo Árbenz succumbed to a similar fate.

For a perspective on how the events that characterized the Middle East were manifest in other parts of the developing world, one need only examine the case of Guatemala. The C.I.A. took a page from its 1953 coup in Iran to follow that playbook during its intervention in faraway Guatemala in 1954. Although the events unfolded on different continents, when the United States over-threw Árbenz, the justifications echoed those heard during the coup in Iran. The consequences were as devastating, though more cata-strophic from a human rights perspective in the Guatemalan case.

Far from exhaustive, this chapter provides a comparative per-spective that helps readers get a glimpse of the convergence of the Cold War thinking and corporate interests at the heart of American foreign policy in the early decades of the Cold War. As I mentioned in previous chapters, the Dulles brothers—Secretary of State John Foster Dulles and C.I.A. Director Allen Dulles—personified this marriage between Cold War politics and private financial interests. While the Dulles brothers were key decision makers in Washing-ton, John Foster Dulles also served on the board of directors of corporations with vast international economic interests.

Cold War hawks started out supporting Árbenz's presidency, but that all ended when he dared to embark on a program of land reforms that threatened the dominance of the U.S.–owned United Fruit Company there. This U.S. multinational corporation was comparable to the Anglo-Iranian Oil Company (AIOC) in Iran. It would be difficult to overstate the influence of United Fruit, which was the biggest employer in Central America and the largest landowner in Guatemala. The power imbalance between the coun-try and the company was extreme: United Fruit was a powerful, independent, multinational corporation backed by the United States, the world's preeminent superpower. Guatemala was a cash-crop-producing Central American country wedged in Washing-ton's backyard.

Jacobo Árbenz and Guatemala's Aspirations

Like the AIOC in Iran, United Fruit had an economic stranglehold on Guatemala. Both companies reaped huge profits while not paying a fair share of taxes. With almost no tax burden, United Fruit had geographic gold, owning the only port to the Atlantic Ocean, Puerto Barrios.[4] The government of Guatemala lacked the power of United Fruit, effectively a state within the state wielding more sway than the authorities. A simple measure of the transnational corporation's dominance is the bottom line: by 1950, the company's annual profits were $65 million, fully twice the revenue of the Guatemalan government.[5]

The parallel with Iran becomes clear with an analogy: oil is to land. Mossadegh's nationalization of the oil industry was met with covert U.S. military intervention, whereas Árbenz undertook agrarian reforms and land redistribution. These undermined United Fruit's monopoly as the country's largest landowner and employer. The Guatemalan dictator Jorge Ubico had been a willing partner to the neocolonialists; before being overthrown in 1941, he sought to suppress wages, going so far as asking United Fruit to pay its workers only fifty cents a day to prevent other workers from demanding higher wages. Known as Central America's Napoleon, Ubico sided with a multinational corporation against the interests of his people. Ubico was not just avaricious; he was cruel. He ascended to power with the United States' backing in 1931, a time of economic turmoil in Guatemala following the New York Stock Exchange crash. His response was to adopt a system of debt slavery and forced labor so there would be plenty of cheap workers for United Fruit and coffee plantations. Far from securing rights for these exploited Guatemalans, he passed laws that made it legal for landowners to practice "disciplinary" executions of unruly workers.[6] "I am like Hitler," he said with twisted pride. "I execute first and ask questions later."[7] In addition to giving away vast swaths of land to United Fruit along with tax exemptions, thereby creating enclave economies within the Guatemalan national economy, Ubico allowed the United States to establish military bases in the country.[8]

The Guatemalan people rose up against this injustice. Schoolteachers led the protests in mid-1944, when World War II set in motion a severe economic crisis while there was an influx of Salvadoran revolutionaries who had fled a botched revolution in their country.[9] Ubico tried an iron fist, declaring martial law and ordering the police to shoot the protestors. But this failed to stop the protests, which instead gained momentum. About a week later, Ubico was forced to resign. Mass celebrations swelled in the streets of Guatemala.[10]

On his way out, Ubico appointed a three-general military junta that included Federico Ponce Vaides, who took over its leadership. The press remained restricted, the police brutal, and the justice system arbitrary. The junta was a victim of its own infighting as its component political factions jockeyed for power and soon lost legitimacy.

Among the coup plotters was Jacobo Árbenz, who fought a long battle of political intrigues before assuming the presidency in a landslide electoral victory almost seven years later, when he was still less than forty years old. Árbenz was the son of a German-Swiss migrant who had arrived in Guatemala in 1901 and married a middle-class Latina woman who gave birth to their son Jacobo in 1913. Their home was comfortable and their income secure, so Jacobo enjoyed a relatively tranquil life—until trouble hit: his father, who ran a pharmacy, became addicted to morphine. When his neglected business went bankrupt, that was the end of Árbenz's dream of attending university. With higher education blocked by its prohibitive cost, Árbenz enlisted in the military academy, where he succeeded exceptionally well, graduating as a "first sergeant"— one of only six cadets to earn that distinction for two decades.[11]

Power and luxury awaited Árbenz if only he had accepted the status quo, which was marked by stark social and economic stratification. Supported by the military, in which he had spent his whole working life, he could easily have ignored and even trampled on the urban proletariat, who were weak, and the rural communities, which were barely mobilized. But Árbenz reached beyond his own comfort and circle to embrace a progressive vision that included a sense of duty to better the lot of the poor, particularly the peasants living in squalid poverty. His greatest achievement was the first genuine agrarian reform in Central America. Árbenz embodied a Greek tragedy: "The more he accomplished, the closer he came to his destruction and the destruction of his dream."[12]

Árbenz was sympathetic toward the country's communists, viewing them as far less interested in lining their own pockets and more in instituting broader social reforms than his military comrades. He saw merit in the teachings of Marx and Lenin, and he was curious about the Soviet Union, for the very obvious reason that its main global adversary, the United States, had caused many decades of harm to the Guatemalan people.[13] At the same time, he had an independent and pragmatic perspective; when he took office, he acknowledged that agrarian reforms had priority over an idealized and speculative socialist revolution.[14]

Standing before a cheering and ecstatic crowd buzzing with nationalist fervor on March 15, 1951, newly elected President Jacobo Árbenz, with the Guatemalan presidential sash draped over his shoulder, reiterated the three fundamental objectives of his presidency:

> To convert our country from a dependent nation with a semi-colonial economy to an economically independent country; to convert Guatemala from a backward country with a predominantly feudal economy into a modern capitalist state; and to make this transformation in a way that will raise the standard of living of the great mass of our people. . . . Foreign capital will always be welcome as long as it adjusts to local conditions, remains always subordinate to Guatemalan laws, cooperates with the economic development of the country, and strictly abstains from intervening in the nation's social and political life.[15]

Nothing about Árbenz's pledges signaled a die-hard communist. The United States, a country borne of a colonial struggle with Great Britain, should have heard in Árbenz's vow an echo of the American Founding Fathers, though seemingly less protectionist. No mention of communism, no salutes to the Soviet Union, just a Guatemalan patriot declaring that Guatemala would serve its own people, not foreign corporations. Right from the start, Árbenz declared his support for transforming Guatemala into a modern capitalist state.[16]

The historians Stephen Schlesinger and Stephen Kinzer pointed out that Árbenz "was not a dictator, he was not a crypto-communist," describing him as a democratic socialist and a Guatemalan national-ist.[17] Neither Árbenz nor his government had flirted with commu-nism or had close ties to the Soviet Union. Guatemala's small Communist Party was not represented in Árbenz's cabinet, though a handful of communists were appointed to lower-level government positions.[18]

According to a report from mid-1948 titled "Communism in Guatemala," by Milton K. Wells, first secretary of the American embassy in Guatemala, the number of communists was estimated at a mere two hundred of a total population of around 3 million.[19] This sense of proportionality was completely lost on Secretary of State John Foster Dulles and his brother, Allen Dulles. Where Guatemalans saw a compassionate leader, the Dulles brothers sus-pected him of having a hidden agenda. Árbenz may have publicly embraced capitalism, but in the eyes of the U.S. government, he was a communist and a Soviet sympathizer bent on undermining American hegemony in Central America. Looking for pretexts, U.S. officials complained about the minute of silence that the Gua-temalan Congress observed in respect for Stalin after he died in March 1953, and the fact that a government-connected newspaper had carried a story about alleged U.S. use of bioweapons in Korea.

Guatemala's Coup in the Making

This paranoia was characteristic of Washington's foreign policy during the early decades of the Cold War, when U.S. leaders con-flated communism with the nationalism upheld by Iran's Mossa-degh, Guatemala's Árbenz, and Egypt's Nasser. For the Eisenhower Cold Warriors, there was not even a sliver of light between asser-tive nationalist leaders opting for semiclosed economic develop-ment and pursuing "neutralism" in foreign policy, on the one hand, and Soviet communism on the other. There were only two choices: with us or against us.

Eisenhower's predecessor, President Harry Truman, stopped providing arms to Guatemala in 1951 while propping up its hostile neighbors, Honduras and Nicaragua, with weapons and military technology. Eisenhower's administration went further by imposing a partial naval quarantine on Guatemala reminiscent of the British

naval blockade of Iran before the 1953 coup. Árbenz was out-
flanked by hostile neighbors. Feeling besieged, he fell back on the
same strategy as Egypt's Nasser, turning eastward to purchase arms
from Czechoslovakia, a Soviet satellite state, in order to defend his
regime. The weapons shipment was delivered by the Scandinavian
cargo ship MS *Alfhem*, thus bypassing America's naval quarantine
of Guatemala.[20]

It was the first time a Soviet bloc country had shipped arms to
the Americas—and its unintended effect was to boost the American
disinformation campaign aimed at portraying Guatemala as a communist beachhead in the United States' backyard. For the Cold
Warriors, this was a boon. A founding C.I.A. officer and the head
of its clandestine operations at the time, Frank Wisner, was initially
upset that the U.S. Navy had not intercepted the arms cargo, but
he then realized that the shipment of weapons was exactly the excuse the C.I.A. needed to intervene.[21] Following the MS *Alfhem's*
evasion of America's naval quarantine of Guatemala and successful
delivery of arms, the U.S. Navy's Caribbean Sea Frontier enforced
a full-scale naval blockade of Guatemala, by both air and sea. The
U.S. Navy stopped all ships and searched them, a clear breach of
international maritime laws.[22]

In 1952 the C.I.A. developed Operation PBFortune to depose
Árbenz through subversion, proxy war, and other violent means.
But this misguided plot was not immediately executed because
Secretary of State Dean Acheson believed that if the truth came
out, it would hurt America's standing in Latin America.[23] As it had
in Mossadegh's case, the Truman administration did not consent to
the C.I.A.'s plan to overthrow Árbenz. It stopped short—despite
having laid out the expansive doctrine of rollback of Soviet communism in 1950–51—and in what could have amounted to a self-
fulfilling prophesy declared the Árbenz administration communist.
This restraint on the part of Truman officials did not continue with
their successors in the Eisenhower administration.[24]

The very fact that the C.I.A designed and instigated action on
Operation PBFortune showed how the agency was going beyond
its mandate to gather and analyze intelligence to take on executive
policy making. The C.I.A.'s powers would expand further in the
coming Eisenhower administration and under the influence of

Cold Warriors like the Dulles brothers. The Eisenhower administration's national security policy conceptualized the Soviet Union as an expansionist power representing an existential threat to the United States, and it rationalized covert military intervention despite death, economic devastation, and other potential negative outcomes.[25]

Compared to its predecessor, the Eisenhower administration was far more inclined to take risks, in terms of both the human toll and reputational costs, to tame assertive nationalist leaders in the developing world. The condescension of the Cold Warriors was extreme. Allen Dulles pointed out how dependent Guatemala was on the United States for its trade and chastised the Central American country for having "[flouted] us and consistently got away with it. It is time they were brought to realize that this could not continue."[26]

There was broad intellectual support in the United States for these coups in developing countries. Rather than finding legitimacy in developing countries' aspirations for independence and control over their destinies, the *New York Times* found fault. In an editorial on the 1953 C.I.A.–sponsored coup in Iran, the Gray Lady scolded would-be leaders and their people: "Underdeveloped countries with rich resources now have an object lesson in the heavy cost that must be paid by one of their number which goes berserk with fanatical nationalism. It is perhaps too much to hope that Iran's experience will prevent the rise of Mossadeghs in other countries, but the experience may at least strengthen the hands of the more reasonable and far-seeing leaders."[27]

Picking up the thread of this narrative, the C.I.A prepared a memorandum titled "The Communist Situation in Guatemala," which included both a budget and a plan to overthrow Árbenz. Painting Guatemala as a communist menace, the agency offered its own brand of condescending pseudopsychology, describing the country as suffering from an "anti-foreign inferiority complex of the 'Banana Republic.' " With blithe contempt for truth, the memo proposed that the C.I.A. achieve the collection of evidence of communist subversion in the country "or fabrication of same."[28] As they had been in their antidemocratic operation in Iran, the Cold Warriors were prepared to depose Árbenz at the cost not only of

Guatemala's blooming democratic process but also of American democracy by misleading the U.S. public about the communist menace in Guatemala.

An all-out propaganda war against Árbenz shifted into high gear. C.I.A. operatives depicted the Guatemalan government as "Communist dominated," charged that the laborers were "organized according to communistic methods," and characterized its relations with neighboring countries as "Communist subversive activities."[29] Only problem? No evidence. Secretary of State Dulles admitted as much to the Brazilian ambassador to the United States, João Carlos Muniz, saying that it would be "impossible to produce evidence clearly tying the Guatemalan Government to Moscow."[30] Two months later, Dulles asked the U.S. embassy in Honduras to come up with evidence that showed attacks against the United Fruit Company in Honduras were sparked by Guatemalan communists. The embassy found "few facts, convicting and convincing evidence scarce," that Guatemala was involved in the attacks.[31]

Even the C.I.A.'s own budget and plan to overthrow Árbenz acknowledged the Guatemalan leaders' legitimate, democratic mandate and widespread popularity, pointing out that "the present Árbenz government commands substantial popular support in spite of evidence of opposition in the capital."[32] Despite repeated efforts to manufacture incriminating evidence, the Dulles brothers and their enablers could not prove that the Guatemalan leader was a Soviet stooge. Árbenz was a democratically elected president who had carried out reforms popular among Guatemalans—and even the C.I.A.'s and State Department's own analysis of Árbenz confirmed these facts.

The truth was as simple as it was undeniable: Guatemalans welcomed Árbenz's agrarian reform law, particularly his defiance of United Fruit, which they knew was an impediment to progress. The analogy between United Fruit and the AIOC did not extend to their respective regions. The Middle East was considered by the United States to be an immediate front line of the global Cold War; Latin America didn't earn that dubious honor until the rise of Cuba's Fidel Castro in 1959. It is on this basis that President Eisenhower justified the meager U.S. foreign aid to Latin America, less than 1 percent of the total foreign aid budget. "Countries like

Burma, Thailand, and the remaining parts of Indochina are directly open to assault. This does not apply in South America," Eisenhower wrote in a letter to his brother in 1954.[33] The normally adventure-prone C.I.A. agreed that "the [Soviet] bloc leadership has been reluctant to allocate to Latin America any substantial proportion of the bloc's total political, economic, and propaganda resources devoted to foreign penetration activities."[34] The horrific proxy wars that engulfed the continent at untold human cost were yet to come, their omens faintly visible in how the United States—a putative champion of democracy—hacked at its roots in Guatemala.

Anticommunist Crusade or Corporate Greed?

The question is: Why did the United States intervene in a country where there was no evidence that communists would infiltrate or that the Soviets were investing significant resources? The answer, in a word: greed.

The U.S. government opposed Árbenz's project of modernization, particularly his agrarian reform bill, which transferred uncultivated land from large landowners and corporations to landless peasants who could then cultivate their own farms.[35] The first to be affected by this reform bill was United Fruit, the biggest landowner of uncultivated land in Guatemala. The Árbenz government did not just seize land; it paid for it. From mid-1953 to mid-1954, it offered United Fruit twice what the company had paid for 400,000 acres of uncultivated land.[36] This was the price at which United Fruit had valued the land, but Dulles's State Department voiced outrage and demanded more than ten times the compensation.[37]

Leaving aside quantifiable factors, the move effected a fundamental power shift in favor of marginalized Guatemalans, especially indigenous people. Árbenz's agrarian reforms raised living standards for many thousands of peasant families. Agricultural productivity and the cultivated area also increased.[38] By June 1954, one-sixth of the population had received a portion of the 1.4 million acres that had been redistributed.[39] Attention to workers' rights was part of the package. The New Labor Code effectively ended Guatemala's supply of cheap, ready-to-be-exploited land and workers.[40] Under Ubico, striking had been punishable by death; Árbenz enshrined it as a civil right. Like Mossadegh and Nasser, Árbenz was an independent-minded nationalist leader. His agrarian reforms put the interests of the people he served above those of U.S.–backed private interests. He mustered the political courage to pursue a progressive national developmental policy that his predecessors hadn't even contemplated.

The Dulles brothers reacted as they had against Mossadegh, fearing that leaders putting national interests first could create a precedent and inspire similar movements.[41] They saw the state-led land distribution as a threat to U.S. interests. The power of a smear was not lost on United Fruit, which launched a lobbying campaign in the United States to depict the Guatemalan government as a communist menace. Lobbying the Dulles brothers, it also spent more than $50,000 in an effort to convince both the U.S. foreign policy establishment and public opinion of the need to oust Árbenz.[42]

Whereas in the Middle East, the key drivers behind Dulles brothers' actions were visceral anticommunism and blind faith in American exceptionalism, in Central America, "Washington's backyard," they had additional corporate ties.[43] John Foster Dulles had previously represented United Fruit as a lawyer. He and his brother Allen allegedly owned a significant amount of stock in the United Fruit Company.[44] Their political ideology aligned perfectly with their personal profit. John Foster Dulles personally drafted the legal rationale for United Fruit to exploit Guatemalan workers and to own huge tracts of land. While working at Sullivan and Cromwell, one of the biggest and most powerful law firms in the world, Dulles was "reputed to be the author of the actual concessions which the firm negotiated" with Guatemala, according to a former United Fruit Company vice president, Thomas McCann.[45]

The transnational corporation had other ties to the government; the list of its top former executives of the era reads like a who's who of the Eisenhower administration: they included John Moors Cabot, assistant secretary of state for Inter-American Affairs, and the former company president Henry Cabot Lodge Jr., American ambassador to the United Nations. During his time as senator from Massachusetts, Lodge was called "the senator from United Fruit." The president's national security advisor, Robert Cutler, was a former member of United Fruit's board of directors.

Ann Whitman, the wife of United Fruit's publicity director, Ed Whitman, was Eisenhower's private secretary.[46] With United Fruit so deeply embedded within the political life of the Eisenhower administration, is it any wonder that the administration was so willing to remove Árbenz from power?[47]

Dusting off Operation PBFortune: Operation PBSuccess

Eisenhower's embrace of covert operations was long in the making. As the Allied commander in World War II, Eisenhower saw the positive results that efficient intelligence could produce, such as deciphering the German Enigma code. Eisenhower viewed covert operations as "humanitarian" and never considered the "long-term effects these operations might have," imagining them as almost "bloodless."[48]

So it was that in August 1953 President Eisenhower authorized Operation PBSuccess, with the explicit aim of overthrowing Árbenz, the same month as the C.I.A.–sponsored coup that removed Mossadegh from power. The ramifications of that authorization would cascade down the decades, costing tens of thousands of lives and dealing a death blow to the nascent Guatemalan democratic process. And the reverberations echoed beyond the borders of Guatemala. The C.I.A. assassination manuals that were prepared for the operation later served as a template for other covert missions, including those in Syria.[49]

At the time—the early 1950s—the C.I.A. was learning by trial and error how to carry out covert operations; assassination, subversion, psychological warfare, and propaganda were all in its toolbox. The lessons learned from the C.I.A.–led coups in Iran in 1953 and Guatemala in 1954 were applied to other theaters across the developing world. The C.I.A. sponsored the training of more than 1,500 foreign mercenaries to be part of the Army of Liberation, led by Carlos Castillo Armas, the soon-to-be president of Guatemala.[50] But this paramilitary force was never intended to fight, because it could not defeat the Guatemalan military; its purpose was just to sit around and serve as the fake rebel force. The agency thus employed psychological warfare and propaganda to destabilize the government and undermine it from within.

Washington's campaign to overthrow the Árbenz government required the harmonization of overt and covert foreign policy. The Eisenhower administration overtly pressured the Organization of American States in March 1954 to add "Intervention of International Communism in the American Republics" to the agenda of its meeting, a move targeting Guatemala. Fearing the loss of America's foreign aid and the possibility of intervention in their own internal affairs, all Latin American countries, with the exception of Guatemala, voted for the motion.[51] The United States successfully cast Guatemala in a communist light, out of step with the rest of the region.

Covertly, the C.I.A. used one of the strongest disinformation tools in its arsenal: a radio station broadcasting from a mobile transmitter called the Voice of Liberation. In what would become a standard playbook, this radio transmission exaggerated the strength of the C.I.A.–sponsored rebel movement, its military victories, and how close it was to seizing the capital. It also blasted anticommunist propaganda twice a day, demoralizing Guatemalan soldiers and creating unrest and instability within the country's cities.[52] The coup was to be carried out on three fronts. First, the plotters planned to assassinate key officials in government to sow discord and chaos in the country and to shock the population. Second, the Eisenhower administration created a diplomatic team that could exert external pressure on Árbenz. Third, the C.I.A.'s psychological warfare exaggerated the military victories of the troops on the ground in order to deepen the demoralization of the Árbenz government.

The invasion of Guatemala was led by Castillo Armas, who went on to achieve his ambition of ascending to the presidency after the coup. A far-right authoritarian military officer, Castillo Armas was born into a lower middle-class family and broke with the central government after his anticommunist patron, Colonel Francisco Arana, Árbenz's main rival for the presidency, died in a shoot-out in 1949 against then-president Juan José Arévalo's supporters. Accused of plotting a coup against the central government, Colonel Arana was killed in mysterious circumstances. After Árbenz's election to the presidency in 1951, Castillo Armas was discharged from the military. He was running a grocery store to make a living when growing discontent led him to conspire with other right-wing officers to overthrow the Árbenz government.[53]

The C.I.A. was along for the ride. Castillo Armas first made contact with the agency in 1950, when he was plotting a coup and attempting to acquire arms from Nicaragua and the Dominican Republic.[54] After the coup failed, Castillo Armas was imprisoned for a year but eventually bribed his way out of jail and fled to Honduras. The C.I.A. contacted Castillo Armas later and asked him to play a leading role in the Truman administration's Operation PB-Fortune. The name proved ironic. The C.I.A. called off the operation but still provided Castillo Armas with a weekly $3,000 retainer to maintain a small paramilitary force and to keep him from taking any premature action.[55]

In 1953 the Eisenhower administration asked Castillo Armas to lead a coup against Árbenz and reinstate a pro-American regime in Guatemala. The invasion force consisted of a single standard battalion—fewer than 500 men—although the United States had trained 1,725 guerrillas.[56] They had the backing of sophisticated psychological warfare as well as American-supplied jet fighters operating out of Honduras. Despite this outside support, the invasion force faced resistance and endured significant setbacks. For example, a force of 122 men, or a quarter of the invasion force, attacked the small frontier town of Zapaca, only to be defeated by a garrison of just 30 Guatemalan soldiers who killed or captured all but 30 of the invaders.[57] While Voice of Liberation was blasting propaganda claims of a large fifth column just waiting to strike deep behind the rebel frontier, peasants and working Guatemalans, on their own initiative, aided the Guatemalan government by putting up roadblocks and supplying army personnel with food.[58]

Despite enjoying popular support and military successes on the battlefield, the Árbenz government experienced internal strife as a result of fear of provoking neighboring Honduras or the United States into a full-scale invasion. Pressed by the Americans, including Ambassador John Peurifoy, and making it clear that the war would continue until Árbenz was gone, the Guatemalan army splintered, and one faction struck a deal with Castillo Armas that forced Árbenz to resign and seek political asylum at the Mexican embassy.

Unlike Iran, which descended into political authoritarianism after the ouster of Mossadegh in 1953, Guatemala was plunged into a thirty-six-year civil war that cost the lives of over 200,000 people in a country whose population was 4.1 million at the start of this epoch of death and destruction.[59]

It was not until 1999 that declassified U.S. documents exposed the C.I.A.'s involvement in Árbenz's removal from power, including the arming of local paramilitaries while the U.S. Navy blockaded Guatemala. As in Iran, the C.I.A.–sponsored coup in Guatemala dramatically altered the trajectory of the state and society in this most populous country in Central America. Before the coup, the Guatemalan people had seen profound improvements affecting their rights, laws, dignity, and independence. As they had in Iran, the Cold Warriors derailed a nascent pluralistic experiment that could have blossomed into a full-fledged democracy in Latin America. The communist threat in Guatemala, as it was in Iran, was grossly exaggerated. Árbenz might have been sympathetic to socialism, but his explicit aim was to build a "modern capitalist economy," not a communist utopia.

Like Mossadegh and Nasser, Árbenz was first and foremost a nationalist who mobilized national resources for the benefit of his people. Promoting inclusive economic progress and demanding that a powerful multinational corporation, United Fruit, treat Guatemalan workers with fairness and dignity, Árbenz bore the brunt of American power. The Cold Warriors were fundamentally angered by Árbenz's independent political orientation. Despite their repeated efforts to gather dirt on Árbenz and depict him as a danger to the Americas, U.S. officials could not link him to Soviet communism.

Guatemala and the Global Cold War

In Guatemala as in Iran, the Cold Warriors used the menace of communism to topple independent nationalist leaders who pursued inclusive development that threatened the vast economic and corporate interests of the United States and its Western allies. Both Mossadegh and Árbenz showed the courage to challenge the imperial interests of the Western powers, particularly the United

States and Britain, and paid dearly for their actions. And in both cases, the C.I.A.–sponsored coups aimed to tame assertive nationalist leaders who pursued state-directed economic paths and "neutralism" in foreign policy.

The two coups took place in different regions and under different conditions—one in a republic, the other in a monarchy—but both aimed to crush independent nationalism. In both cases the United States helped install an autocratic strongman—exactly the result the American Constitution aimed to avoid. Dependent on their superpower patron rather than popular support for survival, the shah and Castillo Armas ruled with an iron fist, suppressed a flourishing open society, and inflicted the abuses of political authoritarianism. Under their rule, the wealth divides in both Iran and Guatemala became far more pronounced.

The Cold Warriors' legacy continues to this day. Unlike the shah of Iran, Castillo Armas did not turn out to be the stable, iron-fisted leader that his C.I.A. patrons had hoped for. His reversal of Árbenz's redistributive land policies sparked waves of leftist insurgency across the countryside. Although Castillo Armas centralized power in his hands, his rule swiftly ended when a member of the presidential guard shot him dead in 1957. Three years later, a group of revolutionary young officers attempted a failed coup against the U.S.–backed José Ydígoras Fuentes. Those officers of the failed coup who were not arrested or killed set up the Revolutionary Movement of November 13, also known as MR-13, which marked the beginning of thirty-six years of civil war in Guatemala. Dirty as civil wars are, the conflict quickly mutated into a calculated campaign of brutal violence and horrific rights abuses against the civilian population by the Guatemalan state.[60]

Those most disenfranchised paid the highest price in this asymmetrical conflict. The final report of Guatemala's Commission for Historical Clarification found that the Guatemalan authorities and their associated right-wing groups were responsible for 93 percent of the documented violations, whereas the guerrillas were responsible for 3 percent of the atrocities.[61] Of the 200,000 dead, 83 percent were Mayan. The massacres, forced disappearances, kidnappings, sexual violence, torture, and summary executions of the largest indigenous group of Guatemala came to be known as the Mayan Genocide or Silent Holocaust.

Of course, the United States was not solely responsible for the brutality and suppression of the civilian population in Guatemala. The heritage of the Spanish conquest and colonization of Mesoamerica—where the majority of the population was disenfranchised and a tiny minority thrived—had deep roots. But whenever progressive leaders and politicians of the Americas like Árbenz tried to break the chains of dispossession, the United States did its utmost to weld them back together.

At least until very recently, the U.S. government sought to crush nationalist leaders in the American hemisphere who pursued independent foreign policies and who sought to build strong sovereign states with inclusive economies. During the first decades of the global Cold War, the United States used various blunt tools to bring about regime change, such as covert and overt military interventions, subversion, funding military training, sending advisers, establishing military bases, and using economic sanctions across the continent. Guatemala was the rule, not the exception. The United States played a key role in the Dirty Wars in Argentina, Cuba, El Salvador, Honduras, Brazil, Chile, Colombia, and Nicaragua.[62]

Eisenhower said he learned from his role in World War II that covert operations were bloodless. Tragically, the decades-long civil war in Guatemala, triggered by the C.I.A.–sponsored coup in 1954, was the longest and bloodiest Latin American conflict of the Cold War, proving Eisenhower gravely wrong, while casting a long, dark shadow over his foreign policy legacy and setting the stage for multiple tragedies repeated across the region and around the world.

Conclusion

T HE JOURNEY THAT THIS book has traversed presents a radically reconstructed postcolonial history of the Middle East. There has been a prevailing and long-standing Western view that this region is chronically chaotic and its people are inherently violent. This distorted perspective undermines the humanity of the people of the Middle East, who, like everyone else, yearn for universal human rights and fundamental freedoms like independence, economic development, and peace.

At the same time, this book has not been a journey of mirages and fantasies. The late 1940s and early 1950s saw the end of the colonial period and its replacement with a more stealthy but no less insidious offspring, namely, neocolonial Western intervention and exploitation. This persisted throughout the Cold War and after, leaving behind a toxic legacy that continues to poison relations within and beyond the region's borders.

In the language of war, hot is meant to convey firepower and casualties, while cold is used to signify the absence of direct military conflict. That may have technically been the case during the Cold War for Europe and North America, but for the peoples of the Middle East and other proxy battlegrounds in the Global South, it was a different story. They bore the brunt of this global

confrontation, suffering physical, psychological, economic, and political devastation.

Arguably, the worst legacy of the Cold War was the deprivation
of Middle Eastern peoples' right to self-determination. This legacy
continues to haunt the politics and societies of the region.

As we have seen, the Middle East, home to civilization's cradle
and historic discoveries, was reduced to being a Cold War chessboard in a game played at the cost of building strong political institutions, real sovereignty, civil and human rights protection, economic
growth, and democracy. The very values that Washington and London claimed to champion were sold out to oil interests and justified
in the name of regional stability.

Some, such as the political scientist Atul Kohli, have dubbed
America's role in the developing world in the second half of the
twentieth century an "informal empire." The weapons in the toolbox were regime change, covert and overt military interventions,
and punishing multilateral sanctions, as opposed to establishing
direct territorial control over newly independent nations. These
were applied in the Middle East and beyond at the cost of independence, sovereignty, and democratic norms and for the benefit
of Western business interests as well as local clients.

The colonial era was over on paper—but in practice, the effects
remained, especially the lack of ability for oppressed peoples to realize their right to choose their form of government and be fully
independent. Washington and London, two vocal champions of
human rights, systematically denied them this right under the pretext of combating the Soviet threat and expansion of communism.[1]
Pro-Western dictators were supported as a result; many of the
same ruling families remain in power today against the wishes of
their own people.

The covert and overt military intervention by the United States
throughout the Cold War and after—the United Kingdom and
France being implicated as well—conspired to thwart the development of nascent institutions that principled leaders tried to cultivate in newly independent Middle Eastern states. For the formerly
colonized peoples, the focus of politics was affirming their independence and sovereignty; for the Western powers, the focus in the
region was building defense pacts, domination, and exploitation.

This destructive engagement was all the more damaging given the context. Western powers were crushing the dreams of newly independent nations just at a moment when America's popularity was high. The United States had almost a clean slate in that its past was free of formal colonial exploitation in the Middle East, so it already enjoyed a better reputation than the European colonial powers. On top of this, the United States emerged from World War II victorious not only militarily but politically. Mohammad Mossadegh in Iran and Gamal Abdel Nasser in Egypt were among those enamored of America's cultural and technological prowess.

Thus, the United States entered with closed minds and clenched fists areas where people were prepared to welcome it with open arms. As a result, the high opinion of America within the Middle East was squandered in what became a steep plunge in popularity precipitated by Washington's new imperial ambitions and aggressive actions.

If it were only the reputation of the Stars and Stripes that suffered, all this might have been mild enough. Instead, countless lives were doomed and economic losses were immeasurable. The high price of intervention continues to be paid to this day in the form of poisoned relations, ongoing conflicts, and unrealized human potential.

American Cold Warriors were obsessed with two political impulses: rolling back communism and keeping the world open like one giant underpriced bazaar for Western shoppers. These policies set in motion a disastrous series of events that radically altered the history of the region and the world.

The overthrow of Iranian Prime Minister Mossadegh in 1953 and the confrontation with Egyptian President Nasser in the mid-1950s were inflection points in the modern history of the Middle East. They demonstrated how botched America's engagement was, how costly the lost opportunity to make valuable partners, and—most important for the future—how to end this warped approach and replace it with a constructive one.

A more nuanced and forward-thinking approach to Mossadegh and Nasser, based on respect for their dignity, independence, and standing among their respective peoples, would have created a safer world for all. If U.S. and European policy makers had had an appreciation of the historical experience of Iran and Egypt, which were dominated and subjugated by foreign powers for decades, they could have acted more judiciously and strategically. This nuanced approach could have led to better policies and better relations between the region and the Western states. Translated into modern terms, the message is clear: it is not too late to embrace the countries and peoples of the Middle East as equals and respect their choices and aspirations and open the path to productive collaboration.

The Legacy and Impact of the Global Cold War

The psychology and motivation of American decision makers were not the subject of this book. Instead, the focus was on the internal politics of the region during the early, formative years of the Cold War. Nor is this book a one-sided account assigning all blame for problems in the Middle East to Western machinations and intervention in the region's internal affairs. Local actors clearly bear a great deal of responsibility for the current malaise.[2]

My argument is far more nuanced than a game of cops and robbers. This book has shown that Anglo-American covert and overt and military interventions in the internal affairs of the Middle East should be fully understood because they strengthened and reinforced the worst sociopolitical trends in the region. These interventions arrested and stunted economic and political development and social change, thereby pushing the region down the path of geopolitical rivalries, militarism, strife, and political authoritarianism.

This is clear even through a cursory examination of the C.I.A.'s coup against the democratically elected leader of Iran, Prime Minister Mossadegh, in 1953. When one has a full understanding of these dramatic and milestone events in the country's development, the causal relationships between events and their consequences become obvious. Such a watershed moment in the history of Iran set the stage first for the repressive rule of the Pahlavi monarchy and then for the clerical takeover in the early 1980s.

Far from being, by virtue of their religion, antidemocratic, the people of Iran had selected a liberal democrat who firmly believed in human rights, fundamental freedoms, and the rule of law. As I mentioned previously, Mossadegh has been compared to Mahatma Gandhi in terms of both his politics and his ethics. His fatal flaw, in the eyes of American Cold Warriors, was his firm commitment to nonalignment in international affairs and his belief in state-led economic development.

No matter how people may judge Iran, all can agree that it is a civilizational force to be reckoned with. How different—and how much better—history would have been within Iran and across the Middle East if Mossadegh had been allowed to remain in office, realize his goals for democracy, encourage a free press, foster a strong economy with a solid safety net for all, profit from the country's own resources, and become a model for its neighbors?

Leaving aside what this would have meant for Iranians, their view of the United States would have been unsullied by neocolonialism and Washington's association with brutality. Instead, the opposite happened: the U.S.–backed shah proved that no violation of the human rights of the Iranian people could be prioritized over America's ability to exploit their resources. If the relationship could be compared to a ship when it came time to lighten its load, the Cold Warriors threw Iranian lives overboard in order to save United States dollars.

Mossadegh had only wanted Iranians to claim what was rightfully theirs, their natural resources and their political independence. The shah sold them out, offering to Western petroleum interests the keys to Persian Gulf resources.

By some measures, especially those used by the C.I.A., the agency's coup in Iran was a resounding success—so much so that it inspired other interventions across the globe, traversing Central and South America, South Asia, and beyond. But as we've seen, with the benefit of history and hindsight, those measures fall far short of the true analysis needed to gauge effectiveness. In reality, the coup took a heavy toll: both sides paid with lives lost, resources squandered, and, above all, stability undermined through the crushing of democracy. A cost-benefit analysis shows America might have reaped a short-term profit in the form of preventing Iran from nationalizing its oil, but the long-term price was too high to justify this. Washington's reputation suffered, Iran regressed, secular politics were undermined, radical Islamist politics gained in popularity, and the region began a decades-long descent into violence that has not ended and shows no signs of abating.

A region proud of being the cradle of civilization was used to nurture an imperial policy that displayed gross disregard for human life even while championing the very tenets of democracy it systematically undermined. Far from just contaminating the countries where it began, the hegemony of the Cold Warriors spread to other states and regions, as we see in the case of Guatemala. The champions of democracy in Washington experimented with their double-standards approach, as these pages have shown, at the expense of the peoples of Iran and Egypt.

Justifying intervention on the basis of Cold War dynamics and fear mongering about the spread of communism led to the war in Vietnam, which cost millions of lives there, destabilized the entire region, and went down in history as the most catastrophic U.S. military defeat in American history.

There were principled individuals whom the United States could have backed but did not, choosing instead, all too often, to sabotage those who were beloved by their countries' peoples while supporting those who were loyal puppets and who were championed by transnational corporations.

America's Cold War obsession and imperial ambitions led to geopolitical rivalries and conflicts in the Middle East and beyond that robbed the region's people of lives and livelihoods. These divide-and-conquer tactics deprived Americans and others in the West of the chance to interact peacefully with, and benefit from, the contributions of Middle Eastern peoples and societies.

Seeds of the Future

We have seen that instead of trying to understand the motivations of secular-leaning nationalists who had their respective countries' interests at heart, the United States allied itself with ultraconservative Islamic-dominated states and Islamist groups and settler colonialism in Israel-Palestine. The fallout would be felt over the skies of Manhattan and Washington, D.C., on September 11, 2001. The breeding ground for this devastation traced its roots to America's pumping billions of dollars into conservative Islamist groups like the Afghan mujahedeen. Many landmines, both actual and meta-phorical, were planted then and have yet to be cleared, continuing to cause damage.

It wasn't enough for the Cold Warriors to destroy America's relations with Egypt; they went further, to the extent of sowing divisions that undermined regional trust while blocking inter-Arab cooperation and trade. If the region's newly independent states could be compared to infants, the decision by the Western powers to divide and exploit them could be compared to a form of child abuse: not only did it do harm in the moment, it also prevented healthy development and set the stage for repeating cycles of political and economic failure. Instead of nurturing early steps toward building strong institutions and a dynamic economic development, the postimperial powers rewarded the tantrums of pliant autocrats.

The lessons were clear: Western-backed local rulers learned that human rights abuses would be ignored as long as Washington's orders were followed. And the peoples of the region learned that their human rights were dispensable to the Cold Warriors and their predecessors as well.

The argument that Arab countries suffer from a special brand of ancient hatreds and tribal conflicts is particularly heinous because it ignores the role of the Western states in contributing to regional fragility and instability. Both European imperialism and the postwar neocolonialism wrecked the Middle Eastern state system and caused structural deformities in the newly independent nations. World War II tore Europe apart, but the United States deliberately promoted political harmony and economic and social reconstruction that easily uprooted enmity. The Middle East would have embraced the same approach had it been offered the option. The Marshall Plan, named after Secretary of State George Marshall, comes to mind.

While the situations in Iran and Egypt differed in important ways, both states were guinea pigs in a geopolitical experiment that left tragedy in its wake. America gambled by investing in the forces of the religious right in the region. The religious fundamentalism so decried in the West was to a large degree nurtured on soil that the United States and the United Kingdom tilled. The Cold Warriors' our-way-or-the-highway mentality left no room for a middle ground. While Egypt pursued a strategy of nonalignment, deliberately eschewing the Soviet Union, Washington drove Nasser into Moscow's arms because it would not countenance anything less than submission to its strategic imperative of fighting communism.

The alternative path was always there for the taking, and even U.S. diplomats in the region and officials in Washington saw its viability. Rather than isolating and alienating Nasser, the Eisenhower administration could have co-opted him simply by accepting nonalignment and providing development assistance. That alternative approach in the long run would have been far less costly than the subsequent spiraling militarism and conflict. Investment in the future of Egypt would have yielded immense dividends across the region, considering Nasser's outsize influence and the country's geostrategic importance. Economic prosperity and cross-border stability would have undermined even the best recruitment tools of the extremists. In place of young people who were preyed on by violent elements hoping to foment destruction, there could have been generations of youth receiving an education, taking on good jobs, and contributing to the collective progress of humanity.

Inadvertently, the United States planted landmines that blew up against it only later. The events of the 1950s and 1960s planted noxious seeds that formed the noxious roots of extremism and terrorism that ravaged the region and the world, including the deadly terrorist attacks of September 11, 2001. Far from anticipating these events, this early chapter in postwar U.S. foreign policy created a Pax Americana, setting the stage for the United States to deepen and expand its overt and covert intervention outside the Middle East to developing nations around the world. Eisenhower bequeathed a dangerous legacy that his successors would carry out far less successfully and far more catastrophically in parts of Latin America, Asia, and Africa.

And absurd though it may be, this political posture, which originated during the Cold War and took its rationale from it, persisted even after the fall of the Berlin Wall in 1989, through the Gulf War in 1990–91, and the U.S. invasion and occupation of Afghanistan and Iraq in 2001 and 2003, respectively. Those events underscored the enduring resolve of the United States to dominate the Middle East and control its petroleum resources with no regard for international law, political norms, or the aspirations of the people of the region.[3]

As has been seen so often in the modern Middle East and the decolonized countries, when indigenous leaders tried to free their nations from the clutches of economic dependency and colonial control, the Western powers stopped at nothing to remove them from power. The hopes and dreams of postwar Middle Eastern countries clashed with the twin U.S. imperatives of rolling back Soviet communism and securing the dominance of liberal capitalism.

The icy flames of the Cold War conflagration spread to other regions as well. It was only a year following the ouster of Mossadegh when Guatemalan President Jacobo Árbenz succumbed to a similar fate. This was a case study in how the events that characterized the Middle East played out in other parts of the developing world. Although the events unfolded on different continents, the justifications rang the same. Predictably, the consequences were similarly devastating.

The Most Penetrated Region in the World

In contrast to Central America and the Global South in general, the Middle East is exceptional in that external powers have intensely and repeatedly intervened in its internal affairs, making it, in the words of the scholar L. Carl Brown, "the most penetrated international relations subsystem in today's world."[4]

Brown made his insightful observation long before the United States had launched a global war on terror following the 9/11 attacks, which led to the invasion and protracted occupation of Afghanistan and Iraq. It is worth emphasizing the catastrophic costs of America's war on terror, which caused more than 4 million in direct and indirect deaths across conflicts in Afghanistan, Pakistan, Iraq, Syria, Libya, Somalia, and Yemen, according to the Costs of War study by Brown University's Watson Institute for International and Public Affairs.[5] Similarly, Russia intervened militarily in Syria in 2015 and saved the Bashar al-Assad regime from being toppled by an Arab Spring revolt. Western powers continue to intervene in the region today by massively supporting authoritarianism and despotism in myriad ways, against the wishes and aspirations of the region's people.

Within the region, the Western policy toward the Israeli-Palestine conflict smacks of a double standard. It is viewed through the prism of long-standing Western support for settler colonialism and apartheid. Many Palestinians and Arabs argue that the case of Palestine proves that imperialism has never really ended.[6] Orchestrated by the Republican Trump administration and promoted by his Democratic successor, Joe Biden, the Abraham Accords, or normalization deals between Israel and pro–U.S. Arab dictators, legitimize Israel's occupation of Palestinian lands and further undermined the struggle for Palestinian self-determination. This confirms a popular view of ongoing Western neocolonialism in the Arab world, in alliance with local despots and tyrants. Following Hamas's attack on Israel in October 2023, which killed 1,139 people, Biden's full-fledged support for Israel's war on Gaza—which has killed at least 23,000 Palestinians at the time of writing, with more than 59,000 reportedly injured, 70 percent of them are women and children—triggered popular shock waves in the Arab (and Islamic) world. For millions of Arabs and Muslims, the complicity of the West with Israeli military occupation and suppression of Palestinian human rights demonstrates that Western imperialism is not a theme of the past but is alive and well today.

The Middle East (its people, history, and politics) is often essentialized and at the same time denied its unique place within the experiences of decolonized states. While other regions have been able—allowed, perhaps—to embark on journeys of transitional justice and democratic governance, the Middle East has lagged and even regressed.

There was a first generation of postcolonial leaders like Mossadegh and Nasser who had a different vision for the Middle East, but their leadership was cut short and their legacies thwarted. They aspired to enjoy real national sovereignty and independence in order to escape dependency, promote development, and become free. They struggled to make a clean break with both European imperialism and postwar neocolonialism.

Iran and Egypt, possessing vast human resources and pursuing modernization efforts, could have inspired other regional countries, probably leading the way in establishing the rule of law, state institutions, and productive industrialization. Instead, they became more militarized and despotic, marked by domestic patron-client relationships that deepened inequalities and abused the trust of millions of people.

Looking back on this history is not an academic exercise. For people of the region, self-determination remains a faraway dream. Many countries in this deeply unstable region lack the capacity to protect their homelands, and they often do not have a monopoly on the use of force in their territories. Saudi Arabia, Iraq, Syria, and other states of the region are dependent on external patrons, which extract a serious price for their roles. This leaves the Middle East with a deficit of respected and forward-looking leaders, even if it has a surfeit of people who long for justice and good governance.

This quest for justice includes the desire to be free from authoritarian control in any form, be it foreign or indigenous. The prodemocracy protests that swept the region in 2010–12 and 2019 were not successful, but this does not mean their aspirations have been quashed, only postponed. Further waves of protests are inevitable.

When that moment comes, a breakthrough beckons if the Western response is informed by the analysis provided in this book. Reflecting on lost opportunities provides lessons for the future. Of course, paths not taken remain untrodden, but it is still worth studying them because this is precisely the way to advance understanding on how to find the road out of the quagmire. Western leaders could have taken the alternative route. If they can put aside short-term gain and privilege long-term progress, they will find there is no more rewarding or valuable approach than to treat the people of the region as equals, afford them the opportunity to develop as is their right, and watch a flourishing region become a force for stability and progress that reverberates around the world.

Notes

Introduction: Narrating History

1. Elizabeth F. Thompson, *How the West Stole Democracy from the Arabs: The Syrian Congress of 1920 and the Destruction of Its Historic Liberal-Islamic Alliance* (New York: Atlantic Monthly Press, 2020).

2. Karla Adam, "Obama Ridiculed for Saying Conflicts in the Middle East 'Date Back Millennia.' (Some Don't Date Back a Decade.)," *Washington Post*, January 13, 2016, https://www.washingtonpost.com/news/worldviews /wp/2016/01/13/obama-ridiculed-for-saying-conflicts-in-the-middle-east-date-back-millennia-some-dont-date-back-a-decade/.

3. Edward Said, *Orientalism: Western Conceptions of the Orient*, rev. ed. (London: Penguin, 1995).

4. Andrew Bacevich, *After the Apocalypse: America's Role in a World Transformed* (New York: Metropolitan Books, 2021). See the *New York Times*'s review of the book: Geoffrey Wheatcroft, "America's Dismal Foreign Policy—and What to Do about It," *New York Times*, July 8, 2021, https:// www.nytimes.com/2021/08/07/books/review/after-the-apocalypse-andrew-bacevich.html.

5. Rashid Khalidi, *Resurrecting Empire: Western Footprints and America's Perilous Path in the Middle East* (London: I. B. Tauris, 2004), p. 33.

6. Kwame Nkrumah, *Neo-Colonialism: The Last Stage of Imperialism* (1965; repr., London: Panaf, 1970), p. xi.

7. Khalidi, *Resurrecting Empire*.

8. There are many books written on imperialism, including this recent provocative gem by Daniel Immerwahr, *How to Hide an Empire: A Short History of the Greater United States* (New York: Farrar, Straus and Giroux, 2019). I cite Kohli's because of its historical depth, conceptual clarity, and diversity of case studies.

9. Atul Kohli, *Imperialism and the Developing World: How Britain and the United States Shaped the Global Periphery* (Oxford: Oxford University Press, 2020), pp. 4, 6.

10. Ibid., p. 291.

11. Ibid., p. 16.

12. See Peter Heather and John Rapley, *Why Empires Fall: Rome, America, and the Future of the West* (New Haven: Yale University Press, 2023).

13. Kohli *Imperialism and the Developing World*, p. 4.

14. For example, over time American leaders recognized the war in Vietnam couldn't be won, yet they also could not withdraw. Kohli argues that maintaining American credibility became a reason to continue the war because credibility was seen as fundamental to the exercise of influence elsewhere in the world. See ibid., p. 256.

15. Ibid., pp. 4, 16.

16. Ibid., p. 17.

17. Kohli seeks to revive the interest in a systematic study of informal empire as a form of imperialism as well as to broaden the scope of the study of imperialism beyond colonialism. He argues that although colonialism ended, imperialism did not. Ibid., p. 6.

18. Ibid., pp. 267, 279.

19. Ibid.

20. Ernest R. May, ed., *American Cold War Strategy: Interpreting NSC 68* (Boston: Bedford/St. Martin's, 1993), vii.

21. Kohli, *Imperialism and the Developing World*, p. 267.

22. Allen Dulles. "Foreign Policy Report: On Understanding and Coping with Communist Bloc Policy in West Africa," June 2, 1961, Allen W. Dulles Papers, https://findingaids.princeton.edu/collections/MC019.09/c034.

23. See Kohli, *Imperialism and the Developing World*.

24. Ibid., p. 2.

25. Farewell address of President Dwight D. Eisenhower, January 17, 1961, box 38, Speech Series, Papers of Dwight D. Eisenhower as President, 1953–61, Eisenhower Library, National Archives and Records Administration.

26. Lisa Anderson, "The State in the Middle East and North Africa," *Comparative Politics* 20, no. 1 (1987): 3.

Chapter One. Mossadegh, Nasser, and What Could Have Been

1. L. Carl Brown, *International Politics and the Middle East: Old Rules, Dangerous Game* (Princeton: Princeton University Press, 1984), p. 16.

2. Timothy Mitchell, *Carbon Democracy: Political Power in the Age of Oil* (New York: Verso, 2011).

3. Ibid., p. 143.

4. Atul Kholi, *Imperialism and the Developing World: How Britain and the United States Shaped the Global Periphery* (Oxford: Oxford University Press, 2020), pp. 1–43.
5. Since 2010, a team of fifty scholars, legal specialists, human rights practitioners, and physicians have participated in the Costs of War project and have kept their own data and assessments. See Stephanie Savel, "How Death Outlives War: The Reverberating Impact of the Post-9/11 Wars on Human Health" paper prepared for Brown University's Watson Institute for International and Public Affairs, May 15, 2023, https://watson.brown.edu/costsofwar/papers/2023/how-death-outlives-war-reverberating-impact-post-911-wars-human-health.
6. Kohli, *Imperialism and the Developing World*, p. 6.
7. S. N. Eisenstadt, "Multiple Modernities," *Daedalus* 129, no. 1 (Winter 2000): 1–29.
8. Mark Mazower, *Dark Continent: Europe's Twentieth Century* (New York: Alfred A. Knopf, 1999), pp. ix–xvi, 395–403, and Charles Tilly, *Contention and Democracy in Europe, 1650–2000* (Cambridge: Cambridge University Press, 2004), pp. 168–205.
9. Mossadegh made mistakes that facilitated the C.I.A.-led coup against him. Although the coup would not have worked without some Iranian support, the C.I.A. manufactured, orchestrated, and facilitated domestic opposition, as will be shown in the following chapter.
10. Svante Karlsson, *Oil and the World Order: American Foreign Oil Policy* (Totowa, N.J.: Barnes & Noble Books, 1986), pp. 280, 279.
11. Kohli, *Imperialism and the Developing World*, pp. 283, 324.
12. Author's interview with Khaled Mohieddin, Cairo, December 12, 2006
13. See Mazower, *Dark Continent*, pp. ix–xvi, 395–403, and Tilly, *Contention and Democracy in Europe*, pp. 168–205.
14. Malcolm Kerr, *The Arab Cold War: Gamal 'Abd Al-Nasir and His Rivals, 1958–1970* (London: Oxford University Press, 1971).
15. Thalif Deen, "American Weapons Used in Gaza Trigger War Crime Accusations against US," Inter Press Service, October 23, 2023, https://www.ipsnews.net/2023/10/american-weapons-used-gaza-trigger-war-crime-accusations-us/.
16. Savel, "How Death Outlives War."

Chapter Two. A Portrait of Mossadegh

1. Ali Ansari, *Modern Iran since 1797: Reform and Revolution* (Abingdon, U.K.: Routledge, 2019), p. 76.
2. Peter Curzon, *Persia* (New York: Macmillan, 1986), p. 480.
3. Ansari, *Modern Iran*, p. 75.
4. As early as the late nineteenth century, therefore, many Iranians already believed that their rulers were inescapably bound to foreign interests.

5. Christopher de Bellaigue, *Patriot of Persia: Muhammad Mossadegh and a Very British Coup* (London: Bodley Head, 2012), p. 31.

6. Sohrab Ahmari, "The Iranian Turning Point," *Wall Street Journal*, May 11, 2012, https://www.wsj.com/articles/SB10001424052702303513404577353640718058390.

7. Peter Avery, *Modern Iran* (Westport, Conn.: Praeger, 1965), p. 273. The truth is that these titles were all abolished.

8. Ali Rahnema, *Behind the 1953 Coup in Iran* (Cambridge: Cambridge University Press, 2015), p. 227.

9. "Dr. Mohammad Mossadegh: Prime Minister of Iran, 1951–1953," *The Mossadegh Project*, May 2021, http://www.mohammadmossadegh.com/biography/.

10. Ali Pirzadeh, *Modern Iran in Perspective* (Cham: Springer, 2019), p. 24.

11. Ervand Abrahamian, *A History of Modern Iran* (Cambridge: Cambridge University Press, 2008), p. 46.

12. Hamid Enayat, *Modern Islamic Political Thought* (Austin: University of Texas Press, 1982), p. 166. For a comprehensive treatment of the Constitutional Revolution, see Janet Afary, *The Iranian Constitutional Revolution, 1906–1911* (New York: Columbia University Press, 1996).

13. Homayon Khozaini, *Mussadiq and the Struggle for Power in Iran* (London: I. B. Tauris, 2009), p. 6.

14. Ibid.

15. De Bellaigue, *Patriot of Persia*, p. 33.

16. Ibid.

17. Mohammad Mossadegh, *Khaterat va Ta'ammolat-e Dr Mohammad Mosaddegh*, ed. Iraj Afshar, 5th ed. (Tehran: Elmi Editor, 1985), pp. 63–64.

18. De Bellaigue, *Patriot of Persia*, p. 35.

19. Mossadegh, *Khaterat va Ta'ammolat-e Dr Mohammad Mosaddegh*, pp. 69, 71; de Bellaigue, *Patriot of Persia*, p. 38; Stephen Kinzer, *All the Shah's Men: An American Coup and the Roots of Middle East Terror* (Hoboken, N.J.: John Wiley & Sons, 2008), p. 54.

20. Stephen Kinzer, *All the Shah's Men*, p. 54.

21. Khozaini, *Mussadiq*, p. 7.

22. De Bellaigue, *Patriot of Persia*, p. 38.

23. Ibid., pp. 41–42.

24. Muhammad Musaddiq, Isqat-i Da'avi', *Majalleh-yi Ilmi* 1, no. 1293 (1914), reprinted in *Musaddiq va masa'il-i Huquq va Siyasat*, ed. Iraj Afshar (Tehran: Zamineh, 1979), pp. 49–55.

25. Supplementary Constitutional Laws of 1907, article 2.

26. For background reading on how and why the council of clerics was proposed, see Afary's excellent book, *The Iranian Constitutional Revolution*, pp. 100–109.

27. Mossadegh, *Khaterat va Ta'ammolat-e Dr Mohammad Mosaddegh*, pp. 74–78.

28. De Bellaigue, *Patriot of Persia*, p. 42.

29. Homa Katouzian, "Mosaddeq's Government in Iranian History: Arbitrary Rule, Democracy, and the 1953 Coup," in *Mohammad Mosaddeq and the 1953 Coup in Iran*, ed. Mark J. Gasiorowski and Malcolm Byrne (Syracuse, N.Y.: Syracuse University Press, 2015), pp. 1–26.

30. Afshin Matin-Asgari, *Both Eastern and Western: An Intellectual History of Iranian Modernity* (Cambridge: Cambridge University Press, 2018), p. 45.

31. Quoted ibid., p. 60.

32. Abrahamian, *A History of Modern Iran*, p. 114.

33. Ervand Abrahamian, *Khomeinism* (Berkeley: University of California Press, 1993), p. 4.

34. Khozaini, *Mussadiq*, p. 3.

35. Arash Norouzi, "Mossadegh and the 1953 Coup in Iran," *The Mossadegh Project*, May 10, 2021, http://www.mohammadmossadegh.com/1953/; de Bellaigue, *Patriot of Persia*, p. 144.

36. De Bellaigue, *Patriot of Persia*, p. 63.

37. Ibid., p. 60.

38. Ibid., p. 66.

39. Touraj Atabaki and Erik J. Zürcher, *Men of Order: Authoritarian Modernization under Atatürk and Reza Shah* (London: I. B. Tauris, 2003), p. 7.

40. Roger Cohen, "A Crass and Consequential Error," *New York Review of Books*, August 16, 2012, https://www.nybooks.com/articles/2012/08/16/crass-and-consequential-error/; de Bellaigue, *Patriot of Persia*, p. 60.

41. Muhammad Musaddiq, *Musaddiq's Memoirs*, ed. Homa Katouzian (London: JEBHE, National Movement of Iran, 1988), p. 284.

42. Farhad Diba, *Mohammad Mossadegh: A Political Biography* (London: Croom Helm, 1986), p. 5.

43. Cited in Gholam Reza Najati, *Mossadegh: The Years of Struggle and Oppression* (Tehran, 1997–98), 1:26.

44. Ervand Abrahamian, *Iran between Two Revolutions* (Princeton: Princeton University Press, 1982), p. 240.

45. Ibid., p. 220.

46. Muhammad Mosaddeq, *Notgh-ha va Maktubat-e Mosaddeq da doreha-ye panjom va sheshom-e Majles* (*The Speeches and the Writings of Mossadegh during the Fifth and the Sixth Parliament*) (Tehran: Mossadegh Editor, 1969), p. 101.

47. Abrahamian, *Iran between Two Revolutions*, p. 89.

48. Ibid.

49. Winston Churchill, *The World Crisis, 1911–1918* (1923–31; abridged ed., New York: Free Press, 2005), p. 76.

50. Daniel Yergin, *The Prize: The Epic Quest for Oil, Money, and Power* (New York: Simon & Schuster, 1991), pp. 138–47, 158.

51. Atul Kholi, *Imperialism and the Developing World: How Britain and the United States Shaped the Global Periphery* (Oxford: Oxford University Press, 2020), p. 275.

52. Mossadegh seems to have imagined nonalignment long before the convening of the Bandung Conference of Afro-Asian states in 1955. This conference was to be an important step toward the eventual creation of the Non-Aligned Movement, which aimed to promote economic and cultural cooperation among Global South nations and to oppose colonialism and neocolonialism by any power. Mossadegh did not have the chance to shape that conference, which was attended instead by the envoys of the shah.

53. J. Emami, Parliamentary Debates, 16th Majlis, November 3, 1951.

54. De Bellaigue, *Patriot of Persia*, p. 123.

55. Mossadegh, *Khaterat va Ta'ammolat-e Dr Mohammad Mosaddegh*, p. 178.

56. The D'Arcy Concession of 1901 gave the British the exclusive rights to prospect for oil in Iran. It was not until 1908 that large commercial quantities of oil were actually discovered; the Anglo-Persian Oil Company was subsequently founded and later renamed Anglo-Iranian Oil Company, but oil had long existed in Iran.

57. Stephen Kinzer, *Overthrow: America's Century of Regime Change from Hawaii to Iraq* (New York: Times Books, 2007), p. 118.

58. M. Reza Ghods, "The Rise and Fall of General Razmara," *Middle Eastern Studies* 29, no. 1 (1993): 22–35.

59. Ibid., p. 28.

60. Ibid., p. 33.

61. Ibid., p. 34.

62. Wm. Roger Louis, *The British Empire in the Middle East, 1945–1951* (Oxford: Clarendon Press, 1984), pp. 682, 689.

63. Timothy Guinnane, "Financial Vergangenheitsbewältigung: The 1953 London Debt Agreement," Working Paper 880 (2005), Economic Growth Center, Yale University, p. 880.

64. Mark Gasiorowski, "The 1953 Coup d'Etat in Iran," *International Journal of Middle East Studies* 19, no. 3 (1987): 262. See also de Bellaigue, *Patriot of Persia*, p. 117.

65. Gasiorowski, "The 1953 Coup d'Etat in Iran," p. 263.

66. The five American companies were Standard Oil of New Jersey (later Exxon), Socony-Vacuum Oil (later Mobil), Standard Oil of California (later Chevron), the Texas Company (later Texaco), and Gulf Oil.

67. De Bellaigue, *Patriot of Persia*, pp. 123–24.

68. Ibid., p. 188.

69. Mossadegh, *Khaterat va Ta'ammolat-e Dr Mohammad Mosaddegh*, p. 180.

70. De Bellaigue, *Patriot of Persia*, pp. 130, 168, 173.

71. "He Oiled the Wheels of Chaos," *Time*, January 7, 1952, https://content.time.com/time/magazine/0,9263,7601520107,00.html.

72. See de Bellaigue, *Patriot of Persia*, pp. 182–85.

73. Amin Saikal, *The Rise and Fall of the Shah* (Princeton: Princeton University Press, 1980), p. 42.

74. The Ambassador in Iran (Henderson) to the Embassy in the United Kingdom, February 28, 1952, in *Foreign Relations of the United States (FRUS)*, 1952–54, X, Iran, no. 164.

75. James Risen, "Secrets of History: The CIA in Iran," *New York Times*, April 16, 2000, https://www.nytimes.com/2000/04/16/world/secrets-history-cia-iran-special-report-plot-convulsed-iran-53-79.html.

76. "Mossie Grabs Britain's Oil—but Navy to the Rescue," *Daily Express*, May 30, 1951.

77. Ibid.

78. Quoted in de Bellaigue, *Patriot of Persia*, p. 159.

79. Louis, *The British Empire in the Middle East*, p. 674.

80. Ibid., pp. 687–88. The United States had also expressed strong disapproval of British plans to use military force in Iran as early as May 1951. See "The Position of the United States with Respect to Iran, NSC Action No. 473," May 17, 1951, Record Group 59, box 4107, National Archives.

81. Gasiorowski, "The 1953 Coup d'Etat in Iran," p. 264. For American and British correspondence regarding Attlee's invasion plans, see, in the Public Records Office, London, "Text of Reply from President Truman," September 26, 1951, FO/371/91591; "Persian Oil Dispute," September 28, 1951, FO/371/91592; "Draft Telegram to Tehran," September 27, 1951, FO/371/91592; "Record of a Conversation with the American Ambassador," October 1, 1951, FO/371/91596; CAB 128/20, pp. 231–34 (British cabinet records).

82. Svante Karlsson, *Oil and the World Order: American Foreign Oil Policy* (Totowa, N.J.: Barnes & Noble Books, 1986), p. 279.

Chapter Three. Saving Iran from Democracy

1. The Secretary of State to the Department of State, November 10, 1951, in *Foreign Relations of the United States (FRUS)*, 1952–54, X, Iran, no. 129.

2. Ibid.

3. See John Ghazvinian, *America and Iran: A History, 1720 to the Present* (New York: Alfred A. Knopf, 2021).

4. Mark Gasiorowski and Malcolm Byrne, *Mohammad Mosaddeq and the 1953 Coup in Iran* (Syracuse, N.Y.: Syracuse University Press, 2004), p. 223. See also Christopher de Bellaigue, *Patriot of Persia: Muhammad Mossadegh and a Very British Coup* (London: Bodley Head, 2012), p. 220.

5. William Inboden, *Religion and American Foreign Policy, 1945–1960: The Soul of Containment* (Cambridge: Cambridge University Press, 2008), p. 6.

6. Walter LaFeber, *America, Russia, and the Cold War, 1945–1996*, 8th ed. (New York: McGraw-Hill, 1997), p. 83. Atul Kohli, *Imperialism and the Developing World: How Britain and the United States Shaped the Global Periphery* (Oxford: Oxford University Press, 2020), pp. 267, 279.

7. Saeed Kamali Dehghan and Richard Norton-Taylor, "CIA Admits Role in 1953 Iranian Coup," *Guardian*, August 19, 2013, https://www.theguardian.com/world/2013/aug/19/cia-admits-role-1953-iranian-coup. See also de Bellaigue, *Patriot of Persia*, pp. 220–21.

8. "Dulles Formulated and Conducted U.S. Foreign Policy for More Than Six Years" (obituary), *New York Times*, May 25, 1959, https://archive.nytimes.com/www.nytimes.com/learning/general/onthisday/bday/0225.html.

9. Richard H. Immerman, *John Foster Dulles: Piety, Pragmatism, and Power in U.S. Foreign Policy* (Wilmington, Del.: Scholarly Resources, 1999), p. 1.

10. Michael J. Devine, "John W. Foster and the Struggle for the Annexation of Hawaii," *Pacific Historical Review*, 46, no. 1 (1977): 29–50.

11. "John Foster Dulles: A Record Clear and Strong for All to See," *Time*, April 27, 1959, http://content.time.com/time/subscriber/article/0,33009,811026,00.html.

12. Ibid.

13. Ibid.

14. "Dulles Formulated and Conducted U.S. Foreign Policy for More Than Six Years."

15. Warren Cohen, *America in the Age of Soviet Power, 1945–1991*, vol. 4 of *The Cambridge History of American Foreign Relations* (New York: Cambridge University Press, 1993), pp. 89–90.

16. Dwight D. Eisenhower, speech at the Moles Annual Awards Dinner, Waldorf-Astoria Hotel, New York City, February 9, 1950.

17. Immerman, *John Foster Dulles*, p. 3.

18. Ibid.

19. David McCullough, *The Path between the Seas: The Creation of the Panama Canal, 1870–1914* (New York: Simon & Schuster, 1977), p. 698.

20. "Dulles Formulated and Conducted U.S. Foreign Policy for More Than Six Years."

21. John D. Wilsey, *God's Cold Warrior: The Life and Faith of John Foster Dulles* (Grand Rapids: William B. Eerdmans), p. 17.

22. Robert Gilbert, "The Impact of Presidential Illness on the Administration of Dwight D. Eisenhower," *Politics and the Life Sciences* 31, nos. 1–2 (Spring–Fall 2012): 16–17.

23. Ibid., p. 19.

24. Stephen Kinzer, *The Brothers: John Foster Dulles, Allen Dulles, and Their Secret World War* (New York: St Martin's Griffin, 2013), p. 115.

25. Melvyn P. Leffler, *A Preponderance of Power: National Security, the Truman Administration, and the Cold War* (Stanford: Stanford University Press, 1992), p. 80.

26. See Ervand Abrahamian, *The Coup: 1953, the CIA, and the Roots of Modern U.S.–Iranian Relations* (New York: New Press, 2013).

27. Mark Gasiorowski, "The 1953 Coup d'Etat in Iran," *International Journal of Middle East Studies* 19, no. 3 (1987): 275.

28. Richard J. Barnet, *Intervention and Revolution* (New York: New American Library, 1968), pp. 226–29; Kermit Roosevelt, *Countercoup: The Struggle for the Control of Iran* (New York: McGraw-Hill, 1979); Barry Rubin, *Paved with Good Intentions: The American Experience in Iran* (1980; repr., New York: Penguin, 1981), chap. 3; and R. K. Ramazani, *Independence without Freedom: Iran's Foreign Policy* (Charlottesville: University of Virginia Press, 2013), pp. 247–50.

29. See Study Prepared by the Staff of the National Security Council, n.d., in *FRUS*, 1952–54, X, Iran, no. 6.

30. Ervand Abrahamian, *Iran between Two Revolutions* (Princeton: Princeton University Press, 1982), pp. 259–60.

31. Ervand Abrahamian, "Iran in Revolution: The Opposition Forces," *Middle East Research and Information Project* 75–76 (March–April 1979): 4.

32. *Ittila'at*, October 12, 1952, and H. Makki, *Parliamentary Proceedings*, 17th Majlis. February 1953.

33. See Ray Takeyh, "What Really Happened in Iran: The CIA, the Ouster of Mosaddeq, and the Restoration of the Shah," *Foreign Affairs*, July–August 2014, https://www.foreignaffairs.com/articles/middle-east/2014-06-16/what-really-happened-iran; and Ray Takeyh, "Clerics Responsible for Iran's Failed Attempts at Democracy," *Washington Post*, August 18, 2010, https://www.washingtonpost.com/wp-dyn/content/article/2010/08/17/AR2010081704944.html.

34. James Risen, "Secrets of History: The CIA in Iran," *New York Times*, April 16, 2000, https://archive.nytimes.com/www.nytimes.com/library/world/mideast/041600iran-cia-index.html.

35. "The Ambassador in Iran (Henderson) to the Embassy in the United Kingdom," February 28, 1952, in *FRUS*, 1952–54, X, Iran, no. 164.

36. James A. Bill, *The Eagle and the Lion: The Tragedy of American-Iranian Relations* (New Haven: Yale University Press, 1988), p. 86.

37. Quoted in Stephen Kinzer, *Overthrow: America's Century of Regime Change from Hawaii to Iraq* (New York: Times Books), p. 124. Kohli, *Imperialism and the Developing World*, pp. 102, 282.

38. De Bellaigue, *Patriot of Persia*, p. 66.

39. Gregory Brew, "The Collapse Narrative: The United States, Mohammed Mossadegh, and the Coup Decision of 1953," *Texas National Security Review* 2, no. 4 (2010): 47. See also de Bellaigue, *Patriot of Persia*, p. 207.

40. C.I.A. National Intelligence Estimate, NIE-75. "Probable Developments in Iran through 1953," November 13, 1952, President's Secretary's Files, Truman Papers, Truman Library.

41. Gasiorowski and Byrne, *Mohammad Mosaddeq*, p. 69.

42. Msvetov, "End of Empire (1985), Chapter 7: Iran," *YouTube*, October 22, 2014, https://www.youtube.com/watch?v=xhCgJElpQEQ.

43. Memo, John Jernegan to Freeman Matthews, October 23, 1952; memo, Henry Byroade to Freeman Matthews, November 26, 1952; Memo of

Conversation, December 3, 1952, National Security Archive, Briefing Book no. 601, https://nsarchive.gwu.edu/briefing-book/iran/2017-08-08/1953-iran-coup-new-us-documents-confirm-british-approached-us-late.

44. Memo, Jernegan to Matthews, October 23, 1952; memo, Byroade to Matthews, November 26,1952; Memo of Conversation, December 3, 1952, National Security Archive, Briefing Book no. 601.

45. Mark J. Gasiorowski, "U.S. Perceptions of the Communist Threat in Iran during the Mossadegh Era," *Journal of Cold War Studies* 21, no. 3 (2010): 190.

46. Report of the National Security Council on the Position of the United States with Respect to Iran, NSC 54, July 21, 1949, in *FRUS*, 1949, The Near East, South Asia, and Africa, VI, pp. 545–51.

47. Christopher M. Woodhouse. *Something Ventured: An Autobiography* (New York: HarperCollins, 1982), pp. 117–18.

48. Risen, "Secrets of History."

49. Andrew Bacevich, "A Prize from Fairyland," *London Review of Books*, November 2, 2017, p. 5. In February 1953 the C.I.A. feared that the shah might soon leave Iran for good amid the chaos, stifling any chance of a smooth transition. Later that month, Secretary of State Dulles received a "top secret" cable from the American embassy in London, which relayed a message from British Foreign Secretary Anthony Eden, stating that the "Foreign Office this afternoon informed us of receipt message from Queen Elizabeth expressing concern at latest developments re Shah and strong hope we can find some means of dissuading him from leaving the country." This extraordinary message seemed to suggest that Queen Elizabeth was appealing to a fellow monarch to remain resolute. A closer look revealed it was all trickery: the message was not from Queen Elizabeth, nor had it any connection to her whatsoever. The British foreign secretary had sent his message on board a ship, the RMS *Queen Elizabeth*, as he headed to Canada for meetings. Aware of the power of the message, however, Washington decided not to tell their British counterparts about the mix-up, or the shah himself. This decision succeeded, and the shah ultimately decided to stay put in Iran. Had this not been the case, the events of 1953 might never have happened. Dan De Luce, "A Message from 'Queen Elizabeth' to the Shah Played Role in CIA 1953 Coup in Iran, Documentary Says," NBC News, June 7, 2020, https://www.nbcnews.com/news/world/message-queen-elizabeth-shah-played-role-cia-1953-coup-iran-n1225981.

50. Risen, "Secrets of History."

51. Ibid.

52. Roger Louis and James A. Bill, *Musaddiq, Iranian Nationalism, and Oil* (London: I. B. Tauris, 1988), p. 80.

53. Ibid.

54. Ibid., p. 110.

55. Risen, "Secrets of History."
56. Memorandum Prepared in the Directorate of Plans, Central Intelligence Agency, March 3, 1953, in *FRUS*, 1952–54, X, Iran, no. 170; Gwen Kinkead, "Kermit Roosevelt: Brief Life of a Harvard Conspirator: 1916–2000," *Harvard Magazine*, January–February 2011, https://www.harvardmagazine .com/2011/01/kermit-roosevelt.
57. Scott A. Koch, *Zendebad Shah! The Central Intelligence Agency and the Fall of Iranian Prime Minister Mohammed Mossadeq, August 1953* (Washington, D.C.: C.I.A., 1998), appendix E, 118–19, 120. This particular appendix detailing divisions within the C.I.A. was not declassified until 2017.
58. Memorandum from the Chief of the Iran Branch, Near East and Africa Division (Waller) to the Chief of the Near East and Africa Division, Directorate of Plans, Central Intelligence Agency (Roosevelt), "Factors Involved in the Overthrow of Mossadeq," April 16, 1953, in *FRUS*, 1952–54, X, Iran, no. 192.
59. Risen, "Secrets of History."
60. Memorandum from Director of Central Intelligence Dulles to President Eisenhower, March 1, 1953, in *FRUS*, 1952–54, X, Iran, no. 169.
61. Kinkead, "Kermit Roosevelt."
62. Gasiorowski, "The 1953 Coup d'Etat in Iran," p. 271.
63. CIA Briefing Note, April 21, 1953, in *FRUS* 1952–54, X, Iran, no. 194.
64. Memo of Conversation, June 6, 1953, in *FRUS*, 1952–54, X, Iran, no. 216.
65. Gasiorowski, "The 1953 Coup d'Etat in Iran," p. 273.
66. Memorandum from the Chief of the Iran Branch, Near East and Africa Division (Waller) to the Chief of the Near East and Africa Division, Directorate of Plans, Central Intelligence Agency (Roosevelt), April 16, 1953, in *FRUS*, 1952–54, X, Iran, no. 192.
67. Gasiorowski, "The 1953 Coup d'Etat in Iran." See the *New York Times* article that details Mossadegh's uproar at the princess's arrival: "Iranian Princess Ordered to Leave: Court Condemns Unauthorized Return of Shah's Sister, a Foe of Mossadegh," *New York Times*, July 27, 1953. This account is from a confidential interview with a U.S. Army colonel, conducted in March 1984. For Ashraf's account of these events see Ashraf Pahlavi, *Faces in a Mirror: Memoirs from Exile* (Englewood Cliffs, N.J.: Prentice-Hall, 1980), pp. 134–40.
68. Risen, "Secrets of History."
69. Ibid.
70. Ibid.
71. Karl Ernest Meyer and Shareen Blair Brysac, *Kingmakers: The Invention of the Modern Middle East* (New York: Norton, 2008), p. 336.
72. Risen, "Secrets of History."
73. Ibid.
74. Abrahamian, *Iran between Two Revolutions*, p. 279.

75. Risen, "Secrets of History"

76. The Ambassador in Iraq (Berry) to the Department of State, August 17, 1953, in *FRUS*, 1952–54, X, Iran, no. 345.

77. "Declassified Documents Reveal CIA Role in 1953 Iranian Coup," NPR, September 1, 2013, https://www.npr.org/2013/09/01/217976304/declassified-documents-reveal-cia-role-in-1953-iranian-coup.

78. Stella K. Margold, "The Streets of Tehran," *The Reporter*, November 10, 1953, http://www.mohammadmossadegh.com/news/the-reporter/november-10-1953/the-streets-of-teheran/.

79. De Bellaigue, *Patriot of Persia*, pp. 233–34.

80. Risen, "Secrets of History."

81. Gasiorowski, "The 1953 Coup d'Etat in Iran," pp. 273–74.

82. Risen, "Secrets of History." See also Gasiorowski, "The 1953 Coup d'Etat in Iran," p. 274.

83. Gholam Reza Afkhami, *The Life and Times of the Shah* (Berkeley: University of California Press, 2009), p. 178.

84. Risen, "Secrets of History." See also Gasiorowski, "The 1953 Coup d'Etat in Iran," p. 274.

85. Ali Rahnema, *Behind the 1953 Coup in Iran* (Cambridge: Cambridge University Press, 2015), p. 227.

86. Ibid., p. 228.

87. Roosevelt, *Countercoup*, p. ix.

88. James Risen, "The Success: C.I.A. and Moscow Are Both Surprised," pt. 4 in "Secrets of History: The C.I.A. in Iran," *New York Times*, April 16, 2000, https://archive.nytimes.com/www.nytimes.com/library/world/mideast/041600iran-cia-chapter4.html.

89. Risen, "Secrets of History."

90. Roosevelt, *Countercoup*, 166.

91. Brew, "The Collapse Narrative," p. 47.

92. Kinkead, "Kermit Roosevelt."

93. Roosevelt, *Countercoup*, p. 207.

94. Ervand Abrahamian, *A History of Modern Iran* (Cambridge: Cambridge University Press), p. 121.

95. Eisenhower is quoted ibid., 125.

96. Abrahamian, *Iran between Two Revolutions*, p. 280.

Chapter Four. From the Cusp of Democracy to the Abyss of Absolute Monarchy

1. "Iran Tells Oil Consortium Pact Will Not Be Renewed," *New York Times*, January 24, 1973, https://www.nytimes.com/1973/01/24/archives/iran-tells-oil-consortium-pact-will-not-be-renewed-companies.html.

2. Arash Norouzi, "AIOC Renamed British Petroleum: William Fraser's Announcement to Stockholders," Mossadegh Project, October 22, 2019,

http://www.mohammadmossadegh.com/news/anglo-iranian-oil-
company/name-changed-to-the-british-petroleum-company-ltd/.

3. John Ghazvinian, *America and Iran: A History, 1720 to the Present* (New York: Alfred A. Knopf, 2021), 99.

4. James Barr, *Lords of the Desert: Britain's Struggle with America to Dominate the Middle East* (London: Simon & Schuster, 2018).

5. Christopher de Bellaigue, *Patriot of Persia: Muhammad Mossadegh and a Very British Coup* (London: Bodley Head, 2012), p. 254.

6. "CIA-Assisted Coup Overthrows Government of Iran," History, November 13, 2009, https://www.history.com/this-day-in-history/cia-assisted-coup-overthrows-government-of-iran.

7. "The Shah of Iran, 1957—A Revised Study," in Despatch from the Embassy in Iran to the Department of State, March 11, 1957, in *Foreign Relations of the United States (FRUS)*, 1955–57, XII, Near East Region; Iran; Iraq, no. 806.

8. Ebrahim Norouzi and Arash Norouzi, "Divvying Up the Loot: The Iran Oil Consortium Agreement of 1954," Mossadegh Project, October 29, 2019, http://www.mohammadmossadegh.com/news/iran-oil-consortium-agreement-1954/.

9. Ervand Abrahamian, *A History of Modern Iran* (Cambridge: Cambridge University Press, 2008), p. 123.

10. Ibid.

11. Ibid., p. 124.

12. Roham Alvandi, *Nixon, Kissinger, and the Shah: The United States and Iran in the Cold War* (Oxford: Oxford University Press, 2014), p. 26.

13. Despatch from the Embassy in Iran to the Department of State, February 10, 1958, in *FRUS*, 1958–60, XII, Near East Region; Iraq; Iran; Arabian Peninsula, no. 721. See also Abbas Milani, *The Shah* (New York: Palgrave Macmillan, 2011), p. 210.

14. Milani, *The Shah*, p. 225.

15. Ibid., p. 226.

16. Dana Adams Schmidt, "West Urges Iran to Rebuff Soviet," *New York Times*, February 12, 1959, https://www.nytimes.com/1959/02/12/archives/west-urges-iran-to-rebuff-soviet-eisenhower-and-others-bid-shah.html.

17. Milani, *The Shah*, p. 228; Roham Alvandi, "Flirting with Neutrality: The Shah, Khrushchev, and the Failed 1959 Soviet-Iranian Negotiations," *Iranian Studies* 47, no. 3 (2014): 439.

18. Alvandi, "Flirting with Neutrality," p. 440.

19. According to former high-ranking Iranian officials, "the Shah had routed hundreds of thousands of dollars to the Nixon campaign," and Swiss banking sources also confirmed that the shah had transferred more than $1 million from his personal accounts to Nixon's Mexican slush fund. See Andrew Scott Cooper, *The Oil Kings: How the U.S., Iran, and Saudi Arabia Changed the Balance of Power in the Middle East* (New York: Simon &

Schuster, 2012), p. 73. See also Asadollah Alam, *Diaries of Asadollah Alam*, vol. 1 *(1347–1348/1968–1969)* (Bethesda, Md.: Ibex, 1992).

20. Mark Gasiorowski and Nikki Keddie, *Neither East nor West: Iran, the Soviet Union, and the United States* (New Haven: Yale University Press, 1990), pp. 148–51.

21. Ibid.

22. Frances FitzGerald, "Giving the Shah Everything He Wants," *Harper's Magazine*, November 1974, https://harpers.org/archive/1974/11/giving-the-shah-everything-he-wants/; Martha Crenshaw, ed., *Terrorism in Context* (University Park: Pennsylvania State University Press, 1995), p. 565.

23. Robert Graham, *Iran: The Illusion of Power* (New York: St. Martin's Press, 1979), p. 143.

24. Gasiorowski and Keddie, *Neither East nor West*, p. 150.

25. Quoted by R. Namvar, *Rezhun-i Teror va Ekhtenaq (Regime of Terror and Strangulation)* (N.p.: n.p., 1962), p. 13 (my translation). For an informative book on SAVAK, see Amin Saikal, *The Rise and the Fall of the Shah: Iran from Autocracy to Religious Rule* (Princeton: Princeton University Press, 1980).

26. Abrahamian, *A History of Modern Iran*, p. 128.

27. British ambassador, report, April 19, 1955, FO 371/Persia 1955/114807, National Archives.

28. De Bellaigue, *Patriot of Persia*, p. 265.

29. Quoted in Ali M. Ansari, *The Politics of Nationalism in Modern Iran* (Cambridge: Cambridge University Press, 2012), p. 173.

30. Quoted in Abrahamian, *A History of Modern Iran*, p. 131.

31. Ali M. Ansari, "The Myth of the White Revolution: Mohammad Reza Shah, 'Modernization' and the Consolidation of Power," *Middle Eastern Studies* 27, no. 2 (2001): 2.

32. De Bellaigue, *Patriot of Persia*, p. 265.

33. Ansari, "The Myth of the White Revolution," p. 2.

34. James Bill, "Modernization and Reform from Above: The Case of Iran," *Journal of Politics* 32, no. 1 (1970): 32. On the White Revolution, see Nikki Keddie, *Roots of Revolution: An Interpretive History of Modern Iran*, with a section by Yann Richard (New Haven: Yale University Press, 2003), pp. 145–61; and Kenneth Pollack, *The Persian Puzzle: The Conflict between Iran and America* (New York: Random House, 2004), pp. 90–92.

35. Abrahamian, *A History of Modern Iran*, p. 131.

36. Ibid., p. 132.

37. On the land and agricultural reform, see Misagh Parsa, *Social Origins of the Iranian Revolution* (New Brunswick: Rutgers University Press, 1989), pp. 48–50; Sussan Siavoshi, *Liberal Nationalism in Iran: The Failure of a Movement* (Boulder, Colo.: Westview Press, 1990), p. 23.

38. Abrahamian, *A History of Modern Iran*, pp. 133–34.

39. Abdullahi An-Na'im, *Islamic Family Law in a Changing World: A Global Resource Book* (London: Zed Books, 2002), p. 108. See also Parsa, *Social Origins of the Iranian Revolution.*

40. Abrahamian, *A History of Modern Iran*, p. 133.

41. Ibid.

42. Ibid.

43. De Bellaigue, *Patriot of Persia*, p. 265.

44. National War College (U.S.), *Intelligence and the National Security Process,* (Washington, D.C.: National Defense University, National War College, 1985), p. 5.

45. Quoted in Tony Smith, *America's Mission: The United States and the Worldwide Struggle for Democracy in the Twentieth Century* (Princeton: Princeton University Press, 1995), p. 255.

46. Mohammad Reza Pahlavi, *Mission for My Country* (London: Hutchinson, 1961), p. 173.

47. Quoted in Fred E. Halliday, *Iran, Dictatorship and Development* (New York: Penguin, 1979), pp. 47–48.

48. Abrahamian, *A History of Modern Iran*, p. 140.

49. Ibid., p. 139.

50. Ibid., p. 140.

51. Ali Gheissari, *Iranian Intellectuals in the Twentieth Century* (Austin: University of Texas Press, 1997), p. 97. For the life and thought of Ali Shariati, see J. Pajum, *Shakhsiat va Andisheie, Doctor Ali Shariati (The Personality and Thinking of Doctor Ali Shariati)* (Tehran: Chapaksh, 1992); and Ali Rahnema, *An Islamic Utopian: A Political Biography of Ali Shariati* (New York: Routledge, 1998).

52. Janet Afary, "Review Essay—The Pitfalls of National Consciousness in Iran: The Construction of a Militant Muslim Ideology," *Journal of Political and Military Sociology* 15 (Fall 1987): 279–84.

53. Hamid Enayat, *Modern Islamic Political Thought*, (London: I. B. Tauris, 2005), p. 155; see also Ervand Abrahamian "Ali Shari'ati: Ideologue of the Iranian Revolution," *MERIP Reports* 102 (1982): 24–28.

54. Mehrdad Vahabi and Nasser Mohajer, "The Islamic Republic and Its Opposition," *Comparative Studies of South Asia, Africa and the Middle East* 31, no. 1 (2011): 110.

55. Graham, *Iran: The Illusion of Power*, p. 19.

56. Ali Fathollah-Nejad, *Iran in an Emerging New World Order* (Singapore: Palgrave Macmillan, 2021), p. 129.

57. Pejman Abdolmohammadi and Giampiero Cama, *Contemporary Domestic and Foreign Policies of Iran* (New York: Palgrave Macmillan, 2020), p. 23.

58. Ibid.

59. Fathollah-Nejad, *Iran in an Emerging New World Order*, p. 129.

60. Ibid.

61. Regarding the causes of the transformation of social and political life in Iran, see Said Amir Arjomand, *The Turban for the Crown* (Oxford: Oxford University Press, 1989), pp. 93–94; Ali Mirsepassi-Ashtiani, "The Crisis of Secular Politics and the Rise of Political Islam in Iran," *Social Text* 38 (Spring 1994): 51–84, 76; Hassan Yousefi Eshkevari, *Nogerai-ye Dini (The Religious Modernism)* (Tehran: Ghazal, 1998), pp. 8–30; and Parsa, *Social Origins of the Iranian Revolution*, pp. 48–50.

62. Abrahamian, *A History of Modern Iran*, p. 147.

63. Ervand Abrahamian, *Khomeinism: Essays on the Islamic Republic* (Berkeley: University of California Press, 1993), p. 24.

64. Fathollah-Nejad, *Iran in an Emerging New World Order*, p. 97.

65. Moshen Milani, *The Making of Iran's Islamic Revolution: From Monarchy to Islamic Republic* (Boulder, Colo.: Westview Press, 1988).

66. Abrahamian, *A History of Modern Iran*, p. 147. Milani, *The Making of Iran's Islamic Revolution*, p. 91.

67. Sparsha Saha, "Iran's Situations: Military Violence, Protests, and Group Dynamics" (Ph.D. diss., Harvard University, 2014), p. 68.

68. Quoted in Baqer Moin, *Khomeini: Life of the Ayatollah* (New York: Thomas Dunne Books, 2000), p. 104.

69. Ruhollah Khomeini, *Islam and Revolution: Writing and Declarations of Imam Khomeini*, ed. and trans. Hamid Algar (Tehran: Mizan Press, 1981), p. 17.

70. Ervand Abrahamian, *The Coup: 1953, the CIA, and the Roots of Modern U.S.–Iranian Relations* (New York: New Press, 2013), p. 215.

71. Simin Fadaee, *Social Movements in Iran: Environmentalism and Civil Society* (New York: Routledge, 2012), p. 55.

72. Baqer Moin, *Khomeini: Life of the Ayatollah* (2000; repr., London: I. B. Tauris, 2009), pp. 135–37.

73. Abdar Rahman Koya, *Imam Khomeini: Life, Thought and Legacy* (Kuala Lumpur: Islamic Book Trust, 2009), p. 36.

74. Mosa Zahed, "The Evolution and Ascension of Iran's Terror Apparatus," in *Terrorism Revisited: Islamism, Political Violence and State-Sponsorship*, ed. Paulo Casaca and Siegfried O. Wolf (New York: Springer International, 2017), p. 67.

75. Koya, *Imam Khomeini*, p. 37.

76. Andrew Scott Cooper, *The Fall of Heaven: The Pahlavis and the Final Days of Imperial Iran* (New York: Henry Holt, 2016), pp. 198–99.

77. Robert Lacey, *The Kingdom* (London: Hutchinson, 1981), p. 416.

78. Cooper, *The Fall of Heaven*, p. 200.

79. Marvin Zonis, *Majestic Failure: The Fall of the Shah* (Chicago: University of Chicago Press, 1991), p. 66.

80. Oriana Fallaci, *Interviews with History*, trans. John Shepley (Boston: Houghton Mifflin, 1976), p. 267.

81. Quoted in Milani, *The Shah*, p. 310.

82. Atul Kohli, *Imperialism and the Developing World: How Britain and the United States Shaped the Global Periphery* (Oxford: Oxford University Press, 2020), p. 283.

83. Alvandi, *Nixon, Kissinger, and the Shah*, p. 30.

84. Memorandum of a Conversation, May 31, 1972, in *FRUS*, 1969–76, Iran and Iraq, E-4, no. 201.

85. F. Gregory Gause III, *The International Relations of the Persian Gulf* (Cambridge: Cambridge University Press, 2009), p. 22.

86. Alvandi, *Nixon, Kissinger, and the Shah*, p. 29.

87. Ibid., p. 172.

88. Abrahamian, *A History of Modern Iran*, p. 152.

89. Ibid.

90. "The Nationalization of Religion," *Mojahed* 29 (1975): 6–10.

91. The shah's extravagant Persepolis party that was widely viewed as self-indulgent and a waste of national resources. It served to undermine his legitimacy, even though the intent was to bolster it. See a contemporary account: Charlotte Curtis, "First Party of Iran's 2,500-Year Celebration," *New York Times*, October 13, 1971. See also a video documentary with contemporary footage: "How Iran Threw the World's Greatest Party in a Desert," SideNote, YouTube, February 8, 2020, https://www.youtube.com/watch?v=6aFoUqCoJ48.

92. Abrahamian, *A History of Modern Iran*, pp. 130–31.

93. Ibid., p. 153.

94. Ruhollah Khomeini, "Proclamation," *Mojahed* 29 (1975): 1–11. See also A. Rouhani, "Proclamation," *Mojahed* 30 (1975): 7.

95. Abrahamian, *A History of Modern Iran*, p. 153.

96. Fathollah-Nejad, *Iran in an Emerging New World Order*, p. 129.

97. Ali Mirsepassi, *Intellectual Discourse and the Politics of Modernization: Negotiating Modernity in Iran* (Cambridge: Cambridge University Press, 2000), p. 94.

98. Ahmad Ashraf, "Bazaar-Mosque Alliance: The Social Basis of Revolts and Revolutions," *International Journal of Politics, Culture, and Society* 1, no. 4 (1988): 541.

99. Roy Mottahedeh, *The Mantle of the Prophet: Religion and Politics in Iran* (New York: Simon & Schuster, 1985), p. 346.

100. Ashraf, "Bazaar-Mosque Alliance," p. 542.

101. Donald Newton Wilber, *Clandestine Service History: Overthrow of Premier Mossadeq of Iran, November 1952–August 1953* (Washington, D.C.: C.I.A, 1954).

102. Ibid.

103. Tamim Ansary, *Destiny Disrupted: A History of the World through Islamic Eyes* (New York: Public Affairs, 2009), p. 334.

104. Quoted in Parsa, *Social Origins of the Iranian Revolution*, p. 193.
105. Sasan Fayazmanesh, "What Kermit Roosevelt Didn't Say," *Counter-Punch*, August 18, 2003, https://www.counterpunch.org/2003/08/18/what-kermit-roosevelt-didn-t-say/.

Chapter Five. What Did the Overthrow of Mossadegh Mean for Iran and the Middle East?

1. Christopher de Bellaigue, *Patriot of Persia: Muhammad Mossadegh and a Very British Coup* (London: Bodley Head, 2012), p. 273.
2. James A. Bill, *The Eagle and the Lion: The Tragedy of American-Iranian Relations* (New Haven: Yale University Press, 1988), p. 63. See also Atul Kohli, *Imperialism and the Developing World: How Britain and the United States Shaped the Global Periphery* (Oxford: Oxford University Press, 2020), p. 276.
3. Quoted in Mostafa Elm, *Oil, Power, and Principle: Iran's Oil Nationalization and Its Aftermath* (Syracuse, N.Y.: Syracuse University Press, 1994), p. 175.
4. "Nonaligned Countries Declaration, 1979 (Havana Declaration)," in *Encyclopedia of the United Nations and International Agreements*, ed. Edmund Jan Osmańczyk (London: Taylor & Francis, 2003), pp. 1598–99.
5. De Bellaigue, *Patriot of Persia*, p. 165.
6. Henry F. Grady. "What Went Wrong in Iran?" *Saturday Evening Post*, January 5, 1952, https://www.saturdayeveningpost.com/wp-content/uploads/satevepost/1952_what_went_wrong_iran.pdf. See also de Bellaigue, *Patriot of Persia*, pp. 165–66, 191.
7. Ambassador in Iran (Henderson) to the Department of State, telegram, January 4, 1952, in *Foreign Relations of the United States (FRUS)*, 1952–54, X, Iran, no. 139.
8. De Bellaigue, *Patriot of Persia*, p. 186.
9. Ibid., p. 273.
10. "Mr. President," he said, "I am speaking for a very poor country—a country all desert—just sand, a few camels, a few sheep." Dean Acheson, recalling his conversation with Mossadegh, Washington, D.C., October 23, 1951, in *A Middle East Mosaic: Fragments of Life, Letters and History*, ed. Bernard Lewis (New York: Random House, 2000), p. 174.
11. Roham Alvandi, *Nixon, Kissinger, and the Shah: The United States and Iran in the Cold War* (Oxford: Oxford University Press, 2016), p. 32.
12. "Ich werde Ihnen Aspirin verkaufen," *Der Spiegel*, January 6, 1974, https://www.spiegel.de/wirtschaft/ich-werde-ihnen-aspirin-verkaufen-a-4c69cc27-0002-0001-0000-000041794683.
13. Abbas Milani, *The Shah* (London: Palgrave Macmillan, 2011), p. 6.
14. Alvandi, *Nixon, Kissinger, and the Shah*, p. 32.

15. Glenn E. Curtis, *Iran: A Country Study* (Washington, D.C: Library of Congress, 2008), p. 27.

16. Marvin Zonis, *Majestic Failure: The Fall of the Shah* (Chicago: University of Chicago Press, 1991), p. 14.

17. Ervand Abrahamian, *The Coup: 1953, the CIA, and the Roots of Modern U.S.–Iranian Relations* (New York: New Press, 2013), p. 52; De Bellaigue, *Patriot of Persia*, pp. 152, 275.

18. Ervand Abrahamian, *Tortured Confessions: Prisons and Public Recantations in Modern Iran* (Berkeley: University of California Press, 1999), p. 106.

19. Ibid., p. 105.

20. Ibid.

21. Ibid., p. 109.

22. Ibid., p. 108.

23. Farhad Diba, *Mohammad Mossadegh: A Political Biography* (London: Routledge & Kegan Paul, 1986).

24. "Corrections and Clarifications," *Guardian*, June 20, 2000, https://www.theguardian.com/theguardian/2000/jun/21/correctionsandclarifications.

25. On this prevailing foreign policy logic, see Bradley R. Simpson, *Economists with Guns: Authoritarian Development and U.S.–Indonesian Relations, 1960–1968* (Stanford: Stanford University Press, 2008). See also Michael E. Latham, *The Right Kind of Revolution: Modernization, Development, and U.S. Foreign Policy from the Cold War to the Present* (Ithaca: Cornell University Press, 2011).

26. Mark Gasiorowski, "The 1953 Coup d'Etat in Iran," *International Journal of Middle East Studies*, 19, no. 3 (1987): 275. See also Stephen E. Ambrose, *Eisenhower*, 2 vols. (New York: Simon & Schuster, 1983), 1:26–27; Dwight D. Eisenhower, *The White House Years: Mandate for Change, 1953–1956* (Garden City, N.Y.: Doubleday, 1963), p. 163; and Kohli, *Imperialism and the Developing World*, p. 255.

27. Milani, *The Shah*, p. 14.

28. Gasiorowski, "The 1953 Coup d'Etat in Iran," p. 275. See also Ervand Abrahamian, *A History of Modern Iran* (Cambridge: Cambridge University Press, 2008).

29. Elizabeth F. Thompson, *How the West Stole Democracy from the Arabs: The Syrian Congress of 1920 and the Destruction of Its Historic Liberal-Islamic Alliance* (New York: Atlantic Monthly Press, 2020).

30. "CIA Admits 1953 Iranian Coup It Backed Was Undemocratic," *Guardian*, October 13, 2023, https://www.theguardian.com/us-news/2023/oct/13/cia-1953-iran-coup-undemocratic-argo.

31. Paper by Robert W. Komer of the National Security Council Staff, October 20, 1962, in *FRUS* 1961–1963, XVIII, Near East, no. 85.

32. Denis Lacorne and Tony Judt, eds., *With Us or against Us: Studies in Global Anti-Americanism* (New York: Palgrave Macmillan, 2005), pp. 192–93. This prism has changed over the last decade. Many young Iranians do

not buy the rhetoric of the Islamic Republic regarding the culpability of the United States as the root cause of the country's severe economic distress.

33. Madeleine Albright, "Remarks before the American Iranian Council, March 17, 2000, Washington D.C.," in *Seizing an Historic Opportunity: Breaking through the US–Iran Impasse*, ed. Hooshang Amirahmadi (Princeton, N.J.: American Iranian Council, 2000), p. 33.

34. "Obama Admits US Involvement in 1953 Iran Coup," *ABS-CBN News*, June 5, 2009, https://news.abs-cbn.com/world/06/04/09/obama-admits-us-involvement-1953-iran-coup.

35. Editorial Board, "Why the Past Haunts Talks with Iran," *New York Times*, April 23, 2021, https://www.nytimes.com/2021/04/23/opinion/iran-nuclear-deal.html.

36. Ibid. See Joost R. Hiltermann, *A Poisonous Affair: America, Iraq, and the Gassing of Halabja* (New York: Cambridge University Press, 2007), and Ray Takeya, *The Last Shah: America, Iran, and the Fall of the Pahlavi Dynasty* (New Haven: Yale University Press, 2021).

37. In a Gallup poll conducted in 2021, roughly 85 percent of Americans expressed an unfavorable view toward Iran, and 40 percent held a very unfavorable view. Gallup, February 3–18, 2021, https://news.gallup.com/poll/116236/iran.aspx.

38. Collective Iranian thinking about America's complicity, however, has shifted over the past decade. In particular, young Iranians who were born after 1979 have no memory of the formative years of the Mossadegh and Shah rule and are familiar only with the clerical rule that has brought them neither prosperity nor freedom.

39. "Doing Satan's Work in Iran," *New York Times*, November 6, 1979, https://www.nytimes.com/1979/11/06/archives/doing-satans-work-in-iran.html.

40. De Bellaigue, *Patriot of Persia*, p. 276.

41. Vernon Walters, *Silent Missions* (Garden City, N.Y.: Doubleday, 1978), p. 247.

42. Lacorne and Judt, *With Us or against Us*, p. 191.

43. Fereydoun Zandfard, *Iran va Jame'-ye Melal* (*Iran and the Society of Nations*) (Tehran: Shirazeh, 1998), p. 1377.

44. "Doing Satan's Work in Iran."

45. For more details, see Gasiorowski, "The 1953 Coup d'Etat in Iran."

46. De Bellaigue, *Patriot of Persia*, p. 277.

47. Maryam Sinaee, "Statistics Suggest Half of Iranians Living in Poverty," *Iran International*, October 8, 2020, https://old.iranintl.com/en/iran/statistics-suggest-half-iranians-living-poverty. See also a study by the Brookings Institution on the relationship between increasing poverty and sanctions: Ali Fatollah-Nejad, "The Islamic Republic of Iran Four Decades On: The 2017/18 Protests amid a Triple Crisis," Brookings Doha

Center Analysis Paper, no. 28, April 2020, https://www.brookings.edu
/wp-content/uploads/2020/04/The-Islamic-Republic-of-Iran-Four-
Decades-On-English-Web.pdf, pp. 20–21.

48. Nick Cumming-Bruce, "The Killing of Qassim Suleimani Was Unlawful,
Says U.N. Expert," *New York Times*, July 9, 2020, https://www.nytimes
.com/2020/07/09/world/middleeast/qassim-suleimani-killing-unlawful
.html.

49. See Ali Fathollah-Nejad, "Analysis: What the Killing of Qassem Solei-
mani Could Mean," *PBS News Hour*, January 3, 2020, https://www.pbs
.org/newshour/world/column-what-the-killing-of-qassem-soleimani-
could-mean-for-iran.

50. On America's rationales behind the assassination of Suleimani, see Gilbert Achcar, "Washington and Tehran's Dance over Iraq: Iraqis Want
Both Countries Out," *Le Monde Diplomatique*, February 2020, https://
mondediplo.com/2020/02/03iraq.

51. Karen Zraick, "What to Know about the Death of Iranian General Suleimani," *New York Times*, July 9, 2020, https://www.nytimes.com/2020
/01/03/world/middleeast/suleimani-dead.html.

52. David D. Kirkpatrick, Farnaz Fassihi, and Ronen Bergman, "Killer
Robot? Assassination of Iranian Scientist Feeds Conflicting Accounts,"
New York Times, December 2, 2020, https://www.nytimes.com/2020/12/
02/world/middleeast/iran-assassination-nuclear-scientist.html.

53. "Ex-CIA Chief Condemns 'Criminal' Assassination of Iranian," WION,
November 28, 2020, https://www.wionews.com/world/ex-cia-chief-
condemns-criminal-assassination-of-iranian-345989.

54. Kambiz Fattahi, "Two Weeks in January: America's Secret Engagement
with Khomeini," BBC, June 3, 2016, https://www.bbc.com/news/world-
us-canada-36431160.

55. Asef Bayat, "A New Iran Has Been Born—A Global Iran," *New Lines
Magazine*, October 26, 2022, https://newlinesmag.com/argument/a-new-
iran-has-been-born-a-global-iran/.

Chapter Six. Nasser

1. This chapter borrows liberally from my biography of Gamal Abdel
Nasser, *Making the Arab World: Nasser, Qutb, and the Clash That Shaped the
Middle East* (Princeton: Princeton University Press, 2018), esp. chaps. 2,
3, and 5.

2. Tarek Osman, *Egypt on the Brink: From Nasser to the Muslim Brotherhood*,
rev. ed. (New Haven: Yale University Press, 2013), p. 51.

3. Author's interview with Khaled Mohieddin, Cairo, December 6, 2006.

4. Quoted in Edward Said, *Orientalism: Western Conceptions of the Orient*
(1978, repr., London: Penguin, 1995), pp. 37–38.

5. Anthony Nutting, *Nasser* (London: Constable, 1972), p. 7.

6. "Mourners Killed as Nasser Is Buried," BBC, October 1, 1970, http://news.bbc.co.uk/onthisday/hi/dates/stories/october/1/newsid_2485000/2485899.stm.

7. Author's interview with Mohamed Hassanein Heikal, Cairo, Egypt, December 10, 2006.

8. "Sunday Times Reporter Interview with President Gamal Abdel Nasser," *Sunday Times*, June 18, 1962, http://nasser.bibalex.org/Common/pictures01-%20sira3_en.htm. See further insights on Nasser and his fellow army officers in Joel Gordon, *Nasser's Blessed Movement: Egypt's Free Officers and the July Revolution* (Oxford: Oxford University Press, 1991); Jean Lacouture, *Nasser: A Biography* (New York: Alfred A. Knopf, 1973), p. 20.

9. Butherina Abdelrahman Tikriti, *Gamal 'Abd al-Nasir: Nasha'at wa-tatawwur al-fikr al-nasiri* (*Gamal Abdel-Nasser: The Creation and Evolution of Nasserist Thought*) (Beirut: Markaz Derasat al-Wihda al-Arabiyya, 2000).

10. Said K. Aburish, *Nasser: The Last Arab* (New York: St. Martin's Press, 2004), p. 11.

11. "A Historical Sketch of President Gamal Abdel-Nasser," http://nasser.bibalex.org/common/pictures01-%20sira_en.htm.

12. "Sunday Times Reporter Interview with President Gamal Abdel Nasser."

13. Ibid. Several memoirs and writings by leading figures in the Egyptian communist movement argued that Nasser did join one or two of the many clandestine communist groups before 1952. Some accounts even mentioned that Nasser was nicknamed "Morris." Nasser's fellow Free Officers counted a lot on cadres affiliated with the Egyptian Communist Party.

14. Tahia Gamal Abdel Nasser, *Nasser: My Husband* (Cairo: American University in Cairo Press, 2013), p. 7.

15. Ibid.

16. Joachim Joesten, *Nasser: The Rise to Power* (London: Odhams, 1960), p. 19.

17. A low-resolution image of the original essay is at http://nasser.bibalex.org/images/fi_megalet_alnadah_01.jpg.

18. Aburish, *Nasser*, p. 11.

19. Anne Alexander, *Nasser: Life and Times* (London: Haus, 2005), p. 14.

20. See Michael E. Gasper, *The Power of Representation: Publics, Peasants and Islam in Egypt* (Stanford: Stanford University Press, 2009), p. 19.

21. I. Gershoni and J. P. Jankowski, *Redefining the Egyptian Nation, 1930–1945* (Cambridge: Cambridge University Press, 1995), pp. 2–3.

22. Gamal Abdel Nasser to his friend Hassan el-Nashar, September 4, 1935, http://www.nasser.org/Common/NasserLife_en.aspx?lang=ar. The letter was written two months before Nasser participated in the student protests against the British and the monarch's rejection of the return of constitutionalism to Egypt. In 1930 the Egyptian monarchy had abolished

the 1923 constitution, which is seen as the most liberal and democratic charter in the country's modern history, even though the monarchy had subverted many of its liberal clauses.

23. Nutting, *Nasser*, p. 7.

24. H. G. A. Nasser, "Biography: A Historical Sketch of President Gamal Abdel-Nasser," n.d., http://nasser.bibalex.org/common/pictures01-%20sira_en.htm.

25. Author's interview with Khaled Moheiddin, Cairo, Egypt, December 12, 2006.

26. Nutting, *Nasser*, p. 15; Aburish, *Nasser*, p. 17.

27. Nutting, *Nasser*, p. 21.

28. Ibid., p. 22.

29. Author's interview with Mohamed Hassanein Heikal, Cairo, Egypt, December 10, 2006.

30. Gerges, *Making the Arab World*, p. 171.

31. P. R. Woodward, *Nasser* (London: Longman, 1992), p. 17.

32. Tikriti, *Gamal 'Abd al-Nasir*, p. 113.

33. G. Abdel Nasser, *Falsafat al-Thawra* (*The Philosophy of the Revolution*) (Cairo: Matab'i al-Dar al-Qawmiyya, n.d.), p. 16.

34. Nasser to his friend Hassan el-Nashar on the events on February 4, 1942, http://www.nasser.org/images/nashar_letters_06.jpg.

35. Author's interview with Khaled Moheiddin, Cairo, Egypt, December 12, 2006.

36. Anwar al-Sadat, *Ya waladi haza amuka Gamal* (*My Son, This Is Your Uncle Gamal*) (Cairo: Madbouly, 2005), pp. 51, 83. Sadat pointed out that Nasser formed the Free Officers and then led the movement as of 1942, the same year in which British forces besieged the king's palace. Members of this organization "shared one sentiment; hatred towards the British control of all walks of life either in the army or outside of it"; ibid., p. 83.

37. Nasser, *Falsafat al-Thawra*, p. 11. Gerges, *Making the Arab World*, p. 170.

38. Gamal Abdel Nasser, *Al-haqiqa al-lati eishtaha* (*The Reality Which I Lived*), pt. 2 (Cairo: Idarat al-Shu'un al-'Ama li-l-Quwwat al-Musallaha, 1955), pp. 4–5, 17, 22. See also Gerges, *Making the Arab World*, p. 170.

39. Other writers and intellectuals agree that Egypt's national security interests converge with pan-Arab interests. See M. El-Sulh, *Misr wal-Uruba* (*Egypt and Pan-Arabism*) (Beirut: Al-Muasassa al-'Arabiyya leil derasaat wal Nashr, n.d.), pp. 22–25. Scholars such as Louis Awad even linked the rise of this pan-Arabism with what he described as Nasser's populist urge: L. Awad, *Aqni't al-Nassiryya al-Saba': Munaqashat Tawfiq al-Hakim and Mohamed Hassanein Heikal* (*The Seven Masks of Nasserism: Debating with Tawfiq al-Hakim and Mohamed Hassanein Heikal*) (Cairo: Madbouli, 1987), p. 49. Gerges, *Making the Arab World*, p. 171.

40. Ahron Bregman and Jihan El-Tahri, *The Fifty Years War: Israel and the Arabs* (London: BBC Books, 1999), p. 39.

41. Nasser, *Nasser: My Husband*, p. 18. Gerges, *Making the Arab World*, p. 173.
42. Author's interview with Mohamed Hassanein Heikal, Cairo, Egypt, September 24, 2006.
43. F. Fahmy, *'Abd al-Nasir min al-Hisar leil Inqilab (Abdel Nasser: From the Siege to the Coup)* (Cairo: Muassar Amoun al-Haditha, 1994), pp. 10–13.
44. Nasser, *Falsafat al-Thawra*, p. 64.
45. Ibid., p. 57.
46. Walid Khalidi, "Political Trends in the Fertile Crescent," in *The Middle East in Transition*, ed. Walter Z. Laqueur (New York: Praeger, 1958), p. 125.
47. Author's interview with Mohamed Hassanein Heikal, Cairo, Egypt, December 10, 2006. See also author's interview with Khaled Moheiddin, Cairo, Egypt, December 12, 2006.
48. Reem Abou-el-Fadl, "Early Pan-Arabism in Egypt's July Revolution: The Free Officers' Political Formation and Policy-Making, 1946–54," *Nations and Nationalism* 22, no. 2 (2015): 291.
49. Nasser, *Nasser: My Husband*, p. 30.
50. T. Aclimandos, "Revisiting the History of the Egyptian Army," in *Re-envisioning Egypt, 1919–52*, ed. Arthur Goldschmidt, Amy Johnson, and Barak A. Salmoni (Cairo: American University in Cairo Press, 2005), p. 70.
51. See the excellent study of the movement by Gordon, *Nasser's Blessed Movement*. See also the official biographer of the Free Officers' revolution, Ahmad Hamroush, *The Story of the July 23 Revolution: The Quest for Democracy . . . The Quest for Socialism* (in Arabic) (Cairo: Dar Ibn Khaldoun, 1982).
52. Author's interview with Sami Sharaf, Nasser's chief of staff and keeper of his secrets, Cairo, Egypt, February 8, 2007.
53. Author's interview with Abd al-Ghaffar Shukr, Cairo, Egypt, October 10, 2007. See also Gerges, *Making the Arab World*, pp. 22–23.
54. Author's interview with the historian and cultural critic Sherif Younis, Cairo, Egypt, October 27, 2006.
55. Joan Wucher King, *Historical Dictionary of Egypt* (Cairo: American University in Cairo Press, 1989), p. 207.
56. Arthur Goldschmidt and Robert Johnston, *Historical Dictionary of Egypt*, 3rd ed. (Cairo: American University in Cairo Press, 2004), p. 83.
57. Author's interview with Khaled Moheiddin, Cairo, Egypt, December 12, 2006.
58. James Brian McNabb, *A Military History of the Modern Middle East* (Santa Barbara, Calif.: ABC-CLIO, 2017), p. 136.
59. Gordon, *Nasser's Blessed Movement*, p. 52.
60. Aburish, *Nasser*, p. 36.
61. Author's interview with Khaled Moheiddin, Cairo, Egypt, December 12, 2006.

62. See Nasser, *Falsafat al-Thawra*.
63. T.R.L., "Egypt since the Coup d'Etat of 1952," *World Today* 10, no. 4 (April 1954): 140.
64. Ibid.
65. Around 18 million of a population of 23 million people worked in the agricultural sector at the time. Of these, 6.5 percent owned 98 percent of the land. Therefore, the remaining 93.5 percent are largely categorized as landless or agricultural laborers. See Stella Margold, "Agrarian Land Reform in Egypt," *American Journal of Economics and Sociology* 17, no. 1 (October 1957): 9; Osman, *Egypt on the Brink*, p. 45; Mourad M. Wahba, *The Role of the State in the Egyptian Economy* (Reading, U.K.: Ithaca Press, 1994), p. 49.
66. T.R.L., "Egypt since the Coup d'Etat of 1952," p. 142.
67. Cited in Gerges, *Making the Arab World*, pp. 83–86.
68. Laila Amin Morsy, "American Support for the 1952 Egyptian Coup: Why?" *Middle Eastern Studies* 31, no. 2 (April 1995): 310.

Chapter Seven. Nasser in "Little Hollywood"

1. Chapters 7, 8, and 9 are based on primary research for my Ph.D. dissertation at Oxford University, which was published in 1994, and which cited and acknowledged all sources. Given the fact that this research covered historical events that won't have changed, there is some overlap between the Ph.D. and these three chapters in this book, which is based on a thesis not previously published.
2. Cited by Jon B. Alterman, *Egypt and American Foreign Assistance, 1952–1956: Hopes Dashed* (New York: Palgrave, 2002), p. 3.
3. Laila Amin Morsy, "American Support for the 1952 Egyptian Coup: Why?" *Middle Eastern Studies* 31, no. 2 (April 1995): 310.
4. Alta F. Fowler of the Office of Near Eastern Affairs to the Officer in Charge of Egypt and Anglo-Egyptian Sudan Affairs, Washington, memorandum, July 28, 1952, *Foreign Relations of the United States (FRUS)*, 1952–54, the Near and Middle East, IX, pt. 2, no. 997.
5. Said K. Aburish, *Nasser: The Last Arab* (New York: St. Martin's Press, 2004), p. 39.
6. Hugh Wilford, *America's Great Game: The CIA's Secret Arabists and the Shaping of the Modern Middle East* (New York: Basic Books, 2013), pp. 133–45. See also Hazem Kandil, *Soldiers, Spies, and Statesmen: Egypt's Road to Revolt* (London: Verso, 2014).
7. Public Record Office, FO 371/118861, 1952 Political Relations between Egypt and the United Kingdom.
8. The Ambassador in Egypt to the Department of State, Cairo, March 17, 1953, *FRUS, 1952–1954, the Near and Middle East*, IX, pt. 2, p. 2025. See also the Ambassador in Egypt to the Department of State, Cairo, April 5,

1954, in *FRUS, 1952–1954, the Near and Middle East*, IX, pt. 2, pp. 2211, 2191, and 2259. Al-Shahid, *My Recollections during Two Administrations* (in Arabic) (Cairo: Dar al-ma'arif, 1976), pp. 256–57.

9. Interview conducted with Muhyi al-Din, cited in Mohamed Odeh, Philip Jallab, and Saad Kamel, *The Story of the Soviets with Egypt* [in Arabic] (Beirut: Dar ibn khaldoun, n.d.), pp. 52–56, 145–46.

10. Strobe Talbott, ed., *Khrushchev Remembers* (London: Book Club Associates, 1971), pp. 431–32.

11. Walter Z. Laqueur, ed., *Communism and Nationalism in the Middle East* (London: Routledge and Kegan Paul, 1956), p. 262.

12. Kennett Love, *Suez: The Twice-Fought War* (New York: McGraw-Hill, 1969), p. 235; Laqueur, *Communism and Nationalism in the Middle East*, p. 262.

13. Muhammad Abd al-Wahab Sayed-Ahmed, "Relations between Egypt and the United States of America in the 1950s," in *Contemporary Egypt: Through Egyptian Eyes: Essays in Honour of Professor P. J. Vatikiotis*, ed. Charles Tripp (London; Routledge, 1993), p. 90.

14. Alta F. Fowler of the Office of Near Eastern Affairs to the Officer in Charge of Egypt and Anglo-Egyptian Sudan Affairs, Washington, July 28, 1952, memorandum.

15. T.R.L., "Egypt since the Coup d'Etat of 1952," *World Today* 10, no. 4 (April 1954): 144.

16. Morsy, "American Support for the 1952 Egyptian Coup," p. 310.

17. William J. Burns, *Economic Aid and American Policy toward Egypt, 1955–1981* (Albany: State University of New York Press, 1985), p. 11.

18. Rashid al-Barawy, *The Military Coup in Egypt* (Cairo: Renaissance Bookshop, 1952), p. 209.

19. Donald Neff, *Warriors at Suez: Eisenhower Takes America into the Middle East* (New York: Simon and Schuster, 1981), p. 177.

20. John Lewis Gaddis, *We Now Know: Rethinking Cold War History* (Oxford: Oxford University Press, 1998), p. 168.

21. Gamal Abdel Nasser, *President Gamal Abdel-Nasser's Speeches and Press Interviews* (Cairo: Information Department, 1960), p. 152.

22. *The Collected Speeches, Declarations, and Statements of President Nasser* (in Arabic), vol. 1 (Cairo: Hai'a al-ist'lamat, n.d.), p. 741.

23. Eugene Rogan, *The Arabs: A History* (New York: Basic Books, 2011), p. 228.

24. Ibid., p.74.

25. Waldemar J. Gallman, *Iraq under General Nuri: My Recollections of Nuri al-Said, 1954–1958* (Baltimore: Johns Hopkins University Press, 1964), p. 27. Mohamed Fadil al-Jamali, *Al-'Iraq al-hadith: Ara'wa mutala'at fi su'unihi al-masiriya (The New Iraq: Opinions and Readings in Its Fateful Affairs)* (Beirut: n.p., n.d.), pp. 18, 117.

26. Gallman, *Iraq under General Nuri*, p. 27.

27. Fawaz Gerges, *The Superpowers and the Middle East: Regional and International Politics, 1955–1967* (Boulder, Colo.: Westview Press, 1994), p. 25.

28. James P. Jankowski, *Nasser's Egypt, Arab Nationalism, and the United Arab Republic* (Boulder, Colo.: Lynne Reinner, 2002), p. 59.

29. A. I. Dawisha, *Egypt in the Arab World: The Elements of Foreign Policy* (London: Macmillan, 1976), p. 11.

30. Abdel-Latif al-Baghdadi, *Memoirs* (in Arabic), vol. 1 (Cairo: Al-Maktab al-Misri al-hadith, 1977), p. 197; *The Collected Speeches, Declarations, and Statements of President Nasser*, p. 418; and Sadat, *Ya waladi haza amuka Gamal*, pp. 138, 140

31. *The Collected Speeches, Declarations, and Statements of President Nasser*, p. 691; Sadat, *Ya waladi haza amuka Gamal*, p. 140; and Salah Nasr, *Memoirs: The 23 July Revolution between Departure and Progress: The Roots* (in Arabic) (Cairo: Mu'assasa al-itihad, 1986), 1:241–43.

32. Gamal Abdel Nasser, *President Gamal Abdel-Nasser's Speeches and Press Interviews* (in Arabic) (Cairo: Information Department, 1959), p. 603; *The Collected Speeches, Declarations, and Statements of President Nasser*, p. 692; Telegram from the Embassy in Egypt to the Department of State, Cairo, October 1, 1955, in *FRUS*, 1955–57, XIV, Arab-Israeli Dispute, no. 321; and Nasr, *Memoirs* (in Arabic), 1:244.

33. Anthony Nutting, *Nasser* (London: Constable, 1972), p. 101; Helen Denkos, *Soviet Foreign Policy in the Middle East, 1955–1975* (translated to Arabic by Abdallah Iskander) (Beirut: Dar al-kalima al-arabiya, 1983), p. 23.

34. *The Collected Speeches, Declarations, and Statements of President Nasser*, p. 692.

35. Humphrey Trevelyan, *The Middle East in Revolution* (London: Macmillan, 1970), pp. 28–29.

36. *The Collected Speeches, Declarations, and Statements of President Nasser*, p. 425.

37. Al-Baghdadi, *Memoirs* (in Arabic), 1:204–5.

38. Ibid.

39. National Intelligence Estimate, November 15, 1955, in *FRUS*, 1955–57, XIV, Arab-Israeli Dispute, no. 411.

40. Memorandum of a Conversation, Department of State, Washington, October 3, 1955, *FRUS*, 1955–57, XIV, Arab-Israeli Dispute, no. 323.

41. Sadat, *Ya waladi haza amuka Gamal*, p. 142.

42. Quoted in Gerges, *The Superpowers and the Middle East*, p. 39.

43. Memorandum of a Conversation, Department of State, Washington, July 29, 1955, and Telegram from the Department of State to the Delegation at the Foreign Ministers Meetings in Geneva, Washington, November 8, 1955, both in *FRUS*, 1955–57, XIV, Arab-Israeli Dispute, nos. 178, 390.

44. Dawisha, *Egypt in the Arab World*, p. 31.

45. For background on the Aswan Dam crisis, see James E. Dougherty, "The Aswan Decision in Perspective," *Political Science Quarterly* 74, no. 1

(March 1959): 21–45; Charles D. Smith, *Palestine and the Arab Israeli Conflict*, 6th ed. (Boston: Bedford/St. Martin's, 2007).

46. Dougherty, "The Aswan Decision in Perspective," p. 22.

47. Burns, *Economic Aid and American Policy toward Egypt*, pp. 8, 13–23

48. *The Collected Speeches, Declarations, and Statements of President Nasser*, p. 656; Sadat, *Ya waladi haza amuka Gamal*, pp. 96–97, 110; and Mahmoud Riad, *The Memoirs of Mahmoud Riad, 1948–1978: The Search for Peace and the Conflict in the Middle East* (Beirut: Arab Institute for Research and Publishing, 1981) p. 46.

49. Quoted in Gerges, *The Superpowers and the Middle East*, p. 51.

50. Diary Entries by the President, Washington, March 13 and 28, 1956; and Memorandum of Discussion at the 279th Meeting of the National Security Council, Washington, March 8, 1956, in *FRUS*, 1955–57, XV, Arab-Israeli Dispute, nos. 187, 226, 178. Memorandum of a Conversation, White House, Washington, March 28, 1956, Subject: United States Policy in the Near East; and Telegram to the Department of State to the Embassy in Egypt, April 3, 1956, in *FRUS*, 1955–57, XV, Arab-Israeli Dispute, nos. 224, 238.

51. Telegram from the Secretary of State to the Department of State, Karachi, March 8, 1956; Memorandum from the Acting Secretary of State to the Secretary of State, Washington, March 12, 1956; Diary Entry by the President, Washington, March 13, 1956; Memorandum by the Director of the Office of Near Eastern Affairs (Wilkins), Washington, March 14, 1956, Subject: United States Policy in the Near East; Memorandum of a Conference with the President, White House, Washington, March 28, 1956; Memorandum Prepared in the Bureau of Near Eastern, South Asian, and African Affairs, Subject: Washington, March 28, 1956, United States Policy in the Near East; and Memorandum from the Secretary of State to the President, Washington, March 28, 1956, in *FRUS*, 1955–57, XV, Arab-Israeli Conflict, nos. 176, 185, 187, 192, 225, 222, 223. See also Burns, *Economic Aid and American Policy toward Egypt*, pp. 36, 72–73, 76.

52. The Embassy in Egypt to the Department of State, April 19, 1956, in *FRUS*, 1955–57, XV, no. 294.

53. Gerges, *The Superpowers and the Middle East*, pp. 52–53.

54. Nasr, *Memoirs* (in Arabic), 1:255; Mohamed Heikal, *We and America* (in Arabic) (Cairo: Dar al-'asr al-hadith, 1967), pp. 113–14. Nasser told the U.S. and British ambassadors later that his decision to recognize China was motivated by a desire to keep an open channel of arms supplies. See Telegram from the Embassy in Egypt to the Department of State, February 15, 1957, in FRUS, 1955–57 XVII, Arab-Israeli Dispute, no. 101.

55. Memorandum of a Conversation, Department of State, Washington, May 17, 1956, Subject: U.S.–Egyptian Relations; Memorandum from the Deputy Assistant Secretary of State (Rountree) to the Secretary of State, May 23, 1956; and Telegram from the Embassy in Egypt to the Depart-

ment of State, Cairo, May 23, 1956, in *FRUS*, 1955–57, XV, Arab-Israeli Dispute, nos. 353, 360, and 363.

56. See the interview with Black in Mohammad Abd el-Wahab Sayed-Ahmed, *Nasser and American Foreign Policy, 1952–1956* (London: Laam, 1989), p. 120; Dwight Eisenhower, *The White House Years: Waging Peace, 1956–1961* (Garden City, N.Y.: Doubleday, 1965), p. 31; Memorandum from the Deputy Assistant Secretary of State (Rountree) to the Secretary of State, Washington, June 6, 1956, Subject: Aswan High Dam, in *FRUS*, 1955–1957,XV, Arab-Israeli Dispute, no. 389; and Burns, *Economic Aid and American Policy toward Egypt*, p. 76.

57. Memorandum of a Conversation, Department of State, Washington, June 25, 1956, Subject: Aswan Dam, Iran, Saudi Arabia; Memorandum from the Director of the CIA (Dulles) to the Secretary of State, Washington, June 27, 1956 Subject: Shepilov's Visit to Egypt; Memorandum of Discussion at the 289th Meeting of National Security Council, Washington, June 28, 1956; and Editorial Note, in *FRUS*, 1955–57, XV, Arab-Israeli Dispute, nos. 410, 411, 412, 452. See also: Dwight Eisenhower, *Waging Peace* (New York: Doubleday, 1965), pp. 33,39. Cited in Gerges, *The Superpowers and the Middle East*, p. 55.

58. Smith, *Palestine and the Arab-Israeli Conflict*, p. 247; Memorandum of a Conversation, Department of State, Washington, July 19, 1956, Subject: High Aswan Dam, in *FRUS*, 1955–57, XV, Arab-Israeli Dispute, no. 478.

Chapter Eight. The Suez Crisis

1. Quoted by Mohamed Heikal, *The Cairo Documents: The Inside Story of Nasser and His Relationship with World Leaders, Rebels, and Statesman* (Garden City, N.Y.: Doubleday, 1973), p. 70.

2. *The Collected Speeches, Declarations, and Statements of President Nasser, 23 July 1952–1958*, vol. 1 (Cairo: Hai'a al-ist'lamat, n.d.), p. 638; Anwar al-Sadat, *Ya waladi haza amuka Gamal* (*My Son: This Is Your Uncle Gamal*) (in Arabic) (Cairo: Madbouly, 2005), pp. 164–65, 169. See also A. I. Dawisha, *Egypt in the Arab World: The Elements of Foreign Policy* (London: Macmillan, 1976), p. 32.

3. *The Collected Speeches, Declarations, and Statements of President Nasser*, 1:547.

4. Ibid., pp. 548–58.

5. Anwar Sadat, *In Search of Identity: An Autobiography* (New York: Harper & Row, 1978), p. 143. See also Ali E. Hillal Dessouki, "Nasser and the Struggle for Independence," in *Suez, 1956: The Crisis and Its Consequences*, ed. Wm. Roger Louis and Roger Owen (Oxford: Clarendon Press, 1989), pp. 37–38; Said Mar'iy, *Political Papers: From the March Crisis to the Disaster* (in Arabic), vol. 2 (Cairo: Al-matab al-Misri al-hadith, 1978), p. 354. Humphrey Trevelyan, *The Middle East in Revolution* (London: Macmillan, 1970), p. 101.

6. Special National Intelligence Estimate, July 31, 1956, Nasser and the Middle East Situation, in *Foreign Relations of the United States (FRUS)*, 1955–57, XVI, Suez Crisis, no. 40. See also Charles Johnston, *The Brink of Jordan* (London: Hamish Hamilton, 1972), p. 8.

7. *The Collected Speeches, Declarations, and Statements of President Nasser*, 1:548, 573, 576–77. Mohamed Heikal, *Cutting the Lion's Tail: Suez through Egyptian Eyes* (New York: Arbor House, 1987), p. 148.

8. Salah Nasr, *Memoirs: The 23 July Revolution between Departure and Progress: The Roots* (in Arabic) (Cairo: Mu'assasa al-itihad, 1986), 1:262; Amin Hewedy, "Nasser and the Crisis of 1956," in Louis and Owen, *Suez, 1956*, pp. 166–67; and Heikal, *Nasser: The Cairo Documents*, pp. 110–11.

9. Memorandum of a Conference with the President, White House, Washington, July 27, 1956; and Telegram from the Department of State to the Secretary of State, at Lima, Washington, July 28, 1956, in *FRUS*, 1955–57, XVI, Suez Crisis, nos. 6, 14.

10. Memorandum of a Telephone Conversation between the President in Gettysburg, Pennsylvania, and the Secretary of State in Washington, July 29, 1956; Memorandum of a Telephone Conversation between the President and the Secretary of State, Washington, July 30, 1956; and Telegram from the Department of State to the Embassy in the United Kingdom, Washington, July 30, 1956, in *FRUS*, 1955–57, XVI, Suez Crisis, nos. 23, 27, 28. Memorandum of a Conference with the President, White House, Washington, July 31, 1956, in *FRUS*, 1955–57, XVI, Suez Crisis, no. 34.

11. *The Collected Speeches, Declarations, and Statements of President Nasser*, 1:583; Nasr, *Memoirs*, 1:262; Mahmoud Fawzi, *Suez: An Egyptian Perspective* (London: Shorouk International, n.d.), pp. 106, 113; Heikal, *Cutting the Lion's Tail*, pp. 146–47, 165; and Telegram from the Embassy in Egypt to the Department of State, July 30, 1956, in *FRUS*, 1955–57, XVI, Suez Crisis, no. 31

12. *The Collected Speeches, Declarations, and Statements of President Nasser*, 1:568. Memorandum of a Conversation with the President, July 28, 1956; Telegram from the Department of State to the Embassy in the United Kingdom, July 30, 1956; and the Embassy in Egypt to the Embassy in the United Kingdom, Cairo, August 1, 1956 (n. 3), in *FRUS*, 1955–57, XVI, Suez Crisis, nos. 16, 28, 45; Abdel-Latif al-Baghdadi, *Memoirs* (in Arabic), vol. 1 (Cairo: Al-Maktab al-Misri al-hadith, 1977), p. 327; Hewedy, "Nasser and the Crisis of 1956," pp. 166–67.

13. Memorandum of a Conversation, British Foreign Office, London, August 1, 1956, in *FRUS*, 1955–57, XVI, Suez Crisis, no. 41.

14. Memorandum of a Conversation, Secretary Dulles's Suite, Waldorf Astoria, New York, October 5, 1956, in *FRUS*, 1975–77, XVI, Suez Crisis, no. 300. Special National Intelligence Estimate, July 31, 1956, in *FRUS*, 1955–57, XVI, Suez Crisis, no. 40. See also Sherman Adams, *Firsthand Report: The Story of the Eisenhower Administration* (New York: Harper, 1961), pp. 196–97.

15. President Eisenhower to Prime Minister Eden, Washington, July 31, 1956, in *FRUS*, 1955–57, XVI, Suez Crisis, no. 35.

16. Special National Intelligence Estimate, July 31, 1956; and Paper by the Secretary of State's Special Assistant (Russell), Washington, August 4, 1956, U.S. Policies toward Nasser, in *FRUS*, 1955–57, XVI, Suez Crisis, no. 62.

17. Memorandum of a Conversation with the President, White House, Washington, July 31, 1956. Memorandum of a Conversation, British Foreign Office, London, August 1, 1956; and Tripartite Statement Issued at London, August 2, 1956, in *FRUS*, 1955–57, XVI, Suez Crisis, nos. 41, 53. John C. Campbell, *Defense of the Middle East: Problems of American Policy* (New York: Harper, 1958), p. 79. See also Robert Bowie, "Eisenhower, Dulles, and the Suez Crisis," in Louis and Owen, *Suez, 1956*, p. 199.

18. *The Collected Speeches, Declarations, and Statements of President Nasser*, 1:583; Nasr, *Memoirs*, 1:573, 583, 652–53; Mar'iy, *Political Papers* (in Arabic), 2:352, 355; Nasr, *Memoirs*, 1:262; Hewedy, "Nasser and the Crisis of 1956," pp. 168–69; Heikal, *Cutting the Lion's Tail*, p. 173; and Report Prepared in the Executive Secretariat of the Department of State, Washington, September 5, 1956, in *FRUS*, 1955–57, XVI, no. 173.

19. Anthony Nutting, *No End of a Lesson: The Story of Suez* (London: Constable, 1967), p. 47.

20. Telegram from the Embassy in the United Kingdom to the Department of State, July 31, 1956; and Message from Prime Minister Eden to President Eisenhower, London, August 5, 1956, in *FRUS*, 1955–57, XVI, Suez Crisis, nos. 33, 64.

21. Quoted in Gerges, *The Superpowers and the Middle East*, pp. 58–59.

22. Ibid., p. 59. Editorial Note; and Message from Prime Minister Eden to President Eisenhower, July 27, 1956, in *FRUS*, 1955–57, XVI, Suez Crisis, nos. 1, 5.

23. Maurice Vaisse, "France and the Suez Crisis," in Louis and Owen, *Suez, 1956*, pp. 135, 138, 143.

24. O. M. Smolansky, "Moscow and the Suez Crisis, 1956: A Reappraisal," *Political Science Quarterly* 80 (December 1965): 581–605; Love, *Suez: The Twice-Fought War*, p. 428; Memorandum of a Conversation, Soviet Embassy, London, August 18, 1956; Annex to Watch Committee Report no. 230, Washington, September 20, 1956, in *FRUS*, 1955–57, XVI, Suez Crisis, nos. 93, 243.

25. Nutting, *No End of a Lesson*, pp. 62, 110.

26. Derek Varble, *The Suez Crisis 1956* (London: Osprey, 2003), p. 21.

27. Humphrey Trevelyan (ambassador to Egypt) to Lloyd, April 19, 1956, FO 371/118846/1.

28. Lindsay Frederick Braun, "Suez Reconsidered: Anthony Eden's Orientalism and the Suez Crisis," *Historian* 65, no. 3 (2003): 539.

29. Annex to Watch Committee Report No. 319, Washington, September 12, 1956, in *FRUS*, 1955–57, XVI, Suez Crisis, no. 214.

30. Judith Miller, "Suez Canal Eases Back to Normal," *New York Times*, August 18, 1984, https://www.nytimes.com/1984/08/18/world/suez-canal-eases-back-to-normal.html.

31. "Egypt Takes Over Canal Operation" United Press International, September 15, 1956, https://www.upi.com/Archives/1956/09/15/Egypt-takes-over-canal-operation/4424125190146/.

32. Mohamed Youness, *Suez Canal: Past, Present and Future* (Cairo: Abu Al Magd, 2006), p. 254.

33. Donald Neff, *Warriors at Suez: Eisenhower Takes America into the Middle East* (New York: Simon & Schuster, 1981), pp. 182–83.

34. Avi Shlaim, "The Protocol of Sèvres, 1956: Anatomy of a War Plot," *International Affairs* 73, no. 3 (July 1997): 514.

35. Nutting, *No End of a Lesson*, pp. 90–95.

36. Mordechai Bar-On, "Three Days in Sèvres, October 1956," *History Workshop Journal* 62, no. 1 (Autumn 2006): 173.

37. Ibid., p. 174.

38. David Ben-Gurion, entry for October 22, 1956, "David Ben-Gurion's Diary: The Suez-Sinai Campaign," in *The Suez-Sinai Crisis: A Retrospective and Reappraisal*, ed. Moshe Shemesh and Selwyn Illan Troen (London: Routledge, 1990), pp. 229–31.

39. Telegram from the Embassy in Egypt to the Department of State, Cairo, October 31, 1956, in *FRUS*, 1955–57, XVI, Suez Crisis, no. 451.

40. Galia Golan, *Soviet Policies in the Middle East: From World War Two to Gorbachev* (New York: Cambridge University Press, 1990), p. 9.

41. Memorandum of a Conference with the President, White House, Washington, October 29, 1956, in *FRUS*, 1955–57, XVI, Suez Crisis, no. 411; Robert Daniel Murphy, *Diplomat among Warriors* (Garden City, N.Y.: Doubleday, 1964), pp. 389, 392; and Adams, *Firsthand Report*, pp. 205–6.

42. Memorandum of a Conversation, Secretary Dulles's Office, Department of State, Washington, October 31, 1956; Memorandum of Discussion at the 302d Meeting of the National Security Council, November 1, 1956; and Letter from President Eisenhower to Swede Hazlett, Washington, November 2, 1956, in *FRUS*, 1955–57, XVI, Suez Crisis, nos. 447, 455, 475.

43. Memorandum of Discussion at the 299th Meeting of the National Security Council, Washington, October 4, 1956; and Memorandum of a Conference with the President, White House, Washington, October 30, 1956, in *FRUS*, 1955–57, XVI, Suez Crisis, nos. 297, 435. Diane B. Kunz, "The Importance of Having Money: The Economic Diplomacy of the Suez Crisis," in Louis and Owen, *Suez, 1956*, pp. 216, 226–27.

44. Editorial Note, November 1, 1956, in *FRUS*, 1955–57, XVI, Suez Crisis, no. 467; Murphy, *Diplomat among Warriors*, pp. 392–93; Adams, *Firsthand Report*, pp. 210–15; and Kunz, "The Importance of Having Money," pp. 227, 230–31.

45. Clive Holes, *Modern Arabic: Structures, Functions, and Varieties* (Washington, D.C.: Georgetown University Press, 2004); Murphy, *Diplomat among Warriors*, p. 349.

46. Golda Meir, *My Life: The Autobiography of Gold Meir* (London: Futura, 1975), p. 250; Michael Bar-Zohar, *Ben-Gurion*, trans. Peretz Kidron (London: Weidenfeld and Nicolson, 1978), pp. 250–51; Yaacov Bar-Siman-Tov, *Israel, the Superpowers, and the War in the Middle East* (New York: Praeger, 1987), pp. 61–65.

47. "Eden's Tragedy: Today He Is a Lonely Man and a Sick Man," *Daily Mirror*, January 10, 1957, https://www.britishnewspaperarchive.co.uk/search /results/1957-01-10?NewspaperTitle=Daily%2BMirror&IssueId=BL%2 F0000560%2F19570110%2F&County=London%2C%20England.

48. John C. Campbell, "The Soviet Union, the United States, and the Twin Crises of Hungary and Suez," in Louis and Owen, *Suez, 1956*, pp. 245–46; Letter from Prime Minister Bulganin to President Eisenhower, Moscow, November 5, 1956; and White House News Release, Washington, November 5, 1956, in *FRUS, 1955–57*, XVI, Suez Crisis, nos. 505, 512; and Yaacov Ro'i, *From Encroachment to Involvement: A Documentary Study of Soviet Policy in the Middle East, 1945–1973* (New York: John Wiley, 1974), pp. 188–91.

49. Memorandum of a Conference with the President, October 29, 1956; Memorandum of Discussion at the 302d Meeting of the National Security Council, November 1, 1956, in *FRUS, 1955–57*, XVI, Suez Crisis, nos. 411, 455.

50. Memorandum of Telephone Conversation between the President and the Secretary of State, Washington, October 30, 1956; Discussion at the 302d Meeting of the NSC, Washington, November 1, 1956, in *FRUS, 1955–57*, XVI, Suez Crisis, nos. 433, 455.

51. See the informative analysis in Lorenz M. Luthi, *Cold Wars: Asia, the Middle East, and Europe* (New York: Cambridge University Press, 2020), esp. pt. 3 and chap. 20.

52. *The Collected Speeches, Declarations, and Statements of President Nasser*, 1:617; Nasr, *Memoirs* (in Arabic), 1:281, 83, 652–53; Mar'iy, *Political Papers* (in Arabic), 2:362; and Mohamed Heikal, *The Sphinx and the Commissar: The Rise and Fall of Soviet Influence in the Middle East* (Harper & Row, 1978), p. 72.

53. Telegram from the Embassy in Egypt to the Department of State, Cairo, November 8, 1956; Telegram from the Embassy in Egypt to the Department of State, Cairo, November 18, 1956; and Telegram from the Embassy in Egypt to the Department of State, December 16, 1956, in *FRUS, 1955–57*, XVI, Suez Crisis, nos. 561, 587, 659. See also Heikal, *The Sphinx and The Commissar*, p. 74.

54. Telegram from the U.S. Embassy, to the Department of State, Cairo, November 8, 1956, in *FRUS, 1955–57*, XVI, Suez Crisis, no. 561.

Chapter Nine. Frustrating Nasser's Arab Nationalism

1. Memorandum of a Conference with the President, White House, Washington, November 19, 20, 1956; and Memorandum of Discussion at the 305th Meeting of the National Security Council, Washington, November 30, 1956, in *Foreign Relation of the United States* (*FRUS*), 1955–57, XVI, Suez Crisis, nos. 589, 596, 626.
2. Memorandum of a Conversation between the President and Secretary of State, Secretary Dulles's Room, Walter Reed Hospital, Washington, November 12, 1956; and Message from the President to the Secretary of State, Augusta, Georgia, December 12, 1956, in *FRUS*, 1955–57, XVI, Suez Crisis, nos. 570, 650. John C. Campbell, *Defense of the Middle East: Problems of American Policy* (New York: Harper, 1958), pp. 128–29. William Burns, *Economic Aid and American Policy toward Egypt, 1955–1981* (Albany: State University of New York Press, 1985), p. 108.
3. Burns, *Economic Aid and American Policy toward Egypt*, p. 108.
4. The Middle East resolution, which became known as the Eisenhower Doctrine, was adopted by the Senate and the House of Representatives on March 5 and 7, 1957, and signed into law on March 9. Editorial Note, in FRUS, 1955–57, XVII, Arab-Israeli Dispute, no. 4.
5. *The Collected Speeches, Declarations, and Statements of President Nasser, 23 July 1952–1958* (in Arabic), vol. 1 (Cairo: Hai'a al-ist'lamat, n.d.), pp. 647, 649, 664; Mahmoud Fawzi, *Suez: An Egyptian Perspective* (London: Shorouk International, n.d.), pp. 116–17; and Telegram from the Embassy in Egypt to the Department of State, Cairo, January 10, 1957, in *FRUS*, 1955–57, XVII, Arab-Israeli Dispute, no. 12.
6. Dwight D. Eisenhower, *The White House Years: Waging Peace, 1956–1961* (Garden City, N.Y.: Doubleday, 1960), pp. 114–16. See also Memorandum of a Conference with the President, November 19, 1956, in *FRUS*, 1955–57, XVI, Suez Crisis, no. 589.
7. Malcolm Kerr, *The Arab Cold War: Gamal 'Abd Al-Nasir and His Rivals, 1958–1970*, 3rd ed. (London: Oxford University Press, 1971).
8. Olivia B. Waxman, "The US Intervened in Syria in 1949: Here's What Happened," *Time*, April 13, 2017, https://time.com/4735438/america-syria-war-coup-history/.
9. Douglas Little, "Cold War and Covert Action: The United States and Syria, 1945–1958," *Middle East Journal* 44, no. 1 (1990): 52.
10. Asher Kaufman, "Between Permeable and Sealed Borders: The Trans-Arabian Pipeline and the Arab-Israeli Conflict," *International Journal of Middle East Studies* 46, no. 1 (February 2014): 95.
11. Central Intelligence Group Report ORE-15, "The Hatay Question," February 28, 1947, NSC Series, Intelligence Files, Harry S. Truman Presidential Library, Independence, Mo.
12. Marshall to Ambassador J. Rives Childs, June 19, 1948, Foreign Relations, 1948, vol. V, pp. 22–23.

13. James Keeley to George Marshall, telegram, November 23, 1948, 890D.00/11–2348, NARG59.
14. Meade to G-2, telegram, December 3, 1948, 350 Syria, box 49, Damascus Post Files, NARG84.
15. Patrick Seale, *The Struggle for Syria: A Study of Post-War Arab Politics, 1945–1958* (Oxford: Oxford University Press, 1965), p. 43.
16. Meade to G-2, telegram, December 3, 1948, 350 Syria, box 49, Damascus Post Files, NARG84.
17. Meade to G-2, telegram, March 18, 1949, 350 Syria, box 49, Damascus Post Files, NARG84.
18. Meade to G-2, telegram, April 15, 1949, Syria Week (part 5), box 77, NARG319.
19. Little, "Cold War and Covert Action," p. 57.
20. Ibid.
21. Aramco, "The Tapline: A Legacy of Triumph," https://www.aramco.com/en/magazine/elements/2021/the-tapline-a-legacy-of-triumph.
22. Ivan Pearson, "The Syrian Crisis of 1957, the Anglo-American 'Special Relationship,' and the 1958 Landings in Jordan and Lebanon," *Middle Eastern Studies* 43, no. 1 (2007): 45.
23. Little, "Cold War and Covert Action," pp. 51–75.
24. Eisenhower, *The White House Years: Waging Peace*, p. 197n14.
25. Ibid.
26. See Salim Yaqub, *Containing Arab Nationalism: The Eisenhower Doctrine and the Middle East* (Chapel Hill: University of North Carolina Press, 2004).
27. Seale, *The Struggle for Syria*, p. 38.
28. William Blum, *Killing Hope: U.S. Military and CIA Interventions since World War II* (Monroe, Maine: Common Courage Press, 1995), p. 86.
29. Bonnie Saunders, *The United States and Arab Nationalism: The Syrian Case, 1953–1960* (Westport, Conn.: Praeger, 1996), p. 49.
30. Blum, *Killing Hope*, p. 87.
31. John Prados, *Safe for Democracy: The Secret Wars of the CIA* (Chicago: Ivan R. Dee, 2006), p. 1.
32. Blum, *Killing Hope*, p. 88.
33. David Lesch, *Syria and the United States: Eisenhower's Cold War in the Middle East* (Boulder, Colo.: Westview Press, 1992), p. 156.
34. Eisenhower, *The White House Years: Waging Peace*, p. 201.; Pearson, "The Syrian Crisis of 1957," p. 50; and Seale, *The Struggle for Syria*, p. 300.
35. Matthew Jones, "The 'Preferred Plan': The Anglo-American Working Group Report on Covert Action in Syria, 1957," *Middle Eastern Studies* 19, no. 3 (2006): 405.
36. "VII. Covert Actions in Support of the Syrian Operation," September 17, 1957; see "G. Elimination of Key Figures," Duncan-Sandys Papers (DSND) 6/35, Churchill Archives Centre, Cambridge, U.K.

37. Elie Podeh, *The Decline of Arab Unity: The Rise and Fall of the United Arab Republic* (Brighton, U.K.: Sussex Academic Press, 1999), p. 126. Sarraj would play a decisive role in the breakup of the Egyptian-Syrian union in 1961.

38. Jones, "The 'Preferred Plan,' " p. 403.

39. Ibid., p. 406

40. "IV. Psychological Program," September 17, 1957, DSND 6/35.

41. Seale, *The Struggle for Syria*, pp. 300–304.

42. Jones, "The 'Preferred Plan,' " p. 411.

43. National Security Council, Long-Range U.S. Policy toward the Near East, January 16, 1958, NSC 5801, U.S. Archives, p. 17.

44. The Outer Island Rebellion was a conflict between the Permesta rebels and the Indonesian government over fair economic distribution. The United States sided with the Permesta rebels in their bid to oust the left-leaning President Sukarno. The C.I.A. used similar tactics of sabotage and sowing chaos to those it used in Iran, Guatemala, and Syria, including deliberately attacking commercial ships in Indonesian waters and other civilian targets as well painting aerial bombers black and obscuring their markings.

45. William B. Quandt, "Lebanon, 1958, and Jordan, 1970," in *Force without War: U.S. Armed Forces as a Political Instrument*, ed. Barry M. Blechman and Stephen S. Kaplan (Washington, D.C.: Brookings Institution, 1978), p. 237.

46. Uri Friedman, "How America Has Come Full Circle in the Middle East," *Atlantic*, January 24, 2020.

47. Douglas Little, "His Finest Hour? Eisenhower, Lebanon, and the 1958 Middle East Crisis," *Diplomatic History* 20, no. 1 (1996): 31.

48. "Complaint by Lebanon in Respect of a Situation . . .," June 11, 1958, United Nations Digital Library, https://digitallibrary.un.org/record/630367#record-files-collapse-header.

49. Sam Pope Brewer, "Lebanon Elects a New President," *New York Times*, August 1, 1958.

50. Gerges, *The Superpowers and the Middle East*, p. 123.

51. 373d Meeting of the NSC, July 25, 1958, U.S. Archives, p. 10; and 381st Meeting of the NSC, October 2, 1958, U.S. Archives, p. 5.

52. David Hirst, *Beware of Small States: Lebanon, Battleground of the Middle East* (New York: Nation Books, 2010), p. 62.

53. Memorandum of a Conversation between the Secretary of State and the Minister of the British Embassy (Lord Hood), Washington, July 14, 1958, and Memorandum of a Conference with the President, July 14, 1958, in *FRUS*, 1958–60, XI, Lebanon and Jordan, nos. 134, 124.

54. Gerges, *The Superpowers and the Middle East*, pp. 110, 119.

55. Memorandum for the Record, Subject: Meeting Regarding Iraq, July 14, 1958, U.S. Archives; and Conference with the President, July 14, 1958.

56. Gerges, *The Superpowers and the Middle East*, pp. 121, 124.
57. Little, "His Finest Hour?" p. 27.
58. Eisenhower, *The White House Years: Waging Peace*, p. 290.
59. Juan Romero, "Discourse and Mediation in the Lebanese Crisis of 1958," *Middle Eastern Studies* 48, no. 4 (2012): 567.
60. "Remarks by the President at the United States Military Academy Commencement Ceremony," https://obamawhitehouse.archives.gov/the-press-office/2014/05/28/remarks-president-united-states-military-academy-commencement-ceremony.
61. NSC, Long-Range U.S. Policy toward the Near East, NSC 5801, January 16, 1958, U.S. Archives, p. 17.
62. Memorandum from the Assistant Secretary of State (Rountree) to the Secretary of State, November 4, 1957, in *FRUS*, 1955–57, XVII, Arab-Israeli Dispute, no 391. Washington to the American Embassy, Baghdad, April 17, 1958, quoted in Mohamed Heikal, *1967: Years of Upheaval: The Thirty Years' War*, 3 vols. (in Arabic) (Cairo: Markaz al-Ahram litarjama wa al-nashr, 1988), 1:850.
63. Telegram from the Embassy in Egypt to the Department of State, August 24, 1957, in *FRUS*, 1955–57, XVII, Arab-Israeli Dispute, no. 367. See also Washington to the American Embassy, Baghdad, April 17, 1958, quoted in Heikal, *1967: Years of Upheaval* (in Arabic), 1:850–51.
64. Gamal Abdel Nasser, *President Gamal Abdel-Nasser's Speeches and Press Interviews* (Cairo: Information Department, 1961), pp. 315, 317.
65. Ahmed Hamroush, *The Story of the July 23 Revolution: Nasser's Autumn* (in Arabic), vol. 5 (Cairo: Maktaba al-madbouli, 1984), p. 61. Baghdadi, *Memoirs* (in Arabic), 2:123–63. Gamal Abdel Nasser, *The Charter* (in Arabic) (Cairo: Ministry of National Guidance, State Information Service, 1962), p. 11.
66. Author's interviews with Khaled Mohieddin, Cairo, December 6, 12, 2006. See also author's interview with Abd al-Ghaffar Shukr, Cairo, Egypt, October 10, 2007.

Chapter Ten. What Have Egypt and the Arab World Lost by the Defeat of Nasser's Secular Nationalism?

1. S. N. Eisenstadt, "Multiple Modernities," *Daedalus* 129, no. 1 (Winter 2000): 1–29.
2. Nader Hashemi, *Islam, Secularism, and Liberal Democracy: Toward a Democratic Theory for Muslim Societies* (New York: Oxford University Press, 2009), pp. 2, 37–38.
3. See Mark Mazower, *Dark Continent: Europe's Twentieth Century* (New York: Alfred A. Knopf, 1999), pp. ix–xvi, 395–403, and Charles Tilly, *Contention and Democracy in Europe, 1650–2000* (Cambridge: Cambridge University Press, 2004), pp. 168–205.

4. Avi Shlaim, *The Iron Wall: Israel and the Arab World* (London: Allen Lane, 2000), pp. 218–64.

5. Tawfiq al-Hakim, *The Return of Consciousness*, trans Bayly Winder (New York: New York University Press, 1985), p. 18. For critical reflections on the war and its aftermath, see Fawaz A. Gerges, *Making the Arab World: Nasser, Qutb and the Clash That Shaped the Middle East* (Princeton: Princeton University Press, 2018), pp. 293–313.

6. Ali Kadri, *The Cordon Sanitaire: A Single Law Governing Development in East Asia and the Arab World* (Singapore: Palgrave Macmillan, 2017).

7. Japan is often described as the only non-European and nonwhite nation that was able to escape colonization through a top-down domestic process of modernization that officially began with the Meiji restoration of 1868. The process was so successful that in just a few decades, Japan was able to industrialize, establish its own colonial empire in East Asia, defeat China and Russia, and even challenge the United States in World War II. Japan was the only non-European country to succeed in this effort, but not the first to try, as Egypt had attempted that path in the early half of the century.

8. A. G. Hopkins, "The Victorians and Africa: A Reconsideration of the Occupation of Egypt, 1882," *Journal of African History* 27, no. 2 (1986): 363–91.

9. Telegram from the Embassy in Egypt to the Department of State, April 19, 1956, in *Foreign Relations of the United State, 1955–57*, XV, Arab-Israeli Dispute, no. 294.

10. Mazower, *Dark Continent*.

Chapter Eleven. From Iran to Guatemala

1. Stephen Schlesinger and Stephen Kinzer, *Bitter Fruit: The Story of the American Coup in Guatemala*, rev. ed. (Cambridge: David Rockefeller Center for Latin American Studies, Harvard University, 1999), pp. 100–101.

2. Eduardo Galeano, *Open Veins of Latin America: Five Centuries of the Pillage of a Continent*, trans. Cedric Belfrage (New York: Monthly Review Press, 1973).

3. Raymond Hinnebusch, "The Middle East in World Hierarchy: Imperialism and Resistance," *Journal of International Relations and Development* 14, no. 1 (2011): 221.

4. Richard H. Immerman, *The CIA in Guatemala: The Foreign Policy of Intervention* (Austin: University of Texas Press, 1982), pp. 68–72, and Schlesinger and Kinzer, *Bitter Fruit*, pp. 67–71.

5. Immerman, *The CIA in Guatemala*, pp. 73–76.

6. Stephen G. Rabe, *Eisenhower and Latin America: The Foreign Policy of Anticommunism* (Chapel Hill: University of North Carolina Press, 1988), p. 43.

7. John Shillington, *Grappling with Atrocity: Guatemalan Theater in the 1990s*, (Madison, N.J.: Fairleigh Dickinson University Press, 2002), 38.

8. Immerman, *The CIA in Guatemala*, pp. 34–37.

9. Shillington, *Grappling with Atrocity*.

10. Cindy Forster, *The Time of Freedom: Campesino Workers in Guatemala's October Revolution* (Pittsburgh: Pittsburgh University Press, 2001), p. 86

11. Piero Gleijeses, *Shattered Hope: The Guatemalan Revolution and the United States, 1944–1954* (Princeton: Princeton University Press, 1991), p. 136.

12. Ibid., p. 134.

13. Ibid., p. 141.

14. Ibid., p. 148.

15. Stephen Kinzer, *The Brothers: John Foster Dulles, Allen Dulles, and Their Secret World War* (New York: St Martin's Griffin, 2013), p. 149.

16. Stephen M. Streeter, *Managing the Counterrevolution: The United States and Guatemala, 1954–1961* (Athens: Ohio University Center for International Studies, 2000), p. 18.

17. Elisabeth Malkin, "An Apology for a Guatemalan Coup, 57 Years Later," *New York Times*, October 20, 2011, https://www.nytimes.com/2011/10/21/world/americas/an-apology-for-a-guatemalan-coup-57-years-later.html.

18. Stephen Schlesinger, "Ghosts of Guatemala's Past," *New York Times*, June 3, 2011; see also Schlesinger and Kinzer, *Bitter Fruit*, pp. 55–59.

19. Immerman, *The CIA in Guatemala*, p. 101.

20. Immerman, *The CIA in Guatemala*, pp. 122–27, 160. See also Schlesinger and Kinzer, *Bitter Fruit*, pp. 106–7.

21. Evan Thomas, "You Can Own the World," *Washington Post*, October 22, 1995, https://www.washingtonpost.com/archive/lifestyle/magazine/1995/10/22/you-can-own-the-world/c772e3f1-2634-4fb1-a223-b681d63a539d/.

22. Nicholas Cullather, *Secret History: The CIA's Classified Account of Its Operations in Guatemala, 1952–1954*, 2nd ed. (Stanford: Stanford University Press, 2006), p. 83.

23. Cullather, *Secret History*, p. 31.

24. Immerman, *The CIA in Guatemala*, p. 109.

25. Heike Bungert, Jan Heitmann, and Michael Wala, eds., *Secret Intelligence in the Twentieth Century* (Abingdon, U.K.: Routledge, 2003), pp. 73–74.

26. Memorandum for the Record, March 8, 1953, in *Foreign Relations of the United States (FRUS)*, 1952–54, Guatemala, no. 36.

27. "The Iranian Accord," *New York Times*, August 6, 1954, p. 16, https://www.nytimes.com/1954/08/06/archives/the-iranian-accord.html.

28. Memorandum for the Record, September 11, 1953, in *FRUS*, 1952–54, Guatemala, no. 51, https://history.state.gov/historicaldocuments/frus1952-54Guat/d51.

29. Ibid.

298 Notes to Pages 238–243

30. Memorandum of Conversation between Ambassador João Carlos Muniz of Brazil and Dulles, May 11, 1954, in *FRUS*, 1952–54, The American Republics, IV, no. 437.
31. Ambassador to Honduras Whiting Willauer to State Department, June 9, 1954, in *FRUS*, 1952–54, The American Republics, IV, no. 466.
32. Memorandum for the Record, September 11, 1953.
33. President Eisenhower to Dr. Milton Eisenhower, December 1, 1954, Eisenhower Diary Series, "December 1954 (2)" Ann Whitman File, Dwight D. Eisenhower Papers of the President of the United States, 1953–1961, Eisenhower Presidential Library.
34. Richard H. Immerman, *John Foster Dulles and the Diplomacy of the Cold War* (Princeton: Princeton University Press, 1990), pp. 181–82.
35. Immerman, *The CIA in Guatemala*, pp. 64–67.
36. Schlesinger and Kinzer, *Bitter Fruit*, pp. 72–77.
37. Kinzer, *The Brothers*, p. 156.
38. Gleijeses, *Shattered Hope*, pp. 149, 164.
39. Ibid., pp. 149–51
40. Lars Schoultz, *Beneath the United States: A History of U.S. Policy toward Latin America* (Cambridge: Harvard University Press, 1998), p. 337.
41. Greg Grandin, *The Blood of Guatemala: A History of Race and Nation* (Durham, N.C.: Duke University Press, 2000), pp. 200–201; Streeter, *Managing the Counterrevolution*, p. 4.
42. Schlesinger and Kinzer, *Bitter Fruit*, pp. 90–97.
43. Kinzer, *The Brothers*, p. 148.
44. Ibid.
45. Ibid.
46. Ibid., pp. 156–57.
47. Ibid., pp. 106–7; see also Immerman, *The CIA in Guatemala*, pp. 111–13, 122–27; and Rich Cohen, *The Fish That Ate the Whale: The Life and Times of America's Banana King* (New York: Farrar, Straus & Giroux, 2012), p. 186.
48. Kinzer, *The Brothers*, p. 115.
49. Annie Jacobsen, *Surprise, Kill, Vanish: The Secret History of CIA Paramilitary Armies, Operators, and Assassins* (New York: Little, Brown, 2019), p. 72.
50. Ibid., p. 74.
51. Gleijeses, *Shattered Hope*, p. 278.
52. Ibid., pp. 100–101.
53. "Castillo Armas: Guest from Guatemala," *Time*, November 7, 1955, https://content.time.com/time/subscriber/article/0,33009,807937,00.html.
54. Cullather, *Secret History*, p. 12.
55. René De La Pedraja, *Wars of Latin America, 1948–1982: The Rise of the Guerrillas* (Jefferson, N.C.: McFarland, 2013), pp. 27–28.
56. Jacobsen, *Surprise, Kill, Vanish*, p. 74.

57. Cullather, *Secret History*, p. 93.
58. Gleijeses, *Shattered Hope*, p. 324.
59. Michael McClintock, *The American Connection: State Terror and Popular Resistance in Guatemala* (London: Zed Books, 1985), p. 50; Historical Clarification Commission, *Guatemala: Memory of Silence* (Guatemala City: Historical Clarification Commission, 1999), p. 17, https://hrdag.org/wp-content/uploads/2013/01/CEHreport-english.pdf.
60. The United States took another terrible step in 1963. Ydígoras Fuentes was going to allow Arévalo to come home and run for president. He had written a book, *The Shark and the Sardines*, that some U.S. officials found intolerable. So President John F. Kennedy green-lighted a coup that brought in a military government and started the massive military repression. Arévalo's return might have set the country on a wholly different path.
61. United States Institute of Peace, "Truth Commission: Guatemala," 1997, https://www.usip.org/publications/1997/02/truth-commission-guatemala. Historical Clarification Commission, *Guatemala: Memory of Silence*.
62. Although the Guatemalan banana plantations that the Eisenhower Cold Warriors defended in early 1950s had lost much of their political influence in Central America by the 1970s, United Fruit (renamed Chiquita) continued to provide funding to far-right extremist groups on America's designated terrorist list. The Bananagate scandal was a case in point, which led to the overthrow of the Honduran government in the 1970s.

Conclusion

1. Atul Kohli, *Imperialism and the Developing World: How Britain and the United States Shaped the Global Periphery* (Oxford: Oxford University Press, 2020), pp. 4, 6.
2. On the ambitions and failures of local leaders, see Fawaz Gerges, *The Hundred Years' War for Control of the Middle East* (Princeton: Princeton University Press, forthcoming).
3. Raymond Hinnebusch, "The Middle East in World Hierarchy: Imperialism and Resistance," *Journal of International Relations and Development* 14, no. 1 (2011): p. 221.
4. L. Carl Brown, *International Politics and the Middle East: Old Rules, Dangerous Game* (Princeton: Princeton University Press, 1984), p. 4.
5. See Stephanie Savel, "How Death Outlives War: The Reverberating Impact of the Post-9/11 Wars on Human Health," paper prepared for Brown University's Watson Institute for International and Public Affairs, May 15, 2023, https://watson.brown.edu/costsofwar/papers/2023/how-death-outlives-war-reverberating-impact-post-911-wars-human-health.
6. See Rashid Khalidi, *The Hundred Years' War on Palestine: A History of Settler Colonialism and Resistance* (New York: Metropolitan Books, 2020).

Index

Note: *Surnames starting with "al-" or "el-" are alphabetized by the subsequent part of the name.*

Abadan oil refinery, 52–53
Abdullah I (king of Jordan), 196
Abraham Accords (2020), 256
Abrahamian, Ervand, 64, 94, 95
Acheson, Dean, 55, 56, 59, 111, 236
Administrative Capital for Urban
    Development, 146
Afghanistan: mujahideen, U.S. allying
    with, 192, 252–53; U.S. war on
    terror in, 19, 36–37, 121, 225, 230,
    254–55
Afshartus, Mahmud, 70
agency of local leaders, 10
AIOC (Anglo-Iranian Oil Company),
    40, 48–49, 51–54, 85–87, 264n56
al-Azhar Mosque (Cairo), 130
Albania, C.I.A. covert operation in, 228
Albright, Madeleine, 117
Al-e Ahmad, Jalal-e, 97, 98
MS *Alfhem*, 236
Algeria, Arab Spring in, 6
al-karama (dignity), 133–34
Allen, George, 161
Al-Qaeda, 33, 37, 220
Alvandi, Roham, 102
Amer, Abdel Hakim, 127, 211, 212

Amini, Mahsa (Zhina), 114, 123
"ancient hatreds" narrative, 8, 14, 179,
    193, 227, 253
Anderson, Lisa, 16
Anglo-American Working Group, 199,
    202
Anglo-Egyptian treaty and reforms
    (Britain-Egypt 1936), 145
Anglo-Iranian Oil Company (AIOC),
    40, 48–49, 51–54, 85–87, 264n56
anti-Americanism, 33–34, 116, 117,
    217–18
anticolonial movement. *See*
    postcolonial leaders
Arab civil war, 210, 212
Arab cold war, 28, 160, 192–93, 209–
    10, 217, 218–19
Arab-Israeli conflict: and Arab cold
    war, 217; and Free Officers, 145;
    Hamas attack (2023) and Israeli
    military response, 34, 256;
    occupation, 7, 30–31, 33–34, 182,
    220; Palestine War (1948), 135–38;
    road not taken, 36, 216–18; Suez
    Crisis, 182–86; and Syria, 196; UN
    Partition Plan for Palestine (1947),

Arab-Israeli conflict (continued)
    194; U.S. role in, 28, 33–34, 217–18,
    252, 256. *See also* Six-Day War
Arab Spring (2010), 6, 30, 134, 257
Aramco, 49, 194, 196
Arana, Francisco, 242
Árbenz, Jacobo, 231–35, 239–40, 244–
    45
Árbenz, Jacobo, coup against, 235–46;
    compared to other C.I.A.-sponsored
    coups, 163, 228–29, 237–38, 244–
    45; in context of U.S. global
    strategy, 3, 229–31, 255; events
    leading to, 235–39; legacy of, 167,
    199–200, 244–46; motivation
    behind, 239–41; Operation
    PBSuccess, 241–44
Arévalo, Juan José, 242, 299n60
armament issue. *See* Czech Arms Deal
Ashraf, Princess (Iran), 72, 73
al-Assad, Bashar, 7, 30, 123, 255
al-Assad, Hafez, 35, 217
Aswan Dam affair (1955–1956), 165–
    70; aid offer and negotiations, 165–
    67; aid offer revoked, 25, 168–69,
    172; Byroade's memo, 167; effects,
    17–18; as flash point, 3, 17, 169,
    249; road not taken, 25, 186–87;
    and Suez Crisis, 186
Atoms for Peace initiative (1957), 88
Attlee, Clement, 57

Ba'athism, 197
Ba'ath Party (Syria), 211
Bacevich, Andrew, 9
al-Badr, Imam Mohammad, 212
al-Baghdadi, Abdel-Latif, 163
Baghdad Pact (1955), 89, 160–61
Bakdash, Khalid, 199–200
Bananagate scandal (1975), 299n62
Bandung Afro-Asian Summit
    Conference (1955), 110, 152, 161–
    62, 264n52
Bani-Sadr, Abolhassan, 97

Bar-On, Mordechai, 181
Barr, James: *Lords of the Desert*, 86
al-Bashir, Omar, 217
Bayat, Asef, 124
Bay of Pigs (1961), 225–26
bazaari (Iranian merchant class), 52, 66,
    103–4, 105
Bazargan, Mehdi, 97
Ben-Gurion, David, 35, 36, 162, 181,
    182
Biden, Joe: and Abraham Accords
    (2020), 256; compared to Cold War
    predecessors, 207; and Hamas
    attack (2023) and Israeli military
    response, 34; and opportunities for
    de-escalation with Iran, 125
Bihbahani, Seyyed Abdollah, 42
Bill, James A., 109
al-Bizri, Afif, 199–200
Black, Eugene, 168
Black Saturday (1952), 140–43
blowback, 106
Brennan, John, 122
Britain: competition with United States
    for Middle East oil and resources,
    86, 120; and Egypt, 128, 134, 141,
    165, 169, 208, 212, 223; imperialism,
    11, 19; informal imperialism, 13,
    28–29, 248; and Iran, 44, 52, 101–2,
    112, 120, 135–36; legacy and impact
    of Middle East interventions, 15,
    250, 253; oil concession of 1909 and
    modifications (Iran), 40, 49, 50;
    policy of equilibrium in the Gulf,
    101–2; and Syria, 2–3, 116, 197–98,
    200. *See also* oil nationalization;
    Suez Crisis
British Canal Zone, 141
Brown, L. Carl, 18, 255
Bush, George W., xi, 11, 36–37
Byroade, Henry, 162, 167, 168–69, 224

Cabot, John Moors, 240
Caffrey, Jefferson, 154

Calvinist Church, 61
capitalism, 62–63, 255
carbon democracy, 18–19
Carter, Jimmy, 119, 121
Castillo Armas, Carlos, 241, 242–43, 245
Castro, Fidel, 225, 238
Challe, Maurice, 181
Chamoun, Camille, 203–5, 206
Chehab, Fouad, 204, 206
Childs, J. Rives, 195
China: and Czech Arms Deal, 161; greater engagement in Middle East, 31; Nasser's recognition of, 167–68
Chiquita. See United Fruit Company
Christianity, 61–63
Churchill, Winston, 48–49, 59, 60, 68–69, 80, 184
C.I.A.: "blowback" term coined by, 106; and clerics' rise, 121; coups in Syria, 169, 193–202, 228, 241; and Czech Arms Deal, 163; expansion under Eisenhower, 236–37; and Iran hostage crisis, 119–21; and Nasser, 158, 163, 205, 225; SAVAK trained by, 90; "The Communist Situation in Guatemala" (1953), 237. See also Árbenz, Jacobo, coup against; Dulles, Allen Welsh; overthrow of Mossadegh
clerics and clerical regime (Iran): and blame for overthrow of Mossadegh, 106–7; causes of rise, 24, 33, 85, 104–6, 250; current protests, response to, 124; and Iran's nuclear program, 88; and paramilitary groups, 123; radicalization, 98–100, 104–5; regional policy of current regime, 124; relationship to bazaari, 97, 105; and Resurgence Party, 102, 103–4; and United States, 118, 120, 121, 123, 124. See also National Front; political Islam and religious fundamentalism

Cold War, ix–xi, 12–15, 19, 207–8, 229–31, 250–55. See also Arab cold war; informal imperialism
Cold Warriors: Cold Warrior-diplomat divide, 26, 155, 157, 167, 224–25; Truman and Eisenhower administrations, 60–61. See also democracy, U.S. undermining of; informal imperialism; individual Eisenhower administration officials by name
colonialism, 11–12, 20, 33–34, 128, 185, 248, 252. See also imperialism
Commission for Historical Clarification report (1999), 245–46
communism: Árbenz's relationship to, 234–35, 238, 244; and Free Officers, 154–55, 161; in Iran under the shah, 97–98; Mossadegh's lack of trust in, 201–2; Naguib's opposition to, 157; Nasser's opposition to, 131–32, 138, 158, 164, 188–89, 193, 201; in Syria, 196, 201. See also U.S. fixation with Soviet role in Middle East
Company Law (Egypt 1947), 156
confrontation with Nasser: compared to overthrow of Mossadegh, 151–52; road not taken, 148–49, 186–89, 205, 223–26, 249–50, 254, 256–57. See also Aswan Dam affair; Czech Arms Deal; Suez Crisis; U.S. fixation with Soviet role in Middle East
conservatism, ultrareligious. See political Islam and religious fundamentalism
Consortium Agreement (U.S.-Iran 1954), 85–87
Costs of War study, 19–20, 37, 255
Cottam, Richard, 68, 78
council of clerics (Iran), 43–44
coups and attempted coups. See specific countries and leaders/rulers
Cromer, Lord Evelyn Baring, 128

Cuba, 93, 225–26, 238
Curzon, Lord George Nathaniel, 39
Cutler, Robert, 240
Czech Arms Deal (1955), 25, 151, 161–
    65, 216

Daily Express, on oil nationalization, 57
Daily Mail, on oil nationalization, 57
Damavand, Mount, 22
Darbyshire, Norman, 69
D'Arcy Concession (Iran 1901), 50,
    264n56
Dayan, Moshe, 162, 181
de Bellaigue, Christopher, 111
democracy: Arab-Israeli conflict's
    effects on, 217–18; carbon
    democracy, 18 19; and geostratcgic
    curse, 32; Iran and Mossadegh, 22–
    23, 26, 67, 94, 123, 144–45, 250–51;
    in Middle East, 256–57; and
    multiple modernities, 21, 215; and
    Nasser, 144–46, 225; postcolonial
    countries' transition to, 27; road not
    taken, 24, 27–28, 214–16, 226, 251;
    in the West, 9, 21, 215, 225
democracy, U.S. undermining of: in
    Egypt, 252; in Guatemala, 252; in
    Iran, 105–6, 116, 252; in Middle
    East, 15–16, 63–64, 116, 248; in
    Syria, 195, 196; U.S. own
    democracy damaged by, 14–15, 20,
    23, 27–28, 89, 206, 238
de Reuter, Baron Julius, 39
Der Spiegel, interview with the shah,
    112
dignity: Iranian struggle for, 81–82;
    Middle East struggle for, 3, 7–8, 82;
    and Nasser, 126–27, 128, 133–34,
    135, 162, 173; U.S. failure to
    recognize universal desire for, 151,
    172
diplomat-Cold Warrior divide, 26, 155,
    157, 167, 224–25
Dirty Wars, 246

Dulles, Allen Welsh, 14, 60, 63–64, 69–
    71, 237
Dulles, John Foster: as anticommunist
    influence on Nasser, 158; and
    Aswan Dam affair, 166, 167, 168–69,
    173; on Chamoun, 204; and Czech
    Arms Deal, 162, 163–64; on
    Lebanon, 204; and overthrow of
    Mossadegh, 60, 69, 86; and post-
    Sévres Protocol sanctions, 184; Suez
    Crisis, 174–77, 185, 190; and Syria,
    198, 199
Dulles brothers: and Árbenz/
    Guatemala, 235, 238, 240; C.I.A.
    under, 237; Cold War mindset, 60,
    172; and corporate interests, 231,
    240; God, country, and family, 61–
    63, 156–57; and Nasser, 157, 163–
    64

Economist, Nasser interview on Aswan
    Dam, 166
Eden, Anthony, 55, 174–75, 177–84
Egypt: abolishment of 1923
    constitution (1930), 281n22;
    agricultural sector in, 283n65; Black
    Saturday (Cairo burning), 140–43;
    and China, 161, 167–68;
    constitution abolished (1923),
    281nn22–23; coup (1952), 137–38,
    143–45, 153, 154, 155, 177; as
    culture capital, 216; economic crisis
    and civil unrest (1930s–1940s), 133;
    Israel's 1955 attack in Gaza, 161;
    land redistribution program (1952),
    147; military, 134, 136–38, 146–47,
    154, 161, 212, 221–23; under
    Muhammad Ali and successors,
    221–23; national security interests,
    281n39; Palestine War (1948), 135–
    38; political Islam in, 4; Sadat's
    alliance with Saudi Arabia, 33;
    secret peace talks with Israel, 160,
    162, 166; and Syrian coups, 208. *See*

also Nasser, Gamal Abdel; road not taken; United Arab Republic; *specific countries for their relations with Egypt*

Egyptian Islamic Jihad, 33

Eisenhower, Dwight D.: Atoms for Peace initiative, 88; on British and French energy problems, 184; Chamoun's request rejected, 204; covert operations and, 241, 246; foreign aid to Latin America, 238–39; foreign policy, 229–31; legacy of, 253; on military-industrial complex, 14–15; and Nasser, 25, 156, 166, 168, 186, 190, 197; on Operation Blue Bat and invasion of Lebanon, 203; and overthrow of Mossadegh, 60, 64, 72, 74, 75–76, 80–81, 228–29; and Saud, 166, 192; and Soviet communism, 62–63, 225; and Suez Crisis, 175–76, 185; and Syria, 197, 198; United Fruit connection, 240–41. *See also* U.S. fixation with Soviet role in Middle East; U.S.-Egyptian relations

Eisenhower Doctrine and U.S. military interventions, 190–213; establishment and effects, 187–88, 190–93; and geostrategic curse, 207–13; Lebanon, 202–6; seeds sown during Suez Crisis, 171; Syria, 194–201

Eisenstadt, S. N., 21, 215

el-Sisi, Abdel Fattah, 146

Eqbal, Manuchehr, 90–91

equilibrium: Britain's policy of, 101–2; of nonalignment, 44, 51–52, 110

Evans, David, 153

Evin Prison (Iran), 114

Exham, Kenneth, 141

Faisal, Emir of Syria, 2, 110, 116

Fakhrizadeh, Mohsen, 122–23

Family Protection Law (Iran 1967), 93

Farouk (king of Egypt), 134, 135, 141–42, 146

Fars province (Iran), 44–45

Fereydun (mythical figure), 22

15 Khordad riots (1963), 99

Financial Times, on SAVAK, 90

Foster, John W., 62

Four Arab Tigers, 221

Four Asian Tigers, 25, 221, 226

Fowler, Alta F., 153

France, 2–3, 19, 93–94, 101, 116, 194–95, 200. *See also* Suez Crisis

Free Officers: and Aswan Dam affair, 165, 172; banning of other parties, 155–56; and birth of authoritarian state, 146–48; Black Saturday, 140–43; and communism/socialism, 154–55, 161; coup (1952), 137–38, 143–45, 153, 154, 155, 177; and Czech Arms Deal, 161; formation and membership, 139–40; internal power struggles, 155–57; priorities and agenda shift, 29; shared sentiment, 281n36; Six Principles and Six Point Program, 144–45; Suez Crisis, 174, 175; and United States, 149, 151, 153–54. *See also individual Free Officers by name*

Fuentes, Ydígoras: *The Shark and the Sardines*, 299n60

fundamentalism. *See* political Islam and religious fundamentalism

Galeano, Eduardo: *Open Veins of Latin America*, 229

Gandhi, Mahatma, 46, 251

Gazier, Albert, 181

geostrategic curse: and Arab cold war, 192–93, 209–10, 218–19; and Nasser's downfall, 210–12; and oil curse, 16; and political authoritarianism, 30–32; road not taken, 219–20; and U.S. informal empire, 28–30, 207–9

Gharani, Valiollah, 89
gharbzadegi (Westoxication), 98
Ghazvinian, John, 59; *America and Iran*, 86
al-Gizawi, Muhammad, 143
global capitalist economy, x, 12, 18, 19, 63, 249
global war on terror, xi, 19–20, 36–37, 225, 255
Grady, Henry F., 111
Graham, Robert, 90
Great Britain. *See* Britain
guardianship of the jurist (Vilayat-e Faqīh), 100
Guatemala, 228–46; agrarian reforms, 231–32, 233, 239–40, 245; Árbenz and Guatemala's aspirations, 232–35; arms purchased from Czechoslovakia, 236; civil war, 244, 245–46; communists in, 234–35; and Dulles brothers, 235, 238, 240; military, 243; New Labor Code, 239; Ubico's dictatorship, 232–33; U.S.-Guatemalan relations compared to U.S.-Iranian relations, 235–36; Voice of Liberation, 242, 243. *See also* Árbenz, Jacobo; United Fruit Company
Gulf War (1990–1991), 230, 254

al-Hakim, Tawfiq, 219
Hamas, 34, 256
Hammarsköld, Dag, 204 `
Hare, Raymond, 175, 183, 188, 191
Harriman, Averell, 54
Hatay province (Syria), 194–95, 196
Heikal, Mohamed Hassanein, 130, 134, 136
Henderson, Loy Wesley, 55, 64, 65, 72, 76, 86, 111
Henry, Patrick, 7
Hezbollah, 30
el-Hilaly, Ahmed Naguib, 142

Honduras, Truman's provision of arms to, 235
Hong Kong, Middle East and Egypt's road not taken compared to, 25, 221
Hosseinie-ye Ershad (Islamic Cultural Centre), 97
hostage crisis (1979–1981), 19, 102, 119–21, 123
humiliation of Nasser. *See* confrontation with Nasser
Hussein (king of Jordan), 201
Hussein, Ahmed, 164
Hussein, Saddam, 7–8, 35, 36, 100, 118, 217, 230

Ilyan, Mikhail, 197–98
imperialism, 11, 14, 19, 63, 253, 256. *See also* colonialism; informal imperialism
Indonesia, MI6 and C.I.A. operations in, 202
informal imperialism: and Christianity, 62–63; in context of British and French imperialism, 19; damage done by, 253–55; of Dulles brothers, 62; and Israeli-Palestinian conflict, 256; joint U.S.-British, 28–29; leaders of developing countries co-opted into, 15; Nasser on participation of major powers as, 158; Nkrumah on, 10–11; and opposition to nonalignment, 65; and overthrow of Mossadegh, 76; and Suez Crisis, 185; as triggering geostrategic curse, 28–29; of United States, summarized, 10–15, 248–50. *See also* Eisenhower Doctrine and U.S. military interventions
instability, 14, 21. *See also* stability and strongmen
inter-Arab civil war, 210, 212
intra-Arab cold war. *See* Arab cold war
Iran: allies and proxies, 123; anti-Iran coalition, 31; Arab Spring in, 6, 30;

al-Assad receiving assistance from, 30; Britain and France requesting loan from, 101; British and Soviet interventions in domestic affairs, 120; Constitutional Revolution (1905–1911), 40–43, 47; and democracy, 22–23, 250–51; distance between people and state, 112; foreign policy doctrine, 124; hostage crisis, 19, 102, 119–20; human rights record, 123; intelligentsia, 66, 95, 106; invasion by Iraq, 118; land reforms in, 92–93, 95; leaders' view of, 124; military, 74, 76–77, 78, 87–88, 99; newspapers, 41, 67, 72, 75, 77, 78, 113; nuclear program, 88, 118, 124–25; as OPEC founding member, 100; palace siege (1942), 135–36; political Islam and religious fundamentalism, 23–24, 95–98, 104–5; population growth, 93; poverty in, 122; Razmara's relations with Soviet Union, 52; revolution (1979), 23–24, 102, 105; road not taken, 24–25, 108, 193–94; secular opposition in, 97–98; Tobacco Rebellion (1890), 39–40. *See also* clerics and clerical regime; Iran under the shah; Mossadegh, Muhammed; oil nationalization; overthrow of Mossadegh; U.S.-Iranian relations

Iranian-English treaty (1919), 120

Iran under the shah, 83–107; authoritarianism under U.S. tutelage, 84–87, 112, 116, 119, 251; blowback, 104–7; economy, 24, 81, 87–88, 100–101; Great Civilization and personality cult, 91–95; installment of shah, 46–47; Khomeini and radicalization of clerics, 98–100; paving way for Islamization, 95–98; regional policy, 124; road not taken, 83–84; SAVAK and crackdowns, 24, 89–91, 104, 106, 113, 118; shah's apparent peak of power, 100–104; shah's paranoia, 87–89; shah's talks with Soviet Union, 89; torture and prisons, 24, 113–14, 119; and U.S. informal empire, 19. *See also* political Islam and religious fundamentalism

Iraq: Al-Qaeda's emergence in, 33; Arab Spring in, 6; conservative monarchies propped up by United States, 192; dependence on external patrons, 257; invasion of Iran, 118; median income compared to Four Asian Tigers, 221; Nasser's galvanization of the masses, 209; as OPEC founding member, 100; and Preferred Plan, 200–201; road not taken, 221; U.S. occupation of, 36–37, 199, 225, 230, 254–55. *See also* Hussein, Saddam

Iraqi Petroleum Pipeline, 196

Islam, political. *See* political Islam and religious fundamentalism

Islamic Cultural Centre (Hosseinie-ye Ershad), 97

Islamic intellectuals (Roshanfekr-e Dini), 97

Israel: Abraham Accords (2020), 256; anti-Iran coalition, 31; Fakrizadeh assassinated by, 122; Gaza, attack on Egyptian troops in (1955), 161; occupation of territories, 182, 218; Palestine War (1948), 135–38; road not taken, 216–18; secret peace talks with Egypt, 160, 162, 166; and shah's covert state-building project, 90; Syrian-Israeli relations, 195, 196, 218. *See also* Arab-Israeli conflict; Six-Day War; Suez Crisis

Italy, C.I.A. covert operation in, 228

Japan: economic revival after World War II, 222; successful modernization preventing colonization of, 296n7

Jeton, Francis, 198

Joint Comprehensive Plan of Action (JCPOA), 125

Jordan: Abdullah I shot for alleged collusion with Israel, 196; conservative monarchies propped up by United States, 192; Israeli occupation of territories, 218; and Preferred Plan, 199–201; water-sharing agreements with Egypt and Israel, 160; and Yemeni civil war, 212

June 1967 war. *See* Six-Day War

justice. *See* struggle for a better future

Kamil, Mustafa, 133, 134

Karlsson, Svante: *Oil and the World Order*, 23

Kashani, Ayatollah Sayyed Abol-Ghasem, 47, 66, 70, 74

Keeley, James, 196

Kennedy, John F., 89, 103, 299n60

Khalidi, Rashid, 11

Khalidi, Walid, 138

Khamenei, Ayatollah Ali, 122

Khashoggi, Jamal, 1

Khomeini, Ayatollah Ruhollah: agency of, 10; Arab-Israeli conflict as excuse for, 217; arrest and exile, 99–100; and hostage crisis, 121; Mirsepassi on, 105; on Mossadegh, 106–7; and nuclear power, 118; on Persepolis party, 102; radicalization of clerics, 98–100; relationship with United States, 122; and road not taken, 24; SAVAK arresting associates of, 104; Shariati's leftist ideas appropriated by, 95–96

Khrushchev, Nikita, 183, 185

King-Crane Commission report (1919), 138–39

Kinzer, Stephen, 234–35

Kissinger, Henry, 102

Kohli, Atul, 248; *Imperialism and the Developing World*, 11–13

Komer, Robert W., 117

Kulthum, Umm, 127–28

Kuwait: and global oil markets, 53; as OPEC founding member, 100

Lakeland, William, 153, 154

Lampson, Lord Miles, 135

Lansing, Robert, 62

Lebanon: conservative monarchies propped up by United States, 192; cosmopolitan potential, 4–5, 35; Israeli occupation in southern Lebanon, 182; median income compared to Four Asian Tigers, 221; Operation Blue Bat and U.S. invasion, 202–6; protests (2019), 6–7, 257; revolution and civil war (1975), 5–6, 35, 220; road not taken, 35–36, 220, 221; student activism (1970s), 5

Le Monde, shah's reforms compared to France's industrial revolution, 93–94

Lewis, Bernard: *What Went Wrong?*, xi

Libya, conservative monarchies propped up by United States, 192

Literacy Corps (Iran), 93, 102

Lloyd, Selwyn, 182

Lodge, Henry Cabot, Jr., 240

Love, Kennett, 67

Maher Pasha, Ali, 135, 142, 156

Majlis, 40, 42, 46, 48, 50, 74, 91

Marshall, George, 195, 253

Masr El-Fatah (Young Egypt) society, 131

Matni, Nasib Al, 203

May, Ernest R., 13

Mayan Genocide (Silent Holocaust), 245–46

Mazower, Mark, 225
McCann, Thomas, 240
McGhee, George, 55–56
Meade, Stephen, 195–96
MEDO (Middle East Defense
  Organization), 157
Meir, Golda, 35, 184
MI6 (Britain), 56, 71, 72, 75, 77–78,
  197–98, 199, 202
Middle East: anti-Americanism, 33–34,
  116, 117, 217–18; and democracy,
  256–57; as most penetrated region
  in world, 18, 255; political transition
  in, 7–8; post-World War I, 2–3;
  road not taken, 215–16, 221–23,
  225–27; unique characteristics of,
  16, 18; view of United States, 3, 10,
  249; violence compared to Europe,
  20–21. *See also* geostrategic curse;
  narratives of the Middle East;
  stability and strongmen; United
  States, Middle East role of; *specific
  countries*
military-industrial complex, 14–15
Mirsepassi, Ali, 104
Mitchell, Timothy, 18–19
modernization: of Egypt, 128–29, 147,
  154, 165, 221–23; of Iran, 67, 92–95,
  96–99, 110–11; multiple
  modernities, 21, 215
Mohammad Ali Shah (shah of Iran
  1907–1909), 42
Mohammad Reza Pahlavi (shah of Iran
  1941–1979): admitted to United
  States for cancer treatment, 119;
  agency of, 10; causes of downfall,
  96; compared to Castillo Armas,
  245; compared to Mossadegh, 83–
  86, 87, 89–90, 91, 94, 112–16, 205,
  251; failure of coup against, 88–89;
  fleeing to Baghdad and Italy, 74, 77;
  Mossadegh as threat to, 49–50;
  Mossadegh on, 48; and overthrow
  of Mossadegh, 67, 72–75, 78, 79–80;

and "Queen Elizabeth" cable,
  268n49; responsibility for existing
  calamity, 35; and Reza Shah (father),
  72, 116; *Toward the Great
  Civilization*, 92. *See also* Iran under
  the shah; U.S.-Iranian relations
Mohieddin, Khaled, 128, 134, 135, 142,
  143, 144
Mohieddin, Zakaria, 142
Mollet, Guy, 174–75, 178, 181, 183,
  184
Molloy, Robert, 198
Morris, William, 112, 113
Mossadegh, Ahmad, 115
Mossadegh, Muhammed, 38–57;
  agency of, 10, 210; on Britain, 120;
  challenges faced as leader, 111–12;
  character traits, 40–41, 42–43, 54,
  112, 114–15, 129; and communists,
  201–2; compared to Árbenz, 232,
  240, 244–45; compared to Gandhi,
  251; compared to Saddam Hussein,
  230; compared to Shariati, 96;
  compared to the shah, 83–86, 87,
  89–90, 91, 94, 112–16, 205, 251; as
  constitutional model, 38–39; and
  Constitutional Revolution (1905–
  1911), 40–42, 47; defiance of, 45–
  47; and democracy, 47–48, 67, 74,
  83, 111, 250–51; initiatives and
  reforms, 48, 67, 110–11, 221; and
  Iranian sovereignty, 44–45, 110,
  256; Iranian view of, 41, 65, 106–7;
  and the Majlis, 40, 42, 46, 48, 50,
  74; origins, 39–40, 134; in Paris and
  Switzerland, 42–44; Security
  Council address (1951), 55, 109–10;
  in solitary confinement, 85;
  strategic and tactical mistakes, 49–
  50, 64–65, 70, 76–77; thesis on
  Islamic law, 43–44; as
  transformative leader, 109–10,
  112; on United States, 54, 64–65,
  120, 138–39, 152, 249. *See also*

Mossadegh, Muhammed (continued)
  Nasser-Mossadegh comparisons;
  National Front; oil nationalization;
  overthrow of Mossadegh
Motahhari, Morteza, 97
Mubarak, Hosni, 35, 127
Muhammad Ali (governor of Egypt),
  221–22
mullahs. *See* clerics and clerical regime
multiple modernities, 21, 215
Muniz, João Carlos, 238
Murphy, Robert, 175
Muslim Brotherhood, 140, 147, 155,
  157, 159, 219

Naguib, Mohamed, 130, 142–43, 144,
  146, 147–48, 155–57, 158–59
Al-Nahhas, Mustafa, 135, 142
Nakba (Palestine War 1948), 135–38
narratives of the Middle East, 1–16;
  articulating constructive, 2–4, 16;
  author's childhood in Beirut, 4–7;
  century-long Arab Spring, 7–9;
  dominant Western narratives'
  cherry-picking, 8–10; of Iran and
  Iran's clerics, 118; shah's imperial
  nationalist narrative, 92; and U.S.
  informal empire, 10–15; value of
  realistic, 1–2; and violence, 20–21,
  247. *See also* "ancient hatreds"
  narrative
Nasir al-Din Shah (shah of Iran 1848–
  1896), 39, 40, 41
Nasser, Gamal Abdel, 126–49; agency
  of, 10, 210; and Arab cold war, 209–
  10; and Arab-Israeli conflict, 217;
  Arab view of, 126, 201; assassination
  attempt, 159; Black Saturday, 140–
  43; Byroade on, 167, 224;
  opposition to communism, 131–32,
  138, 158, 164, 188–89, 193, 201;
  compared to Árbenz, 236, 240, 244;
  compared to Churchill, 184;
  compared to the shah, 205; coup

(1952), 137–38, 143–45, 153, 154,
  155, 177; Czech Arms Deal, 25,
  161–65, 216; and democracy, 26,
  123, 144–45, 214, 225; and dignity,
  126–27, 128, 133–34, 135, 162, 173;
  downfall, 210–12; Egyptian view of,
  127, 128, 129, 130, 159, 164, 223;
  Eisenhower on, 166, 190, 197;
  engineering compromise settlement
  in Lebanon, 205–6; flaws and
  motivations, 127–28; as hero, 173–
  74, 183, 185; as inspiration, 127,
  172, 225; modernization and
  initiatives, 128–29, 147, 151–52,
  165, 211, 223; Naguib's power
  struggles with, 147–48, 155–57,
  158–59; nationalism and leadership,
  26–27, 214; and Non-Aligned
  Movement, 129, 162, 174, 178;
  paranoia and insecurity complex,
  140, 210–11; *The Philosophy of the
  Revolution*, 138; radicalization of,
  135–39; recognition of communist
  China, 167–68; responsibility for
  existing calamity, 35; road not taken,
  32–33, 34–36, 215, 219–20; shift to
  regional/international agenda, 165,
  209; upbringing and family, 130–34,
  152; views of United States, 25–26,
  138–39, 148, 151–54, 162, 249; and
  Voice of the Arabs, 209, 216. *See also*
  confrontation with Nasser; Nasser-
  Mossadegh comparisons; Six-Day
  War; Suez Crisis
Nassereddin Shah Qajar (shah of Iran
  1848–1896), 39, 40, 41
Nasseri, Nematollah, 90
Nasserism, 138
Nasser-Mossadegh comparisons:
  adolescence, 134; agency, 210;
  appealing to U.S. sense of justice
  and fairness, 174–75; British tactics
  toward, 178; character traits, 129;
  consolidation of power, 163;

democracy, 123, 144–45, 214; developmentalism, 26, 214, 221; domestic agenda, 151–52; hopeful view of U.S. aid and support, 26, 152, 225; and industrialization, 221; King-Crane Commission and, 138–39, 249; and nationalization, 172–73; as new generation of postcolonial leaders, 188; and nonalignment, 148–49; priorities, 123, 166; regional ambitions, 139, 174, 209; semisecular nationalism and religion, 129; upbringing, 123, 129, 139; U.S. approach toward, 152, 160, 175; on violence, 135–36, 137–38, 178; willingness to go down fighting, 164, 177. *See also* U.S. reasons for targeting Nasser and Mossadegh

National Front (Iran), 47–48, 50–51, 52, 65–68, 74, 81

nationalism. *See* secular nationalism

nationalization, 23, 128–29, 172–76, 211. *See also* oil nationalization

National Security Council (U.S.), 13, 56, 60, 69, 155

NATO (North Atlantic Treaty Organization), 60

negative equilibrium, 44, 110

Nehru, Jawaharlal, 109, 110, 129, 164

neo-colonialism/neo-imperialism. *See* informal imperialism

Netanyahu, Benjamin, 1

neutralism. *See* nonalignment

New York Times: and C.I.A. propaganda against Mossadegh, 67; John Foster Dulles's obituary, 62; and Fakhrizadeh's assassination, 122; on Iran hostage crisis, 119; on overthrow of Mossadegh, 237; on U.S.-Iran crisis, 118

Nicaragua: Castillo Armas's attempts to acquire arms from, 243; Truman's provision of arms to, 235

9/11 (September 11, 2001 terrorist attacks), xi, 19, 36, 37, 252–53, 254

Nixon, Richard, 87, 89, 101–2

Nixon Doctrine, 101–2

Nkrumah, Kwame, 10–11, 109, 129

Non-Aligned Movement, 110, 129, 162, 178, 264n52

nonalignment: and Mossadegh, 44–45, 48, 65, 69, 148–49, 251, 264n52; and Nasser, 148–49, 152, 188–89, 254; U.S. opposition to, 13, 65, 69, 148–49, 152, 235

normalization deals, 256

North, Oliver, 118

NSC-68, 13, 56, 60

nuclear program. *See* Iran

Nutting, Anthony, 128, 134, 178, 179, 181

Nye, Joseph: *Soft Power*, 153

Obama, Barack, 8, 117, 122, 124, 207

oil: 1933 agreement (AIOC-Iran), 49; 1933 U.S.-Saudi oil exploration agreement, 10; 1973 crisis, 100–101, 220; carbon democracy, 18–19; as driver of U.S. informal imperialism, 18, 57, 164, 230, 254–55; as driver of Western and foreign intervention, 230; Eisenhower on, 184; Iran's economy fueled by, 24; oil curse, 16; and overthrow of Mossadegh, 64; and road not taken, 24; Saudi oil boom, 33; and shah's monopolization of power, 87–88; shah's oil concessions, 85–87; and Suez Crisis, 174–76, 184, 185; Trans-Arabian Pipeline, 194–96. *See also* oil nationalization

oil nationalization, 48–54; history of exploitation, 48–49; importance to Mossadegh, 45, 48, 50–51, 54, 109, 110–11; Iranian support for, 110–11; Mossadegh's appeal for U.S. help, 54–57; and overthrow of

oil nationalization (continued)
Mossadegh, 51–54, 64, 76; parallels
to Zahhāk myth, 22; reversal and
consequences, 71, 80, 85–87, 251–
52; U.S. tactics compared to during
Suez Crisis, 175; and U.S. fixation
with Cold War, 56, 64
OPEC (Organization of the Petroleum
Exporting Countries), 87, 100
open economy. *See* global capitalist
economy
Operation Blue Bat and invasion of
Lebanon (1958), 202–6
Operation Buccaneer (proposed), 57
Operation PBFortune (1952), 236
Operation PBSuccess (1953), 241–44
Operation Straggle (1956), 197–98,
200
Operation TP-AJAX (1953). *See*
overthrow of Mossadegh
Operation Wappen (1957), 198–202
Organization of American States, 242
Organization of the Petroleum
Exporting Countries (OPEC), 87,
100
Orientalism, 179
Outer Island Rebellion (Indonesia),
202
overthrow of Árbenz. *See* Árbenz,
Jacobo, coup against
overthrow of Mossadegh, 58–82;
Albright's half-apology for, 117;
botched first attempt and aftermath,
72–75, 76–77; and Churchill's
return to power, 59–60; C.I.A.
sabotage and propaganda, 65–68,
84; C.I.A.'s acknowledgment of role
in, 116; compared to coup against
Árbenz, 237–38, 244–45;
consequences for international
institutions, 23; consequences for
Iran, 24, 81–82, 105–6, 116–21, 244,
250–52; consequences for U.S.
foreign policy, 17–18, 23, 75–77,

167, 228–29, 241, 250–52; covert
design of, 58–59; Eisenhower and
Dulles brothers' role, 60–64; as
flash point, 3, 17, 169, 249; Iranian
support for, 77–78, 106–7, 261n9;
lack of straightforward link to
confrontation with Nasser, 215;
Mossadegh's strategic
miscalculation, 64–65; planning of,
68–72; protests and ouster, 77–79;
road not taken, 24–25, 34, 83–84,
115–16, 226, 249–51, 256–57; and
Kermit Roosevelt, 79–80, 163; Suez
Crisis compared to, 178, 182; and
Truman, 59–60; U.S. failure to take
responsibility for, 117; U.S.
motivation for, 64, 76, 86, 115; U.S.
tactics for confrontation with
Nasser compared to, 152; and
Zahedi, 70, 72–73, 91. *See also* Iran
under the shah

Pahlavi dynasty, 24, 47, 72, 77, 96–97,
113, 250. *See also* Mohammad Reza
Pahlavi; Reza Shah
Pakistan: road not taken, 34; and U.S.
fixation with Soviet role in Middle
East, 14
Palestine. *See* Arab-Israeli conflict
Palestine War (*Nakba* 1948), 135–38
pan-Arabism, 32, 136–39, 185, 191–93,
209–13
Parti Populaire Syriens (PPS), 197
Partition Plan for Palestine (UN 1947),
194
path not taken. *See* road not taken
Pax Americana, 14, 185, 254. *See also*
informal imperialism
Peres, Shimon, 181
Persepolis party (Iran), 102–3, 115
Peurifoy, John, 243
political Islam and religious
fundamentalism: and defeat of
secular nationalism, 4, 32–33, 34–

36, 104–5; dominant Western narrative on, 9; in Iran, 23–24, 95–98, 104–5; road not taken, 34–35, 36, 219; and Saudi Arabia, 29, 32–33, 121, 187, 188, 219; U.S. backing of, 29, 33, 121, 192, 193, 219, 252–53. *See also* clerics and clerical regime (Iran)

Ponce Vaides, Federico, 233

positive equilibrium, 51–52

postcolonial leaders: aspirations and struggles, 256; Allen Dulles on, 14, 63; effects of Bay of Pigs invasion on, 226; and leftists/Marxists, 201–2; Mossadegh as, 65, 109–10; and U.S. fixation with Soviet role in Egypt, 230. *See also individual leaders by name*

PPS (Parti Populaire Syriens), 197

Preferred Plan, 199–202

prisons: as indicative of Middle Eastern struggle for a better future, 7–8; in Iran, 24, 113–14, 119

Protocol of Sèvres (1956), 180–82

Qaddafi, Muammar, 7, 112, 217

Qajar dynasty (Iran), 39–40, 41, 46, 47, 112, 113

Qavam, Ahmad, 48

"Queen Elizabeth" cable, 268n49

Qutb, Sayyid, 10

al-Quwatli, Shukri, 195–96, 229

Rabin, Yitzhak, 137

Radio Tehran, 78

Raisi, Ebrahim, 123

Razmara, Haj Ali, 51–52

Reagan, Ronald, 118

religious fundamentalism. *See* political Islam and religious fundamentalism

Resurgence (Rastakhiz) Party (Iran), 94–95, 102, 103–4

Revolutionary Command Council (Egypt), 147, 154, 155–56, 173

revolving-door governments, 197

Reza Khan. *See* Reza Shah

Reza Shah (shah of Iran 1925–1941), 46–47, 72, 113

Riahi, Taghi, 74

road not taken, 214–27; Arab-Israeli conflict, 36, 216–18; Aswan Dam affair (1955–1956), 25, 186–87; democracy, 24, 27–28, 214–16, 226, 251; Egypt, 25–28, 186, 187–89, 193–94, 214–19, 221; geostrategic curse, 218–20; global war on terror, 36–37; Iran, 24–25, 108, 193–94; Israel, 32–33, 34–36, 216–18; Lebanon, 35–36, 220, 221; Middle East generally, 215–16, 221–23, 225–27; Pakistan, 34; political Islam, 34–35, 36, 219; Suez Crisis, 186, 187–89; Syria, 221. *See also* confrontation with Nasser; overthrow of Mossadegh; Six-Day War

Rommel, Erwin, 135

Roosevelt, Franklin Delano, 76

Roosevelt, Kermit, 71–75, 78–80, 107, 163, 199; *Arabs, Oil, and History*, 71; *Countercoup*, 79–80

Roosevelt, Theodore, 71

Roshanfekr-e Dini, 97

Rouhani, Fuad, 87

Rouhani, Hassan, 124

Rountree, William, 209

Rumsfeld, Donald, 118

Russell, Francis, 176

Russia: greater engagement in Middle East, 31; military intervention in Syria (2015), 255. *See also* Soviet Union

Sabri, Ali, 153

Sadat, Anwar, 10–11, 33, 35–36, 134, 143–44, 164, 165–66, 173

Said, Edward, 8, 179

al-Said, Nuri, 204

al-Sarraj, Abdel Hamid, 198, 199–200, 201

Saud (king of Saudi Arabia), 166, 177, 192, 201

Saudi Arabia: and anti-Nasser Arab bloc, 218–19; and Arab Spring, 30; arms, aid, and security protection from United States, 12; compensating for absence of Iranian oil, 53; conservative monarchies propped up by United States, 192; death sentence executions, 123; dependence on external patrons, 257; founding member of OPEC, 100; oil boom, 33; oil exploration agreement (1933), 10; as OPEC founding member, 100; religious fundamentalism in, 29, 32–33, 121, 187, 188, 219; Sadat's alliance with, 33; and U.S. informal empire, 19

Saudi Trans-Arabian Pipeline, 194–96

SAVAK (Iranian secret police), 24, 89–91, 104, 106, 113, 118

Schlesinger, Stephen, 234–35

Schwarzkopf, Herbert Norman, 73, 90

Schweizer Illustrierte, on Persepolis party, 103

secular nationalism: defeat and marginalization in Egypt, 4, 32–33, 188, 193, 219; defeat in Iran, 4, 32, 34, 99, 104–5; and Eisenhower Doctrine, 193; of Mossadegh and Nasser, 129; road not taken, 34

Security Council (UN), 55, 109, 183, 204

self-determination, 9, 11, 34, 115, 226, 248, 256, 257

Serageddin, Fouad, 141

Serry Amer, Hussein, 142

Seven Sisters of oil industry, 54

Sèvres Protocol (1956), 180–82

the shah. *See* Mohammad Reza Pahlavi

shah of Iran. *See* Mohammad Ali Shah; Mohammad Reza Pahlavi; Nasir al-Din Shah; Reza Shah

Shariati, Ali, 95–96, 97, 98

Shukr, Abd al-Ghaffar, 140

Silent Holocaust (Mayan Genocide), 245–46

Singapore, Middle East and Egypt's road not taken compared to, 25, 221

Sirri Pasha, Hussein, 142

Six-Day War: causes, 25, 29, 32–33, 127, 169; effects, 32–33, 187, 210–13, 219–20; road not taken, 32–33, 34–36, 218, 219–20

Six Principles and Six Point Program, 144–45

South Korea, Middle East and Egypt's road not taken compared to, 25, 221

Soviet Union: Aswan Dam aid to Egypt, 172; and Azerbaijan, 120; Czech Arms Deal, 25, 161–65, 216; Egyptian-Soviet relations, 154–55, 205, 224; Iranian domestic affairs, interventions in, 120; and Iran's Razmara, 52; and Lebanon, 206; and Nasser's suppression of Marxists and socialists, 29; shah negotiating nonaggression pact with, 89; shared goals with United States in Middle East, 29; Suez Crisis, 174, 178, 180, 183, 184–85; Syrian intervention (2015), 255; Turkey-Syria border crisis, resolution of, 201. *See also* Cold War; U.S. fixation with Soviet role in Middle East; U.S. influence on Egyptian-Soviet relations

stability and strongmen, x–xi, 8, 18, 31, 193, 245

Stalin, Joseph, 62, 155, 235

Stone, Howard E., 198

strikes: Egypt's antigovernment strikes (1930s–1940s), 133; Iran's industrial strikes (1950s), 90–91; Nasser's crackdown on socialist-inspired strike (1952), 155

struggle for a better future, 6, 7–8, 9, 31, 81–82, 225, 257

Student Day (Iran 1953), 87

Sudan, Arab Spring in, 6

Suez Canal, 145, 172

Suez Canal Company, 172–73, 177, 180

Suez Canal Users' Association, 176–77

Suez Crisis, 171–89; and Aswan Dam affair, 17–18, 25, 169; and Baghdad Pact, 160; compared to U.S. tactics in Iran's oil nationalization, 175; and Eisenhower Doctrine, 171–72, 187–89; events precipitating, 176–79; and invasion, 182–84; lessons drawn by Nasser, 191, 225; nationalization by Nasser, 172–76; prices of, 184–87; Protocol of Sèvres (1956), 180–82; response of Israel, France, and Britain to nationalization, 179–80; road not taken, 186, 187–89

Suez War (1956), 182–86

Sukarno, 109, 129, 164

Suleimani, Qassim, 122, 123

Sullivan and Cromwell, 63, 240

Supplementary Oil Agreement (Iran-Britain; not ratified), 51–52

Sykes, Lord Mark, 179

Sykes-Picot Agreement (Britain-France 1916), 179

Syria: and al-Assad, 30, 123, 217, 255; coups in, 169, 193–202, 228, 241; dependence on external patrons, 257; Hatay province, 194–95; recognition of Israel, 195, 196; road not taken, 221. *See also* United Arab Republic; *specific countries for their relations with Syria*

Syrian National Congress, 2

Syrian Social Nationalist Party, 197

Taiwan, Middle East and Egypt's road not taken compared to, 25

Taliban, 36, 37

Tehran hostage crisis (1979–1981), 19, 102, 119–21

Tehran Radio, 78

Thompson, Elizabeth F., 2, 116

Time: buying into C.I.A. propaganda against Mossadegh, 67; Mossadegh cover (1952), 55

Tito, Josip, 102, 129, 164

torture: by SAVAK (Iran), 90, 113–14; by United States, 20

Trans-Arabian Pipeline, 194–96

Trans-Iranian Railway, 93

Trosin, Walter, 116

Truman, Harry: arms provision to Guatemala, Honduras, and Nicaragua, 235; and coup against Árbenz, 236; fixation with Soviet role in Middle East, 13, 56, 60, 62; on oil, 64; and oil nationalization, 54–57, 59

Trump, Donald, 1, 8, 31, 121–22, 125, 217, 256

Tudeh party (Iran), 65–68, 70, 74–75, 81, 90

Tunisia: Arab Spring in, 6; monarchy in, 192

Turkey's border crisis with Syria, 194–95, 199, 201

Ubico, Jorge, 232, 233, 239

Ukraine, C.I.A. covert operation in, 228

ulama. *See* clerics and clerical regime (Iran)

undermining of Nasser. *See* confrontation with Nasser

United Arab Republic (UAR), 200, 203, 208, 210–12

United Fruit Company, 231–32, 238–41, 244, 299n62

United Kingdom. *See* Britain

United Nations: Partition Plan for Palestine (1947), 194. *See also* Security Council

United States, Middle East role of:
Abraham Accords (2020), 256;
allying with Saudi Arabia, 29; anti-
Iran coalition, 31; and authoritarian
populism, 9; backing acquiescent or
subservient ruling elites, 23, 115,
252; backing brutal authoritarian
rulers, 29; backing conservative
monarchies, 192; and Britain, 28,
86, 120; carbon democracy, 18–19;
early positive relations, 3, 10, 139;
in Israel's occupation and settler
colonialism, 28, 33–34, 217–18, 252,
256; key flash points, 17–18, 169–
70; Middle Easterners' view of, 3,
10, 249; military interventions, 208;
as negative inspiration for lesser
powers, 20; occupation of Iraq, 36–
37, 199, 225, 230, 254–55; and
religious fundamentalism, 29, 33,
121, 192, 193, 219, 252–53; and
Saddam Hussein, 118, 123; and
Soviet Union, 18, 29, 35, 120, 207–
8, 230, 235, 254. *See also* anti-
Americanism; confrontation with
Nasser; democracy, U.S.
undermining of; Eisenhower
Doctrine and U.S. military
interventions; informal imperialism;
narratives of the Middle East; 9/11;
overthrow of Mossadegh; road not
taken; Suez Crisis; U.S. fixation
with Soviet role in Middle East;
U.S.-Egyptian relations;
U.S.-Iranian relations; *specific Middle
East countries*
U.S. fixation with Soviet role in Middle
East: and Aswan Dam affair, 166;
and coup against Árbenz, 235, 237–
39, 242, 244–45; and coup in Egypt,
153; and coups in Syria, 193–202,
228, 241; and Czech Arms Deal,
151; Dulles brothers, 61–64, 156–
57, 163–64; Egyptian-Soviet

relations, 151, 152, 163, 190, 205,
219, 254; and global capitalist
economy, x, 12; and Nasser's
nationalism, 148, 167, 169–70, 209–
10; and nonalignment, 13; and oil
nationalization, 56, 64; and
overthrow of Mossadegh, x, 64–65,
68, 75–76, 111, 148, 244–45; and
Suez Crisis, x, 173–74, 176, 187; and
U.S. foreign policy generally, 13–15,
56–57, 249
U.S. reasons for targeting Nasser and
Mossadegh: and capitalism, 101,
254–55; challenging corporate
interests and moving to socialism,
230; for desire for independence
and sovereignty, x, 23, 29, 76, 110,
218, 229; and oil, x, 18, 57, 164, 230;
U.S. imperial ambitions, x, 35, 186
U.S.-Egyptian relations, 150–70; after
1952 coup, 148–49; anti-Nasser
Arab bloc, 218–19; and Arab cold
war, 209–10; Baghdad Pact, 89,
160–61; Czech Arms Deal, 156,
161–65, 166; democracy
undermined by U.S., 252; Egyptian-
Israeli relations soured by, 216–18;
and Egypt's internal power
struggles, 155–60; Eisenhower
Doctrine, 190–93, 208; and
informal imperialism, 12–13; and
Lebanon, 204–6, 208; Nasser's
attempts at friendly relationship,
25–26, 152, 186, 190, 225; and
Nasser's downfall, 212; promising
beginning, 152–55; road not taken,
25–28, 186, 187–89, 215, 217–19;
under Sadat, 33; summarized, 150–
52, 169–70; and Syria, 201, 208;
U.S. diplomats' cautions, 224–25;
U.S. failure to engage with Nasser,
25–28, 190; U.S. failure to perceive
common ground, 151, 176, 186;
U.S. hostility and deceptiveness,

208–9. *See also* Aswan Dam affair; confrontation with Nasser; Suez Crisis; U.S. fixation with Soviet role in Middle East; U.S. reasons for targeting Nasser and Mossadegh
U.S.-Iranian relations: after World War I, 120; clerics and clerical regime, 118, 120, 121, 123, 124; compared to U.S.-Guatemalan relations, 235–36; costs of economic and financial sanctions, 122; covert missile sales, 118; current, 117, 121–25; hostage crisis, 102, 119–21; and informal imperialism, 12–13; Iranian views of United States, 119, 123; Iran's nuclear program, 88, 118, 125; and Khomeini, 123; Nixon Doctrine and arms transfers, 101–2; and prison system, 113–14; under Razmara, 52; under the shah, 11–12, 19, 29, 83–90, 97, 112, 116, 119; summarized, 120–21; U.S. failures to take responsibility for, 117–18. *See also* oil nationalization; overthrow of Mossadegh; U.S. reasons for targeting Nasser and Mossadegh

Vatolina, L. N., 155
Vietnam War, 229, 252, 260n14
Vilayat-e Faqīh (guardianship of the jurist), 100
Voice of the Arabs, 133, 209, 216

Wafd government (Egypt), 142

Walker, Peter, 100
wars, costs of, 19–20, 21, 37
Wells, Milton K.: "Communism in Guatemala," 235
Westoxication (*gharbzadegi*), 98
White Revolution (Iran), 92–94, 96–99
Whitman, Ann, 241
Whitman, Ed, 241
Wilber, Donald, 66, 69
Wilson, Woodrow, 60, 138
Wisner, Frank, 236
women's rights in Iran, 93, 111, 124
world economy. *See* global capitalist economy

Ydígoras Fuentes, José, 245, 299n60
Yemen: civil war, 212, 219; and Nasser, 209
Young Egypt (Masr El-Fatah) society, 131

Zahedi, Fazallah: Afshartus's kidnapping and murder attributed to, 70; and coup against Mossadegh, 74, 75, 77, 78; exile, 91; imprisonment and execution of Mossadegh supporters, 94; and oil nationalization, 71, 80; Kermit Roosevelt's decision to install as prime minister, 73
Zahhāk myth, 22
al-Za'im, Husni, 195–96
al-Zawahiri, Ayman, 33
Zhou Enlai, 161